MINORITY PROBLEMS
IN SOUTHEAST ASIA

MINORITY PROBLEMS
IN SOUTHEAST ASIA

By VIRGINIA THOMPSON
and RICHARD ADLOFF

AUTHORS OF

The Left Wing in Southeast Asia

NEW YORK / RUSSELL & RUSSELL

ISSUED UNDER THE AUSPICES OF THE
INTERNATIONAL SECRETARIAT
INSTITUTE OF PACIFIC RELATIONS

To
R.L.Y. and H.N.Y.

FOREWORD

In less troubled times the destinies of the diverse and colorful minority peoples within the larger nations, many of which are themselves in their political infancy, of Southeast Asia would be of interest only to small groups of anthropologists and administrators. Today, however, many of these apparently inconsequential communities have begun to take on a new importance for the student of world politics and even military strategy. There may not be an exact equivalent in Southeast Asia to the Sudeten German problem which had such a fateful influence on the destiny of Czechoslovakia, but no serious student of Southeast Asian affairs today, since the rise of Viet Minh power in northern Indochina, can afford to overlook the potentially disruptive, if not subversive, role which strategically placed minorities in Thailand, Burma, Indochina, and Malaya may play in the future. One need only consider the efforts of the Chinese Communists to develop inside their southern borders a "Free Thai" movement, or the possible future significance of large Chinese communities in such cities as Bangkok, Saigon, Singapore, and Djakarta, to recognize that the problem is far from academic.

The present introductory survey, which does not claim to be comprehensive, is intended to awaken a wider interest in the problem before it becomes a matter of acute international tension or conflict. It also serves to supplement other studies in the international research program of the Institute of Pacific Relations, such as the volumes by Dr. Victor Purcell on *The Chinese in Southeast Asia* and on *Malaya: Communist or Free?* and by Mr. Bruno Lasker on *Human Bondage in Southeast Asia* and by Dr. Kenneth P. Landon on *The Chinese in Thailand*.

NEW YORK
August, 1954

WILLIAM L. HOLLAND
Secretary-General
Institute of Pacific Relations

CONTENTS

Foreword—*by William L. Holland* vi

Introduction 1

Chapter One: THE CHINESE 3
   The Economic Stake 4
   Education 8
   Political Activities 8
   Peking's Attitude Toward the Chinese of Southeast Asia 11
   Peking's Relations with Southeast Asian Governments 15
   The Policies of Southeast Asian Governments in Regard to China . . 18
   Malaya and Singapore 32
      Population and immigration, 32—Political activities, 35—Education, 41

   Thailand 44
      Population and immigration, 44—The citizenship issue, 47—Education, 47

   Indonesia 48
      Population and immigration, 48—The citizenship issue, 51—Education, 52

   Burma 54
      Population and immigration, 54—The citizenship issue, 55—Education, 55

   Indochina 56
      Population and immigration, 56—The citizenship issue, 57—Education, 58

Chapter Two: THE INDIANS 59
   India's Policy 59
   The Attitude of Southeast Asian Governments Toward India and Indians 63
   The Position of Pakistan 64
   Remittances 68
   Burma 69
      Population and immigration, 75—The Azad Hind, 77—Postwar political activities, 79—The economic stake: Investments and banking, 83; Trade and industry, 87; Labor and occupations, 87—Cultural activities and social welfare, 89—Intergovernmental relations, 89

   Malaya and Singapore 93
      Population and immigration, 94—Political activities, 98—The economic stake: Investments and banking, 108; Trade and industry, 109; Labor and occupations, 111—Cultural activities and social welfare, 114—Intergovernmental relations, 119

Chapter Two: THE INDIANS—Continued.

Indonesia 122
    Population and immigration, 122—The economic stake, 123—Inter-
    governmental relations, 123

Thailand 125
    Population and immigration, 125—Political activities, 125—The eco-
    nomic stake, 127—Cultural activities, 127—Intergovernmental rela-
    tions, 128

Indochina 129
    Population and immigration, 129—Political activities, 129—The eco-
    nomic stake, 130—Intergovernmental relations, 131

Chapter Three: INDIGENOUS MINORITIES 135
The Eurasians 135
    Indonesia, 138—Malaya, 143—Burma, 146—Indochina, 149—Thai-
    land, 150
The Arakanese 151
The Malays of South Thailand 158
The Ambonese 165

Chapter Four: BUDDHISTS *vs.* BUDDHISTS 170
Cambodia 170
    Thailand and Cambodia, 173—The Viet Minh and Cambodia, 174—
    Internal politics, 177—Relations with France and Vietnam, 179—King
    vs. Opposition, 183—Royal achievements, 188—Cambodia's prospects,
    193

Laos 197
    Birth of the Issarak, 198—The French reoccupation, 199—Constitu-
    tional developments, 202—Return of the emigrés, 203—Viet Minh and
    Pathetlao, 208

The Thai of Tonkin 211
The Buddhist Bloc and the Thai "Autonomous" State 219

Chapter Five: CHRISTIAN MINORITIES 229
Indonesia 235
Indochina 248
Burma 258
Thailand 267
Malaya 273

Chapter Six: CAUSES AND REMEDIES 280

Bibliography 287

Currencies (official rates) 289

Index 291

INTRODUCTION

IN Southeast Asia the student of minority peoples is faced with such an embarrassment of riches that any selection made from them is necessarily somewhat arbitrary. No choice, however, is possible in regard to alien minorities, for indisputably the Chinese and Indians are outstanding in this category. The difficulty here lies in according proper attention to the primordial position of the Chinese without simply reworking ground that has already been admirably covered by other students of the subject. Consequently, an attempt has been made in this study to present the Chinese chiefly as a regional minority and to supply current information as to their activities. Inasmuch as no analogous work on the Indian minority has yet been published, a fuller treatment has been accorded this group, though the writers are well aware that the Indians offer nothing like so important a field for analysis as do the Chinese.

As to the indigenous minorities, the choice among innumerable candidates is hard to make. Some outstanding minorities, such as the Karens of Burma, have been omitted for the reason that they are already the subject of numerous books and articles. Other omissions are the primitive tribes of the area—the Sakai of Malaya, the Méos of Indochina, the jungle peoples of Indonesia, to mention only a few of them. For the time being, at least, these tribal groups have comparatively little influence on the course of major events in Southeast Asia and their study seems more appropriately left to the anthropologist. While it could be argued that the Eurasians are similarly placed as regards shaping important trends in the area, they have been included in this work because they present a problem common to the whole region and one that has a special emotional appeal. In each of the Southeast Asian countries other than Malaya (where two of the three main population components have already been dealt with as alien minorities), an ethnic group has been chosen to illustrate how minorities, through their geographical location or their religious affiliation or both, can create an internal situation that has international complications.

The "Buddhist vs. Buddhist" struggle which is taking place in the heart of the Indochinese peninsula illustrates the process by which minorities are being currently created in Southeast Asia. Thailand and China, perennially sovereign powers, albeit of very unequal strength, are jockeying for control of their coreligionists who live in the areas between them. One group which seems likely to be subordinated to either Thailand or China is a complex of relatively primitive tribes—the Thai of Tonkin. The two others, Cambodians and Laotians, are far more evolved peoples just emerging from a colonial status to independent nationhood. All three are geographically so situated as to be subjected to strong and conflicting international pressures, which are

I

more likely than not to place them again in a position of dependency—this time to one or the other of their Buddhist neighbors.

The Christian groups in Southeast Asia are of special interest because to the long-standing problem of their religious separateness certain new facets have been added as a result of the withdrawal of colonial powers and the rise of new national states.

Generally speaking, the writers have attempted to throw light on little-known communities in Southeast Asia by supplementing work already done in the field as well as breaking fresh ground, and also to analyze—through the study of such microcosms—some of the difficulties which the minorities themselves and the new Southeast Asian states face in their relations with one another and with the world at large.

July 1954,

Chapter One

THE CHINESE

APART from its influence on the foreign relations of Southeast Asian countries, the Chinese minority offers an internal problem of fantastic complexity to the nations of the area. Certain aspects of this problem are common to the whole region, such as an increase in the proportion of local-born to the immigrant Chinese population, the growing urbanization of the Chinese community as a whole, the increasing domination by the Chinese of the region's economy, and the ever stronger attraction which the area holds for Chinese immigrants and for the two regimes each claiming to be the government of China. Though the status of the Chinese varies from country to country, all the governments of the area have been setting restrictions on their immigration, education, and political and economic activities. Generally speaking, four factors determine the relations between the resident Chinese and the governments and peoples of Southeast Asia: Chinese economic domination, their cultural unassimilability, the attitude of the local Chinese toward their homeland, and relations between the Southeast Asian governments and the Peking and Formosa regimes.

Since the war, the Chinese have been subjected to increasingly restrictive measures throughout Southeast Asia, but the severity and effectiveness of these has varied with the degree to which the native nationalists are in control of their countries and feel their national existence threatened by the Chinese. Thailand, because of its independent status in a traditionally colonial area and because its nationalism reached an emotional peak in the decade preceding World War II, has longest and most severely imposed restrictions on its Chinese population. In Burma, the number one scapegoat has always been the Indian community, and the Chinese there have been regarded—until lately— almost as kinsmen and not as either a political or an economic menace. The Vietnamese, too, feel themselves ethnically and culturally akin to the Chinese, but cannot forget China's domination of their country, even though this ended in A.D. 931. Moreover, the grip which the Chinese hold over much of the local economy, and—more recently—the predatory behavior of the Chinese occupation troops stationed in Tonkin just after World War II, as well as the current proximity of Red China's troops on their northern frontier, all have conspired to revive the tradition of China as Viet Nam's perennial enemy. However, because of Chinese intervention in Viet Nam's civil war and of

3

French backing for the Bao Dai regime, neither Ho Chi Minh's Republic nor the State of Viet Nam has been free to impose restrictions on the domiciled Chinese. Similarly in Malaya, it has been the prevailing armed strife and the continued British domination of the country which have shaped a policy toward the Chinese that has fluctuated sharply since 1950. Indonesia, free only since December 1949 to deal with its Chinese problem, has moved deliberately in imposing restrictions, presumably because the Chinese there form only a very small proportion of the total population and are not concentrated in any one area, and because China itself is far away.

For a short time after the Japanese surrender the Chinese enjoyed remarkable freedom of action throughout the area. In part this was due to the sympathy inspired by their persecution during the Japanese occupation, in part to the role which they had played in the local resistance movements, and in part to China's new status as one of the great powers. But the treaties made by China early in 1946 with the governments of Thailand and Indochina, which improved the legal status of the local Chinese, were progressively ignored as the power of the Kuomintang rapidly deteriorated. Yet even before that became evident, all Southeast Asian countries were showing a marked reluctance to welcome to their shores fresh waves of Chinese immigrants. International agencies, such as UNRRA and IRO,[1] which were trying to repatriate to Southeast Asia those Chinese who had returned to China just before the Pacific war broke out, experienced great difficulties in inducing the countries to take back their former Chinese residents. By no means all of them succeeded in getting permission to return, and everywhere preference was given to skilled workers and professional men.

The Economic Stake

The economic grip of the Chinese upon Southeast Asia's economy is probably the basic cause of the indigenous peoples' resentment and fear of the Chinese minority. Their position is the more remarkable when one realizes that the Chinese form only 6 per cent of the region's total population. Chinese are to be found throughout the entire economic gamut. Their importance in the different occupations varies from country to country but everywhere they dominate commercial life, especially the retail trade.

Certain shifts in the economic position of the Chinese have occurred in the postwar period, owing to governmental controls and regulations, armed strife, rural crime, and in some countries the withdrawal of competitors. While it is as yet impossible to assess accurately what effects these new factors will ultimately have on the status of the Chinese, specific trends are already clear. One major category of official controls aims at reserving to the native peoples eco-

[1] Katrine Greene, "Repatriating China's Expatriates," *Far Eastern Survey*, Feb. 25, 1948.

nomic activities which the Chinese have long controlled. Probably an equally important influence is that exercised by the insecurity of life and property, which is a by-product of the war and of the rapidly changing postwar political and economic conditions throughout the area.

In two countries of Southeast Asia the Chinese have had a lucky break. In postwar Burma, the decline in the number and economic activities of local Indians has given the Chinese an opening which they have been quick to seize, with the result that their economic importance in the country has markedly increased.[2] In Viet Nam, the withdrawal of many Vietnamese from French-held areas has permitted the Chinese to move into their places. As early as May 1947 (as the writers can testify), many shops and other enterprises in Saigon which formerly had had Vietnamese proprietors had already been taken over by the Chinese. As to the north, according to a French source, by mid-1948 "all the commerce in Tonkin [had] passed into Chinese hands."[3]

Government controls over Chinese immigration, while not wholly effective, have nevertheless succeeded in cutting down the number of unskilled Chinese laborers in the area and incidentally in increasing the percentage of local-born Chinese in the total Chinese community. Chinese labor has never been important in Thailand, Indochina, and Burma, and in Malaya and Indonesia it has been used mainly on plantations and in mining. Notwithstanding governmental restriction of specified occupations to the indigenous people, the Chinese have always tended to better their economic status through their superior industry, perseverance, and business acumen. Today, examples of a dizzy rise from coolie to millionaire are less frequently encountered among the Southeast Asian Chinese than formerly, mainly because the second generation of Chinese starts from a higher economic level and many of them now enter the professions. This trend, plus the marked decline in coolie immigration, has left a void in the ranks of unskilled labor which, in part, is being filled by the local people. In Malaya, notably, the Malays have in growing numbers overcome their traditional reluctance to work for wages. This change can be traced to the pressure of inflation, a belated recognition of their economic backwardness, and the desire for a higher standard of living. Where the Chinese remain as laborers, they tend to dominate the newly formed trade unions, as in Malaya, Thailand, and—to a certain extent—Indonesia.

As the Chinese move up the rungs of the economic ladder, they are encountering obstacles deliberately placed in the way of their further advance. In Thailand, a long-standing official policy of reserving specified occupations to the Thai people, first evidenced in 1939, has been reinforced, beginning in

2 "Chinese businessmen in Burma have come to play an increasingly important part in the country's economy." (D. Mandelbaum and E. Law Yone. *Far Eastern Survey*, Oct. 21, 1950.) "Almost one-third of Burma's trade is now controlled by the Chinese community, both foreign and domestic, in the north as well as in the south." (Pan-Asia despatch, Rangoon, Aug. 20, 1952.)

3 *Indoclim*, Paris, June 10, 1948.

1949, by a further series of laws. Many countries have legislation restricting or forbidding alien ownership of land. Some of these laws date back to colonial days, as in Indonesia, where the ban has long been total; in Viet Nam, where aliens have never been permitted to own rural lands or mines though they may own urban property; and in Thailand, which is progressively curtailing the areas where foreigners may possess real estate. In Burma, where 40 percent of the Chinese population are artisans, the problem has not arisen, for Chinese landownership there had been confined almost wholly to market gardening. The great exception to this general trend in Southeast Asia is Malaya, where Chinese squatters are now being given titles to land.

The foregoing restrictions have probably affected only a segment of the total Chinese population in Southeast Asia, as farming usually is not remunerative enough to attract the Chinese and most of them are not sufficiently educated for, or interested in, high government service. What has closely affected them are controls which the respective governments are now trying to impose on Chinese business. Chief among these are the official monopoly of the rice trade in Burma, Thailand, and Indochina; the reservation to nationals of a majority of the licenses granted to exporters and importers in Indonesia, Cambodia, and Burma, and in the case of Viet Nam to French firms; and the development in all these countries of co-operative societies designed to eliminate the alien middleman and moneylender. Furthermore, the area's trade with China, in which Chinese merchants had already been adversely affected by postwar conditions, was dealt an official death blow by the United Nations embargo on trade in strategic materials with Red China in May 1951.

Partially effective governmental controls, along with changing conditions, have forced the Chinese into new patterns of living and into illegal activities. This development seems likely to alter adversely their relations with the native peoples but unlikely to endanger their economic hold over the area. The increasing urbanization of the Southeast Asian Chinese has accentuated their aggressiveness, social aloofness, and disproportionate wealth as compared with the country's nationals, whose own standard of living has declined in the postwar period. Foreign-exchange and other controls have transformed many of the Chinese into smugglers and black marketeers, and such operations have increased both their wealth and their unpopularity.

Attempts to control the Chinese have almost everywhere run into the bewildering maze of overlapping Chinese organizations which exists in every country of the area, and they have been frustrated by Chinese evasion, ability, and indispensability. The Burma Chinese have conducted a flourishing overland contraband trade with Red China;[4] Thailand's Chinese have made fortunes out of smuggling rice to the black markets of Hong Kong and Malaya; the Chinese merchants of Singapore, Penang, and the Indies profited

[4] *Le Monde*, Aug. 21, 1952; Pan-Asia despatch, Rangoon, Aug. 20, 1952.

by running the Dutch blockade of Indonesia; and Viet Nam's Chinese traders have been impartially the main provisioners of the French-held cities and of Viet Minh troops. Licensing systems have been thwarted by the willingness of inexperienced indigenous businessmen, whom they were intended to benefit, to sell their import and export permits to the Chinese who possessed what they lacked—organization, contacts, experience, and capital. While the Chinese have held their own in the processing industries, such as rice milling and saw milling, there have been instances where Chinese have been forced out of business. This was the case with many Chinese moneylenders in rural Java, where the government has turned a deaf ear to Chinese pleas for enforcing the repayment of peasant indebtedness.[5] But usually the Chinese of Southeast Asia have adapted themselves and found compensation elsewhere for their losses. Merchants fleeing from Red China brought large amounts of capital into Thailand where, according to a prominent local Chinese leader, they were thereafter largely responsible through their speculative investments for the rapidly rising cost of living in the Thai capital.[6]

The angry exasperation inspired by such activities was voiced by Indonesia's President Sukarno in a speech made on November 17, 1951. Naming no names, he unmistakably attacked the Chinese—whom he had hitherto treated with restraint—when he said:

There are foreigners utilizing the people's difficulties to get as much profit as possible. . . . Government regulations have frequently been violated, outsmarted, avoided and sabotaged. As a result they destroy the government's authority and our economic welfare, and endanger their own cause. As a result of their improper attitude, these foreigners have aroused a hostile attitude . . . have sown the seeds of race hatred, because the difference between rich and poor coincides incidentally with the difference in nationalities. . . . It is very easy for such a social difference to turn into a racial controversy—namely, a controversy between nations . . . Such a situation is really dangerous . . . They forget the history of Tanggerang and Kebumen.[7]

Sukarno's strong statement contained both a warning and a confession. Aside from the doubtful capacity of Southeast Asian governments to eliminate or even control Chinese economic activities, none has as yet proved the ability of its own nationals to replace the services which the Chinese have performed. No amount of legislation, as the government of Thailand has found, can induce enough of its people to take up jobs which the Chinese can no longer legally fill. More important is the grave problem of agricultural credit. Development of the co-operative movement is widely believed to be the answer to this problem, but during the long educative process which a successful expan-

[5] George McT. Kahin, *Nationalism and Revolution in Indonesia* (Cornell University Press, 1952), p. 475.

[6] *Bangkok Post*, Aug. 26, 1950.

[7] *Report on Indonesia* (New York, Republic of Indonesia Information Office), Nov. 18, 1951.

sion of co-operative societies requires, who is to replace the Chinese (and Indians) as the financiers of Southeast Asia's crops? Burma's prewar co-operative movement foundered—as did partially that of Cochin China—because of an over-rapid and inadequately supervised development. And its postwar government has had to write off, at great loss to the national treasury, the great bulk of agricultural loans it had made to peasants.

Though there is no accurate gauge of their present economic status, the Chinese seem, through sheer ability, to have adapted themselves to the changing economic and political environment of the area. Unable to count upon the support of a home government, double-taxed by both regimes in Viet Nam, subject to extortion from "agents" of both Peking and Taipeh in Malaya and Thailand, and the target of discriminatory legislation everywhere but in Burma, the Chinese have not only survived but also apparently prospered.

Education

The interest shown in Chinese education by Southeast Asian governments is a postwar phenomenon, except in Thailand. On the negative side this interest is tied in with the apparently well-founded fear that Chinese schools are being used as a medium for the dissemination of Communist propaganda; on the positive side, the newly independent states have recognized that education is a major means of creating national unity and of training future citizens among ethnically diverse and very largely illiterate populations.

Until very recently the colonial governments offered a limited amount of public instruction to no more than a small fraction of the indigenous peoples; they generally ignored Chinese education and exercised surveillance over only the handful of Chinese schools which applied for grants-in-aid. Thailand, as the perennially independent country of the area, was naturally the first to try to curb the increasingly nationalistic Chinese schools established in the country. But in the postwar years all the Southeast Asia governments that are hostile to the Peking regime have changed their educational policy regarding the local Chinese. Burma and Indonesia, which have diplomatic relations with Red China, persisted longer in their laissez-faire attitude toward Chinese schools, but in the past two years they, too, have come to recognize the potential danger for their regimes represented by the absence of any effective controls. Repressive measures, such as the closing of offending schools, deportation of Communist teachers, and seizure of subversive textbooks and literature, have been resorted to by all the governments. Only in Malaya (and especially in Singapore) has the size and caliber of the local Chinese community required that a more constructive approach be made.

Political Activities

Relations between the Chinese and the governments of Southeast Asia have generally been less good than those between the local Chinese and the indigenous peoples, especially in the rural districts where the Chinese shopkeeper, moneylender, and middlemen have performed vitally needed services. In Burma and Cambodia the Chinese have come nearest to being assimilated to the native population through more frequent intermarriage and through a greater adaptation to local dress, language, and customs.

This relatively favorable relationship is, however, in process of deteriorating. The decline began during the war when the Japanese deliberately fostered such estrangement, and the results of their policy were evident in the Sino-Malay and Sino-Thai riots that followed soon after V-J Day. Differences between the Chinese and the local people as regards temperament, economic function, language, and religion, which had passed largely unnoticed in the compartmentalization that was characteristic of the colonial governments, became accentuated when those administrations were liquidated by the Japanese. During the postwar independence struggles, almost nowhere in Southeast Asia did the local Chinese actively help the native nationalists, and, in Indonesia, Chinese sympathies seemed clearly to be on the side of the Dutch. Elsewhere the Chinese, caught between conflicting forces, have adopted a wait-and-see attitude, apparently anxious only for the re-establishment of order and a stable government under which they could pursue their own interests profitably. In 1949 the victory of communism in near-by China introduced another explosive and disruptive element into an already tense situation. It increased local hostility to and fear of the Chinese in proportion as Southeast Asians suspected them of constituting a potential fifth column that might pave the way for military invasion or economic domination of the area by Peking.

Much has been written about the political sympathies and activities of the Southeast Asian Chinese which, in great part, is surmise, wishful thinking, propaganda, or generalization from isolated data. However, in the welter of opinion, there appears to be general agreement on the following points:

The long-standing cleavage between Kuomintang and Communist sympathizers among the overseas Chinese of the area has both widened and changed in character since the war. Particularly after the Communist victories in China and Korea, the ranks of the latter group swelled, reaching their peak during 1949-50. The main motive for this change-over was far less adherence to Communist ideals than a nationalist upsurge. This was stimulated by the evident strength of Red China, which, it was hoped, could and would support the overseas Chinese vis-à-vis the governments of Southeast Asia. Ideological inroads, however, have been made, chiefly among Chinese labor groups and youth: the former seemingly have been worked on by professional Communist agents, whereas the latter have responded to the patriotic fervor engendered by teachers in local Chinese schools—themselves in great majority China-born, young, underpaid, and overworked.

The new alignment has cut across the line dividing the local- from the China-born, though the latter obviously have stronger ties with the mother country and the former a greater interest in the land of their birth. Nor has it clearly followed economic stratification among the overseas Chinese. Though prosperous merchants are naturally less inclined than laborers to support the Peking regime, millionaires like Tan Kah Kee of Singapore have become pro-Communist for motives of patriotism or opportunism or both. Wherever Communist Chinese or Soviet embassies have been established, as in Burma, Indonesia, and Thailand, there has been a marked increase in local Communist activity, especially among laborers and students, but nowhere in the area does a Chinese Communist Party have legal existence. According to most students of the current scene, in no country of Southeast Asia does the Chinese Communist Party have more than a few thousand active members.

By 1951, disillusionment with the Peking regime obviously began setting in, as was shown by the decline in the sale of China Victory Bonds, shrinking remittances to China, and firmer resistance to extortion from local Communist agents. In October there were bigger celebrations of the Double Ten Nationalist Chinese holiday than for several years past, and a number of overseas Chinese "loyalty" missions went to Formosa. Letters and reports from relatives of adverse conditions in the homeland, and the forced conversion at low official rates of money sent them from overseas, went far to dispel the hopes held by Southeast Asian Chinese that the Peking regime would be more honest, more disinterestedly concerned for their welfare, and less oppressive than its predecessor.

By force of circumstances rather than by inclination, the overseas Chinese have become more rooted in Southeast Asia. Such aspirations as they may have had for a transformation of the area into a "Chinaya," or appendage of China, still persist, but probably only a military invasion by Chinese Communist forces could revive that dream. While it cannot be said that they have as yet given their loyalty to the country of their adoption, they have come increasingly to realize that they must reach a working partnership with the area's nationals. The great majority of Southeast Asia's Chinese are still waiting to see what the local nationalists will offer them in return for shifting their allegiance, but the nationalists for their part want evidence of loyalty before allotting the Chinese an important stake in their country.

The major issue on which this problem has become focused is the granting of citizenship to the domiciled Chinese. Yet even those Southeast Asian countries which have taken action with a view to putting an end to dual nationality for the Chinese have not resolved it. For neither the Kuomintang nor the Communist regimes of China have renounced their age-old contention that the overseas Chinese are their nationals, and that whatever action is taken by the individual countries of the area is legally void because unilateral.

From India it was reported in July 1954[8] that Chou En-lai had told Nehru and Nu that Communist China was prepared to drop its dual citizenship claims on overseas Chinese living throughout Southeast Asia. When urged by Nu to include such a pledge in the joint communiqué issued after their Rangoon meeting, Chou was said to have insisted upon its emanating from Peking official sources after his return home. It is noteworthy that no statement was then issued, and even the reported concession made by Chou to Nehru was later denied.

From the viewpoint of the overseas Chinese there has recently been added a further complication to an already thorny problem—that is, the requirement that should they choose to remain aliens they must register as such with the embassy of China. Now in Burma and Indonesia such embassies represent the Peking government, but in Viet Nam and Thailand the only official representatives of China are those of the Nationalist regime. Many of the local Chinese are not unnaturally reluctant to commit themselves to one or the other government by registering with its diplomatic mission.

Peking's Attitude Toward the Chinese of Southeast Asia

Communist China has shown itself greatly concerned to win the co-operation and the loyalty of China's overseas nationals. As a broad policy this differs little from that perennially pursued by Nationalist China, but the scope of Peking's activities and their relation to the Communist plan for world revolution give it far greater importance. Southeast Asian Chinese, who form about five-sixths of the approximately twelve and one-half million Chinese living abroad, are a main target for Peking's propaganda, which is directed at all levels of that community. Appeals are made to young men to return to the homeland, and indoctrination of overseas Chinese children is attempted through the medium of local schools. Patriotic contributions and an increase of family remittances are asked of prosperous Chinese living abroad. Leaders of local Chinese Communist parties and fellow travelers are periodically called to Peking to receive directives and training in carrying out the strategy of world revolution. The goal of world peace to be achieved through leadership of a strong and united China is stressed as an objective likely to arouse the enthusiasm of all elements among overseas Chinese.

Although Peking has set up in China an organization and propaganda organs for the overseas Chinese far bigger and more efficient than any comparable Kuomintang machinery, its efforts have in part backfired because Communist China's basic policy suffers from the same handicaps as did that

[8] Associated Press despatch, Bombay, July 19, 1954.

of the Nationalist regime. Primarily this is because both governments have asked almost everything from their nationals living abroad, and have given them virtually nothing in return. Secondarily, in championing the cause of the "oppressed" overseas Chinese, both of China's regimes have antagonized all the Southeast Asian governments—nationalist as well as colonialist—which already had a backlog of resentment and fear toward the Chinese living in their midst.

The bureaus for overseas Chinese established at Peking, in Hainan, and in some of the south China provinces have as their special function the protection and servicing of Southeast Asian Chinese returning to their homeland.[9] Their "benevolent" activities range from providing facilities for travel to admission into Chinese educational institutions and the settlement of disputes relating to the property of overseas Chinese in China. The offer of free land in China to such overseas Chinese as had failed to make a good living in Southeast Asia has brought back many of the laboring class. The opportunity to receive a higher education in China has lured thousands of youths unable to acquire traditional Chinese culture in Southeast Asia. In July 1953, Radio Peking announced that China's Ministry of Education was reserving 10 percent of the admissions to Chinese universities for overseas students, and that the motherland needed 10,000 of its overseas sons to return to China "where big jobs and key positions" awaited them.[10] In Malaya and Viet Nam, the recent introduction of compulsory military service has prompted thousands of Chinese to elect soldiering in the service of China as preferable to that of Southeast Asian governments. Since New Year's Day 1954, propaganda posters appeared almost simultaneously throughout Burma, Malaya, and Indonesia, promising free education and exemption from military service to overseas-Chinese youths returning to China.[11] Chinese Communists control newspapers, distribute films, and sell books and periodicals at very low prices. These find a ready public among the newly literate southeast Asians, who, regardless of their ideologies, are avid for learning and short of reading matter.

To reach the still younger generation, Peking's long arm has reached into the Chinese schools of Southeast Asia as did that of the Kuomintang government before it. The fact that everywhere in the region Chinese education has been the concern almost exclusively of the Chinese community and not of the local educational authorities has made infiltration easier.

The fund-raising tactics used by the Peking government have fallen into two patterns.[12] The first and more innocuous method was a direct appeal to

[9] G. William Skinner, *Report on the Chinese in Southeast Asia* (mimeo.; Cornell University, 1950), p. 81.

[10] United Press despatch, Singapore, July 9, 1953; *Straits Times*, July 29, 1953.

[11] *Bangkok Post*, May 3, 1954.

[12] S. Y. Lee, "Defeat Through Default: A Failure of New China Abroad," *South-East Asia Review* (Bangkok), January 1952.

Chinese patriotism for donations. In prewar years, particularly after the outbreak of the Sino-Japanese war, Southeast Asian Chinese had contributed enormous sums to the Kuomintang exchequer. Disillusionment with the Nationalist government and with its use of such funds was evident in the early postwar period. Up to February 1946 the Bank of China used to receive U.S. $5 million monthly from Southeast Asian Chinese; by December of the same year the amount had shrunk to $2 million, and the Nationalist government was reported to be seriously worried at this progressive decline.[13] Probably this meant no corresponding diminution in the amount of family remittances sent to China, for overseas Chinese were said to be using foreign bank drafts and other nonofficial channels. Inauguration of the Communist regime at Peking was followed by appeals to overseas Chinese to buy "Victory Bonds," and initially these yielded substantial results. Late in 1949 Radio Peking stated that remittances from Southeast Asian Chinese were then providing the Communist regime with its second largest source of foreign exchange.[14]

When purchase of these bonds began falling off, the time-honored practice of squeeze was resorted to. Chinese businessmen in Southeast Asia began receiving what came to be known as standard "letters from home." The short-term effects of such letters were satisfactory in that they brought in sizable amounts to the coffers of Peking, but the long-term results have been poor. Not only have remittances fallen off (in part because of the restrictions placed on such remittances by Southeast Asian governments), but more important, the prosperous overseas Chinese have been soured by the confiscatory exchange rate imposed by the Communist authorities and resentful of the harsh measures that have been taken toward their families in China.[15]

Usually after the fifth "letter from home," the donors have either stopped remitting or simply sent enough to cover the day-to-day needs of their relatives. Apparently despairing of any further considerable sums from this source, the Peking government in December 1952 resorted to a new squeeze play called "surrender of surplus overseas remittances." For its purposes, overseas Chinese remitting money to China have been classified into three groups—the rich, middle class, and poor.[16] Relatives of those falling into the

[13] Associated Press despatch, Nanking, Dec. 11, 1946.

[14] *Bangkok Post*, Jan. 8, 1950.

[15] In October 1951, a semiofficial survey of Bangkok remittance houses revealed that there had been a big drop during the year in the sums sent to China. Local Chinese were believed to be sending then only $35–40 (Hong Kong) a month. The Thai government admitted to the difficulties of enforcing a total ban on Chinese remittances. In Malaya for six months beginning late in 1949, there was a cessation of remittances to China. But by February 1950 over 800 remittance firms in the Federation and 167 in Singapore were able to resume operations. Since that time remittances have averaged between Str. $2–5 millions monthly, of which more than half has been sent from Singapore. Each remitter could send only Str. $35–40 a month.

[16] *Bangkok Post*, Dec. 19, 1952.

first two of these categories were required to report all remittances which they have received since 1946; failure to report would entail imprisonment, and informers were to be rewarded. This retroactive measure, which lent itself to ruthless and arbitrary application, could not but further alienate a vitally important segment of the overseas Chinese population—the prosperous middle class. That such was the case was indicated by a meeting of overseas Chinese delegates called at Peking in June 1953, reportedly to devise ways in which the steadily waning support for the Communist government could be off-set.[17]

Peking twice before this had been the scene of conferences to which Southeast Asia Communist leaders and their faithful followers were summoned. At the World Federation of Trade Unions meeting in November 1949, labor in Southeast Asia was reportedly assigned the task of spearheading the revolts which—it was announced—were finally to liberate the area from the vestiges of economic and political domination by Western imperialists. To the conference held in September 1952 delegations of the so-called peace committees in each Southeast Asian country were invited, and resolutions were passed urging an immediate end to the Korean War and to the revival of Japanese militarism, and calling for the formation of an Asia-wide peace bloc. Though this conference was in part inspired by that of ANZUS, it was but the most recent and the biggest in a series of "peace" progaganda moves which began with the Stockholm Peace Appeal, just prior to the start of the Korean conflict in 1950.

To reconcile the contradictory pictures of Communist China as the strategist of Asia's revolution and as top dove of Asian peace, Peking propagandists have had to choose their audience and their timing. Though secrecy surrounded the proceedings of the conferences of 1949 and 1952, presumably the hard core of Communist Party delegates were given directives of revolution, while the fellow travelers and the world at large heard only the dove cooing, if the blaring of Radio Peking can be so delicately described. How far such propaganda has been effective can, of course, only be surmised. Peace, naturally, has a universal appeal and a particularly strong one to Southeast Asian nations which have lived through the Japanese occupation and years of subsequent strife and which require uninterrupted tranquillity in order to carry out their many development plans. While the effect of Peking's peace propaganda on the Southeast Asian masses cannot be gauged, the reactions of the area's governments are more clearly discernible. These reactions have been conditioned by the individual country's physical proximity to China, the importance and activities of its Chinese minority, the country's prevailing ideology, and finally by its relations with Peking.

[17] United Press despatch, Singapore, *Times of Indonesia*, June 9, 1953.

Peking's Relations with Southeast Asian Governments

As regards the newly independent countries of Southeast Asia, Peking has used high-pressure methods and has shown a tactless determination beyond any displayed by the Kuomintang, even in its most aggressive days. Radio Peking has been relatively tender toward the two countries which have recognized the Mao government, but even with them it can hardly be said to have exercised diplomacy. The envoys sent by the Chinese Communists to Rangoon and Djakarta have, reportedly, antagonized even those national governments which had enthusiastically hailed their arrival.

In the case of Burma, the Chinese ambassador brought along as a member of his staff a Chinese who had previously been expelled from Rangoon for having given aid and comfort to the Burmese Communist rebels,[18] and his aloofness at social functions further alienated the sociable Burmese. At the Peking WFTU conference in November 1949, Premier Nu was denounced as a stooge of the Western imperialists.[19] Radio Peking has from time to time reproached Burma for its failure to oust the Kuomintang troops from the Shan States. Perhaps the most clumsy of all was the dissemination in Burma, during the spring of 1951, of a map printed in China which showed parts of north Burma as Chinese territory.[20] And it was reported in mid-1953 that Chinese Communist backing for an autonomous Kachin state, along the Burma-India-Yunnan frontier, was causing serious anxiety to the Rangoon authorities.

At the Colombo conference of Asian prime ministers held in April 1954, Nu expressed anxiety about China's expansionism and "demanded guarantees to ensure that the withdrawal of French rule from Indochina would not automatically be followed by Chinese infiltration."[21] That same month, however, Burma signed a three-year trade agreement with Peking. In May Premier Chou En-lai, reportedly at Nehru's suggestion, made a visit to Rangoon for the purpose of allaying Burmese fears of Chinese aggression. Whether or not as a result of this visit, Burma's Defense Minister, U Ba Swe, said that the time was now ripe for negotiating a nonaggression pact with Peking, and concessions were made to local Chinese residents in regard to the amount of money they would be allowed to remit to close relatives in China.[22] Never-

[18] Skinner, *op. cit.*, p. 29.

[19] Mandelbaum and Law Yone, *op. cit.*

[20] *New York Times*, May 17, 1951. The disputed border area involves about 75,000 square miles. Negotiations between China and Britain regarding it were interrupted by the Pacific war. The dispute flared up again in December 1947 when a Kuomintang minister voiced China's claim to Burmese territory north of 25° 35" N. lat. The Burma government hastened to reassure its people that the question would be resolved through normal diplomatic channels and that Burma would not surrender any territory. (Associated Press despatch, Rangoon, Dec. 22, 1947.)

[21] *Manchester Guardian Weekly*, July 1, 1954.

[22] Henceforth, Chinese remittances could amount to one-third to one-half of monthly earnings. (*The Burman*, May 9, 1954.)

theless, there are indications that Premier Nu was not wholly convinced of the Communists' peaceful intentions. Late in May he was said to have greatly influenced the Indian decision to let the Soviet Union know that a too-ambitious Communist policy in Southeast Asia would spell danger.[23]

In Indonesia, Peking's ambassador was very active in promoting the cause of local Communists, both Chinese and indigenous; he was believed to have stirred up some of the labor troubles plaguing the Indonesian economy; and he wanted a larger staff and more consulates than the Indonesians were willing to have in their country. His zeal further included communizing the local Chinese schools.[24] In Djakarta, as in Rangoon, the Chinese embassy was believed to have close contact with Peking's agents throughout the area and with the Soviet embassy at Bangkok. More than elsewhere in southeast Asia, the Chinese Communists in Indonesia have been active in the distribution of films and reading matter, the infiltration of the Chinese Chambers of Commerce, and the control of the local Communist party and the main labor federation (SOBSI).

Thailand, for every good Marxist reason, was the main target of Peking's attacks. Not only did the Thai refuse to recognize the Mao government but they have cultivated increasingly cordial relations with the Kuomintang regime on Formosa. Premier Pibul has been denounced by Radio Peking as a fascist, cruelly oppressing the local Chinese, and slavishly subservient to Washington. Since a Communist victory in Asia was inevitable, Radio Peking warned, the Thai had better get on the winning side. In April 1953 Radio Peking made such strong charges against the Thai government[25] that the *Straits Times* described them editorially as "the most serious Far Eastern development since the Korean invasion." Peking's specific accusations were that—

(1) Thailand was "allowing" the U.S. to build strategic military airfields throughout the country and strategic highways from Thailand to Burma for the purpose of supplying KMT forces in the latter country;

(2) The Thai had sent troops to fight in Korea for aggressive purposes and to assure themselves of American military aid; and

(3) The number of United States military advisers in the country had tripled, and that they were there in order to control Thailand's armed forces.

The Soviet embassy, the underground Chinese Communist Party, and the Chinese-dominated Central Labor Union of Bangkok were believed to be

23 United Press despatch, London, June 2, 1954.

24 When it was learned in July 1952 that the ambassador Wang Jen-shu had been appointed to the Peking Politburo after an absence of six months from his post in Djakarta, an Indonesian diplomat reportedly expressed the hope that "Perhaps Peking will send a better man to Indonesia" (*Times of Indonesia,* July 2, 1952).

25 *Bangkok Post,* Apr. 30, 1953.

the agencies through which Peking received intelligence and transmitted policy directives.

As to the Viet Minh Republic, Mao's recognition of it in January 1950 dispelled any lingering doubts as to the closeness of the ties between the two regimes. Later that year, completion of the Naning railroad and loss by the French of their posts at Caobang and Langson obliterated for all practical purposes the frontier between Yunnan and Tonkin. Reportedly the Viet Minh had already concluded agreements with Peking which permitted the former to open military camps in Chinese territory where Chinese instructors gave military and political training to Ho's troops. South China, which had for decades served as a place of refuge for Vietnamese revolutionaries, now came to play a role in the Indochina conflict analogous to that of Manchuria in the Korean War.[26] Though the equipment furnished the Viet Minh fluctuated in quantity and kind with the fortunes of Chinese arms in the Korean conflict, it was a welcome addition and adequate enough to outfit new units and to permit the Viet Minh to pass from guerrilla to open warfare. An unknown number of Chinese advisers, perhaps 300, were believed to have been sent at about that time to instruct the Viet Minh forces in the field. Despite repeated rumors to the contrary, no evidence that Chinese soldiers were with Ho's troops had come to light as of early 1954, and the long-threatened Chinese invasion of Indochina had not yet materialized. Chinese aid to the Viet Minh, until the siege of Dien Bien Phu in early 1954, appeared to be aimed chiefly at maintaining the Republic's fighting strength rather than at enabling it to achieve a decisive victory.[27] And even in making possible the victorious assault on Dien Bien Phu, Chinese policy has seemed related more nearly to furthering its own objectives at the Geneva Conference than to supporting Viet Minh interests. Presumably Peking felt that the Viet Minh were doing well enough without open help from China, which might arouse American counterintervention and a hostile Asian reaction and also might encounter opposition from a Moscow reluctant to see China dominate the area.

Early in May 1954 the U.S.S.R. and Red China jointly issued an invitation to the Viet Minh to send a delegation to the Geneva conference. However, the latter were reportedly not overpleased by the settlement reached through the efforts, in part, of Chou En-lai, especially as regarded Laos and Cambodia. A Chinese Communist spokesman at that conference asserted that China "has made no intervention of any kind in the Indochina war."[28] A few days later a United States government agency made public what was alleged to be a Chinese Communist guidebook, dated December 15, 1953, for the use of

[26] Le Monde (Paris), Jan. 30, 1952.
[27] Ellen J. Hammer, The Struggle for Indochina (Stanford University Press, 1954), p. 249.
[28] Associated Press despatch, Geneva, May 4, 1954.

some of the thousands of "volunteers" helping the Viet Minh. Both the Soviets and the Red Chinese asserted that this document was a forgery.

In contradistinction to its direct moves re Indochina, Peking has held relatively aloof from the Communist-led revolt in Malaya. Geographical distance is certainly a factor, and Malay hostility to the Chinese is another. So far as is known from this distance, the Communist insurgents there have received no outside aid, though individual agents are believed to have been helping them with strategy and indoctrination. In addition to a normal propaganda barrage about oppression of the local Chinese by British imperialists, Radio Peking proposed to Prime Minister Attlee in March 1951 that a delegation of the Chinese Relief Committee for Overseas Refugees from Malaya be permitted "to investigate the conditions of the persecuted Chinese in Malaya." Not surprisingly this was refused, and the amount of indignation that this remarkable proposal engendered among the Malayan Chinese suggested that it had completely missed its mark as propaganda. Late in 1952, after the Truman-Attlee conference at Washington, Radio Peking reported the holding of "complaint meetings" in China at which it was claimed that the British were brutally maltreating the Chinese in Malaya and had already deported 35,000 of them.[29]

In November 1953 a conference held at Peking, attended reportedly by 412 delegates of overseas Chinese, caused another wave of adverse reactions in Southeast Asia. Not only was it touted as the biggest conference of its kind since the Communist regime had come to power in China, but it was said to have assigned 30 seats in the All-China People's Congress to delegates from Southeast Asia's Chinese and to have prescribed the method by which they were to be nominated.[30]

The Policies of Southeast Asian Governments in Regard to China

While the policy of the Southeast Asian countries toward China has varied as to pattern, it is inspired in each case by the same mixed motives—fear of Chinese aggression, particularly since the end of the Korean War, admiration for a strong and independent Asian nation, the desire to trade with China, and the dread of becoming entangled in the East-West power struggle.

The factor of physical proximity to China has been of more political and military importance than economic significance, and it has counted heavily in determining the policy of the three northernmost states of the area. China's frontier with Burma and Indochina traverses a rugged, inaccessible region, hard to exploit profitably. From the political and military angles, these very factors are weighty. Dissidents or revolutionaries fleeing from the governments of their respective countries have long sought refuge on both sides of the border. Currently, southern China is still sheltering Vietnamese out of favor

[29] New York Times, Dec. 19, 1952.
[30] Reuter despatch, London, Times of Indonesia, Nov. 25, 1953.

with both regimes in Indochina and also the Kachin rebel, Naw Seng. Conversely, Kuomintang troops pushed back by the advancing Communist army crossed over by the thousands into Burma and Indochina, where they created an international problem of an explosive nature.[31] The setting up by Red China, during 1953, of two "autonomous governments" among the Thai and Kachins who live on both sides of the frontier between Yunnan and Indochina and Burma fell into the normal Communist pattern of creating satellite border states. They were designed to attract political opponents of the governments of Thailand, Burma, and Indochina, which, thus far, have been unable to control those regions and which have been deeply concerned not to provoke an invasion of their territories by the Chinese Communist forces stationed along the Yunnanese frontier. Although the borderlands are of undeniable strategic importance, it is the far richer southern areas of Southeast Asia which are the great prize and to which the vast stream of Chinese immigration and China's dream of hegemony has long been directed.

Obviously the first issue to arise in determining Southern Asia's policy toward "the New China" was that of formal recognition of the Peking government. Massing of Communist troops along the southern frontier of China late in 1949 frightened Burma into remembering that it had 1,000 miles of undemarcated boundary with that country in the north. Rangoon hastily recalled its ambassador to the Kuomintang government and, in December 1949, became the first non-communist country to recognize Mao. By mid-1950, embassies were exchanged, as later were cultural missions, between the two countries. Realism rather than ideology motivated this move, for Burma had been fighting a Communist revolt of its own for over two years. Burma's Chinese community was small and regarded as neither a political nor an economic menace.

In contrast to Burma, Indonesia had no fear of a Chinese invasion and did not take the initiative in recognizing the Peking regime. Nevertheless, in March 1950, impelled by mixed motives of sentiment and principle, it accorded this recognition. Chinese had not been prominent in the Madiun Communist revolt of 1948, which, moreover, had been ended a year and a half before. Indonesian nationalists seem to have been favorably influenced by the Chinese Communists' fight against the Japanese, against a corrupt regime, and against a foreign economic imperialism. Moreover, they saw it as analogous to their own struggle to wrest independence from the Dutch. Since neutrality was the cornerstone of Indonesia's foreign policy, it was only logical that its government should seek to offset its economic dependence on the West by closer relations with a great and rising power in Asia.

Not many months passed, however, before Indonesia began to experience the disadvantages of its action. China wanted to open 12 consulates in the

---

[31] See also p. 24 ff.

archipelago, while the Indonesians were willing to accept only 3—at Makassar, Medan, and Surabaja. The Indonesians felt that an embassy staff of 80 was excessive, and in July 1951 refused entry permission to 16 additional Chinese diplomats whose names had not previously been cleared with the Djakarta government. China's ambassador protested formally; the New China News Agency called this an "unfriendly act," but the Indonesians stood firm in regard to what they considered an infringement of their sovereignty.[32] That segment of the press which supported the government's action contrasted disapprovingly the freedom allowed in Indonesia to China's diplomatic mission with the restrictions placed on the movements of the Indonesian chargé d'affaires at Peking, and claimed that in books written by the Chinese ambassador he had accused Sukarno and Hatta of being traitors to their people. Relations became obviously strained, and the departure for China of an Indonesian cultural mission was postponed. It was not until September 1953 that Indonesia sent to Peking its first ambassador to China. Earlier that same month Dr. Sunario, Foreign Minister in the newly installed Ali government, denied a press report that he had said Indonesia would support the admission of Red China to the United Nations and the return of Formosa to that government.[33]

For some months after receiving Mao's bid for recognition in mid-October 1949, the Thai government maintained an ostrich-like attitude. Suddenly, early in 1950 Peking launched a fierce radio attack on the Pibul regime, apparently inspired by Bangkok's playing host to American Far East diplomats in February.[34] The Thai broadcast several replies to Peking's charges, in which their policy toward the local Chinese was described as one of "extreme moderation," and they announced their government's decision not to recognize Peking nor to sell Thai rice to China. This marked a turning point in Thailand's traditional foreign policy of playing off against each other the two strongest forces in Asia. Thereafter the Thai were definitely committed to the Western bloc and with it the Kuomintang regime. Though all Kuomintang consulates in Thailand were closed by May 1, 1950, and only its embassy remained open, the Thai maintained a chargé d'affaires attached to the Formosa government. Relations between Bangkok and Taipeh rapidly improved to such a point that the latter did not protest against the increasingly restrictive measures which the Thai were imposing upon the local Chinese.

In June 1950, the outbreak of the Korean War forced the Southeast Asian governments to reconsider their policy toward China. After some hesitation, Premier Nu announced on July 8 that Burma would support the United Nations Security Council resolution but would be unable to offer any effective aid. While Burma's adherence to the United Nations stand on Korea had

[32] *Report on Indonesia*, July 31, 1951.   [33] Antara despatch, Djakarta, Sept. 2, 1953.
[34] *Bangkok Post*, Jan. 28, 1950.

only moral importance for the international scene, internally it represented a major policy decision for the government. Conservative opposition leaders rang the changes on Burma's perennial fear of a Chinese invasion, which they claimed Nu's action would precipitate. The Socialists and labor unions split over the issue, and the extreme left wing broke away to form a new political party (the Burma Workers and Peasants Party) whose program came to follow the Communist line. Chinese Communists did not cross the border, the government did not fall, and Nu made propitiatory gestures to Peking by steadily supporting its demand for a seat in the United Nations. There had been no break with Burma's neutral foreign policy, he asserted. But more realistically he pointed out that if Burma wanted United Nations support in the event of a Chinese invasion, then Burma would have to support the United Nations.[35]

Indonesia, the only other country which had recognized the Mao government, maintained a neutral attitude longer. But eventually it followed Burma's lead, though with more reservations and greater internal trauma. Reluctant to take sides and confused as to the issues involved, the Indonesian government reiterated that its most urgent task was to solve domestic problems so that the country could defend itself in an emergency.[36] Not until Indonesia became a member of the United Nations in September 1950 did it face a showdown. Two months later, its chief delegate to the United Nations explained Indonesia's abstention from the vote on the Kuomintang's charge that the U.S.S.R. was threatening the independence of China. Said Dr. Palar:

We are convinced that Nationalist China cannot continue its struggle and we expect that Mao's China is soon to replace Nationalist China . . . We are very sad about this question. We know that Nationalist China has always supported us in our struggle for freedom.[37]

Alternately Indonesia tried to propitiate one side and the other. On December 8, 1950, Indonesia joined 12 other countries in an appeal to Peking to halt its advancing forces north of Korea's 38th parallel. A peace proposal for Korea suggested by ex-Premier Natsir to Peking through the Chinese ambassador at Djakarta in July 1951 went unanswered. A year later Indonesia rejected President Truman's invitation to take part in a neutral inspection of United Nations prison camps in Korea.

Communist victories in Indochina during the early months of 1954 aroused Indonesia, as they did every other Southeast Asian country, to reconsider its relations with Red China. At the Colombo conference of Asian prime ministers held in April, Premier Ali sided with the elements that regarded colonialism as a greater menace than communism to Southeast Asia. And in May his

---

[35] Martyrs' Day speech, July 19, 1950.   [36] *Report on Indonesia*, June 20, 1950.
[37] *Report on Indonesia*, Nov. 30, 1950.

government announced that it was considering sending an invitation to India and Burma to join in formulating with Communist China a nonaggression pact for the purpose of offsetting the Southeast Asia Treaty Organization.[38] Some observers saw in this project evidence of the government's fear of China's expansionism, while others believed that it reflected primarily Premier Ali's concern to check the internal hostility between the Masjumi party and the local Communists.

The Thai government, on the other hand, not only immediately supported the United Nations resolution of June 30 on Korea but, the next month, took a unique place among Asian nations by promising to send 4,000 troops to fight the Communists in Korea. Premier Pibul overrode the feeble opposition offered this pledge by the Democrats, who disagreed not in principle but on the ground that so great a military effort was too much for a small country like Thailand. Not only were more troops than promised actually dispatched to the Korean front and rice sent to the South Koreans, but Pibul intensified his campaign against the local Chinese. Those steps, capped by economic-aid agreements which Thailand signed with the United States in the fall of 1950, spurred Red China to fresh radio attacks on the Thai government. Late in November 1950, Peking for the first time evinced an interest in the local Communists. Its radio broadcasted a declaration allegedly made by the Thai Communist Party, which appealed for a united front against the Pibul administration and charged the United States with turning Thailand into an advanced base for aggression against the Viet Minh and China. In December Pibul retaliated by directing his delegate to the United Nations to announce that Thailand would support the bombing of Manchuria. And in January 1951 Pibul sounded a clarion call over the Bangkok radio for patriotic resistance to the Chinese Communist aggression. For good measure he recalled that it was the Chinese who, centuries before, had driven the Thai out of China and who now monopolized the trade of Thailand.

In the spring of 1951 there arose a third major issue in Southeast Asia's foreign relations with China, which for the first time required that a stand be taken by Indonesia and Malaya. This was the United Nations limited embargo on trade with Communist China. On May 7, 1951, ten days after he became Foreign Minister, Subardjo caused a flutter in the Western dovecotes by declaring that "Indonesia would sell to the devil" if it would serve his country's interests. There is little doubt but that he echoed a majority sentiment among Indonesian nationalists, who greatly feared the effects of such an embargo on Indonesia's shaky economy and on its "independent" foreign policy. Eventually the government decided to abide by the United Nations embargo, and the internal political effects of this compliance were somewhat neutralized by official stress on the fact that they stemmed from Indonesia's

38 *New York Times*, May 30, 1954.

membership in the United Nations—a body to which the country owed much during its independence struggle—and did not represent an independent decision. As a gesture to mollify Peking, Indonesia announced it would raise its diplomatic mission in China to embassy status.

About a year later Peking's proposal to exchange Indonesia's rubber for rice and light machinery met with a cool reception at Djakarta because of what a highly placed Indonesian official described as the "unpleasant" sequel to a Chinese-Indonesian arrangement of April 1951.[39] At that time trade talks had been informally held at Djakarta, during which the Indonesian government was reportedly assured of receiving 200,000 tons of rice from China in 1951. By the end of that year Indonesia was disillusioned not only by the failure of the promised tonnage to materialize but by a report that Red China had in the meantime signed an agreement for immediate delivery of 100,000 tons to India. In August 1953 the Chinese made a notable effort to impress Indonesians by a display of their wares at the Djakarta trade fair. More than this, however, the continuing slump in world rubber prices and the signing of an armistice in Korea revived Indonesian interest in trading with China. Trade missions were exchanged, and early in 1954 a three-year trade agreement was signed by the two countries. This agreement, however, only laid down general principles for the exchange of commodities between the two countries. When it came to the application of such principles, negotiations, which opened on June 28, 1954, were said to have bogged down within three weeks owing to Indonesia's reluctance to include among its exports to China petroleum and rubber.[40] Earlier in July, the Ministry of Economic Affairs denied rumors that Indonesia had already shipped rubber to Red China.

Since Red China's need for rubber transcended its other trade interests in Southeast Asia, its major effort to break the United Nations embargo inevitably centered on Malaya as the world's largest rubber producer. It has even been suggested that China's apparent failure to supply more aid to Malaya's insurgents was caused by its concern not to hamper rubber production in the peninsula. Until this issue came to the fore, Malaya had accepted passively British foreign policy toward China, even though some voices were periodically raised to regret the psychological lift which Britain's recognition of the Mao regime in 1949 had given to Malaya's Communist rebels. But Malaya's docility was sorely tried by the ban on rubber shipments to Communist China, which had been increasing by leaps and bounds since the outbreak of the Korean War. Then, too, both British and Chinese businessmen were as one in resenting Malaya's colonial status, which made the country impotent to follow Ceylon's example in refusing to impose the United Nations embargo. Yet in June 1953, when the Singapore Chinese millionaire, K. C. Lee, urged

[39] *Times of Indonesia*, May 29, 1952.   [40] *New York Times*, July 18, 1954.

lifting the 26-months-old ban on rubber shipments to Red China, Singapore commercial leaders reportedly termed his plea "premature."[41] For Thailand, Burma, and Indochina, which were far less important rubber producers than Malaya and Indonesia, the ban did not become a real issue.

Because the Associated States of Indochina had at that time acquired only limited sovereignty in their foreign relations, France still called the tune in their policy toward China. The Chinese, to whom the United Nations had assigned the duty of receiving the Japanese surrender in the northern part of Indochina, aroused French hostility during the winter of 1945–46 by the support which they gave in general to the Republic's government at Hanoi and in particular to its pro-KMT faction, the Dong Minh Hoi. To secure evacuation of Tonkin by Chinese Nationalist occupation forces in February 1946, the French had made important concessions concerning—among other points—the position of the Chinese living in Indochina, notably as to their legal and fiscal status.

Progressively, an increasing number of those concessions became dead letters, as exigencies arising from the conflict between France and the Viet Minh transcended all other considerations and the Kuomintang government rapidly declined in strength. A dispute between France and Nationalist China regarding sovereignty over the Paracel Islands ended inconclusively early in 1947, and in June 1948 France restored its prewar administration of the Chinese Congregations. Protests from the Kuomintang consuls in the country followed, and negotiations were transferred to Paris. There the matter was settled amicably; the Congregations were given a name less wounding to Chinese pride, and election of their chiefs was made more liberal. But in fact the tight control which the Congregation organization permitted to the French was retained. Any thought which France may have entertained in 1949 of recognizing the Peking regime was dispelled by Mao's recognition of the Viet Minh Republic in January 1950. As of mid-1954, no pro-Communist journals had been tolerated in the French-held parts of Indochina, and Formosa's consuls were stationed at Saigon, Pnom-Penh, Hanoi, and Haiphong. A Vietnam good will mission, headed by former Premier Tam, was feted in Formosa in June 1954. To their routine duties these consuls added the onerous responsibility of liaison between the French authorities and the thousands of Kuomintang troops who were interned for some months after fleeing across the Indochina border from the Communist advance in south China.

The promptness with which the French interned the refugee Nationalist soldiers (who were later returned to Formosa) and the smallness of their number in Thailand obviated the possibility that their presence in those two countries might serve as a pretext for a Red China invasion. But in Burma the problem posed by the presence of a far larger number of Kuomintang

[41] *Straits Times,* June 12, 1953.

troops—estimates of their strength ranged from 8,000 to 20,000—revived fears of a Chinese Communist invasion, especially as some of Burma's Communist insurgents were believed to have contacts with Peking and as the Kachin rebel, Naw Seng, was known to have tried to recruit followers in Yunnan. Too weak militarily to eject or intern the Kuomintang troops, Burma tried to neutralize their presence by diplomacy. Having no longer diplomatic relations with the Nationalist Chinese government, Rangoon indirectly tried to exercise pressure on the Kuomintang regime to withdraw its troops from Burma, but Formosa disclaimed responsibility for the activities of General Li Mi, commander of the Nationalist refugee troops in north Burma. The latter simply stayed on, became the *de facto* government in certain areas of the Shan States, lived off the land to the distress and resentment of the local people, and cornered the region's lucrative opium trade.[42]

In the summer of 1951 two unsuccessful attempts made by the Kuomintang forces to invade southern China rearoused Burmese fears and suspicions. A few months later Radio Peking tried to confirm them by utilizing a visit made by Li Mi to Formosa as a chance to attack the United States for aiding his troops in Burma from bases in Thailand. In the January 1952 session of the United Nations General Assembly, Vishinsky repeated and embellished these charges, which were denied by both Bangkok and Washington. High Burmese officials joined in the chorus—with the important difference that they did not accuse the United States government but individual Americans of backing the Kuomintang venture. Not until a year later was a report circulated that the Central Intelligence Agency was the responsible organization and that the American ambassador at Rangoon had resigned in protest against its "bungling" of the affair.[43] But the Rangoon government, ever fearful of Peking's reprisals, turned down a British proposal that a United Nations Commission should investigate the situation. At a press conference at New Delhi in October 1951, Premier Nu was careful to stress that Red China had been very "correct" in its attitude toward Communist insurgents in Burma. He also added: "I don't think they give aid to Burma's rebels."[44]

On Burma's internal political situation, failure to dislodge the Kuomintang troops in the country had serious repercussions. Opposition forces cited the alleged presence of American officers and advisers with the Kuomintang forces and called for a volunteer brigade to oust them. From bitter experience the Burmese authorities realized that these volunteers might easily become the nucleus of still another anti-government armed force. Premier Nu pointed out that the problem was hardly a new one since the Kuomintang troops had

[42] *Le Monde*, Aug. 2, 1952.

[43] J. and S. Alsop, "Abortive Invasion of Yunnan Province," *New York Herald Tribune*, Feb. 12, 1953.

[44] *Bangkok Post*, Oct. 25, 1951.

been in the country since March 1950, and reassuringly announced an offensive against them by government forces. A few days later he proclaimed the success of this offensive, though the public must have realized the improbability of achieving such rapid results. Since no one was allowed into the area to check on the situation, the government weathered the storm. Throughout 1952 left-wing opposition parties assiduously fostered pro-Chinese sympathies in Burma, and a sizable Burmese delegation attended the Peking World Peace Conference in the fall.[45]

If the Kuomintang troops had been content with the status quo, the problem posed by their continued presence in the Shan States might have remained localized. But late in 1952 the Chinese Nationalists began expanding their area of operations in Burma. In so doing they deposed the ruler of Mongshu, hoisted the Kuomintang flag over a town they captured, and went so far as to ally themselves informally with some Karen and Mon insurgents—all of which inevitably gave rise to clashes with the Burmese army. Practical considerations, rather than ideology, seem to have induced them to take this fateful step. Two abortive attacks allegedly made on Yunnan in January 1953[46] may have permanently discouraged some of the Kuomintang troops from further attempts to re-establish themselves in China and decided them to settle down in Burma. Apparently they have given guns and military training to the Karens and Mons in exchange for food supplies, which the Chinese Nationalists badly needed, and for wolfram, which they have been able to sell at a profit.[47]

In Rangoon newspapers, reports of American equipment and personnel among the Kuomintang forces began to appear with increasing frequency. And when the Eisenhower administration announced that it would withdraw the Seventh Fleet from Formosa, the Burmese interpreted this to mean that formal and large-scale American support would now be available to the Kuomintang troops in Burma. Consequently the pressure internally brought to bear upon the government to "prevent Burma from becoming a second Korea" mounted to an irresistible level. Premier Nu, who in mid-February 1953 had made a speech warmly defending the American aid program,[48] within three weeks felt compelled to call for its termination, and eight days later in the U.N. General Assembly, the Burmese delegate charged the Formosa regime with aggression against his country. This sudden about-face had at least the merit of making the American government finally aware of how deeply the Burmese resented and feared the presence of foreign troops on their soil, and of the need to get the Formosa authorities to withdraw them. On April 22 the U.N. General Assembly unanimously condemned the presence of Chinese

45 *The Burman*, Aug. 11, 1952.   46 Associated Press despatch, Rangoon, Mar. 1, 1953.
47 *The Burman*, Jan. 20, 1953.   48 *Christian Science Monitor*, Feb. 13, 1953.

Nationalist troops and called on them to lay down their arms and leave the country or march into internment camps.

The role played by Formosa was ambiguous, to say the least. The Kuomintang government consistently denied the Burmese charge that it had issued directives to Li Mi, and it maintained that his army was in Burma contrary to its wishes. Obviously the Formosa regime did not want to withdraw its troops who were already strategically poised for an attack on the mainland.

In May 1953 the United States took the initiative in arranging the first of a series of meetings at Bangkok between delegates of Burma, Thailand, and Nationalist China. Within a month, agreement was reached on the procedure for evacuating Chinese troops from Burma, but its acceptance by Formosa and by the Chinese officers in the field proved quite a different matter. The Formosa authorities claimed that they had control over only a small proportion of the Chinese guerrillas in Burma, the majority of whom they asserted were local recruits. The Chinese "jungle generals" were then called to Bangkok in a vain effort to secure their co-operation. They even proposed that such Chinese troops as preferred to remain in the country be concentrated in a neutral zone in Burma, with the United States guaranteeing a cease-fire between them and the Burmese army.[49] Following Formosa's rejection of two more evacuation proposals in September, the Burmese delegation quit the Bangkok meetings, Burma's army reopened a campaign against the local KMT troops, and the Rangoon government once more brought its case before the U.N. Despite its good offices as negotiator in the dispute, the United States—as Chiang Kai-shek's main supporter—came in for a large share of the blame in Asian eyes for Formosa's delaying tactics and obstructionism.

The American and Thai delegations continued their meetings with the Chinese Nationalists at Bangkok, but it was probably Burma's decisive actions that finally induced Formosa to agree to the evacuation of the 2,000 troops in Burma who it admitted were KMT regulars. For six months, beginning October 5, 1953, some 2,000 KMT soldiers and their dependents were withdrawn to Formosa, but not without serious hitches and delays. When it was learned that, among these evacuees, some very recently recruited Shans were being palmed off as KMT soldiers and that only a few obsolete weapons were being surrendered, the Burmese not unnaturally revived their charge that Formosa was acting in bad faith. Obviously a large quantity of modern arms still remained in the hands of the 8,000 to 10,000 Chinese guerillas, who were disowned by the Formosa government but who were continuing to support Karen and Mon rebels and preying upon Burmese villagers. Not only did the Burmese government have to divert its limited military forces from putting down indigenous revolts (which received fresh stimulus from the Chinese guerillas' local activities) to the task of ousting the KMT troops, but their con-

[49] *New York Times,* July 23, 1953.

tinued presence was a standing invitation to Communist China to invade an area that was increasingly troubled by internal unrest.

In 1946 the frontier areas, long administered separately from Burma by the British, had thrown in their lot with the Burmese nationalists, and in return for their loyalty had been granted considerable autonomy by the constitution of independent Burma. During the long period of internal revolts, beginning in March 1948, the frontier peoples in the Shan, Chin, and Kachin States had with few exceptions supported the central government of Premier Nu. Slowly the government forces began forcing the rebels out of central Burma and into the peripheral areas. By 1950 some of them had moved into the northern frontier states at about the same time that the KMT troops were seeking refuge there from Yunnan.

As the KMT troops began digging in, they contributed directly and indirectly to the friction that was building up between various elements of the frontier peoples. In large part this friction was the natural consequence of the new concepts of political and social freedom engendered by Burma's independence struggle. In each of the frontier states, the younger generation was increasingly resentful of the arbitrary powers exercised by the hereditary chieftains—the sawbwas in the Shan States and the duwas in the Kachin villages. By 1952 the opposition had become strong enough to convince the sawbwas that they should turn over their powers to a more democratically constituted government. In these troubled waters the KMT tried to fish, with such disruptive results that the central government felt it must set up a military administration over part of the Shan States in December of that year. For in some of the 32 Shan States the KMT had forcibly replaced the hereditary chief and substituted their own sawbwa, while in others they had sided with the incumbent sawbwa against the opposition to him. The Burmese government believed that Li Mi was exploiting the political crisis of 1952 as part of his general plan to occupy all of the Shan States.[50]

Among the Kachins, trouble developed along different lines. After the British withdrawal in 1947, the Kachin Hills Area was divided administratively. The Kachin State, as constituted in independent Burma, consists of the northwestern portion, whereas the southeastern sections fall into the Shan States region. In the latter area, reportedly, the sawbwas have "lost their authority and are faced with a communist movement that receives considerable Kachin support."[51] In the Kachin State proper, conflicts between rival duwas and ethnic groups have merged into a struggle between political parties. Duwa Sima Sinwa Nawng, head of the state since 1948 and strong advocate of co-operation with the central government, was forced to resign in July 1953 despite his undeniable popularity with the Kachins and support by the Kachin Youth

[50] *Bangkok Post*, June 26, 1953.
[51] E. R. Leach, *Political Systems of Highland Burma* (Harvard University Press, 1954), p. 258.

League. Unfavorable economic conditions as well as political considerations were largely responsible for his downfall. Wartime devastation, serious unemployment, and a decline in the transfrontier trade had induced Duwa Sima soon after independence was achieved to initiate a five-year plan for the industrialization of his state. However, it proved to be so impracticable that the central government, in addition to doling out annual subsidies to the state treasury, had to take over and revise the plan late in 1952. Furthermore, the People's Economic and Cultural Development Organization, founded by Duwa Sima, included reportedly pro-Communist elements whose expulsion was demanded by the AFPFL. Duwa Sima's economic and political naïveté, not his lack of good intentions, eventually permitted a rival organization, the Kachin National Congress led by Duwa Zaw Lun and supported by the AFPFL, to oust him as head of the state. In local terms this has meant—at least temporarily—the ascendancy of the plains people (Shans and Burmese) over the Kachin element, and has created unrest that may lead to further political instability. The Rangoon government is mindful that "the Chinese have never admitted Burmese rights over the country east of the Irrawaddy and north of Myitkyina,"[52] and that for some years Communist China has been exploiting Kachin trouble spots.

Since 1950, rumors of Communist agitation in the northern frontier areas have been rife. When the Bangkok government began clamping down on the Viet Minh agents and Chinese subversives in Thailand, Communist headquarters in Southeast Asia were reportedly transferred to Burma, where the Viet Nam Republic's delegation and the embassy of Communist China enjoyed greater freedom of action. In an inaccessible spot in the Shan States, an outstanding international Communist agent—a Vietnamese whose aliases included, among others, Nguyen van Long—was believed to have established a center for gathering intelligence and disseminating propaganda throughout the frontier zones. Periodically, incursions into Burmese territory by Communist agents and troops have been reported, as has been the recruiting of an underground army, the Nai-Zain Tat[53] and the distribution of pamphlets denouncing Premier Nu and Duwa Sima.

Coinciding with the latter's downfall came an increase in Peking's propaganda for the creation of a "greater Kachin state" that would comprise the 300,000 Kachins in China and the 70,000 living in India as well as the 200,000 established in Burma. Further, some of the duwas having authority over Kachins living on both sides of the national frontiers were said to have been spreading Communist ideas among their tribes, and many disaffected Kachins had migrated to China where they were receiving Marxist indoctrination and training.[54] On May 24, 1954, a Rangoon daily, *The Nation*, reported from

[52] *Ibid.*, p. 241.   [53] *The Burman*, Oct. 9, 1951, May 13, 1953.
[54] *New York Times*, Aug. 13, 1953.

Myitkyina that Burmese Communists aided by Chinese Communist agents were planning to hold a conference in north Burma for the purpose of winning over the Kachins. According to the same source, this conference was to be attended by Indian Communists from Assam (whose permanent agent was stationed at the headquarters of a new underground movement located 100 miles south of Myitkyina), thus suggesting a liaison with the Red Chinese who claimed the northern section of the Kachin State.

The establishment in March 1954 of the so-called "Free Karen State" along Burma's eastern frontier, from Monghsat to Mergui, seems to fall into what has become a Chinese Communist pattern, evident earlier in the creation of the "autonomous" Kachin, Free Laotian, Cambodian, and Thai states. The latest comer to this galaxy of borderland satellites seems to offer double advantages to the Communists, by consolidating a wedge of dissidents between the anti-Communist governments at Rangoon and Bangkok. A memorandum, reportedly announcing to the Thai government formation of the new "state," claimed that the Karens were of the same ethnic stock as the Thai and had migrated south at the same time as other Thai from Yunnan.[55] It also asserted that the newly installed "government" was supported by Mon as well as Karen insurgents against the central Burmese administration. Presumably the Communists hope that, if they succeed in capturing leadership of the dissidents in Arakan and in the Malay states of south Thailand, the organization of hostile groups along all the Burmese and Thai frontiers will reduce the Nu and Pibul regimes to impotency.

Regardless of whether or not they began propitiously, relations between all the Southeast Asian governments except, of course, the Viet Minh and the Peking regime have deteriorated until partially and perhaps temporarily improved as a result of Chou En-lai's visits to India and Burma in the spring of 1954. But only Thailand has courted the Formosa Kuomintang. As the tempo of Thai restrictions and arrests of Chinese accelerated, so did Peking's radio attacks. The Chinese Communists particularly resented the fact that it was a Thai-sponsored resolution at the United Nations General Assembly meeting in November 1951 that ruled out discussion for that session of the admission of Red China to membership. At the same time, progressively cordial relations were established between Thailand and Formosa. In Bangkok the Kuomintang was allowed to start a propaganda magazine and exhibits in March 1951; in May, Thailand's diplomatic mission to Formosa was enlarged; in October,

<hr>

[55] Reuter despatch, Mar. 24, 1954. Early in April the new "state" notified the Thai government that it had been set up by an act of the Karen "Parliament"; a "Cabinet" had been formed under a military administration; and it would seek recognition from the United Nations. The territory claimed for this "state" was 3,840 sq. km. in area, its president was said to be the forty-five-year-old chief of its High Military Council (Saw Hunter Tamuy), and its army composed of 6 Karen divisions (24,000 soldiers) and one Mon division (4,000). (*Bangkok Post,* April 12, 1954.)

the government permitted local Chinese a big celebration of the Double Ten anniversary, and that same month made an agreement with Taipeh to establish airline service between Formosa and Bangkok. On its side, the Kuomintang became the first foreign regime to recognize the Thai military government which came to power as a result of the November 28, 1951 *coup d'état*. Since that time a number of good will and business missions have been exchanged between Bangkok and Taipeh. In May 1954 Generalissimo Chiang —without apparent irony—bestowed high honors upon two of Thailand's police officials who had been most active in prosecuting the local Chinese. The following month the Formosa regime pledged its support for Thailand's appeal to the United Nations to send an observation team to study the Indochina border war situation.

The changing political climate of Southeast Asia enabled Chiang to hold a successful meeting of overseas Chinese delegates in Formosa shortly after the Peking conference of September–October 1952. More than 200 delegates from 22 countries attended at their own expense, and endorsed resolutions to float U.S. $100 million worth of bonds as backing for a Nationalist invasion of the China mainland. Other pledges included the imposition of an economic blockade against Red China, increased unity among overseas Chinese in the global anti-Communist struggle, and support for the Kuomintang government. For its part, the Taipeh regime eased economic controls with a view to encouraging greater investments by overseas Chinese in Formosa, and drafted a policy platform promising to improve diplomatic relations with the governments of the countries where overseas Chinese reside.

This conference, the first of its kind, did not receive much publicity at the time. Nevertheless, it was the first concrete evidence backing Chiang's claim to the loyalty of Chinese living abroad. And in contrast to the earlier Peking conference, delegates to it represented the wealthiest group of Chinese in the world, influential out of proportion to their numbers both in world trade and among their own communities. Probably most of them were still Chinese nationals, and all had family and cultural links with China. As hardheaded businessmen, their pledge of sweeping economic sanctions against Communist China must be taken with many grains of salt. But their presence in numbers larger than had been anticipated and their promise of monetary support for a Nationalist invasion of the mainland indicated an evolution of great importance. For it showed that many influential Chinese had not only turned their backs on Communist China but believed that Chiang's effort to liberate the home country was worth backing with cash. In October 1953 the markedly increased celebration of the Double Ten anniversary by the Chinese of Southeast Asia—with the possible exception of Indonesia—seemed to confirm the anti-Communist trend. Nevertheless, there can be no doubt that the prestige of Red China in general and Premier Chou in particular has been greatly enhanced in the eyes of the local Chinese as a result of the Communist victories in Indochina and of the outstanding role played by the Chinese Communists at the Geneva conference. While communism's success in Vietnam could not but increase the apprehensions of Southeast Asian governments in regard to China's aggressiveness, they noted with satisfaction that Chou En-lai returned home by way of India and Burma rather than via Moscow. His statement that "revolution cannot be exported," and his proposal made on June 27, that Asian chiefs of state meet occasionally to ease the threat of war and to prepare a "mutual respect" pact among themselves (similar to the one he had signed with India on April 29), met with a favorable reception.

Southeast Asians in general admire the Peking regime's role in the international sphere because of the fact that an Asian nation has so rapidly become powerful enough to stand up to the colonial and capitalist West. Quite different, however, is their attitude toward China as the homeland of their own Chinese minorities. For the latter not only remain culturally Chinese but they personify and aggravate the threat that China's growing aggressiveness represents for the sovereignty which southeast Asian nations have so recently won.

MALAYA AND SINGAPORE

Population and Immigration

Of the nine to ten million Chinese living in Southeast Asia, the most important group—not only numerically and proportionately but also economically and culturally—are those living in Singapore and Malaya. The total number of the Malayan Chinese is only slightly larger than that of the Chinese population of Indonesia, but their numerical relation to the indigenous population, geographic concentration, educational standard, and growing political importance, and above all, the role which they play in the country's economy, account for their primacy among the Southeast Asian Chinese.

Altogether, the Chinese of Singapore and the Malayan Federation are estimated at 2,795,000, and they present the extraordinary phenomenon of an alien population slightly outnumbering the indigenous Malays. This numerical advantage will inevitably grow in the future, for the Chinese segment of the population is increasing annually at the rate of over 3 percent as compared with about a 2 percent rate of growth among the Malays.[56] Some 90 percent of the Chinese in the Malay peninsula have settled in a belt about 40 miles wide down the west coast, and in Singapore they form three-fourths of the population. Generally speaking, the Malayan Chinese are urban, almost 54 percent of them being classified in the 1947 census as town dwellers, and over 40 percent of them resided in towns of 40,000 or more inhabitants. Malaya-

[56] T. E. Smith, *Population Growth in Malaya* (London, 1952), pp. 77, 61.

born Chinese constituted nearly two-thirds of the total Chinese population of the country in 1947.[57]

As in Thailand, the motivation behind the restrictive measures imposed by Malaya on Chinese immigration and settlement has been politico-economic, but the timing and stress have been different. The quota allotted to Chinese male immigration in 1933 (followed by that on female immigration in 1938) was inspired by the world depression and was never seriously enforced. Malay hostility to the Chinese, which derived from Japan's wartime policy and flowered as a result of the improved status conceded to the local Chinese in the Malayan Union scheme, made it politically inadvisable to permit unrestricted Chinese immigration. But above all it was the Chinese Communist revolt, which broke out in 1948 in the Malay peninsula, that impelled the authorities to control not only Chinese entry into the country but travel and residence as well. Because of the postwar shipping shortages and Malaya's distance from China, it was not difficult to enforce immigration laws, which now limited legal entry of Chinese almost exclusively to the families of residents. Indeed, from 1946 to 1949, there was a small net outward movement of Chinese from Malaya to Hong Kong and China amounting to about 13,000 annually.[58] And in 1950 there was a large-scale exodus of Chinese youths whose aim was to serve the "New China" and who also were anxious to escape being called up for military service under Malaya's new manpower regulations. During 1952–53 the exodus of Chinese returning to China continued at a steady pace: from July to December 1952 those leaving numbered 4,694 as compared with 4,882 for the comparable period in 1953.[59] But in the spring of 1954 Communist successes in Indochina, coupled with enforcement of the national service registration required of youths from the ages of eighteen to twenty, suddenly swelled the monthly departures to an average of about one thousand. Moreover, few if any of those leaving for China bothered to apply for a re-entry permit.[60] In May thousands of Singapore Chinese school children rioted in protest against compulsory registration for the military draft.

Until October 1950, all that was required of a Singapore Chinese wishing to travel abroad was a certificate of local residence. That month the governor-in-council suddenly added the requirement of a re-entry permit for each trip made outside Malaya. Following forceful representations by Singapore Chinese businessmen regarding the delays and red tape that this would entail, the requirements were somewhat modified in the spring of 1951. This flurry not only illustrated the strength of the Singapore Chinese business community but also their favorable position there, compared with that of their compatriots

---

[57] M. V. Del Tufo, *Malaya—A Report on the 1947 Census of Population* (London, 1949), p. 84.
[58] *Economic Survey of Asia and the Far East—1950* (United Nations), p. 43.
[59] *Straits Times*, July 9, 1953.
[60] United Press despatch, Singapore, *Bangkok Post*, May 3, 1954.

in the revolt-ridden peninsula, where far more drastic measures affecting the Chinese were taken.

In the Federation, new immigration regulations came into force on August 1, 1953. The bill embodying these regulations had been three years in the drafting, it had had a long and difficult passage through the legislature, and in its final form it was vainly opposed by every unofficial Chinese member of the Federal Legislative Council. By its provisions, immigration into Malaya has been restricted to aliens belonging to the artisan or professional classes who are assured of a position in the country entailing a minimum monthly salary of Str. $500. The right of unrestricted re-entry has been confined by the same law to Federal citizens and British subjects born or normally resident in the Federation. All others must apply individually for permission each time they wish to return to Malaya after an absence abroad. Obviously the new law aimed at protecting the living standards of Malayan workers by closing the doors to jobless immigrants no longer needed, it was felt, to supply the labor force of a country in which half the population is under twenty-one years of age. Though this law would affect Indians more than Chinese it was the latter element which, characteristically, fought its passage. They claimed that it was the government's failure to provide adequate school facilities which prevented many aliens from acquiring the knowledge of English or Malay required to qualify for Federal citizenship. The Malayan Chinese Association (MCA) went so far as to assert that this bill "is apparently being used as a political weapon to reduce the number of Chinese living in Malaya."[61]

As to the Chinese already living in the Federation, their position was drastically affected by other measures taken as a result of the armed uprising that began in early 1948.

The Briggs Plan, launched in 1950, gave official recognition to the relationship between the Communist revolt and the food, money, and shelter which the insurgents were afforded—voluntarily or otherwise—by the Chinese squatters who lived along the fringes of the jungle or on the outskirts of the peninsular towns. For over a year the resettlement of these squatters was held up by the expense involved, opposition on the part of the Malay states to acquiring additions to their Chinese populations, and the inevitable disruption of agricultural production and of the rubber estates' labor force (to both of which the squatters were important contributors) that would ensue.

However, by the end of 1952 this major upheaval, involving a fourth of the Federation's Chinese population of two millions, was accomplished, and its political and economic consequences promised to be momentous. Military strategy required that the settlers be brought together in compact villages straddling the main channels of communication; health conditions necessitated sanitation measures; giving the displaced Chinese a constructive alterna-

[61] *Straits Times*, Nov. 24, 1952.

tive to communism entailed granting them land titles, meeting halls, schools, and a village council.[62] Thus the Chinese squatters were given a stake in the country, accessibility, amenities, and a village organization which not only had they never before known but which were advantages superior to those enjoyed by the traditionally law-abiding and loyal Malay kampong (village) dwellers.[63]

From the viewpoint of pure justice this was certainly inequitable. Moreover, it marked an important revision in the British government's long-established pro-Malay policy, and it had the practical effect of weighting the delicate Sino-Malay political balance definitely in favor of the Chinese. Undertaken primarily as a military measure, the large-scale resettlement of some 500,000 Chinese squatters has accelerated the change, already rapid, of the political face of Malaya. It is believed to offer a new avenue for Communist infiltration, as many of the resettled Chinese are bitter over the forcible nature of their transplantation. It has certainly added new fuel to the Malays' fear and distrust of the Chinese.[64]

Political Activities

In Malaya the citizenship problem has affected the Federation seriously, but it has not been felt in Singapore, because of the latter's continued status as a British crown colony. In the Federation the citizenship issue has touched the very heart of the Sino-Malay problem, and in its initial handling both the Chinese and British showed remarkable ineptitude. The Malayan Union scheme failed to resolve the dual loyalties of the alien Asians in that it created a local citizenship that was not tantamount to nationality. Such citizenship was conferred with a fairly liberal hand on the domiciled non-Malays, but later, by the federal constitution of 1948, the qualifications for acquiring it were so tightened, in deference to Malay wishes, that only about 350,000 Chinese undertook to become citizens under its provisions. Though the advantages such citizenship would confer were never specified, the stringent qualifications for acquiring it aroused resentment among the Straits-born Chinese and have been a major cause of their persistent opposition to the federal constitution and of their failure to support the government actively during the Communist revolt.

After prolonged discussion the Communities Liaison Committee finally worked out a compromise under which citizenship would automatically be accorded to non-Malays born in the Federation, one of whose parents had also been born there. Provision was made for the acquisition of citizenship on the

[62] By April 1953 about 100 of the new villages were self-governing.
[63] E. H. G. Dobby, "Resettlement Transforms Malaya," *Economic Development and Cultural Change* (University of Chicago), October 1952.
[64] J. E. King, "Malaya's Resettlement Problem," *Far Eastern Survey*, March 1954.

part of aliens not born in the Federation but long resident there. Since the new laws opened the gates almost exclusively to second-generation Malayans they have not wholly satisfied those local Chinese who want birth in Malaya to confer citizenship automatically, and who are holding out for less-stringent language qualifications and for elimination of the sultans' arbitrary power to cancel the privileges of non-Malay citizens.

The foregoing concession made to the Malayan Chinese represented the most realistic approach to the problem as yet attempted in any Southeast Asian country. Actually, it was the product of joint statesmanship on the part of British and Chinese leaders. It reflected a belated British acknowledgment that their pro-Malay policy had not paid off in terms of crushing the long-drawn-out Communist revolt, and that Chinese co-operation would have to be won by positive inducements which the Malays must be persuaded to ac-cept. Further British steps in their new wooing of the Chinese included in-ducements to enter the Malayan Home Guard, police and armed forces, but perhaps the most significant move was the opening of the Malayan Civil Service in December 1952 to qualified non-Malay Asian aspirants in the pro-portion of one to four Malay appointees. As it has worked out, however, this concession has been of more moral than practical advantage to the Chinese. The higher salaries paid by private and commercial firms are held responsible for the small number of non-Malay Asians applying for admission to the Malayan Civil Service.[65]

The local Chinese, for their part, moved even more slowly and less directly, hampered as they were by lack of political experience and inclination. The vast majority among them still remained uninterested in politics, negative in their attitude, and absorbed by business matters. But in May 1948 their leader-ship, after a brief alliance with radical elements, formed a strong communal organization, the Malayan Chinese Association (MCA), led by Sir Cheng-lock Tan. Before that time this Straits-born rubber baron had headed the leftist coalition of the Council of Joint Action, but he came gradually to recog-nize that Sino-Malay co-operation was the prerequisite to creation of a truly Malayan nationality on the mainland. Later the Chinese made other contribu-tions to racial harmony: the Singapore Chinese Chamber of Commerce ac-cepted the principle of conscription for military service and the MCA voted to welcome non-Chinese to associate membership in that body.

At about the same time the Malays seemed to recognize that a dog-in-the-manger attitude toward the Chinese would not advance the status of their community or longer elicit active British support. However, while many of the Chinese did not go along with the MCA's policies, the Malays were even more divided among themselves as to which path they should follow. Dato Onn bin Jaafar, the outstanding Malay leader, was moving too fast for the

[65] *Straits Budget*, May 27, 1954.

majority of his compatriots as regards concessions to non-Malays. And in September 1951 he broke away from the United Malays Nationalist Organization (UMNO), which he himself had founded, to organize the Independence of Malaya Party (IMP). The MCA proceeded to enter into an informal alliance with the conservatives who now dominated the UMNO. This was a surprising move as regarded both parties. It had been assumed that most members of the UMNO felt that even the status quo (which assured them of a majority in the Federal Legislative Council[66] and required the consent of their state governments to any major policy decision) merely enabled them to hold their own vis-à-vis the Chinese. They were alarmed lest the citizenship provisions in the constitution should be revised in favor of non-Malay Asians, if elections were to be held for the Federal and Municipal councils as the MCA wanted.

As to the Chinese attitude toward the UMNO-MCA alliance, Sir Cheng-lock seemed to be reversing his established policy. For instead of supporting the IMP as had been expected, he stole its political thunder. He was farsighted enough to realize that the intercommunal IMP did not truly represent Malay opinion. Co-operation with the Malays, he believed, must be achieved through the UMNO, with whose leaders he could strike a fundamental bargain whereby the Malays would trade political power for economic advantages. Both the leaders of the UMNO and of the MCA, united by a feeling of antagonism toward Dato Onn, were able through "communal gerrymandering" to work out a practical system for electing candidates of the dominant ethnic group in each ward. The success of these tactics was first shown in the seven municipal elections held in 1951, where the MCA-UMNO combine decisively routed the IMP candidates.

Despite such a clear-cut victory at the polls, by no means all the Chinese or the Malays were pleased by the MCA and UMNO leadership of their communities. If some Malays felt that the UMNO's leaders had sold their political birthright to the Chinese too cheaply, many of the Chinese themselves—particularly those in Singapore—felt dissatisfied with their end of the bargain. For one thing, setting the Malays on their economic feet would be a very expensive undertaking. Two local authorities, T. N. Silcock and Ungku Abdul Aziz,[67] estimated that it would "require a sum equal to the whole present federal revenue—about Str. $300 million—levied almost every year from the Chinese and devoted to Malay welfare for 10 to 15 years." They also felt that this change could not be brought about without a major economic operation. Secondly, the Singapore Chinese were very proud of the noncommunal aspect of local politics as contrasted with the strongly communal organizations that dominated such political life as existed in the Federation. True, they were not

66 Out of a total membership of 75 there were only 16 Chinese on that council.
67 *Nationalism in Malaya* (mimeo.; New York: Institute of Pacific Relations, 1950), p. 46.

pleased by the smallness of the Chinese electorate for the Singapore Legislative and City councils. Although by December 1950 there had been a notable increase in the number of Chinese running for election, there were still only 4 Chinese candidates, as compared with 13 Indians, and only 48,000 of the estimated 250,000 eligible to vote had registered.[68] But in December 1951, the British eased the language and residence qualifications for Singapore Chinese to become British subjects and thus eligible to vote in local elections. While this move undeniably increased the political potential of the Singapore Chinese, it foreshadowed a bitter struggle between two rival groups among them. After the MCA, which had established a branch at Singapore in 1950, decided to enter local politics in 1952, it met with strong opposition from the oldest Chinese organization in the colony—the Straits Chinese British Association.

By this time, too, British military successes in the Federation were dissipating the unifying force that had been supplied by the common danger arising from the Communist revolt. Need for Chinese support in putting down the revolt diminished, and with it Britain's concessions to the Chinese. As the pendulum of British policy swung back toward supporting the Malays, Dato Onn likewise reverted to his earlier role of voicing the now reawakened fears of his compatriots, and even the UMNO began looking with suspicion at its ally, the MCA. In August 1952, the Malays turned down a gift of Str. $500,000 offered by the MCA for their economic uplift, and their leaders refused to meet Victor Purcell, British adviser to the MCA, who had been invited by the MCA to visit Malaya.[69] The next month Dato Onn, in a very forthright statement to the central committee of the IMP, asserted that all talk at that time of friendship and co-operation between one community and another in Malaya was "nothing but sham."[70] In April 1953 he went so far as to assert that the Chinese were trying to turn Malaya into the thirtieth province of China and prophesied that "we shall yet see a major clash of conflicting interests between the Malay and Chinese communities."[71]

As to the MCA's aims, Sir Cheng-lock has consistently maintained that they embrace improvements for the Malays as well as greater rights for the Chinese. In the first issue of the *Malayan Mirror*, official organ of the MCA, which appeared on June 15, 1953, he spelled out more precisely than he had before the objectives of that organization:

1. In regard to citizenship in Malaya, the principle of *jus soli* should be adopted without qualification.

[68] *Straits Times*, Dec. 2, 29, 1950. Three years later a memorandum from the Straits Chinese British Association to the Rendel Commission stated that there should be over 200,000 Chinese on Singapore's electoral rolls but that only 10 percent of that number was registered.

[69] *Straits Times*, Sept. 4, 1952.

[70] *Ibid.*, Sept. 19, 1952.

[71] Associated Press despatch, Kuala Lumpur, quoted in the *Burmese Review*, Apr. 20, 1953.

2. All public services, including the Malayan Civil Service, should be fully opened to non-Malays.
3. Elections to the Federation, State, and Settlement councils should be held as soon as the citizenship question was settled.
4. Food production, especially rice, should be officially encouraged; non-Malays should be urged to grow more paddy.
5. The economic strength of the Malays, especially the peasantry, should be increased.
6. All ethnic groups in Malaya must regard themselves primarily as Malayans without, however, losing their cultural and linguistic affinities.

Nevertheless, throughout 1953 Sino-Malay relations continued to deteriorate. Specifically, Malay fear of the Chinese was stimulated by the latter's determination to found their own university at Singapore, by the recrudescence of Chinese secret-society activities, and, above all, by the political ascendancy which the MCA was acquiring both in Singapore and the Federation. These developments seem also to have made the British feel that they had probably gone too far in favoring the Chinese at Malay expense. In addition to improving educational facilities for the Malays through training programs and scholarships) and supporting the Rural and Industrial Development Authority's efforts to raise the rural Malays' standard of living, the government was reportedly considering legislation requiring business firms to employ a certain percentage of Malay labor.[72]

In April 1953 the Chinese provided fresh ammunition to their opponents by failing to air a scandal involving the disappearance of lottery funds from the Singapore branch of the MCA. Such funds had apparently been used to finance some members' business operations that were unrelated to the MCA's avowed activities, and in any case MCA lotteries were felt to have given that association undue political advantage over rival parties. Two months later (June 1953) the government announced a ban beginning in August on all lotteries sponsored by political parties. On the surface this measure was non-discriminatory as it hit the UMNO, the Peninsula Malays' Union, and the Malayan Indian Congress as well, but it fell hardest upon the MCA, which operated by far the biggest lottery[73] and which depended financially in large measure upon lottery proceeds.

The lottery ban, besides so angering the MCA that it announced an end to all its welfare activities on behalf of the Malays, provoked a widespread anti-government reaction among the Chinese community generally. Chinese indignation was further fanned by circulation among troops in Malaya of a British officer's book, *Jungle Green,* which contained derogatory comments on

[72] *New York Herald Tribune,* Apr. 7, 1953.
[73] Each drawing had provided prize money totaling over U.S. $800,000.

the Malayan Chinese.[74] Already the Chinese were incensed by what they felt to be restrictions upon their citizenship status and immigration facilities, and by the government's plan for national schools to be financed by a Registration and Licensing of Businesses Ordinance that would bear hardest upon their community. Chinese leaders pointedly asserted that the economic power of their compatriots had declined markedly during the past twenty years and that it was the Europeans who now dominated big business in the country.[75] Sir Cheng-lock stated his belief that the motive behind the government's lotteries ban was to weaken the MCA-UMNO alliance which was seeking independence for Malaya.[76] In part to disprove that allegation and in part to still the UMNO demand for federal elections in 1954, the British High Commissioner in October 1953 appointed two outstanding members of the Alliance to posts in the Federation's cabinet.

This gesture, however, did not appease the Alliance, which found new grievances in the recommendations made by the Rendel Commission on constitutional reform in Singapore and by the Federal Elections Committee on the mainland, both published in February 1954. Although the changes proposed by the Rendel Commission were surprisingly advanced in many vital respects, they did not wholly meet Chinese demands, notably as regards the creation of a distinctive Singapore citizenship and in the use of languages other than English in the proposed, mainly elected assembly. As to the Federation, the Alliance was so little "prepared to compromise on any of the main issues—the ⅗ elected majority in the Council, elections by November 1954, and the eligibility of government officials for election to the legislature"[77]— that it announced in May 1954 that it would boycott any elections held under the proposed new Federal constitution. Whether the Chinese will prefer obstructionism, which some elements among them tried unsuccessfully once before, or whether they will choose to utilize such political concessions as have been made them, remains to be seen. As Mr. Carnell comments:

About 73 percent of the Chinese in the Federation are now entitled to citizenship. Similarly in Singapore, though admittedly only about one Chinese in two is en-

---

[74] In January 1954, as a result of protests by the MCA and the SCBA, the author and publisher of *Jungle Green* promised to delete "16 epithets considered offensive to the Chinese" from subsequent editions.

[75] In a pamphlet entitled *Chinese Economic Domination of Malaya Is a Myth*, the publicity chief of the MCA, Tan Siew Sin, said that the future was dark for the local Chinese. Of the country's more than 3 million acres of cultivated rubber, more than half was owned by Europeans while the rest was shared between the Malays (22 percent), the Chinese (20 percent), and the Indians (6 percent). At one time, he claimed, the Chinese owned most of the local tin mines, but by 1939 only one-third remained in their hands and this proportion had now been reduced to one-fifth. While the Chinese still controlled the retail trade, all the big export and import business was in European hands.

[76] *Straits Times*, June 25, 1953.

[77] F. Carnell, "Constitutional Reform and Elections in Malaya," *Pacific Affairs*, September 1954.

titled to vote, the Chinese easily can make up the vast majority of the potential electorate. It is beyond doubt that power in Singapore, and their fair share of power in the Federation, is within the grasp of the Chinese if they choose to take it. For that reason the two new constitutions are likely to set them the greatest political challenge they have yet encountered.

Education

Despite the comparatively high standards of Chinese education in Malaya, less than half of the Chinese children of school age receive even primary schooling. In 1950 more than 700,000 Chinese children in the Federation attended its 1,340 Chinese schools (of which 1,085 were run by the Chinese community) and fewer than one-third of the entire Chinese population there were literate. In that same year there were 285 registered Chinese schools in Singapore, with an enrolment of 73,000—a small proportion of that city's Chinese population of some 790,000 but more than half the total number of students enrolled in all of Singapore's schools.[78]

Fewer than one-third of Singapore's Chinese schools were government-aided,[79] and the proportion was even lower in the Federation. Despite stiffly rising costs, those grants-in-aid were still on the prewar level, averaging Str. $8.54 per student per year. An inevitable result has been the substandard quality of Chinese education both in Singapore and on the mainland; the fees charged by Chinese schools (Str. $4 to 12 monthly) are comparatively high; their teachers are underpaid[80] and undertrained, and lack security of tenure; and their management is subject to the rather casual supervision of their deficit-underwriting board of directors. The curriculum of these schools has been patterned after that of the homeland, and many of their teachers have been brought to Malaya from China.

The new deal in primary education for Singapore, formulated in the Neilson Plan of 1947 and supplemented by the Frisby Plan of 1949, included Chinese along with other children but not Chinese schools as such. But neither in Singapore nor in the Federation was the budgetary allocation for education large enough to realize this objective, and no official policy for Chinese schools was laid down. Regarding secondary schools no real problem existed, for the great majority of Straits Chinese were already sold on an English education that was the open sesame for remunerative employment in Malaya. But the question debated by the whole community has been the linguistic medium for primary education, and to a lesser extent its curriculum, as Straits-born and

---

[78] *Straits Times,* Nov. 21, 1950; *Bangkok Post,* Dec. 9, 1950.

[79] In 1953, the government spent about Str. $2 million of the $20 million of its education budget on Chinese schools.

[80] As of December 1953, salaries of full-time primary teachers in Singapore's Chinese schools ranged from Str. $140 to $200 a month, and for secondary teachers from Str. $240 to $400 a month.

China-born alike are determined that their children shall preserve a distinctively Chinese cultural heritage.

In 1951 the Federation asked for and received two reports which it had hoped would provide guidance on educational policy. Their answers to the moot question of Chinese schooling were diametrically opposed. That of Leonard Barnes advocated the elimination of all vernacular schools and proposed a national school whose avowed purpose was Malayanization of the younger generation and whose non-Malay Asian students at the age of six would begin the study of two other languages—English and Malay. On the other hand, the Fenn-Wu Report, while subscribing to the same long-term objective, insisted that education must not be prostituted to political ends. Its authors urged the strengthening of Chinese schools through a 100 percent increase in government subsidies; improvement in the management, curriculum, and teaching staff; elimination of political jingoism through close official supervision; and the adding of English in the third year, and of Malay in the sixth, as required auxiliary languages in addition to Chinese. Messrs. Fenn and Wu stressed the intense suspicion prevailing among the Malayan Chinese in regard to British policy toward their traditional culture, and their fear that—for want of a truly all-Malayan culture—the education dispensed in the proposed national schools would become largely Malay. (In August 1950 the closing of two of Singapore's outstanding Chinese schools for allegedly disseminating Communist propaganda, and the establishment in the Federation of a three-to-one ratio in favor of the Malays in the allocation of state scholarships to the University of Malaya, had gone far to confirm that Chinese suspicion.)

In regard to taking action on the two reports, Singapore characteristically moved faster than the Federation. As of January 1954 not one national school had yet been built on the mainland, although the Federal Legislative Council had approved of the scheme eighteen months before. The building of some non-national schools in the interval seemed to disprove the official explanation of financial stringency as the cause of such inactivity. Some observers have concluded that a more valid reason was the strong criticism of the principle of national schools voiced by the UMNO-MCA alliance.

In Singapore, on the other hand, a committee was appointed in June 1952 to suggest ways in which Chinese primary schools could be integrated with the colony's educational system, as the indispensable preliminary to drafting legislation making primary education compulsory. And even before this committee was appointed, the Singapore Education Department had reversed its prewar policy by allotting a substantial place to Chinese-language study in the curricula of English schools. In December 1953, after long study of the question, the Singapore government accepted the proposal made by some prominent Chinese to establish bilingual schools. Existing vernacular schools in the colony could, if they so wished, receive from the government double the current grants-in-aid by giving equal weight in instruction to English and Chinese and by directing their courses of study to the objective of turning out good citizens of Singapore. Most of the additional grants were to be devoted to increasing teachers' salaries and to improving their status. In this respect the MCA had already led the way by donating Str. $100,000 to that end. Singapore at the time had no normal school in which to train the 1,300 or more Chinese teachers in the colony, of whom 957 were China-born.

The first reaction of most sections of the Chinese community to the proposal to establish bilingual schools was favorable, but soon an adverse reaction set in. Despite assurances to the contrary, fears were voiced in the Chinese press that the new system might be used by the government to eliminate Chinese culture and the language on which it rested. Other objections of a practical nature were raised even by those who accepted the principle of the bilingual school. One prominent Chinese pointed out that the Chinese schools were in such great economic distress (because they were having to admit more and more children for whom no accommodation could be found in government schools) that they were in no position to implement the new system without prior and substantial financial aid. Another straw in the wind was the rejection as unsuitable in December 1953, by the Federation of Singapore Chinese Schools, of some new textbooks prepared by the Education Department to create a Malayan outlook among the students attending vernacular schools.

But it was in the domain of higher education that the government and the Chinese community were to clash openly. For some years, throughout Southeast Asia, failure to resolve locally the problem of higher education for graduates of local Chinese schools has impelled many Chinese youths to leave for China. In 1951, 1,000 Singapore Chinese reportedly left for university education in the home country, and by mid-1952, the monthly average of such departures was said to be more than 200. Although two-thirds of the student body in the University of Malaya, since its establishment in 1949, has been Chinese—despite the scholarship ratio strongly favoring Malay candidates—conservative Chinese were still dissatisfied and wanted facilities for the traditional higher education to be made available locally. For a time the promise to establish a Chair of Chinese Languages and Literature at the University of Malaya partially met this demand. But by January 1953, when there was little evidence that that chair would be established in the near future, and when it was rumored that English would be the medium of instruction even for such higher Chinese studies, a group of Singapore's Chinese millionaires banded together to found a truly Chinese university in the colony.

British officials promptly objected to setting up the proposed Nanyang University on the grounds that Malaya's Chinese students could be educated to gain admittance to the existing university and that a separate Chinese university would perpetuate communalism. Supporters of the Nanyang project argued that there were in the country "nearly 400,000 Chinese students who, unless permitted to attend a Chinese institution, would have no opportunity to secure higher education"[81] outside of Communist China. To prove the noncommunal character of the proposed university, they promised that courses therein would be given in English as well as Chinese, and that eventually it would include departments for Malay and Indian studies. The British, while unconvinced, have not formally opposed establishment of Nanyang University. In fact, its imminent materialization prodded them into setting up the long-promised Department of Chinese Studies at the University of Malaya in the fall of 1953. Should Nanyang University fulfil one of the objectives of its founders—that of attracting students from all over Southeast Asia—it may at least partially offset the appeal which education in Communist China now makes to the Chinese youths of the area.

THAILAND

Population and Immigration

Perhaps second in importance in Southeast Asia to the Malayan Chinese come those of Thailand, where the Chinese form 16.7 percent of a total population of some 18 million. Any attempt to estimate the number of Thai Chinese encounters the unresolved difference in interpretation of the term "national" between Thailand and China. Until very recently the Thai have considered all persons born in their country to be, automatically, citizens, whereas China has maintained that children of a Chinese father are Chinese no matter where born. In February 1953 the Thai National Assembly passed a law designed to solve the old and thorny problem of dual nationality for the local Chinese. By its terms children born in Thailand of Thai mothers are considered as Thai unless they have already registered as aliens; children born of alien parents in Thailand are deemed to be foreigners. Neither the Communist nor the KMT governments of China has accepted this ruling. A currently accepted round figure for the Chinese segment of the Thai population is 3 millions.

In Thailand the Chinese live more widely scattered than in any other Southeast Asian country except Indonesia, for only briefly during the war did they experience forced concentration as regards their residence and they have not been obliged, as elsewhere in the area, to seek refuge in the cities from armed strife. Nevertheless, slightly less than half of the Thai Chinese live in the lower Menam delta, while another major agglomeration resides in the Kra Isthmus.[82] In the capital city of Bangkok, the Chinese account for over 31

81 R. Butwell, "A Chinese University for Malaya," *Pacific Affairs*, December 1953.
82 Skinner, *op. cit.*, p. 3.

percent of the population, the big up-country towns have large Chinese colonies, and "almost all villages have at least a few resident Chinese families."

In 1947 the Thai government reduced Chinese immigration to 10,000 annually, and in January 1949 that number was drastically cut to a mere 200. Moreover, the Thai have found other methods of reducing the entries. Chinese already in the country on temporary permits are now allowed to apply for admission under the quota, which, in 1952, was almost entirely filled by Chinese already living in Thailand.[83] Chinese now wanting to enter Thailand must possess not only a passport but a visa issued by a Thai consul; new arrivals have to register with the Chinese embassy, along with two relatives willing to sign as guarantors; and Chinese residents leaving the country must return within the time limit affixed to their passports on pain of forfeiting their re-entry privilege. In October 1950 the Thai Parliament passed an Aliens Registration Ordinance, which required foreigners to carry an identity card more complete than formerly, the annual renewal of which cost a larger fee than before. Furthermore, aliens had to notify the police whenever they left their place of residence for more than two weeks. Pleas from local Chinese organizations succeeded in getting the registration deadline postponed from January 1 to July 1, 1951, but very few complied with the regulation during that period of grace. By mid-1951 when the law was finally enforced, it was estimated that there remained about 100,000 unregistered alien Chinese who had entered the country illegally and were therefore afraid to declare themselves.[84] By early 1954 only 700,000 aliens had registered. In an effort to increase revenues from this source and to exert a closer control over aliens generally, those under eighteen and over sixty years of age were no longer exempted from paying the registration fee. The following month it was announced that a special Bureau for Aliens would soon be established.

Obviously many thousands of Chinese were still coming into Thailand both overland and by sea, despite establishment of immigration control posts in the northern provinces and the stationing along frontier areas of a special police force trained for alien surveillance. The influx continued, although hundreds of Chinese were arrested for failure to carry registration cards and to pay their fees and taxes, and hundreds more—including about 50 Chinese educators convicted of teaching communism, as well as criminals—were deported. By early 1950 the expense of such deportations (about 800 baht per person), the refusal of the Hong Kong government to receive any more deportees from Thailand, and finally the suspension of regular shipping services between south China ports and Thailand, caused the Bangkok administration to set up a detention camp at Petchabun for "undesirable aliens." Coincidentally

---

[83] R. Coughlin, "The Status of the Chinese Minority in Thailand," *Pacific Affairs*, December 1952.

[84] *Bangkok Post*, June 28, 1951.

with the deportations there was a small voluntary exodus of Chinese from the country. In 1950–51 a few hundred Chinese repatriated themselves; most of them went back to take advantage of Peking's offer of free land to returning overseas Chinese, some were students who wanted to pursue a higher education in China, and still others simply wished to visit relatives in the homeland.

Inevitably the Thais' fear of the Chinese has grown with the successes of the Communists in China, and periodically nationalistic Members of Parliament have tried to impose further restrictions on Chinese immigration and residence. In early November 1951, ten of them unsuccessfully sponsored a motion to oust aliens from the Bangkok area. The military government which came to power as the result of a *coup d'état* later that month soon embarked on an openly anti-Chinese program. Early in 1951, aliens were forbidden to live in areas specified as strategic, and, more important, the registration fee for aliens (of whom only 170,000 Chinese had registered by that time) was increased from 20 to 400 baht annually. Although this and other like measures were carefully framed so as to apply indiscriminately to all aliens, they naturally affected—as indeed they were meant to do—the Chinese far more than other foreigners. Strong protests from all the local Chinese organizations have been unavailing. According to a neutral observer, this measure has seriously damaged Sino-Thai relations because it was a common grievance, and it evoked an anti-Thai sentiment among the Chinese never before aroused among them to such a degree.[85]

But in spite of this and a series of increasingly harsh and arbitrary measures directed against them by the Thai government, the local Chinese are believed to be aligning themselves more and more with the Nationalist cause and not with the Peking regime, even though the latter is ever more sharply denouncing the Pibul administration. Indications of such a reorientation are the notably enlarged celebration at Bangkok of the Double Tenth in October 1953, the continued shrinkage in remittances to China (which have sunk far below the amount permitted by the Thai government),[86] and the strongly pro-Chiang sentiments of the newly elected officers of Bangkok's influential Chinese Chamber of Commerce.[87] Obviously, it is not loyalty to the Thai government that is responsible for this trend, but rather the excesses committed by the Peking regime, which have alienated its erstwhile supporters in Thailand.

---

[85] Coughlin, *op. cit.*

[86] On Apr. 7, 1953, the *Bangkok Post* reported that local remittance houses were sending only 5 million baht monthly as compared with 30 million previously, and that the average remittance amounted to 150–175 baht per month although the government permitted individuals to remit up to 2,000 baht monthly.

[87] *Christian Science Monitor*, Oct. 7, 1953.

The Citizenship Issue

In contrast to their forceful handling of alien immigration and residence, the Thai have postponed a showdown on the Chinese citizenship issue. The concession they made in the Sino-Thai treaty of January 1946, in agreeing to an exchange of diplomatic representatives with China for the first time in history, was widely expected to lead to pressure on the part of China for more concessions to the Chinese in Thailand. But the rapidly weakening position of the Kuomintang removed pressure from the Thai, who were able to pursue their anti-Chinese program with relative freedom. An unexpected quirk in the situation occurred after the Communist victories in China began to arouse Thai fears of a local Chinese fifth column. When the government wanted to deport local-born Chinese as undesirable aliens, its long-held contention— that all persons born in the country were Thai citizens, hence undeportable —backfired. So in January 1952 the government sponsored a bill prohibiting dual citizenship for all persons born in Thailand, authorizing the deportation of any citizen whether naturalized or born of alien parents, and denying Thai citizenship to any Thai belonging to the foregoing categories who remained in the country of his alien parents longer than ten years. In late 1952 the government drafted an amendment to this bill which by making the children of aliens legally foreigners has also made them automatically ineligible for service in the Thai armed forces.

Education

In Thailand there has been a running battle for the past twenty years between the government and the Chinese community for control of the local Chinese schools. For a few months after the war, the Chinese enjoyed a brief respite from controls, and the number of their schools in Thailand grew to about 400. The Sino-Thai treaty of January 1946 contained a provision that Chinese schools in Thailand would thenceforth receive the same treatment as schools maintained by other national groups, although children in all primary grades were required to learn the Thai language. But by the time Pibul returned to power, in April 1948, the Kuomintang government had obviously become incapable of insisting on implementation of that provision. Thus, the Thai government was able to resume its prewar policy of aggressive nationalism vis-à-vis the Chinese schools, which it was determined to reduce in number while Siamizing the curriculum of those surviving.

Some of the Chinese schools which had mushroomed in the early postwar period collapsed from financial famine, but far more were officially closed down. By 1950 there were slightly fewer than 300 Chinese schools left in the country, all of them primary, and with a total enrolment estimated at about

80,000.[88] In the four years 1948–51, almost 50 Chinese school teachers were deported for teaching Communist doctrines, and the Thai police chief pledged that he would rigorously pursue this policy.[89] The government has made no secret of its intention to limit the number of Chinese schools to 50 for the whole country—three in Bangkok, three each in Thonburi, Korat, Chiengmai, and Ubol, and two in each of the other provinces. In February 1951 the Education Department announced that it was going to increase the number of hours which Chinese schools must devote to teaching the Thai language—that is, as much time would be given to learning Thai as Chinese—and that standardized textbooks would be issued after consultation with Chinese school officials.[90]

Thai policy toward Chinese education has been the object of persistent attack by Radio Peking. At first the Thai Ministry of Education replied in counterbroadcasts in which its officials harped on the theme that local Chinese schools were subject to the same laws as those which governed all private schools, and that schools were closed down only because they had hired unlicensed teachers, or had neglected to teach the required amount of Thai, or had included political courses in their curriculum adjudged to be contrary to the interests of the Thai government.[91] Under the provisions of a newly passed Anti-Communist Act, many Chinese schoolteachers (as well as journalists) were among those arrested and slated for deportation on suspicion of having participated in the alleged antigovernment plot of November 1952.

There is little doubt but that Thailand is determined to continue, if not intensify, its present policy toward Chinese education in the hope that eventually it can force the majority of Chinese children in the country to attend Thai schools. In May 1954 the cabinet approved regulations drafted by the Ministry of Education for better control of the teachers and owners of private schools.

INDONESIA

Population and Immigration

Indonesia's Chinese population is almost as large as that of Malaya, but it makes up only about 2 percent of the total population of the archipelago, and a larger proportion lives in the Outer Islands than on Java. From 1920 to 1930 (the year of Indonesia's last census), the number of Chinese increased in Java from 384,000 to 582,000 and in the Outer Islands from 425,000 to 651,000. Probably the Chinese of Java are the most assimilated of all the Southeast Asian Chinese; only 20 percent of them were born in China compared with about 50 percent of the Outer Island Chinese. The Javanese Chinese have be-

[88] Skinner, *op. cit.*, p. 9.   [89] *Bangkok Post*, Dec. 15, 1951.
[90] *Ibid.*, Feb. 5, 1951.   [91] *Ibid.*, Mar. 15, 1951.

come increasingly urbanized since World War II, partly as the result of violent anti-Chinese outbreaks, such as the massacres of Tanggerang and Kebumen. The Chinese are now believed to account for one-sixth of the population of Djakarta and about 10 percent of the other city dwellers on the island of Java.

Most of the archipelago's Chinese are merchants, but many of them are engaged in industry, mining, and agriculture—particularly in rubber. No longer wage laborers for the most part, the Chinese are now associated with the management or ownership of many Indonesian agricultural enterprises, and they have also penetrated into the professional classes.

After sovereignty was transferred to Indonesia's government in December 1949, a token annual immigration quota of 4,000 was allotted to the Chinese, in which preference was to be given to professional men. In March 1951 the Republican authorities announced that they would establish an immigration office at Hong Kong in order to screen the large number of Chinese who, having fled from Indonesia during its independence struggle, now wanted to return. In view of the circumstances under which they had left, a warning was issued that re-entry permits would not be readily accorded. A great increase in the number of illegal immigrants was the official reason assigned by the Indonesian government when, in November 1951, it ordered the registration of all aliens residing in the country, including women and children. But for unspecified "practical" reasons, the registration regulation was not enforced, even after blood was shed in north Sumatra where some hundreds of Chinese squatters (who had entered the country illegally) refused to obey a government order to move off the land they were unlawfully occupying.[92] As recently as January 1954 the Djakarta authorities once again announced that the government would soon promulgate "an emergency law on registration and other matters concerned with foreigners staying in Indonesia."[93] For similarly unexplained "certain reasons" the government did not get around to promulgating an immigration law. In April 1953 the chief of the Immigration Department stated that even without definitive legislation the government would tolerate no flouting of its provisional restrictive regulations and that it had definitely reversed the open-door policy of its Dutch predecessors. It was a favor on the part of the authorities, he added, that foreigners were allowed to stay in the country.[94]

In larger numbers than in any other Southeast Asian country, Chinese youths in Indonesia have responded to Peking's appeals to return to China. Every passenger ship leaving Indonesian ports for Hong Kong reportedly carries Chinese students, and the number thus leaving in 1953 totaled about

[92] *Times of Indonesia*, Mar. 23, 1953.   [93] *Ibid.*, Jan. 29, 1954.
[94] *Ibid.*, Apr. 22, 1953.

5,000.[95] One reason for this proportionately large youthful exodus has been the almost-unhampered propaganda activities of the Communist Chinese diplomats among Chinese school children in Indonesia. Another has been—until recently—the passive attitude of the Indonesian authorities toward these departures. However, in June 1952 the formalities required for students' exit permits were tightened, reportedly at the request of some 200 Chinese parents. Subsequently the Indonesian government issued a warning that only in exceptional cases would China-bound students be allowed to return to Indonesia. Indicative of this slightly stiffer official attitude was a query made by Ambassador-elect Mononutu on the eve of departure for his Peking post. Why was it necessary, he asked in Surabaja, for Chinese students to go to China for their education when there were sufficient schools for them in Indonesia?[96]

The answer seems to lie not only in the inducements of immediate university training and eventual high posts offered in China, but in the "assimilationist" policy recently initiated by the Djakarta authorities. Throughout 1953, representatives of minority groups, especially the Chinese, complained of forcible assimilation measures and of increasing discrimination against them by the Indonesian government. Probably responsible for this sterner official attitude vis-à-vis the Chinese were the increasingly troublesome factional disputes and extortionate practices among the Chinese communities not only in Java but in Borneo (September 1952), Sumatra (March 1953), and Celebes (June 1953). The Indonesian government's reaction seems to have stemmed not from ideological sympathy with either the pro-KMT or pro-Communist elements, or with the victims of Chinese strong-arm methods. Rather, it appears to have derived from irritation at the Chinese defiance of the country's laws and from misgivings regarding the loyalty of even those Chinese who had elected to become Indonesian citizens.

On both sides, however, conciliatory efforts were made to reverse the deterioration of Sino-Indonesian relations. During 1952–53 there were formed among citizens of Chinese origin at least three political parties whose avowed aims included aid in Indonesia's rehabilitation, as well as the elimination of discrimination through active participation in local politics.[97] For its part, the Indonesian government in 1953 assigned for the first time since independence two cabinet posts to the local Chinese. While these moves may well prove helpful, the crux of the Chinese problem in Indonesia remains so long as the problem of their dual citizenship is unsolved. The proportion of Chinese who

[95] *Christian Science Monitor*, Jan. 23, 1954.   [96] *Times of Indonesia*, Sept. 29, 1953.
[97] Commonly known by the abbreviation of their Indonesian names as PERWITT, PDTI, and PERTIWI. A fourth organization called BAPERKI was set up in March 1954 as a nonpolitical association designed to serve as a citizenship consultative body. A few months later BAPERKI changed its stand, and decided to present its own candidates in the forthcoming national elections. This about-face laid BAPERKI open to the charge of being a reactionary, narrowly communal organization.

have opted to or automatically become Indonesian citizens has been variously estimated at 50 to 75 percent of the whole community,[98] but this involves little change in their attitude toward Indonesia as long as in the eyes of any Chinese regime they also remain citizens of China.

The Citizenship Issue

Mainly because a solution of the Chinese citizenship problem has been tied in with the even more troublesome status of the Indo-Europeans and linked to Indonesia's fluctuating relations with the Mao government, the Djakarta authorities have been cautious and dilatory in their approach. In 1950, after several postponements had already occurred, all domiciled aliens were given until the end of 1951 to decide their citizenship. It was decreed that if, during that time, the Peranakans (local-born Chinese, who form 70 percent of the country's Chinese population) did not opt for Chinese citizenship by so registering with the embassy of China, they would automatically become Indonesian. According to a British student of the problem,[99] the Peranakans in 1950, "like the other minorities, were awaiting an assurance from the government that they would receive equal treatment with other Indonesian citizens before making up their minds." What probably chiefly concerned them was whether or not Indonesian citizenship would automatically eliminate the Dutch-imposed ban on their acquisition of landed property. By the December 31, 1951, deadline, only 25 to 30 percent had taken the positive step of opting for Chinese citizenship.

Reports in the local press early in 1954 that the government was drafting a law that would require Indonesian citizens of Chinese origin to reaffirm their choice of Indonesian citizenship and produce certificates attesting to their birth in Indonesia aroused the local Chinese to action. In February 1954 a committee was formed by leading Indonesia-born Chinese to sound out opinion among the China-born element on the citizenship issue. Within a few days this committee reported strongly against the government's new bill, on the grounds that it was practically impossible for the majority of local-born Chinese to produce the required birth certificates[100] and, more important, that forcing those who had automatically become Indonesian citizens to restate in positive terms their wish to be so considered would create among them an undesirable feeling of insecurity.[101]

The government's long-standing desire to put an end to the dual-citizenship

---

98 The number of Chinese who have acquired Indonesian citizenship has never been accurately assessed. "Official" figures reported in the local press on different dates in March 1954 were highly contradictory.

99 Victor Purcell, The Chinese in Southeast Asia (Oxford University Press, 1951), p. 709.

100 Under the Dutch regime, civil registration for Chinese born in Java was not instituted until 1918 and for those born in the Outer Islands not until 1926.

101 Times of Indonesia, Feb. 24, 1954.

status of the great majority of local Chinese who had become Indonesian citizens simply by failing to declare themselves formally citizens of China was strengthened by a report in November 1953 that seats had been reserved for the Indonesian Chinese in the All-China People's Congress. In consequence, the newly appointed ambassador to Peking, Mononutu, was instructed to open negotiations on the subject. But after six months he was reported to be dissatisfied with the results of his efforts. Although the Peking authorities had expressed willingness to hold formal talks on the citizenship issue, not even the basis for such talks had been reached by May 1954.[102] It June it was announced that negotiations on the dual-citizenship question would begin the following month in Peking, but once again they were postponed at the request of the Chinese government. At the same time it became known that Indonesia had asked Peking to accept, in advance of the formal negotiations, the principle that local Chinese would be permitted to choose Indonesian instead of Chinese citizenship if they so desired.[103]

Education

In Indonesia, for various reasons, the postwar development of Chinese education has followed a course contrary to that in Malaya. Prewar Dutch policy differed from that of the British in Malaya in that it offered more facilities for higher education to the Chinese in the Dutch schools both of Holland and the Indies, and for lower education in the local Dutch or Malay schools. Authorities differ as to the number of Chinese children who received an education in the three different school systems of the prewar Indies, the highest estimate being that half those of school age were enrolled.[104] Chinese schools provided almost 50 percent of the primary education available to Chinese children in that period.

In threading a way through the maze of statistics embracing all the prewar and postwar systems in which the Chinese have been involved, it appears that the number of Chinese schools and of the pupils attending them has increased since the Japanese surrender. Finkelstein stated, as of 1951, that there were 800 Chinese schools, with 250,000 pupils and 6,500 teachers.[105] Certainly this distribution was uneven; Djakarta schools were notably overcrowded because of the influx of Chinese refugees into that city. How far the growth of such schools has been the result of official encouragement is not known, but in any case the authorities have not discouraged them. In June 1950 it was reported that schools for minority groups, including the Chinese, would soon be established in Indonesia.[106] An important factor in the situation has been the lin-

102 *New York Times,* May 6, 1954.   103 *Ibid.,* July 20, 1954.
104 Purcell, *op. cit.,* p. 531.
105 L. S. Finkelstein, "Education in Indonesia," *Far Eastern Survey,* Aug. 22, 1951.
106 *Report on Indonesia,* June 30, 1950.

guistic assimilation of the Peranakans (local-born), which has inevitably forced them to send their children to either Dutch or Indonesian schools. The offspring of the Tetoks (China-born), on the other hand, constitute the majority of Chinese children of school age in Indonesia and consequently of the student body in Chinese schools. In view, however, of the closing down of most Dutch schools in recent years and of the low standards prevailing in Indonesian schools, the Peranakans are increasingly attending Chinese schools.

In Indonesia, as in other countries of Southeast Asia, the majority of Chinese schools are run by committees of prominent businessmen or by regional associations. Only the very few among them that receive official grants-in-aid are required to teach the indigenous language for a specified number of hours each week. Thus, the government exercises no control over the vast majority of Chinese schools in the archipelago, which teach the curriculum used in Communist China and which are in large part staffed by young China-born men who reportedly stress Communist indoctrination.[107] According to an article in the *Christian Science Monitor* of May 31, 1952, most of the Chinese secondary schools are given over to Communist indoctrination, the Chinese Students Union of Djakarta is pro-Peking, and there is only one Kuomintang-oriented school in the capital city. How successful this use of schools for propaganda purposes can be was shown in June 1952 when 771 Chinese youths went to China from Indonesia. This was said to be one of the largest groups of overseas Chinese ever to have gone to Red China up to that time.[108]

Belatedly recognizing the dangers inherent in this lack of supervision, the Indonesia government early in 1952 banned the use of a communistic geography textbook in Chinese schools.[109] In May and June of that year the police raided Chinese schools in Java and reportedly seized many manuals and pamphlets which were being used there although not approved by the Indonesian Ministry of Education. One of these texts, it was said, contained an attack on the local authorities. Justifying the seizure on the ground that schools should be free from politics, "the authorities stressed that they would not tolerate communist cultural infiltration" in primary and secondary schools "where the twigs are easily bent."[110]

In 1952–53 the official prohibition on disseminating political propaganda in Chinese schools was being so obviously flouted that the government closed down some of them in Java and Borneo, set up an Inspectorate of Foreign Schools, and tried to arbitrate disputes among the Nationalist and Communist Chinese regarding the use of Chinese school buildings. Recently the pro-KMT Chinese have become more active, but they are hampered by lack of official

107 Skinner, *op. cit.*, p. 66.
108 Associated Press despatch, Hong Kong, *Bangkok Post*, July 4, 1952.
109 *New York Herald Tribune*, Feb. 13, 1952.
110 *Times of Indonesia*, May 26, 1952.

recognition. And the ineffectuality of the Indonesian government's efforts to control the propaganda flowing from Peking's embassy and consulates is indicated by the continuing large stream of Chinese students going from Indonesia to China. Thanks to the co-operation of the Indonesian Communist Party and to a widespread and vast outpouring of published materials, the Chinese Communists have been making more headway in Indonesia than elsewhere in Southeast Asia. And, as one American journalist observed in January 1954, their main target is the local Chinese youth:

It is conservatively estimated that in Indonesia half of these (Chinese schools) fly the Communist China flag and that at least 75% of all Chinese teachers are pro-Communist. The Indonesian government tries to control the textbooks used, but officials admit they have no control over the teachers.[111]

BURMA

Population and Immigration

Burma may be said to have the least important Chinese population of the area. In 1951 the Chinese there constituted only a little more than 1 percent of the total population, which was estimated at about 16 million. As in Thailand and Indonesia, the Chinese are to be found in the southern portion of the country, about half of them living in and around the Irrawaddy delta. According to the 1931 census (racial breakdowns are not available for the partially completed 1941 census), Chinese constituted 4.7 percent of the urban and 0.9 percent of the total population of Burma. Insecurity of life and property in the rural districts, particularly since 1946, has tended to concentrate the Chinese in such towns as Rangoon (where there are 30,000 to 50,000) and Moulmein (15,000). A special feature of this recent urbanization is that the Burma Chinese no longer live together in Chinatowns but, rich and poor alike, are now scattered throughout the urban centers.[112]

Into Burma, Indochina and Indonesia, the stream of Chinese immigration has never been so intense as into Malaya and Thailand, either for reasons of relative inaccessibility or because of colonial control measures. Altered political and economic conditions in the postwar period have fundamentally transformed this situation. The largely seasonal prewar migration of Chinese into northern Burma has declined, owing to adverse economic conditions in the frontier area, but the thousands of Kuomintang troops which have infiltrated there since 1950 may leave a residue of permanent settlers. A nightmare which used to haunt Burmese nationalists in the late 1930's—that the Burma Road might serve as a channel by which hordes of Chinese from Yunnan would pour into Burma—has in recent months been revived. Actually

---

[111] *Christian Science Monitor,* Jan. 23, 1954.
[112] Pan-Asia despatch, Rangoon, Aug. 20, 1952.

there has been considerable new Chinese immigration, dating from the Communist victories in China, but its proportions are not accurately known. Vaguely simple statements like the following excerpt from the Rangoon *Tribune* obviously refer to immigrants other than Chinese Nationalist troops: "New Chinese faces are seen everywhere in Burma; this means that there has been a great influx of Chinese into the country."[113]

No official controls, beyond the Emergency Immigration Act of 1947 designed to restrict the entry of Indians into Burma,[114] have since been set up, nor have there been any reports of popular clamor to revive the negotiations between the Burmese premier and China initiated late in 1941 to check the flow of Chinese into Burma. Either the Burmese have not regarded nonmilitary Chinese immigration as a menace or they recognize the futility of trying to stem it under present conditions.

The Citizenship Issue

Since Burma became independent in 1948, it has followed much the same course as has Indonesia—the government has set successive deadlines for the registration of aliens and then postponed their enforcement. Since Indians were the chief objective in this forcing of the citizenship issue, the local Chinese have not been seriously affected, except for the handful among them who want civil service appointments. The government has been lax in enforcing not only the deadline for alien registration but also such requirements for acquiring citizenship as a fluent speaking knowledge of Burmese.

Education

Burma remains the only country in Southeast Asia where Chinese education reportedly is still free of both official surveillance and aid. A Registration of Private Schools Act, providing for the registration of all private schools other than those teaching purely religious subjects and having 20 or more students enrolled, was indeed passed on August 8, 1952. But by the end of the six-months period for registration, so few schools had registered under this act that apparently neither the government nor the education authorities concerned take it very seriously.[115]

Considering the small size of the Chinese community in Burma, the number of Chinese schools in Rangoon (28) and up-country (180) is remarkable. According to a recent observer,[116] eight of these Rangoon schools and three of the provincial schools are secondary ones, but the great majority of the others are primary schools of poor quality, both as regards teaching and pupil attendance. Only the handful of schools whose students want matriculation

---

[113] July 12, 1952.
[115] *The Burman*, Jan. 14, Feb. 16, 1953.
[114] See p. 77.
[116] Skinner, *op. cit.*, p. 27.

certificates conform to the regulations laid down by the Burmese Ministry of Education, but authorities differ as to the language aspect of the curriculum. According to Skinner, there is no requirement for the teaching of Burmese, but Purcell claims that such pupils as wish to go on to higher education spend half an hour daily studying Burmese—the same amount of time as is given to the learning of English.[117]

In any event, the lack of government supervision has left the field open for a contest of strength between the pro-Kuomintang and pro-Peking elements among the Burmese Chinese community for control of the Chinese schools, and by 1950 the latter had won hands down. Nevertheless, according to an informant in Rangoon, this struggle, which has focused on the choice of textbooks to be used in Chinese schools, has rocked the Chinese community in the capital. Naturally, the Chinese ambassador has thrown his weight on the side of importing the textbooks now used in Red China, and the unpopularity of the Nationalist government (as a result of the Li Mi troops' activities in the country) has compelled the pro-KMT elements to put up with this. A survey made in early 1953 disclosed that of the 236 Chinese schools then existing in Burma, 230 were using communist textbooks printed in China.

INDOCHINA

Population and Immigration

In Indochina, the Chinese account for 3.1 percent of the total population of Viet Nam and 7.1 percent of that of Cambodia and Laos. Even more than in Indonesia has this element of the population gravitated toward the cities since the Japanese surrender in 1945. At present some 400,000 out of the 2 million residents of Saigon-Cholon are Chinese, this city thus containing the next largest concentration of Chinese in Southeast Asia after Singapore. Their total number in Tonkin has probably been reduced since the outbreak of local warfare in December 1946. Those who have remained are concentrated principally in Hanoi (where they number some 15,000) and Haiphong (about 35,000). In 1948 it was estimated that the Chinese population of the main cities of Viet Nam had doubled since the war's end.[118] In the absence of reliable recent statistics, it is believed that the total Chinese population of Indochina is now about one million.

From 1946 to 1948 there was an average net immigration yearly of nearly 20,000 Chinese.[119] That no official move was made to control this influx was thought to be attributable to clauses in the Franco-Chinese treaty of February 28, 1946, which guaranteed to the Chinese their prewar rights of entry and departure and the most-favored-nation privileges of travel and residence in

[117] Purcell, op. cit., p. 696.   [118] Indoclim, July 10, 28, 1948.
[119] Economic Survey of Asia and the Far East—1950, p. 45.

Indochina. These sizable additions to the local Chinese community occurred in the south, for the strife in northern Viet Nam is believed to have seriously reduced the total Chinese population there. Considerable displacements of populations have certainly occurred in the north—some voluntarily to escape the fighting and other evacuations compelled by the authorities—and some members of the Chinese occupation forces or their numerous camp followers may have remained behind. No accurate information on this subject can be expected until peace is restored to the region.

In Cochin China and Cambodia, however, we are on firmer ground. At the Dalat conference of 1948, Vietnamese delegates complained of the Chinese "pacific invasion" of their countries. Tran thien Veng, then a minister for Cochin China, bewailed the mass arrivals of Chinese by land and by sea, and demanded the reimposition of prewar restrictions on immigration and a census of the existing Chinese population. In reply, High Commissioner Bollaert stated that 8,000 Chinese—twice the prewar figure—were then arriving each month in Cochin China, and that little control was exercised over them other than an easily evaded requirement that new arrivals register at the Chinese consulate within 48 hours.[120] The French, preoccupied with the military situation, probably lacked the means to check this inflow, and perhaps the will to do so. Vietnamese were leaving the French-held areas or refusing to work for the French, either from patriotic motives or from fear of Viet Minh reprisals, and the Chinese were extremely useful.

But by July 1949 the French viewpoint had changed. There was no longer any compulsion to respect the treaty made with the Kuomintang in 1946, and Communist victories in China made some restrictive measures urgent. Thenceforth no Chinese could legally enter Indochina without a passport visaed by French consular officials at the foreign point of departure. An American observer in 1950[121] reported that by then Chinese immigration into Cambodia had virtually ceased and that the French were detaining such Chinese students as wanted to return to China. Apparently no difficulty was experienced in arriving at an agreement on a joint immigration policy for Viet Nam, Cambodia, and Laos at the Pau Conference[122] of 1950: each of the Associated States was to have its own immigration service, the French were to be included in any discussion of immigration problems common to all, and the French High Commissioner was to retain the right to expel any foreigners whom he regarded as a threat to the security of French troops.

The Citizenship Issue

By now most of the Southeast Asian countries have taken some action on the question of Chinese citizenship. The outstanding exceptions are the As-

[120] *Indoclim*, July 10, 1948.   [121] Skinner, *op. cit.*, p. 19.

[122] Held in the French Pyrenees to regulate the economic relationship of France and the three Indochinese states.

sociated States of Indochina, which apparently have not yet had to face up to the problem and which continue to operate under provisions of the Franco-Chinese treaty of February 1946. Allied to this question is that of the juridical status of the Chinese in Cambodia, and failure to resolve this has delayed ratification of the Franco-Cambodian treaty of 1949.[123]

Education

According to Skinner, the literacy rate among the Indochina Chinese is probably lower than elsewhere in Southeast Asia.[124] This view, reached in 1950, solely on the basis of observation of Chinese schools in Cochin China and Cambodia, did not take into consideration their counterparts in the north, where the war made inspection very difficult. Nevertheless, it probably holds good for all of the country, since the more prosperous and numerous Chinese in south Indochina would presumably have the most highly developed school system. The only Chinese schools in the south are those run by the three biggest Congregations in Cholon.

Chinese students wanting education beyond the primary level perforce attend French secondary schools, and French textbooks have even been introduced into Chinese schools. French officials keep a close watch over the activities of Chinese students. Reportedly Communist activities have been checked, recalcitrant schools closed down, and students wishing to return to Red China refused permission to depart.

[123] See p. 180.   [124] Skinner, *op. cit.*, p. 21.

Chapter Two

THE INDIANS

INDIA and Indians occupy a position in Southeast Asia which at present differs radically from that of China and the Chinese. In the first place, Indians are an important minority only in Burma and Malaya, and even in those countries their importance has declined since the war, both comparatively and absolutely. Though, like the Chinese, they are to be found throughout the economic scale, there are fewer millionaires, more laborers, and fewer ubiquitous and prosperous merchants, and they do not improve their status with as much facility as do the Chinese. Since they are even less assimilable to the native peoples and more transient in Southeast Asia, their smaller numbers and relative unimportance have made them a minor target for nationalist antipathy as compared with the Chinese, except in Burma. And even in that country, since the war, the hostility which they previously inspired has largely evaporated with their declining role. Nevertheless, both in Burma and Malaya, Indian immigration has been controlled by law, as have the operations of Indian moneylenders.

A development that has altered radically the status of the Indian minority in Southeast Asia is the rise of India as a world power, together with the great personal popularity of Nehru as a regional leader. Although, occasionally, fears of an eventual Hindu or even Pakistani imperialism are voiced, the great subcontinent is far enough from most of Southeast Asia, and its leaders are sufficiently motivated by nonaggressive ideologies, for Southeast Asian countries to feel almost none of the apprehensions that haunt them in regard to Red China.

In the absence of current and accurate statistics for most countries of Southeast Asia, it is difficult to estimate the number of Indians now (mid-1954) living in the area. A reasonable guess would be in the neighborhood of 1,246,000. Approximately 80 percent of them are agriculturists or agricultural laborers, and the rest merchants and moneylenders, with a sprinkling of professional men. The majority come from south India, though there is also a considerable number of Sikhs, some Punjabis, and a few Parsees.

India's Policy

In prewar days, India's interest in its nationals living in Southeast Asia was slight, except in times of crisis such as the anti-Indian riots of 1938 in Burma

59

and the plight of Malayan Indians during the world depression of the early 1930's. Occasionally the Congress expressed general concern for them, as in the following resolution passed at its annual session in 1936:

The Congress sends greetings to our fellow countrymen overseas and its assurances of sympathy and help in their distressful condition and in the continuing deterioration in their status in the territories in which they have settled. The Congress is ready and willing to take all action within its power to ameliorate their condition, but desires to point out that a radical amelioration in their status must ultimately depend on the attainment by India of independence and the power to protect her nationals abroad.[1]

Nor did the Congress, in its overwhelming preoccupation with the winning of sovereignty for India, develop contacts with Southeast Asia Indians for political purposes. A Foreign Department was indeed set up by the Congress in 1936 with the aim of creating and maintaining contacts with Indians overseas and any other international organizations which might help the cause of India's freedom. But this department showed no activity beyond sending a circular to Indians abroad, inviting them to keep in touch with the Congress and printing a pamphlet (cited above) designed primarily to inform the people of India about their overseas compatriots and to awaken interest in their problems. In 1937 Nehru made an unofficial visit to Malaya and Burma, but the patriotic enthusiasm he aroused was never followed up with organization or propaganda.

For many years, some Indian intellectuals toyed with the idea of a federation to be led by India and to be dedicated to Asian freedom and welfare.[2] Nehru gave substance to this dream when he convened the Asian Relations Conference of 1947 at Delhi. There the inherent weaknesses in this vague and idealistic approach soon revealed themselves: China, fundamentally uninterested in such a union, sparred with India for leadership of any Asian body that might come out of the meeting; the smaller Asia countries were preoccupied with winning their own independence and anxious not to offend the great Western powers; and the Islamic countries were embarrassed by the refusal of India's Muslim League to participate in the meeting. According to Werner Levi,[3] this conference "marked the apex of Asian solidarity and the beginning of its decline," but it had the merit at least of showing what could not yet be done in Asia. The general liquidation of Western colonial holdings in Asia during the next two years delivered the *coup de grâce,* for it eliminated Asia's strongest cohesive force—anticolonial fervor.

In January 1949, Nehru called a second Asian conference, but this time for a specific object—to underscore Asian solidarity in the face of renewed Dutch

[1] D. Y. Dev, *Our Countrymen Abroad* (New Delhi, 1940), p. 90.
[2] See W. Levi, *Free India in Asia* (University of Minnesota Press, 1952), p. 34.
[3] *Ibid.,* p. 39.

aggression in Indonesia. Of the nations invited, not all accepted. Thailand, after first refusing to attend, sent only an observer. This reluctance to attend, as well as the weakness of the resolutions passed at the meeting, far from demonstrating Asian unity, betrayed the anxiety of Southeast Asian countries not to antagonize the West. Still another conference called by Nehru, to consider aid to Burma, though it was confined to Commonwealth nations, foundered for a different reason—Burmese resentment, as an infringement of their sovereignty, of the conditions made for accepting the proffered aid. Nehru by this time appeared to be disillusioned with the conference method as a means of attaining his goal, and he actually opposed calling another such meeting after the Korean War broke out. He had come to realize, says Levi, that Asia could not be welded into a political unit, at least not then, for its strength was moral, not military, and its problems were so various that they had to be worked out by the individual countries concerned through international agencies.

Nevertheless, the Indochina crisis in early 1954 moved Nehru to convene still another conference for the purpose of achieving a united stand among south Asian nations on the eve of the Geneva meeting held by the great powers on the same issue. At this Ceylon conference, more than at any similar meetings held previously, the points of disagreement rather than of unity became evident, and the meeting had to be extended by additional sessions in order to produce even watered-down resolutions that were mutually acceptable. Although all were agreed on the desirability of an immediate cease-fire in Indochina, Nehru's proposal that the big powers be urged to declare a policy of nonintervention in Indochinese affairs met with opposition. However, the main bone of contention was whether colonialism or communism was the greater menace to the newly independent countries of south and Southeast Asia. Pakistan, Ceylon, and Burma were unwilling to follow India's lead in condemning colonialism without simultaneously condemning communism as an equally dangerous form of imperialism. On this issue Nehru could no longer claim to speak for a united south Asia,[4] though he remained the architect and chief advocate of the "independent" or neutralist foreign policy to which all the countries represented at the Ceylon meeting still adhered.

Whether or not the reaction of the other Colombo premiers altered Nehru's viewpoint toward the menace of communism to the newly independent countries of south Asia is not yet clear. Certainly Nehru brought influence to bear on Chou En-lai during their Delhi meeting (midway in the Geneva conference) to commit himself to a nonaggression, nonintervention agreement. Apparently it was at Nehru's instigation that Chou went to Rangoon to reassure

---

[4] A participant in the conference told an American correspondent that "we have been witnessing dilution of straight Nehruism." (*Christian Science Monitor*, May 3, 1954).

Premier Nu of China's pacific intentions. It is also widely believed that Indian pressure was largely responsible for Red China's aboutface in regard to Laos and Cambodia at the Geneva conference. And, finally, Nehru expressed willingness to help guarantee the cease-fire in Indochina. On the other hand, from his conviction that any collective defense organization for Asia simply increases international tensions, Nehru has not been receptive to proposals made by the United States, Britain, or Ceylon to lay the foundations for any such grouping.

Despite his repeated assurances to the contrary and his partially revised stand on the Indochina question, Nehru seems not to have renounced the aim of making India the leader of Southeast Asia, nor to have given up direct intervention wherever he feels that overseas Indians have unjustly suffered from discrimination. However, time has modified the tactics he uses, and on many occasions he has shown great patience with and understanding of Southeast Asian problems. Suspicion of a potential Hindu imperialism, he is aware, exists among the area's supersensitive nationalists, particularly those of Burma. Fears are aired periodically in Southeast Asia as to what course India might follow should Nehru die or the parties opposing him come into power. He also realizes the unpopularity of the area's Indian minorities, which is based on their undisguised self-interest, transiency, cultural unassimilability, internal divisions, and failure to contribute to the welfare of the country they inhabit. Although public opinion in India since the war has shown a new and lively interest in Indians overseas, Nehru far more than his compatriots has become aware of the complications involved in supporting Indian minorities and, at the same time, freedom movements in Southeast Asia.

During two visits he made to Southeast Asia since the war, Nehru preached unity to his fellow countrymen, and identification of their interests with those of the country in which they live. To the chettyars of Burma and Malaya, he made it clear that the government of India could not prevent the nationalization by Southeast Asian states of land and industries which affected them, and that it could only ask for reasonable compensation within the bounds set by the economic conditions of the country concerned.[5] To the governments of the region he has given repeated assurances that he disapproves of dual nationality for overseas Indians and of the unrestricted immigration of Indian laborers. He never pressed the harassed government of Burma for repayment of its debt to India nor for modification of its immigration policies.

On the positive side, Nehru has consistently championed the cause of Asian independence, actively in the case of Indonesia and with progressive reservations as regards Malaya and Indochina. In international bodies such as the ECAFE and Colombo Plan group, he has stressed the economic needs of Southeast Asia. Numerous good will missions composed of prominent In-

[5] C. Kondapi, *Indians Overseas* (New Delhi, 1951), p. 520.

dians have been sent to Southeast Asian countries to underscore the cultural
—especially religious—bonds between them and India. An Indian Council of
Cultural Cooperation, of which a section is devoted to Southeast Asia, was
formed in August 1949 and has promoted other cultural exchanges. Nehru
has been eminently successful in making Indian economic experience and
know-how available to less developed Asian countries. And many Southeast
Asian students have been offered scholarships for study in India.

During 1954, Nehru tried to exert a moderating influence on Peking, mak-
ing himself the spokesman for southeast Asian countries fearful of possible
Red Chinese aggression in the area and worried about the status of their own
Chinese minorities.

Probably most important of all is the moral leadership which Nehru has
given to the idealistically minded nationalists of the area, especially those of
Burma and Indonesia. India's attainment of sovereignty in 1947 inevitably
enhanced her role as a great and rising power in Asia, but it has been above
all else the personality of Nehru that has inspired affection and veneration
throughout the region and raised high the prestige of his country.

The Attitude of Southeast Asian Governments Toward India and Indians[6]

The enthusiasm shown by Southeast Asia's governments for India's cultural and political leadership is in marked contrast to the distaste or indifference they feel towards their domiciled Indian communities. On the political
plane, Burma and Indonesia almost invariably follow India's lead in international affairs, and in domestic policy the similarity of their ideals and practical problems often results in analogous programs. This is less true of Thailand,
which has thrown in its lot with the Western powers, and of Malaya, which
has a distinctive internal problem and no foreign policy independent of that of
Britain. Even distant Viet Nam has indirectly acknowledged the prestige of
India's leadership, for both regimes in that country have sought recognition
by India. From the economic standpoint, trade between India and Southeast
Asia has grown during the postwar eclipse of Japanese competition. And on
the cultural level, the Buddhist nations of Thailand, Burma, Cambodia, and
Laos naturally feel closer to India than do the Muslim countries of the area.
Nevertheless, Indonesia and, to a lesser extent, Malaya recognize their cul-
tural heritage from India.

This amicable relationship and the declining importance of Southeast Asia's
Indian minorities are postwar phenomena. By and large, India and the Indians are not feared as are China and the Chinese, but neither are they re-

[6] Relations between the several countries of Southeast Asia and India are taken up in detail
hereinafter; see pp. 69 ff. In view of the fact that the state of Pakistan did not come into existence until 1947, members of the Indian community in Southeast Asia, whether Hindu or
Muslim, are generally referred to in this study as Indians.

spected to the same extent. The character of the Indian minorities in the area has changed little, despite a larger percentage of local-born and, in Singapore and Malaya, their greater participation in public life. In part this is due to the greater attraction that sovereign India now holds for its nationals abroad, who have always had very close social, religious, and to a lesser extent political bonds with the motherland. In part it derives from the policies of Southeast Asian countries, which have not inspired Indians with the confidence required for them to transfer their allegiance to the land of their residence.

With few exceptions, Indians have taken all their customs with them to Southeast Asia; they do not identify themselves with the local people, nor adopt their dress, nor intermarry with them. They live as foreigners far more rigidly than do the Chinese.[7] Having entered in the wake of early British or French imperialism, they have become associated with Western aggression in the minds of the indigenous peoples, and their brief collaboration with the Japanese in the Azad Hind movement did nothing to endear them to those peoples. Indian businessmen and moneylenders have waxed visibly rich, have repatriated their wealth to India, and have not been noticeably philanthropic toward either local charities or the poor among their own compatriots.[8]

As to the less prosperous Indians, clerks and laborers among them are regarded as either depressing local wages or taking jobs which legitimately should be held by the indigenous peoples. While much the same might be charged against the equally materialistic Chinese, the latter have shown far more public spirit and philanthropy, as well as greater solidarity at clan and regional levels.

The Position of Pakistan

Pakistan's almost total eclipse by India as leader of Southeast Asia is astonishing when one considers the fact that nearly half the area's population is Muslim. The Indonesians and Malays are almost solidly Muslim, and there are sizable minorities of coreligionists in Burma and Thailand.

The Malays of Malaya have evinced no interest at all in Pakistan, and even the Indian Muslims living there have only spasmodically organized themselves into local Muslim Leagues. Pakistan, for its part, has shown little interest in them. In Burma, only a minority of the Muslim community has wanted to identify itself with Pakistan. And in southern Thailand, the Islamic minority seems to have paid no attention to, and received none from, Pakistan. The chief concern of all these Muslims is the preservation of their

[7] Madan Gopal, "Indians in Southeast Asia," *Eastern World* (London), July 1952.

[8] Even so fervent a nationalist as Kondapi has admitted this failing: "The Indian trading and professional classes should assume a more sympathetic attitude to the Indian working class. Cases are not wanting where Indian big business has joined hands with the European capitalists to trample upon the interests of their less fortunate brethren." (*Op. cit.*, p. 520.)

distinctive Islamic culture in areas where other religions and ethnic groups are paramount. But Pakistan has done virtually nothing to give their aspirations leadership and a focal point. Moreover, Pakistan's acceptance of military aid pacts with the United States and Turkey in 1953 appeared to many south Asian nations to be a serious breach in the neutralist united front which they had expected Pakistan would support in international politics.

Indonesia represents Pakistan's most serious failure in respect to the potential leadership of Islamic south Asia. Here is an overwhelmingly Muslim country which might normally be expected to see in Pakistan the world's foremost Muslim state. Indonesia has been tactful rather than cordial with Pakistan, and is obviously anxious not to offend it. When President Sukarno, after leaving Delhi, visited Karachi early in 1950, he became the first head of state to go to that country. Various good will and cultural missions have been exchanged between Pakistan and Indonesia. On March 5, 1951, the simultaneous signing of friendship treaties with India and Pakistan was announced. The next day, Foreign Minister Rum said that Indonesia was ready to help mediate the Kashmir dispute should his country be asked to do so.[9] No such request was forthcoming. In mid-July, however, Sukarno and Hatta tried again —their first open attempt to ease the tension between what were often described as Indonesia's two best Asian friends. They sent a message to Nehru and Liaquat Ali Khan expressing the hope that the Kashmir question would be satisfactorily settled through United Nations mediation.[10] The replies they received were politely non-committal.

On October 8, 1951, Premier Nu of Burma invited Premier Sukiman of Indonesia to a tripartite conference with India to be held at Rangoon later that month. Embarrassed by the omission of Pakistan from the proposed conference, yet not wishing to decline outright, the Indonesian government accepted the invitation but urged postponement "because of pressing business at home."[11] On the eve of the Ceylon conference of south Asian premiers held in April 1954, Foreign Minister Sunario and the chairman of the Indonesian Parliament's foreign affairs section again vainly offered their country's good offices in helping to mediate the Kashmir dispute.[12] On this delicate issue, however, India more than Pakistan has been disinclined to accept offers of mediation made repeatedly by Asian nations friendly to both parties in the dispute.

In Indonesian-Pakistani relations, the Kashmir question has required only tightrope walking on Indonesia's part. A much more fundamental difficulty has been Indonesia's reluctance to adhere to Pakistan's ideal of the Muslim state and bloc. Indonesia had voiced misgivings as to sending representatives to the various Islamic conferences called by Pakistan in 1949 and 1951. When

[9] *Report on Indonesia*, Mar. 6, 1951.   [10] *Ibid.*, July 17, 1951.
[11] *Ibid.*, Oct. 29, 1951.   [12] *New York Times*, Apr. 11, 1954.

Pakistan proposed in May 1952 that a conference of Muslim premiers be convened at Karachi, the chairman of Indonesia's Parliamentary foreign affairs committee insisted, as a condition of acceptance, that there be—

no attempt to create an Islamic bloc. Indonesia is not an Islamic state and should work with all the young countries of Asia—Islamic, Hindu, and Buddhist. Such a conference should be purely for reaching an understanding, not for making any binding decisions.[13]

Ex-Premier Natsir (leader of the liberal wing of Indonesia's biggest Muslim party), after returning from a tour of the Middle East the next month, urged that his country be represented at the Karachi meeting because it promised to be more social than political in character and would strengthen the Arab-Asian bloc in the United Nations. (Indonesia has attended meetings of the international Islamic economic organization and sent delegates to its third annual conference held at Karachi in April 1954.)

To a certain extent, the long-standing personal friendships which bind leaders such as Sjahrir and Hatta to Nehru count for something in Indonesia's reaction to Pakistan's policy. But more important is the Western secular education to which Indonesia's present leaders have been exposed. Time and again, Indonesians—pious Muslims though they be—have reiterated that their country is a national state, not a theocratic one, and that they want no part in any bloc based exclusively on a common religion. For practical political results, they prefer to work with the United Nations' Arab-Asian group, which, they feel, can more efficiently help other Muslim countries to attain independence.

Pakistan, for its part, has two major and largely unexpressed grievances against Indonesia. First of all, the Pakistanis feel that the Indonesians are lax Muslims. As one Pakistani, who had lived for some time in Indonesia, expressed it:

Foreign Muslims hardly feel themselves in an Islamic atmosphere, as local nationalism scarcely differentiates between Muslims and other foreigners. . . . Few (Indonesian) Muslims enter a house with the Islamic greeting and many do not trouble to answer it, looking on those who do as fanatically minded. . . . It may be said that the Javanese way of life is un-Islamic, and another startling manifestation is that the Indonesian National Airways serves ham sandwiches to every passenger.[14]

In rejoinder, Indonesia might point to the thousands of Indonesian pilgrims who go to Mecca each year and to other thousands who have studied at Egypt's Al-Azar University. But there is no denying that almost without ex-

[13] *Ibid.*, May 6, 1952.
[14] F. Hossein, "Problems Indonesia Is Facing Today" and "Future Prospects of Indonesian Islam," *Islamic Literature* (Lahore), August and March 1952.

ception the country's present leaders are secular-minded, have written religious freedom into the constitution, and believe in the separation of religion and state.

Pakistan cannot forget that the Islamic states were the first to recognize the Indonesian Republic, nor forgive Indonesia for now trying to strike political bargains in cases where gratitude might be expected to make it give altruistic support. Reportedly Indonesia, in return for backing Pakistan on the Kashmir question, wanted the assurance that Pakistan would actively support Indonesia's claim to Irian (Western New Guinea).[15] A minor point, but a straw in the wind, was the resentment felt by some Pakistanis that the Indonesian delegates to its Islamic conference persisted in wearing European and not their national dress. Political rather than religious considerations determine Indonesia's foreign policy, and this is the fundamental issue on which it parts company with Pakistan.

Burma, like Indonesia, wants Pakistan's good will, but finds the viewpoint of India's leader more congenial. Unlike that of Indonesia, however, Burma's situation is complicated by physical proximity and religious differences that are tied up with minority problems in both countries.

The presence in Arakan of a large and transient minority of Muslims from Chittagong and their alleged involvement in large-scale rice-smuggling from Burma into East Pakistan has long been a sore point with the Burmese.[16] Since 1948, separatist tendencies on the part of some Arakanese Buddhists have been fostered by Burmese Communist insurgents. This manifestation of regionalism, which is directed against the government of Burma, has—despite contradictory objectives—periodically gotten mixed up with the demand on the part of the Indian Muslims in north Arakan for annexation to Pakistan. Recently a further complication has been added by reports of persecution by Pakistanis of Arakanese Buddhists living in Pakistan and involvement of this situation with the unrest prevailing in East Bengal. Complex as the situation remains, a trend toward alignment along religious and racial lines on both sides of the border is discernible. Fortunately the manifest determination of the governments of both Burma and Pakistan to maintain good and correct relations have thus far kept this powder keg from blowing up. In January 1953 opposing views in regard to the sovereignty of 21 islands in the Naaf River marking the boundary between Burma and Pakistan were amicably discussed by the two governments. As to the outbreaks at Dacca in the early summer of 1954, the Burmese voiced no suspicion that they might have any relationship with the Mujahid problem. And the Rangoon press generally sympathized with the position taken by Fazlul Huq as the spokesman for the legitimate grievances of his people.[17]

[15] Ibid.   [16] See pp. 151–158.
[17] The Burman, June 3, 1954.

Aside from the Arakan troubles, Burmese-Pakistani relations have been cordial, though overshadowed by Burma's far closer ties with India. (Rather surprisingly, at the Asian premiers' meeting at Colombo in April 1954, Burma found itself in agreement with Pakistan rather than with India in regard to the greater danger for the region represented by communism as compared with colonialism.) In remaining on good terms with both, Premier Nu, like his Indonesian colleague, has run up against the obstacle of the unsettled Kashmir question. When Nu, fearing Chinese aggression, put out feelers to neighboring Southeast Asian countries in 1951 for a mutual-aid pact, he found that the chief stumbling block was the reluctance of India and Pakistan to join it together. He told a correspondent of the *Manchester Guardian*[18] that "the Kashmir dispute is thus hamstringing efforts to establish collective limited security in southeast Asia," and Nu had to content himself with signing a treaty of friendship with Pakistan in January 1952. A year and a half later Nu warned that there might be repercussions throughout Southeast Asia if India and Pakistan did not in time solve their differences over Kashmir.[19]

In mid-1953 the Burmese premier again offered to try bringing India and Pakistan together and once more he failed. So when Ceylon proposed in February 1954 to Burma and Indonesia that they jointly offer their mediation services to India and Pakistan in the Kashmir dispute, two influential Rangoon dailies[20] simultaneously and independently warned the Burmese government against accepting the Ceylonese suggestion. In the absence of a specific invitation to mediate from the main parties to the dispute, they argued, Burma would undoubtedly be blamed for meddling and for the probable failure of such efforts to settle the thorny Kashmir question.

Remittances

Money sent by overseas Indians to the homeland has long been a vital support for the joint-family system in India, and a major incentive to the emigration of Indians to Southeast Asia. Since the war, however, these remittances have ceased to be the yardstick they once were of the close ties between Indian nationals abroad and their mother country. All Southeast Asian countries have imposed restrictions on the export of funds, and those not tied to sterling have consequently limited Indian remittances within the general context of their financial regulations.[21]

Even the most sensitive Indian nationalists can find in these restrictions no discrimination against Indians, and in many cases Southeast Asian countries have responded to the pleas of the government of India for relaxation of such

[18] Issue of Jan. 7, 1951.

[19] Associated Press despatch, Rangoon, quoted in the *Bangkok Post*, Aug. 15, 1953.

[20] The *New Light of Burma* and the *Rangoon Daily*, issues of Feb. 24, 1954.

[21] Burma was part of the sterling bloc until the summer of 1952, when these ties were severed and its own monetary unit, the kyat, replaced the rupee.

financial controls in specific cases. The Burma government, while generally limiting remittances to Pakistan to Rs. 40 per person per month,[22] made a special concession in the case of families of Pakistanis caught in rebel-held areas. Indonesia, too, as the result of strong representations on the part of India, eased the application of its monetary restrictions to resident Indians, who were the chief source of income for Hindu refugees from Pakistan.[23] Indochina proved to be a special case, for during the war years there had accumulated some 10 crores (100 million) of rupees in local banks, for want of remittance facilities. After the Japanese surrender, prolonged negotiations between the French and Indian authorities finally resolved the problem, and by November 1949 remittances through normal banking channels were re-established. However, with the internal devaluation of the franc, to which the Indochinese piastre is pegged, there was alleged to be a considerable decline in the total value of such Indian assets.[24]

With regard to Malaya, more detailed information is available, though official figures have never told the whole story inasmuch as it has been the habit of Indians returning to India to carry their savings on their persons in the form of cash or jewelry.[25] Moreover, it is hard to compare the prewar with the postwar periods because of inflation and fluctuating economic conditions. In 1951, for example, the virtual doubling of remittances to India from Singapore and the Federation of Malaya over the previous year was undoubtedly a result of the current rubber boom and the larger earnings of Indian laborers in the country.[26] Although there probably has been a real increase in remittances as compared with those of the prewar years, the sums involved are of less importance in determining the degree to which ties are maintained with the homeland than are their regularity and proportion as compared with other immigrant communities.[27] The *Social Survey of Singapore* for 1947 found that, in that pre-boom year, the majority of Indian wage earners remitted money to dependents in the homeland, and that—though the longer they stayed in Singapore the less frequently did they remit—nevertheless Indians remitted more than did the Chinese in similar circumstances.

BURMA

Problems arising from the presence of a large Indian minority in Burma were not acute until after the country's separation from India in 1937. True,

[22] *The Burman* (Rangoon), Jan. 21, 1952.   [23] Kondapi, *op. cit.*, p. 369.
[24] *Ibid.*, p. 368.
[25] *Economic Survey of Asia and the Far East—1950*, p. 60.
[26] Average monthly remittances in 1949 were Str. $686,000 from Singapore and $1,097,000 from the Federation; in 1950 the figures were slightly higher; and in 1951 the monthly amount rose to $1,280,000 from Singapore and $2,077,500 from the Federation. (Reuter despatch from Kuala Lumpur, quoted in the *Bangkok Post*, Jan. 7, 1952.)
[27] Between 1934 and 1938, the average annual amount remitted to India from Malaya ranged between Rs. 7 and 12 millions.

the world depression of the early 1930's had changed the character of the Indian economic stake in Burma and had placed the Burmese in an increasingly disadvantageous position vis-à-vis the Indians, but its consequences were not apparent so long as Burma remained an Indian province and under the same British colonial administration. In the years just preceding World War II, not only was there a rapid growth in nationalism on the part of both Indians and Burmese but it found new channels for its expression. Burmese nationalists were now able to take action which their counterparts in India regarded as hostile to Indian interests. And in Burma, violence flared up between Burmese and Indians, which had the additional disruptive effect of widening the breach between the Hindu and Muslim elements in the local Indian community.

Although there were fewer Muslims than Hindus in Burma, the former were more firmly rooted in the country. Descended from Muslim immigrants married to Burmese wives, they were scarcely distinguishable from the Burmans.[28] In 1941, for the first time, they were allowed to be listed in the census taken that year as Burma Muslims, rather than under their former name of Zerbadis, in order to show their identity with the "sons of the soil." Most of the Hindus, on the other hand, were immigrant laborers, and though some of the more prosperous among them were permanently resident in the country and for all practical purposes had severed ties with India, they remained generally aloof from the Burmese. While they had in common an absorption in money-making, the Hindus were divided among themselves by caste and by differences in economic and cultural levels. The existence of Burmese and Indian chauvinism wrought further division in a community already badly split.

Minor differences between the Hindu and Muslim Indians had long existed, but never before the riots of 1938 had they taken the form of violence, and in this instance they were fanned into flame by their admixture with Burmese nationalism. Burmese Buddhists alleged that their religion had been insulted by the republication of a book written by a Burma Muslim, which had first appeared in 1929 and which at that time had attracted little notice. The 1938 riots began in Mandalay with an attack on Indian merchants and soon spread to Rangoon and throughout the country, becoming involved en route with various irrelevant issues, such as strikes of the oil-field workers, bus drivers, and students.

These riots were estimated to have caused more than 200 deaths, chiefly of Indian Muslims, and property losses were officially placed at Rs. 18 million. Far more serious, they not only embittered Indo-Burmese relations but widened the rift between Indian Muslims and Hindus. During the riots some Hindus had ostentatiously sided with the Burmese by giving food to the

[28] F. B. Leach, "Burma's Indian Minority Problem," *Great Britain and the East*, Oct. 15, 1940.

pongyis (monks), joining Buddhist processions, and even claiming the existence of a blood tie between themselves and the Burmese Buddhists. From
such incidents, which were often purely local and without any communal
bias, antagonism between the two groups spread to wider issues. India's political controversies were imported into Burma and fostered aggressively by
both Hindus and Muslims. Thereafter, processions organized on Congress
holidays were regarded by the opposing camp as anti-Muslim demonstrations
and, similarly, celebrations of the Prophet's birthday or of the All-India Muslim League's anniversaries were taken by the Hindus as directed against themselves. The newly appointed agent of the government of India in Burma and
the two main Indian organizations in Rangoon—the Burma Indian Association and the Burma Indian Chamber of Commerce—helped in restoring
superficial harmony, but they did not succeed in reuniting the community as
a whole nor in undoing the harm done by the riots to Indian prestige in
Burma.

Nor did the nationalistic measures passed during the next three years by the
Burma Legislature succeed in uniting the local Indian community, which
they affected adversely at all economic levels. The Land Purchase Bill em-
powering the state to buy land from absentee nonagriculturist landlords and
to distribute it to the agrarian proletariat, as well as the Tenancy Act, which
aimed to reduce land rents drastically, naturally affected Indians, as they
formed the bulk of the nonfarming landowner class. Thanks to inefficient administration of these two agrarian laws, and to representations made to the
government by the Nattukottai Chettyar Association in Burma, they had a
less damaging effect on Indian landholding interests than had been originally
anticipated. However, such measures, together with the recent anti-Indian
riots, convinced most of the chettyars that they must pull out of Burma, and
whenever possible Indian bankers and landlords began liquidating their holdings. In 1938 the largest sum in the history of the two countries was remitted
to India, and thousands returned to the motherland.[29]

The Buddhist Women's Succession and Marriage Act, of concern only to
the comparatively few Indians married to Burmese wives, determined that all
questions of divorce, property, and inheritance should thenceforth be regulated according to Burmese Buddhist law, and no longer according to codes
applying to non-Buddhist husbands. Another piece of legislation, the Rangoon
Municipal Bill of 1940, provided that not less than half of the members of the
Rangoon Corporation Council should be Burmans. Rangoon's Indian community, which at that time formed over half the population of Burma's capital and paid 55 percent of municipal taxes, contended that this bill would reduce Indian representation in the city's government far below the level justified by its numerical strength and revenue contributions. The bill was even-

[29] John Christian, *Modern Burma* (University of California Press, 1942), p. 257.

tually modified somewhat, owing to intervention by the government of India, which—spurred on by organs of public opinion in India—was in a favorable position to defend Indian interests in Burma in two far-reaching fields, trade and immigration.

In the treaty separating Burma from India, it was agreed that from April 1937 to April 1940 Burma would impose no duties on Indian imports or restrictions on Indian immigration into Burma, and thereafter not without giving a year's notice of her intention to abrogate the existing arrangement. Burma duly gave such notice as soon as it was legally possible to do so. While India could hardly object to Burma's altering disadvantageous trade relations in order to fill her war-depleted treasury through the imposition of customs duties on the increasing amount of imports she was receiving from India, the government of India used this chance to work for better treatment of Indians domiciled in Burma. As early as April 1939, a resolution was passed in the Indian Legislative Assembly against renewal of the trade agreement with Burma, and asking the government of India to regulate rice imports from Burma. Under the wartime conditions of 1940–41, when India was taking more than half of Burma's rice, almost all her mineral oils, and about 60 percent of her timber exports, Burma could not expect to find substitute markets for those three commodities, which constituted over 70 percent of her total exports. But as they formed only about one-tenth of India's total trade, that country was in a better position than Burma to negotiate an advantageous treaty. How little the politicians of Burma understood their country's economic dependence on India was shown by a remarkable statement made by a former Minister of Commerce, and supported by the Burmese-language press, that it mattered little to Burma if India did not keep on buying her rice.

Negotiations dragged on from July 1939 until the spring of 1941. In the meantime, Burma's dependence on imports from India had increased, while India was making herself more independent of Burma as a market for her products. An export tax, which Burma had placed on her rice shipments to India shortly before the expiration of the old trade agreement, further aroused India's desire for retaliation and for a more intensive local cultivation of paddy that might enable her eventually to do without Burma's rice. Finally, on April 3, 1941, the pact was signed, to India's advantage: Indian goods were to receive a 15-percent preference over non-Empire goods and a 10-percent advantage over those of British origin, and the government of India was empowered to levy duties on imports from Burma.

The immigration agreement, which was negotiated only after the trade pact was signed, was a corollary to it and affected an even wider range of Indian interests in Burma. In September 1940, almost as soon as he came to power, Premier U Saw announced that his government intended to end unrestricted immigration into Burma from India and China. However, he awaited the report of the Baxter Committee, which had been appointed in 1939 as a result of the 1938 Riot Enquiry Committee's recommendation. The 1938 committee had reported that perhaps the most compelling cause of the anti-Indian outbreaks had been the unrest and discontent caused by the dominant position of Indians in Burma and by their unrestricted entry into the country. In view of the amount of emotion aroused by a subject on which little accurate knowledge existed, a committee of experts, headed by the financial adviser, James Baxter, was asked to ascertain the volume of Indian immigration; to what extent it was seasonal and transient; in which occupations Indians were mainly employed in Burma; whether in such occupations Indians had displaced Burmans or could be replaced by them; and finally, whether in view of such findings, Indian unskilled labor was essential for Burma's requirements.

Unfortunately for its reception by both Burmese and Indian opinion, the text of the Baxter Report was not published until that of the immigration agreement on which it was based had been made known, in July 1941. Generally speaking, the agreement rested on two main principles—the right of Burma to determine the composition of her own population, and that of Indians who had identified themselves with the interests of Burma to enjoy the same privileges as the permanent population. By its terms, two classes of immigrants were defined—first, those who could remain indefinitely in Burma and be employed there, and second, those whose entry permits would be controlled by the Burmese government and issued only to persons with specified financial guaranties and literacy qualifications. In addition, the government of Burma announced that it would soon institute a system for registering Indians domiciled in the country.

In India an outburst of indignation greeted publication of the treaty terms. On August 14, 1941, the Federation of Indian Chambers of Commerce, the Imperial Indian Citizenship Association of Bombay, and the Madras All-Parties Meeting sent a joint memorandum of protest to the viceroy. Gandhi himself strongly condemned the agreement as an undeserved slur on both Burma and India, and could not believe that it had been made in response to "a vital cry from the great Burmese nation."[30] Responding to the strong feeling this agreement had aroused locally, the government of India succeeded in persuading London to postpone its approval.

Less vehement protests came from the comparatively inarticulate and disunited Indian community in Burma. In part this was due to the official level at which the negotiations were conducted: the Baxter Report was not published beforehand, and the negotiating delegation from India arrived so precipitately that local Indians had no time to organize or present their case. The only group of domiciled Indians who had a chance to express their views to

[30] *Rangoon Times,* Aug. 26, 1941.

the delegation were representatives of the Burma Indian Chamber of Commerce, which was composed of the outstanding local merchants, bankers, and industrialists. Since the Burma Legislature had to pass on the agreement, the single member representing Indian industrial labor was able to voice his views, but he was the only one of the eight appointed Indian legislators who did not represent big business. In the uneasy political situation, the Indian members of the Legislature were accused by the Burmans of not identifying their interests with those of the country, and of using their votes simply to interfere in the domestic issues of the indigenous peoples. Neither the small shopkeepers and merchants, nor rural labor, nor the retired Indian civil servants living in Burma were consulted. The Indians as a whole seemed to have accepted the inevitability of some sort of restriction on their immigration into Burma, but felt that negotiations had been conducted with undue secrecy and that those who were most affected by them had been the least consulted.[31]

The immigration issue pointed up the complexities underlying the position of Indians in prewar Burma. Most salient among these was the divergency of economic interests in a community already divided by religion and subdivided by caste. Big businessmen among the Indians naturally wanted unrestricted immigration because it assured them of a large and cheap supply of labor, and they had channels through which they could express themselves and the means by which they could bring pressure on the British governments of Burma and India. In the late 1930's, both these governments were yielding to increasingly strong nationalist movements which, through lack of understanding of the foregoing and through an unfortunate personality conflict, seemed to be in mutual opposition. Nationalistic Indians in India, wounded by what they felt to be groundless discrimination on the part of Burmese nationalists against their compatriots in Burma, apparently did not grasp that they were doing a disservice to the bulk of the Indians there by opposing the immigration-restriction agreement. Nor did the superheated Burmans, for their part, realize that the majority of the Indians in Burma had every reason to side with them in opposing an influx that could only depress wages and lower their already poor standard of living. To the Burmans, all the Indians were an alien and unsympathetic people, who were exploiting Burma's resources solely for their own profit. The personal misunderstanding which arose between Jawaharlal Nehru and Premier Ba Maw at the time of the former's visit to Burma in 1937 further widened the breach.

Nationalist pressure led to periodic intervention in Burmese affairs on the part of the government of India, which remained the senior partner in their economic relationship. It is noteworthy that when, in 1931, the question of Burma's separation from India arose, the Chief Secretary of the government of Burma reported that Indian opinion in Burma conceded the right of Bur-

[31] *Ibid.,* June 26, 1941.

mans to separation and desired only that the legitimate interests of Indians resident in Burma should be protected.[32] In applying this informal mandate, the government of India interpreted Indian interests to be almost wholly those of the propertied class, and such modifications as it obtained in nationalistic Burmese legislation favored the chettyars, big traders, and shipping companies. For the protection of Indian labor, the government of India had indeed appointed an agent in Burma, but that did not take place until 1939 and his powers were limited in comparison with those of his counterpart in Malaya.[33] Uneducated, absorbed in earning money, and expecting little from India, the majority of the Indians in Burma before the war took little interest in the politics of their homeland.

Even among the few educated Indians in Burma, there seems to have been little transplantation of the political struggle that was going on in India. Before 1937 a Provincial Congress Committee existed in Burma, which regularly sent delegates to the annual Congress meeting in India. But after 1937, this committee was dissolved and was replaced by a Burma committee dedicated to work for the independence of Burma. However, the new committee continued to elect members to the All-India Congress Committee, of whom two were Indians and one a Burman in 1939.

That same year, two other Indian organizations were founded in Rangoon —the All-Burma Muslim League and the Burma Hindu Sabha; both had direct, though perhaps not official, connections with the parent organizations in India. There were also various regional Indian associations, such as the Young Chulia Muslim League, composed of Tamil Muslims from Madras, and the All-Burma South Indian Association. But such groups evinced less concern with politics in India than with the improvement of the social and economic status of Indians in Burma.

Population and Immigration

Until war broke out in the Far East in 1941, the Indian population of Burma was on the increase, as was its proportion to the country's total population, though at a less rapid rate than in the early years of the century. In 1931, the last year for which complete census figures are available, the Indians numbered 1,018,000, or almost 7 percent of the country's population. The war caused a big numerical decline: at the time of the Japanese invasion, approximately 500,000 Indians fled from Burma, of whom the Burmese government believes some 10,000 perished en route. Owing to immigration restrictions, insecurity, and adverse economic conditions in Burma since the end of the war, the Burmese Indian population has by no means regained its former size or importance.

[32] Christian, *op. cit.*, p. 65.   [33] Kondapi, *op. cit.*, p. 464.

Burmese nationalist sentiment ran so strongly against additions to the local Indian population that an agreement (Saw-Bajpai) restricting their immigration was reached with the government of India in 1941, but the war prevented its being carried out. In the latter years of the war, the Burmese government-in-exile at Simla conducted intermittent and inconclusive negotiations with New Delhi for revision of the 1941 agreement, which had been unpalatable to Indians.

In the months that immediately followed the British reoccupation of Burma in 1945, Indian businessmen—notably the chettyars and the heads of Scindia Navigation Company—brought considerable pressure to bear on the governments of Burma and India for the prompt resumption of unrestricted Indian immigration into Burma. The Scindia Company was interested in the transport of Indian workers, and the chettyars in the relative cheapness of Indian labor in Burma. However, since the Indian government had no intention of relaxing the ban it had imposed in 1938 on the emigration of unskilled labor (with the exception of 16,000 laborers to be recruited by the Civil Affairs Service, Burma, for temporary rehabilitation work), Burmese nationalist ire was not aroused. The two governments concerned and the Colonial Office agreed that only evacuees who were not unskilled laborers should have the right to return to Burma, but this decision on principle encountered practical difficulties—shortage of shipping, the scarcity of lodging and food, and the inability of many evacuees to establish proof of previous residence in Burma. (The first of the drawbacks just mentioned also affected 200,000 Indians who, having stayed in Burma during the war, wanted repatriation to India.) In the light of these problems, the ardor of evacuees to return to Burma was considerably cooled. Figures differ as to the number of Indians who did so in the early postwar years. According to the Burmese Minister of Labor and Industry in the spring of 1947, almost 246,000 Indians had by that time entered Burma since the re-establishment of civil government, but the government of India figures showed a maximum of 140,000.[34] The expense of this two-way repatriation was borne by the government of India, and many complaints arose as to the inefficiency or corruption, or both, of the Burmese Immigration Department.[35]

Improvement in shipping conditions made it increasingly difficult for both of the governments concerned to control Indian entries into Burma in the absence of any legal authority. A second agreement, reached after prolonged negotiations in December 1945, was disapproved by the Burma Executive Council in March 1946. In November 1946 the Indian government laid down special conditions for the recruitment of skilled laborers in India for service in Burma. The Protectors of Emigrants at Indian ports were instructed to

[34] *Times of India*, June 29, 1947.   [35] *The Burman*, June 28, 1946.

permit emigration only on the basis of a written contract normally for a two-year period and for monthly wages of not less than Rs. 46, plus such cost-of-living allowances as the Burma government might sanction; a security deposit was also required.[36]

On its side, the Burmese government prepared and passed an Emergency Immigration Act in June 1947, which required all persons entering Burma to possess a properly visaed passport or a permit issued by the Controller of Immigration. Vehement protests from India at this "unilateral and harsh" action were unavailing. The government of Burma stood on its rights, claiming that the new law was not discriminatory, in that it applied equally to all foreigners, and that it was only designed to meet an emergency. India's objections stemmed essentially from hurt pride, and the blow was felt more keenly in that it came from another Asian nation whose refugees India had harbored during the war. In reality, neither India nor Burma wanted a resumption of the prewar flow of Indians into Burma. Between May 1945 and April 1947, fewer than 3,000 new emigrants had been sponsored by the government of India,[37] and probably only about one-quarter of those who had fled from Burma to India in 1942 had returned by the spring of 1947. According to the 1953 census of Rangoon, there were then in that city only 40,396 Indians and Pakistanis out of a total population of 737,079. (As had been the case before the war, the great majority were men who came to Burma without their families.)

The one group of Indian immigrants which Burma has actively encouraged are doctors. Most Burmese government doctors in the postwar period have resigned to take up more remunerative private practice.[38] Unable to fill these vacant posts locally, the Burmese government sent a mission to recruit doctors in India. Results were encouraging: 600 applied for the 280 positions advertised.[39]

The Azad Hind

After the great exodus of early 1942, the Indians remaining in Burma were the object of considerable intimidation and abuse by the Burmans. The stores of Indian shopkeepers were looted, and Indian laborers in the delta were subjected to a veritable pogrom. Relief came from the Japanese, who had their own uses for Burma's Indians, either as laborers or as espionage and sabotage agents. Many came to Rangoon for Japanese protection, and the Indian landowners who remained in Burma were given a chance to prove their claims to

[36] Kondapi, op. cit., p. 52.

[37] Economic Survey of Asia and the Far East—1950, p. 47.

[38] Of the 670 doctors in government service in prewar days, only about 280 remained as of early 1952 (The Burman, Feb. 10, 1952).

[39] Ibid., June 13, 1952. Under the Colombo Plan, India has been giving training to Burmese technicians and military personnel in its educational and defense establishments.

property. The Japanese military authorities at first organized them into an Indian Residents Association, then in August 1942 formed at Rangoon a committee of the Indian Independence League (IIL). All who agreed to join the Japanese in fighting for India's "liberation" were promised release from prison and the princely wage of Rs. 5 a month. The following October, Tokyo Radio announced that 400 prisoners of war had accepted the offer, but almost 2,000 others remained in Rangoon's Central Jail. At first the IIL functioned rather anemically as a protective and relief organization, and it was not catapulted into publicized activity until Subhas Chandra Bose came to Rangoon in June 1944.

Because of the strength of anti-Indian feeling among the Burmese, it took some persuasion and time for the Japanese to win Ba Maw's consent to having Burma used as Bose's operational base. But by August 1943 the Burmese government was prodded into reversing a law promulgated in October 1942 which forbade the entry of additional Indians into Burma, and thenceforth, at least in principle, Indians even became eligible for Burmese citizenship. Mass rallies were held, and Burmese nationalists as well as Bose urged the Indians to rise up in arms against Britain. A few Indians were given military training, but their number was kept low, probably both as a result of their lack of enthusiasm and because of policy, pending the time when Burmese opinion could be adjusted to the idea of the transfer to their country of the bulk of the Indian forces then undergoing training at Singapore.[40] Judging from a concentrated effort to win support from the Burma Muslims, it appears that the Japanese counted more on their support than on that of the Hindus, particularly after Bose transferred his headquarters to Rangoon in October 1943 and received formal recognition by the government of Burma.

In February 1944 the Azad Hind regime received tangible proof of Japanese benevolence when one of its representatives was dispatched to administer the Andaman and Nicobar Islands. This, like Bose's much-publicized offer to ship Burma's surplus rice to starving Bengal, was a good propaganda stunt for Indians in the homeland, and it was also a curtain raiser for the Manipur campaign that took place a few months later. While Bose was calling upon his compatriots in Southeast Asia to shed their blood for the liberation of the motherland, he was much more insistently asking them to give him funds. In October 1943 he stated that the Rangoon chapter of the IIL was collecting Rs. 10 millions as a voluntary contribution to the cause. And at a conference called in Rangoon on April 8, 1944, of representatives of all IIL branches in the country, he flatly declared—undoubtedly under Japanese prompting— that supporters of India's freedom had no moral right to expect all-out aid from Japan until they had mobilized themselves behind the Indian National Army to the last man, rupee, and grain of food.

[40] See pp. 98–99.

A few days before this conference, the Bank of Azad Hind was established in Burma with the obvious aim of getting hold of the local Indians' financial resources for the projected campaign to liberate India. It was apparently hoped that a purely Indian bank would overcome the Indians' natural reluctance to place their funds in Burmese hands. The recent transfer by Japan to the Burmese government of all enemy-owned assets discouraged any excuses the Indians might advance on the grounds that they were British subjects. Although the local Indians were already deeply indebted to the Japanese for protection against Burmese hostility and powerless to resist their pressure, yet the Indians left in Burma had all suffered so disastrously from the events of 1942 that they were unable to provide large funds even if they had been so inclined. The group of Burma Indians in whose hands most of that community's wealth was concentrated were the very ones who stood to gain most by a return of British control. This element of the Indian population (as well as Indian black marketeers) were the most vulnerable to the Bose-Japanese squeeze because of their unpopularity with the Burmese.

The Indian policy of the Japanese in Burma was simple, and added up to the greatest possible financial and military exploitation. That of the Burmese government, however, was complicated by long-standing ethnic hostility, the geographic necessity of Burma's serving as a base for Bose's operation in India, and the fear of retaliation after the war from an India immeasurably strengthened by wartime industrialization, a large sterling balance, and increased armed forces. By this time, even the most chauvinistic Burmese nationalists had come to realize that economically their future was tied up with that of India, and that their treatment of Indian nationals in Burma would necessarily affect that relationship in postwar years.

Postwar Political Activities

The Azad Hind movement gave the Burma Indians a greater unity than they had ever before achieved, and a larger identification of their aspirations for independence with those of the Burmese nationalists. This development, taken in conjunction with the reduction in their numbers, the actual if not legal elimination of the chettyars, and the docility displayed by Indian labor to Burmese leadership, had the effect of wiping out almost all Burmese hostility toward the Indian minority by the end of the war. On the positive side, again, outstanding Indian organizations such as the All-Burma Indian Congress and the All-Burma Muslim League actively supported the Anti-Fascist People's Freedom League (AFPFL) in its struggle for Burma's independence from Britain. And individual Indian leaders fostered the budding cordiality of the Indo-Burmese relationship. The agent of the government of India (called its representative after 1944) was Dr. C. Rauf, a Burma-born Indian; his brother, M. A. Raschid, later acquired Burmese citizenship and entered the Cabinet. Both these men were *personae gratissimae* to the local nationalists. Most important of all, Nehru allayed Burmese fears on the question of Indian immigration, and several times urged his compatriots in Burma to put an end to their dual-nationality attitude. The local Indians responded in kind by rejecting their prewar communal representation in the Burmese Legislature and by confirming their faith in the promise of independent Burma to safeguard minority rights.

Inevitably there lingered some misgivings on the part of Indians and Burmese alike. The Burma Indian Chamber of Commerce, which had enjoyed a privileged status under British rule, was uneasy about the role it would play in sovereign Burma and irked by the restrictions placed on foreign trade.[41] General Aung San, for his part, openly distrusted Indian big business and told the writers, in April 1947, that its rapacity and economic imperialism in regard to Burma were held in check only by Nehru. In a press interview at New Delhi in January 1947, Aung San reportedly[42] made this comment:

There are some Indians in the AFPFL . . . but Indian vested interests, like any other vested interests, are not in favor of independence. The rest of the people are with us.

The first disturbance of this honeymoon period occurred in January 1947 when, in the so-called London agreement, a Burmese national was defined as a British subject or subject of an Indian state who was born in Burma and who had resided there for a total period of not less than eight out of the ten years immediately preceding either January 1, 1942, or January 1, 1947. This definition was hastily concocted in order to pave the way for the election of a constituent assembly three months later. Nehru was said to have protested against it to Aung San and to have received the assurance that it was provisional and would not determine the franchise for Indians under the new constitution.[43] That the fears of the Indians were not wholly allayed was shown by their forming of a committee to study clauses affecting minorities in the constitutions of other countries,[44] with a view to making representations to the AFPFL committee then drafting Burma's constitution.

Indian suspicions were indeed confirmed when the new constitution of 1948 drew a distinction for purposes of citizenship between those of indigenous and those of alien origin. Indians who opted for Burmese citizenship were required to renounce their Indian nationality; failing this, they were required to register as aliens by April 4, 1949. The deadline was postponed several times. By September 1949, more than 150,000 of the approximately 250,000 Indians resident in Rangoon had acquired Burmese citizenship.[45]

[41] *The Burman*, Dec. 19, 1946.   [42] *Burmese Review* (Rangoon), Jan. 13, 1947.
[43] *The Burman*, Feb. 11, 1947.   [44] *Hindustan Times*, Mar. 22, 1947.
[45] Kondapi, *op. cit.*, p. 420.

More recent figures are not available, but it is known that thousands of Indians have left Burma since late 1949 because of the insecurity of life and property and also because of their strong sentimental attachment to India. Probably most of those who have remained in Burma recognize that failure to choose Burmese citizenship will close many avenues of employment and impede promotions.

The Burma government, for its part, has from time to time tried to reassure the domiciled Indians. To offset the effect of its unilateral action in promulgating the Emergency Immigration Act of June 1947, it issued a soothing communiqué the following September to the effect that Burma welcomed Indians as citizens, that it appreciated their renunciation of special privileges and protection, and that its constitution guaranteed fundamental rights to all classes of citizens, regardless of birth, religion, sex, or race, and also equality of opportunity.[46] As to government service, "a due share of appointments" would be given to Indians, and they would be allowed to use English until they had had time to learn Burmese, which had now become the official language. Although preference in appointments would naturally be given to Indians who acquired Burmese citizenship, there would be no other type of discrimination shown against those who preferred to remain Indian nationals.

The citizenship issue was both more and less complicated for the Burma Muslims than for the Hindus, and it became an increasingly divisive one. Though they were more rooted in the country, Burma's common frontier with newly independent Pakistan stimulated their consciousness as Muslims. Moreover, in July 1947 they lost an able leader when Razak was assassinated. But even before his death, the ranks of the Burma Muslims were beginning to be split by differences on internal issues and international alignments. Under Razak's leadership, the Burma Muslim Congress (BMC) had expanded throughout the country, and had joined forces with the AFPFL, but some of its members were looking westward as early as May 1946. In the local press, Razak gave out the following warning:

To those Muslims whose outlook is tinged with Pakistanism, I would like to say that such a thing is not within practical politics, nor is it wise in Burma. We should strive to make ourselves a strong and respected community, but we must not hamper national progress.[47]

At a Burma Muslim Congress held at Rangoon in December 1946, a resolution was passed urging all Burma Muslim organizations to sink their differences and merge into one body, and also to participate actively in the Burma freedom movement by joining the AFPFL. Already a rival body was

[46] *The Burman*, Sept. 25, 1947.   [47] *Ibid.*, May 20, 1946.

beginning to form, which came out into the open after Burma attained independence in January 1948. In April of that year, the AFPFL requested the Burma Muslim Congress to withdraw from membership in it on the ground that of late the latter had failed to follow AFPFL directives and that its religious complexion was incompatible with the purely political objectives of the AFPFL. The parting was amicable, and the BMC showed no inclination to join either the right- or left-wing opposition to the government. In June 1948, a meeting of the pro-AFPFL members of the BMC was held under the chairmanship of U Khin Maung Lat, at which it was decided to transfer the Congress's religious functions to the Ulama Society and to seek readmittance to the parent body. This precipitated a definite split among the Burma Muslims, and the dissenters, led by U Kyaw Nyun, broke away to form the Burma Muslim League. The AFPFL rewarded its Muslim prodigal sons in February 1949 by assuring them that they would not be "treated as Indians and hence are not required to put in claims to be treated as Burmese nationals,"[48] and two years later, U Khin Maung Lat was appointed Minister of Judicial Affairs.

Reaction to this appointment was not slow in coming. Boh Tilla, then president of the Muslim League, asserted that Maung Lat's elevation was an honor to his community and not to the organization he headed, that the BMC had lost its political identity when it adhered to the AFPFL, and that it had done nothing to protect the rights of Burma Muslims. A spokesman for the Muslim League followed through by spelling out that organization's objectives, which, stated in general terms, were for a separate communal status that would preserve its Islamic culture and laws. Specifically he asked for a special category for Burmese Muslims in the forthcoming census, formation of Muslim units in the nation's armed forces, a government grant for the "uplift" of the Muslim religion, adequate representation in Parliament, the opening of Muslim schools in Burma's main towns, and the same statutory rights as other indigenous minorities, such as the Frontier Peoples.[49] Those who opposed these objectives pointed out that granting such privileges to one religious group would probably entail similar concessions being made to Hindus and Christians.

In the Parliamentary elections of 1951, both the BMC and the BML put up their own candidates, and dismissed from their membership all those whom each body suspected of disloyalty. In 1952 the whole Burma Muslim community was rocked by a proposal sponsored by Khin Maung Lat to amend the law relating to Islamic marriages. At the annual Burma Muslim Congress held in June 1954, Khin Maung Lat made one of his routine pleas for the development of "Union Consciousness." During the course of his speech he aroused some dissension by voicing his regret that most of the

[48] Ibid., Feb. 21, 1949.   [49] Ibid., Mar. 9, 1951.

Burma Muslims still clung to their foreign dress and had not yet adopted the Burmese costume.[50]

This schism between the Burma Muslims has been unfortunate in itself and also for its effect on other resident Indians. Although there has been no repetition of the 1938 riots, communalism has reinfected the whole community, partly as an inadvertent result of official Burmese action, which seems to have been inspired by the desire to give dignity and unity to the religion of the majority of Indian residents in Burma. In June 1951, the Ministry of Religious Affairs sponsored a meeting of representatives of the various Hindu sects in Rangoon, at which it was decided to set up a committee for the purpose of organizing a permanent body. Two years passed before the All-Burma Hindu Central Board was formally established and backed financially by the Burmese government. It was founded as a nonpolitical organization whose aims were to unite and represent all Hindu sects in the country and to propagate the fundamental teachings of Hinduism.[51]

The Economic Stake: Investments and Banking

Chettyars were the wealthiest element in the Indian population of prewar Burma. By 1937 they had come to own, either outright or through mortgages, a huge proportion—amounting to perhaps one-quarter—of Burma's best riceland. Chettyar capital invested in agriculture alone, in 1930, was estimated at Rs. 500 million (that is, a little over $180 million at the then current exchange rate), and was considered to have been chiefly responsible for the rapid development of rice production in Lower Burma.[52] The remaining chettyar investment, roughly Rs. 250 million, was largely in urban property and businesses.[53]

When the Japanese invaded Burma in early 1942, most of the chettyars fled to India, leaving behind a few agents and one functioning bank which, in 1943, was transformed into the People's Bank of Burma. The Japanese, not wishing to alienate the Indians, for whom they had uses and who had propaganda value for them, began by recognizing chettyar land titles but soon had to shift ground. Neither they nor the chettyars' agents in Burma were in any position to dislodge the Burmese farmer-tenants, who had simply taken over the land. Ba Maw, the wartime premier, later legalized the existing state of affairs, and in so doing he released the Burmese peasant from a great burden of debt.

To many persons this liquidation of alien and absentee landlordism seemed a happy solution of Burma's vexing agrarian problem. However, they reck-

50 *Ibid.*, June 21, 1954.
51 *Ibid.*, Aug. 24, 1953.
52 J. Russell Andrus, *Burmese Economic Life* (Stanford University Press, 1947), p. 75.
53 *Ibid.*, p. 306.

oned without the chettyars, who—years before the war—had foresightedly filed their land titles in India. Legally, at the end of the war, 3 million acres of Burmese paddyland valued at Rs. 60 to 80 crores were owned by about 5,000 Indians, chiefly chettyars. Some 250,000 Indians in Rangoon were said to own 70 percent of the buildings and 50 percent of the cinemas there.[54] Burmese nationalists have long been aware of the dangers of such a huge economic stake in the hands of aliens.

Even before formally becoming a sovereign state, Burma moved to strengthen its inadequate prewar legislation that had been designed to effect land reforms. The Tenancy Act of 1947 fixed the rent that a landlord might receive at roughly twice the amount of land tax. On January 3, 1948, the day before Burma became independent, the Transfer of Immovable Property Restriction Act was promulgated. This forbade the transfer of immovable property to any foreigner for a term exceeding one year. Originally the term "foreigner" did not include British subjects domiciled in Burma, but in February 1948 the act was amended to include all noncitizens of Burma.

Three more laws in 1948 had even farther-reaching effects. The Land Nationalization Act prohibited noncultivators from owning land, and cultivators from possessing more than 50 acres. Although enforcement of this law was to be gradual, its ultimate effect on Indian landowners was easily foreseeable. The maximum compensation to be paid dispossessed landlords was set at 12 times the land tax being currently paid, which ranged from Rs. 1 to 5 per acre, and in no case should it exceed Rs. 60 per acre. India proposed sending a delegation to discuss this compensation question, but in February 1949 the government of Burma asked that its arrival be postponed. Seven months later, the Burma government appointed a committee to determine the basis of compensation and methods of payment.

The Land Alienation Act of 1948 aimed to prevent the sale of land to persons other than Burmese nationals. The Disposal of Tenancies Act, of the same year, empowered the government to lease to tenants of its own choosing the maximum area that a single tenant could cultivate efficiently.

While the Burma government claimed that these laws were not discriminatory, in that they applied equally to all aliens, their combined effect naturally could not but be highly detrimental to Indian interests in the country. In the first place, judging from past experience, payment of even the small rents set by the government was likely to be irregular, and the restrictions placed on remittances to foreign countries would prevent most of what was collected from being sent out of Burma. Kondapi claimed[55] that recent Burmese land legislation has reduced the value of Indian landed property in Burma (estimated at Rs. 100 crores) "most arbitrarily and has deprived Indians of their

---

[54] Kondapi, *op. cit.*, p. 300. [55] *Ibid.*, p. 300.

legitimate income therefrom. The lack of Burmese capital to purchase the property has worsened the situation." The government of India was quick to request Burma to postpone enforcement of these acts pending an over-all agreement to be negotiated between the two countries.

Moneylending from capital largely provided by the chettyars themselves was their main activity, of which landownership was an undesired consequence. This had come about during the world depression and resulted from high interest rates, ranging from 15 to 36 percent, together with Burmese insouciance. In prewar days, according to Andrus, the chettyars were "much the most important part of Burma's financial community, judging by volume of business and economic impact on the country as a whole."[56] On the eve of World War II, there were six Indian banks functioning in Burma, which were financing an increasing proportion of the trade of local Indian merchants. Burmese moneylenders, often landlords, who charged even higher interest rates and who had less capital at their disposal, were quite unable to compete with the Indian bankers or to cope with the demand for loans.[57]

During the war, the Japanese kept a strict control over all banks; chettyar operations were virtually static; and the only Indian bank extant confined itself to operations connected with the Indian National Army. Since the end of the war, the government of Burma has tried to curb moneylending by law and to take the place of the chettyars as a source of agricultural credit. But the Moneylenders Act of 1945, which attempted to supplant the Usurious Loans Act by a more effective enforcement of registration, maximum interest rates, and the keeping of accounts, could not be put into force "for administrative reasons."[58] By advancing many times the amount offered in prewar days to Burmese farmers—in 1950–51 such agricultural loans were estimated at Rs. 36.5 millions—the government has gone deeply into debt and the rice crop still suffers from inadequate financing. But according to the ECAFE report for 1950,[59] "the activities of foreign—mainly Indian—moneylenders have thus been practically stopped."

Besides granting agricultural loans on a vast scale, the government has been trying to develop peasant organizations and revive the co-operative movement, so as to liquidate tenancy and eliminate the alien middlemen and rice millers. Peasant organizations have suffered from a struggle, as yet unresolved, for their control between the government and the Communists; insurgents have distributed land with a free hand to peasants in the regions which they control; and the co-operative movement, handicapped by a prewar history of failure and by postwar inefficiency and corruption in its administration, has not succeeded in winning public confidence. Currently there is a five-year plan for further development of co-operatives, which is to be guided by ILO

[56] Andrus, op. cit., p. 305.
[57] Ibid., p. 311.
[58] Burmese Review, Oct. 7, 1946.
[59] Op. cit., p. 181.

experts and whose outcome is dependent upon termination of the civil war in Burma. A great load of debt has indeed been lifted from the Burmese peasantry, but it may have to be paid by the entire population in taxes. In 1951 the government had to write off all agricultural loans and land taxes outstanding up to 1949 at an estimated loss of about Rs. 109 millions. And the end was not yet in sight. As the Burmese delegate explained on November 21, 1951, at the United Nations General Assembly session in Paris:

Both the agricultural credit system existing since 1910 and the recently created private development bank have proved inadequate . . . as a result of land nationalization in Burma, private capital is no longer forthcoming for land restoration or for land reclamation.

Furthermore, the question of compensation for nationalized land has not yet been settled. Chettfars have long wanted to cease owning land in Burma, but they are concerned about the form and method of compensation. In June 1950 a conference on the question was held at Rangoon, representatives from India attending as observers. They wanted to know if the Burma government would pay cash for a portion of their holdings, compensating them for the remainder in interest-bearing nontransferable bonds, and also whether chettyars would be included as members of the land committees (set up to supervise the distribution of nationalized land) in those areas where their holdings were considerable. The government hedged in replying to these questions, and made no definite commitments beyond promising nondiscrimination and a gradual enforcement of the nationalization law.[60]

In December 1953 a small "unofficial" delegation (which was nevertheless headed by the Indian ambassador to Burma) came to Rangoon for the purpose of persuading the Burma government to pay more compensation for Indian landholdings in Burma than was provided under the terms of the Land Nationalization Act. The Burmese government stood firm and, three months later, again disappointed chettyar interests by failing to include in an economic agreement it then signed with the Indian authorities any settlement of the question of Indian property in Burma. Early in March 1954 a deputation of Indian landowners in Burma complained to the Deputy Minister for External Affairs of India that the Land Nationalization Bill of 1954, soon to be discussed in the Burmese Parliament, was actually if not legally discriminatory. While Burmese landowners were usually smallholders, Indian landowners owned bigger units of land in lower Burma and, consequently, stood to lose far more heavily. Under the law's provisions, they claimed, 12,000 Indian landowners would receive compensation amounting to only one crore of rupees for their properties covering 3 million acres which they valued at between 90 and 100 crores of rupees.[61]

[60] *The Burman*, June 12, 1950.
[61] United Press despatch, New Delhi, Mar. 8, 1954.

The openly expressed dissatisfaction of the chettyars in regard to the compensation to be paid them under the Land Nationalization Act (which worked out to an average of 24 kyats per acre of agricultural land), reawakened some anti-Indian feeling among the Burmans. One well-known Rangoon journalist denounced the chettyars' "insatiable greed";[62] others proposed that the Indian government be asked to write off the debts still owed by wartime Burmese evacuees in India, allegedly inflated because of the Delhi officials' mismanagement of the evacuee camps, and still others wanted the Rangoon government to demand from India compensation for the aid it had given to resident Indians during the war.[63] Even some of the local Indians felt called upon to disassociate themselves from the chettyars' avarice. Burma Hindus, at a meeting held in Rangoon in May, passed a resolution requesting the "Indian central and state governments and all newspapers to ignore the Indian landlords' unjustifiable demands outrightly."

The Economic Stake: Trade and Industry

During the colonial period in Burma, Indian businessmen prospered there because of their long experience in commerce and their familiarity with British ways and law. Indians came to control "more than half of Burma's rice export, and were important in the export of several other commodities, as well as being the leading importers of most items. They owned many sawmills, rice mills, and miscellaneous but important factories like those manufacturing matches, soap, and knit goods."[64] An index to their prosperity is the fact that, in 1931, 49 percent of those who paid income tax in Burma were Indians.

After the war, Indian businessmen suffered at the hands of, first, the returning British and then the Burmans. A Civil Supplies Board set up in 1946 to control imports allotted Britishers a large share of the quotas. At the same time, the Agricultural Projects Board scaled down participation by Indian merchants in the purchase and export of rice from the prewar percentage of 65 to 36 percent.[65] When the Burmans began to assume control of their own government in 1947, they allotted 50 percent of import licenses to Burmese firms which, in prewar days, had handled less than 10 percent of such business, and later the government took over the entire rice trade. The big Indian trading houses have managed to thrive with the expanding trade between India and Burma, but the small Indian merchant has felt acutely the government-supported competition from newly established Burmese traders.

The Economic Stake: Labor and Occupations

According to the census of 1931, only 14 percent of Burma's male wage earners were Indians, but they predominated in the fields of banking, trade,

---

[62] "Mr. Burman" writing in *The Burman*, Apr. 9, 1954.
[63] *Ibid.*, May 27, 1954.
[64] Andrus, *op. cit.*, p. 351.   [65] Kondapi, *op. cit.*, p. 347.

government employment, and unskilled labor. Among the important facts established by students of labor conditions in the country during the 1930's was that the Burmese were not much affected by Indian competition as far as agriculture and unskilled labor were concerned, and that this was progressively the case as the decade passed. India's ban on the emigration of unskilled laborers in 1938 simply strengthened an established trend.

In the postwar years, because of the failure to rehabilitate Burma's war-damaged economy and later because of the civil war, the country's labor needs have been sharply curtailed and there has been an intensification of the displacement of workers that began during the Japanese occupation. Many agricultural laborers took refuge in the towns, and to the chronic problem of underemployment was added that of urban unemployment. The closing of many sawmills, a drastic curtailment of the mining and petroleum industries, and a reduction in the transport services threw thousands of workers out of jobs. By May 1949 there were estimated to be at least 5,000 unemployed Indians.[66]

Along with a decline in the employment of Indian laborers has come an eclipse of Indian leadership in the trade unions. Before the war, one seat in Burma's House of Representatives was assigned to Indian labor, and on the eve of World War II, Indian stevedores and transport workers organized their own unions. Since the war, however, they seem to have accepted Burmese leadership of the organized-labor movement. As of 1947 there were only 5,000 Indians belonging to the Trade Union Congress of Burma, which had a membership of some 30,000. According to the secretary of the Congress,[67] the Indians had no leaders of their own who might have disputed Burmese domination of that organization, which prided itself on its interracial character.

The passivity shown by Indian laborers has been matched by that of Indian employees in Burma government service. When the Burmese in 1947 announced their intention of reducing the number of nonnationals employed in the civil service, Indians holding such posts numbered nearly 4,000. Faced with the alternative of losing their jobs or of assuming Burmese citizenship and learning the Burmese language, about 1,000 Indians had returned to India by February 1949. During that same month there occurred a nationwide strike of government workers, called by the All-Burma Ministerial Services Union, in which the Indians' attitude not unnaturally succeeded in pleasing neither side. Kondapi offers the following version of these developments:[68]

On the advice of the Indian Embassy, the 1,000 Indian employees in Rangoon remained neutral by staying away from work but declaring that they were not deliberately on strike and reaffirming their loyalty to Burma. The Government of Burma on Feb. 7 declared that all who failed to return to duty by Feb. 10 would

[66] *Ibid.*, p. 366.
[67] Interview with Thakin Hla Kywe, Rangoon, Apr. 22, 1947.
[68] *Op. cit.*, p. 366.

be dismissed. . . . On Feb. 11 the Burmese Government dismissed 600 Indian and Pakistani employees (on the eve of their release from service) in spite of their neutrality towards the strike. . . . By May 1949 nearly 1,500 Indians employed in government service were retrenched. In certain cases, pensions were arbitrarily reduced.

Cultural Activities and Social Welfare

Under the British colonial regime, a wide variety of Indian languages was taught in Burma's Anglo-Vernacular schools—Hindi, Urdu, Tamil, Telugu, Bengali, Gujarati, and Punjabi. After the war, it was generally expected that Burmese nationalists would eliminate such instruction, but the Educational Policy Enquiry Commission appointed by the government in 1946 partially and temporarily endorsed the status quo ante bellum:

... immigrants have no moral right to demand that the state should help them to preserve their old nationality. But in view of the past situation in Burma, we believe that the same concessions as given to the national minorities should be made to them—that is, use of the vernacular be permitted as the main language in the primary stage for a reasonable period of time. . . . In secondary schools, the main language definitely must be Burmese. In all schools compulsory teaching of Burmese must begin at least in Standard II.

This liberal policy has saved the language question in Burma from becoming the problem that it represents in Malaya. The only Indian community that appears to have been agitated about education is the Burma Muslims, and their main concern has been with religious instruction. In May 1946, Moulvi Hashim of the Arabic College at Yindaw appointed a committee to draw up a syllabus of religious education "to be in keeping with the times." He felt that Burma Muslims "have been reading the Koran without much comprehension of its lofty ideals, and this calls for urgent reform."[69] The government, far from opposing such a move, has shown itself to be in sympathy with an improvement in Koranic learning.[70]

The Ramakrishna Mission of India, partially subsidized by the Indian government, has long carried on benevolent work in Burma. Its hospital at Rangoon, open to all races and creeds, suffered great damage during the war. In January 1947 it was able to reopen an outdoor dispensary, but not until several years later was the hospital repaired and able to resume operations.[71]

Intergovernmental Relations

Before the war, official relations between Burma and India were complicated by the long historical association of the two countries, their economic and

[69] *The Burman*, May 20, 1946.
[70] See p. 265.
[71] For an account of the activities of the Ramakrishna Mission in Rangoon see *The Burman*, June 28, 1954.

cultural ties, and the rapid growth of chauvinistic nationalism in each. For many years a separate administration for Burma was mooted, and it was generally regarded as sooner or later inevitable. From the outset their union had been based on nothing but administrative convenience for the British, as the problems of Burma were essentially different from those of India. Originally the demand for separation was based on the complaint that Burma was being treated as a "Cinderella of the Provinces" and on an ever louder clamor of "Burma for the Burmese."

The early opponents of separation were simply those who, while agreeing that a separate status for Burma was ultimately desirable, claimed for Burma the right to remain with India as long as she wished and to cut adrift at her own chosen time. The later antiseparationists, who were returned to the Legislative Council in large majority at the crucial election of 1932 (which was based specifically on that issue), were the extreme nationalists who feared that separation might deprive Burma of sharing in any political advance made by India. What finally neutralized their opposition and caused them to refrain from insisting that a vote be taken on this issue in the Council was the financial argument in favor of separation—namely, that Burma, through the collecting of her own customs duties and income tax, would considerably increase her revenues. This anticipated boost in the country's finances was realized as a result of the separation, although Burma had to assume responsibility for her own defense, for repayment of sums that had been spent by the government of India in Burma, for pensions to civil servants, and for certain unremunerative communications services. As a result of the separation, moreover, politicians, now for the first time vested with limited governmental responsibilities, were able to give vent to their rising hostility toward the Indians domiciled in Burma.

Outstanding developments in postwar Burma have been the serenity of relations with India and the liquidation of the minority problem represented by resident Indians. These achievements are the more remarkable in that the unifying element of common opposition to British rule by Burmese and Indian nationalists was eliminated through Britain's political withdrawal from both countries, giving free rein to nationalism in each. Two important trends —the decline in Indian immigration and the withdrawal of chettyar interests —antedated the war, and were simply strengthened by Burmese legislation enacted after independence was won. The new and probably decisive influence has been the reorientation of Indian leadership, which has shown a remarkable understanding of sovereign Burma's problems and an identity of interests with Burma in foreign policy.

Nehru's vision and personality primarily, and the changed scene in Asia secondarily, have been responsible for the great improvement in Indo-Burmese relations. Though it could be said that the wartime exodus, which nearly halved the Indian population of Burma, and the willingness of the chettyars to withdraw from the country if compensated for their losses, have of themselves gone far to solve the Indian minority problem, more important has been Nehru's determination not to make political capital out of the situation. He has come out frankly against dual nationality for overseas Indians and unrestricted Indian emigration to Southeast Asia. He has not protested against Burmese legislation harmful to chettyar interests nor pressed for compensation to them or for payment of Burma's debt to India. Recognizing Burma's financial straits as the consequence of its multiple civil wars, he has even prodded the Commonwealth countries into giving economic aid to his hard-pressed neighbor. Although Burma, on becoming independent, did not follow India's lead by remaining within the Commonwealth, Nehru early in 1949 convened a Commonwealth conference at Delhi to devise ways of helping the lamb that had strayed from the fold. And he was not discouraged by Burma's initial refusal to accept as a condition of the proposed loan a prior settlement of its conflict with the Karens. Two months later he acceded to Premier Nu's request to help Burma obtain a loan from Britain. At the Colombo conference of January 1950, Burma was granted a two-year loan of £6 million from a Commonwealth sterling fund to which both India and Pakistan contributed.

The friendship which Nehru has inspired in both of Burma's postwar premiers, Aung San and Nu, has been reinforced by religious ties and common objectives in foreign affairs. Premier Nu, an ardent Buddhist, has made pilgrimages to the Buddha's shrines in India, arranged for an exchange of sacred relics, and generally stressed India as the fountainhead of the religion which almost all the Burmese profess. Furthermore, India's religious philanthropy, exemplified by the Ramakrishna Mission, has long done charitable work in Burma that is widely appreciated in that country.

In the field of foreign affairs, both countries—strongly conscious of their common colonial past—continue to regard Western imperialism as a grave threat to their newly won independence and to advocate a neutral policy between the two world power blocs. Yet India and Burma alike need not only time to carry out the welfare and development projects that are the keystone of their domestic policies, but also the skills to implement them and the capital to finance them which are available only in the West. Only in small part have they been helped toward their objectives by the handful of technicians and the small funds supplied by United Nations and Commonwealth agencies, and irresistible internal pressure requires them to make drastic changes at a more rapid rate. Their deep-rooted fear of aligning themselves with the "imperialistic" West was partially offset by the victory of Mao's armies in China, which has placed Chinese Communist troops uncomfortably near their northern frontiers and rallied the wavering forces of indigenous communism.

Though both often reiterated their cherished "independent" policy, India and Burma have gravitated against their expressed will into the orbit of the only powers able to supply what they felt they must quickly have.

This struggle between fear and need came to a head in 1951. Burma followed India's lead in failing to participate in the Japanese peace treaty conference held at San Francisco in September of that year, and later refused to renew an agreement for economic aid from the United States until all the strings providing military assistance were detached. Public opinion generally, and the opposition parties in particular, felt so strongly on these issues that it would have been dangerous for the Burmese premier to have acted otherwise. Yet by the end of 1951 the results of the elections held throughout the year— inconclusive and incomplete as they were—permitted the government unobtrusively to change its course. The premier felt his hand sufficiently strengthened to take more severe measures against the Burmese Communist insurgents and also to turn unofficially toward the West in much the same way India was doing. In 1952, Burma accepted increasing MSA funds and even decided to join in the Colombo Plan.[72]

The following year, however, American aid became such an internal political liability to Premier Nu (because of the Burmese belief that the United States was supporting the presence of Chinese Nationalist troops in northern Burma) that he had to end official acceptance of it.[73] Nonetheless, relations between the two governments remained cordial and many of the American technicians already in the country stayed on as employees of the Burma government. In protesting to the United Nations against the Formosa regime's refusal to evacuate its troops from the Shan States, Burma had the strong support of India's delegation and the whole-hearted sympathy of the Indian press. At the Asian Socialist Congress held in Burma during June 1954, the leader of the Indian delegation went so far as to propose closer co-operation between Burma and India as the nucleus of a wider Asian mutual aid system.[74]

Improvement in Indo-Burmese political relations has not been accompanied by a proportionate increase in Indo-Burmese trade. On the contrary, though commercial exchanges are picking up, India has not regained its prewar position of taking more than half of Burma's exports and supplying over half of its imports, despite the preferential tariff that Burma accorded India in 1946. In part, this was due to India's food self-sufficiency program and wheat imports, which have reduced her dependence on Burmese rice, and, in part, to Burma's far smaller postwar production and exports. As of 1950, India supplied 36.28 percent of Burma's imports, but occupied only third place (13.75 percent) as a taker of Burmese exports. In September 1951, following conclu-

[72] *Times of Indonesia* (Djakarta), June 4, 1952.
[73] See pp. 24–28.
[74] *The Burman*, June 6, 1954.

sion of a treaty of peace and friendship, Burma and India signed a commercial agreement for a five-year period which, it was hoped, would reverse the trade decline that at one time threatened to become "unfortunate for the countries' international relations and affect all questions (other than rice) pending between them."[75]

Economic differences continue to account for the only serious discords that mar Indo-Burmese relations. India feels that Burma demands too high a price for its rice, and the Burmese were offended by uncomplimentary remarks on this score reportedly made at Rangoon by R. A. Kidwai, Food Minister of India.[76] As to the domiciled community, black marketeering, false pretexts for remitting money to India, and currency manipulation by some Indian merchants in Rangoon have revived Burmese hostility toward them and caused the government to enact a Public Property Protection Act.[77]

Yet thanks to the persistent friendship between Premiers Nu and Nehru, political and cultural relations between the two countries remain remarkably close. Burma's debt to India was finally settled on an amicable basis within the context of a rice-purchasing agreement signed in March 1954. By the terms of this agreement, Burma's debt to India was to be paid out of the proceeds from the sale of 900,000 tons of rice, and the Indian government as a gesture of good will wrote off Rs. 2 crores of the debt. In May 1954 Nehru told the Council of States that the compensation Burma proposed to pay for nationalized land might not perhaps have done "full justice" and might even have caused "considerable distress" but it was entirely the concern of the Burmese government.[78] The only important outstanding business between India and Burma is a final regulation of the immigration question and chettyar claims—on neither of which is Nehru apparently pressing for a settlement. Although, at the Ceylon conference of Asian premiers in April 1954, Nu differed with Nehru on the relative danger to world peace of colonialism and communism, there is little doubt but that Nu still subscribes to the great tribute he paid to Nehru in August 1953: "I consider him to be the most remarkable man of our times."[79] Nehru, for his part, has shown special solicitude for Nu's viewpoint. Informed observers, such as Robert Trumbull, believe that India would fight to save Burma should the latter be seriously threatened by a Communist invasion.[80]

MALAYA AND SINGAPORE

Geographical distance from India has made Malaya's ties with that country more attenuated than Burma's. For many years, however, they were main-

[75] *Burmese Review*, Mar. 6, 1950.
[76] Associated Press despatch, New Delhi, Aug. 27, 1953.
[77] *The Burman*, Dec. 26, 28, 1953.   [78] *Ibid.*, May 5, 1954.
[79] *Ibid.*, Aug. 30, 1953.   [80] *New York Times*, June 6, 1954.

tained as a result of the common status of India and Malaya as British colonies in the East and of Malaya's need for Indian laborers. But the factor of distance caused the administrative knot joining the two to be severed as long ago as 1867 and the flow of Indian immigration into Malaya to be regulated by subsequent agreements between the two countries.

Population and Immigration

As of June 1941, the Indians in Malaya totaled slightly over 700,000, or 13.4 percent of the country's total population. Five-sixths of them were Tamils from Madras, the remainder Malayalees and Telugus from south India, Punjabis and Sikhs from the north, and a small number of Bengalis. Some 466,000 Indians lived in the Federated Malay States, 150,000 in the Straits Settlements, and 130,000 in the Unfederated Malay States. Indians were concentrated chiefly in the states of Selangor and Perak, where they represented 28 and 20 percent, respectively, of the local population. As of 1941, probably one-quarter of the resident Indians were Malaya-born, and only a third of them were females.

Intergovernmental regulations controlled carefully not only the entry of Indian laborers into Malaya but also their treatment while in the country. Although this arrangement assured generally fair treatment for Indian workers during their Malayan sojourn, it had several drawbacks. As regards long-term disadvantages, it encouraged their transiency in Malaya and also their tendency to look to paternalistic intervention from the government of India rather than to organize for their own advancement. Indian immigrants usually stayed only seven to eight years in Malaya, then returned to India either for a visit or permanently. Proportionately more Indians than Chinese had wives in the homeland. Even though, in the decade preceding 1941, estate managers were doing more to encourage their Indian laborers to bring families to Malaya, the net effect of the government's policy was to accentuate the transient character of the local Indian population, with the result that few Indians were absorbed into Malayan society.

A short-term defect of the official regulation of Indian immigration became obvious during the world depression of the early 1930's. At that time, surplus Indian laborers were shipped back to India, thus posing a tough problem for that country, which also was in the throes of the depression and where adverse economic conditions had given the primary impulse to emigration. Rising Indian nationalism seized on such instances of repatriation to denounce the government of Malaya for returning destitute Indians like "sucked-out oranges," and demanded that permission to recruit laborers in India thereafter should be made conditional upon granting Indians in Malaya a status equal to that of other communities there. A deadlock in the negotiations between the governments of India and Malaya ensued, and in 1938 India imposed a ban upon the emigration of unskilled workers to Malaya that has never since been lifted.

Indian nationalist arguments were based upon the assumption that it was the Malayan government's refusal to give resident Indians a stake in the country that was responsible for the rootlessness of the Malayan Indian community. In part this was probably true. Britain's pro-Malay policy ruled out the possibility of granting security of tenure to Indians wishing to settle on the land, and this was believed to be a main reason why all prewar attempts to create Indian agricultural colonies in Malaya were unsuccessful. What this assumption overlooked, however, was the strong sentiment which has always bound overseas Indians to the homeland, and these ties have obviously been strengthened during and since the war. Factors which have contributed to this development are the wartime hardships imposed by the Japanese (which depleted the Indian population), the growth of national consciousness among all the peoples of Malaya, and the enhanced prestige of an independent India. Straws in the wind are the number of Indians returning to India either for a visit or permanently, and the amounts of money which they have remitted to the homeland.

The Japanese occupation had a more disruptive effect on the life of Indians than on that of the other communities in Malaya. Cut off from export markets, the rubber industry went into an eclipse. Rubber tappers, who formed the bulk of the Malayan Indian population, suffered first from unemployment and food shortages and later from forced labor. During 1943, many Indian rubber workers were compelled to work on the Death Railway in Thailand. Of the total of 73,502 laborers of all races taken from Malaya to work on that project, some 85 percent were south Indians, and of these, 20,825 are believed to have died during its construction.[81] "... although the Chinese suffered more than Indians and Malays from deliberate brutality and homicide, they did not experience the enforced family separation or disruption of the normal means of earning a living to quite the same extent as did the Indians."[82] Consequently, even more than in Burma did the Indians in Malaya seek repatriation after the war. During 1946 the government of India aided some 18,000 Indians to go home from Malaya.[83] It is not surprising, therefore, that the 1947 Malayan census enumerated somewhat under 600,000 Indians in the country, representing a decrease of about 22,000 as compared with 1931 and a proportional decline from 14 to 10 percent of the total population.

Ninety-five percent of the Indians living in the peninsula, as of 1947, were concentrated in a belt 40 miles wide along the west coast, inhabiting generally the same region as did the Chinese.[84] Nearly 40 percent of them were town

[81] Kondapi, op. cit., p. 175. [82] Smith, op. cit., p. 84.
[83] Straits Times, Jan. 17, 1947.
[84] E. H. G. Dobby, Southeast Asia (London, 1950), p. 137.

dwellers, whereas in 1931, only 21.5 percent of the urban population of the Federated Malay States was Indian.[85] This increased urbanization of the Malayan Indians is the more striking when considered in conjunction with the decline in the Indian population as a whole. It is in the rural areas, especially those of Perak, Selangor, and Negri Sembilan, that the decrease is most marked, for on Singapore Island and in most towns of the peninsula, the Indian population has increased normally.[86] Although in 1947 Indian births considerably exceeded deaths, the net movement of Indians out of the country reduced the increase in the Indian population to less than 2 percent. Because of the improved sex ratio among the Malayan Indians,[87] there was an appreciable increase in the number of Indian children. Approximately half of the Malayan Indians at that time were local-born. Thus it is apparent that, though smaller, the Indian population of Malaya has become more settled.

In part, this decrease in Malaya's Indian community has been due to post-war policies of the governments of both Malaya and India. The latter has remained strongly opposed to the emigration of unskilled laborers, and the Malayan government and local Indian opinion have also been generally against unrestricted Indian immigration. In 1948, out of 7,274 requests from Indians to enter Malaya, 3,555 were rejected on the ground that the applicants would not prove beneficial to the economic life of the country.[88] That same year, the Malayan government issued only 7,128 permits to all new immigrants, and in 1949 it reduced the number to 1,427. Despite appeals from some Indian merchants in Malaya, no entry permits were granted to newcomers after May 1949 unless they could produce evidence of an assured livelihood in the country.

Three years of study, drafting, and debate in the local legislatures preceded the enforcement of a new immigration law on August 1, 1953. By its provisions, immigrants were required to be in possession of guaranties of positions in Malaya paying a minimal monthly salary of Str. $500, and re-entry permits would be granted freely only to aliens who could show proof that they had lived for seven of the preceding ten years in Malaya. In answer to Chinese and Indian protests, voiced both before and after passage of this immigration bill, the government stated that it was not an anticommunal but an economic measure designed to safeguard the living standards of all laborers domiciled in the country. Unemployment, officials pointed out, was already becoming a problem, especially among the white-collar workers of Singapore, and the greatly increased influx of Indian immigrants over the past few years was aggravating this situation. In the Federation, Dato Onn told the Legislative

[85] C. A. Vlieland, "The Population of Malaya," *Geographical Review*, January, 1934.

[86] Del Tufo, *op. cit.*, p. 35.

[87] The ratio was 516 females per 1,000 males in 1931 to 692 in 1947 (Del Tufo, *op. cit.*, p. 58).

[88] Kondapi, *op. cit.*, p. 190.

Council, immigrants from India had averaged 1,800 a month in 1951, 3,200 in 1952, and 4,300 for the first six months of 1953.[89] The local employment exchanges reported that they were quite unable to take care of this increased inflow, especially as it was found that Indians described on their passports as students, merchants, and technicians were in reality only unskilled laborers. Between June and December 1952, only 4,784 of the 9,696 who had registered with the exchanges in Singapore had been placed in jobs.

Although some Indians recognized that it was in their own interest that Malaya should no longer be flooded with cheap labor, others among them resented being compelled to pay their employees higher wages, and the community as a whole tended to regard the new restrictions on immigration as anti-Indian. Characteristically, their protests were channeled to the government of India for action.

To only a very slight degree did political considerations determine in this respect the policy of the government of Malaya. And these were a result of the Communist revolt which had broken out in the spring of 1948 and in which far more Chinese than Indians were involved. Under the Emergency Regulations of July 1948, all persons in Singapore and the Federation were required to carry identity cards, and severe penalties were imposed on those failing to produce them upon request. Some Indians, detained under the provisions of those regulations, were given the option of repatriation to India. Up to February 15, 1949, 56 Indians had so opted; none was forcibly repatriated. About 30 Indian bankers were arrested in 1949 for alleged payment of protection money to the terrorists; they, too, were allowed to return voluntarily to India after they had promised not to attempt to re-enter Malaya so long as the emergency lasted.[90] In November 1952, another 20 Indian detainees returned to their home country.

A booklet[91] prepared in the office of the economic adviser to the government of India in 1951, drew an optimistic picture of the increased permanency of the shrunken Indian population then residing in Malaya. Authorities differ as to what elements made up this more settled population. The booklet's author claimed that it was the immigrants of the interwar period who had become a "permanent and useful element in the population," while T. E. Smith concluded that it was the prosperous Indian, rather than the laborer, who tended to settle in Malaya and that it was the second-generation Indians who formed the shopkeeping, clerical, and professional classes of that community.[92] Silcock and Aziz pointed out that there have been few channels of advancement in Malaya by which Indian laborers could rise into the local middle class.[93] Doctors, lawyers, teachers, and clerks, they claimed, came from

[89] *Straits Times,* July 16, 1953.   [90] Kondapi, *op. cit.,* p. 239.

[91] S. Nanjundan, *Indians in Malayan Economy* (New Delhi, 1951).

[92] *Op. cit.,* p. 84.   [93] *Op. cit.,* p. 6.

the middle class of south India or, with few exceptions, were recruited from descendants of that class in Malaya. Chettyars are notoriously transient, and merchants, they added, have been little more than agents of firms in India or of local houses retaining very close ties with the homeland. All, however, were agreed that of all the Asian aliens living in Malaya, the Indians were culturally, politically, and economically the most attached to their mother country.

Political Activities

In prewar days, the only contact with the government open to the average Indian was through the Malayan government's Department of Labor. Like the Chinese, the Indians could not enter the Malayan Civil Service, though they could and did join the Straits Civil Service. The only Indian representative on public bodies consisted of one unofficial Indian member named to the Federal Council of the Federated Malay States, one to the Straits Settlements Legislative Council, and one to the Johore State Council. Appointed by, and usually subservient to, the government, these three Indians could by no stretch of the imagination be called representatives of a people who then formed almost 14 percent of the total population.

A few Indian-language newspapers were published and a considerable number of communal, sectional, professional, and other organizations existed, but the Malayan Indians had no strong institutions comparable to those of the Chinese. Into what was virtually a leaderless community stepped the Central Indian Association of Malaya (CIAM) in 1936. This body aroused antagonism not only among the British but also among the Indians themselves by its aggressive championship of better labor conditions, education, and political privileges for Malayan Indians. For a time it succeeded in awakening an interest in politics and in the poor of the community on the part of some prosperous Indians, but it also drove a wedge between the local-born and immigrant elements. By its involvement, first, with Congress politics in India and later with the Malayan Communist Party in labor strikes on the peninsular plantations, the CIAM became discredited with both the government and the employer class in Malaya. It did not survive beyond the outbreak of the Pacific war, but the Japanese used its leadership, as well as that of other existing Indian organizations, as nuclei for a movement set up to further their own interests. It is noteworthy that the president and vice-president of the CIAM (N. Raghavan and S. C. Goho) were the men to whom the Japanese first turned to organize Indian Independence Leagues (IIL) in Malaya.

After the fall of Singapore on Feb. 15, 1942, a central committee was organized in Malaya to launch and direct the movement for India's freedom sponsored by the Japanese. Hand-picked Malayan Indians attended the various formative conferences held at Tokyo and Bangkok in early 1942. Japan's original choice of personnel, both Japanese and Indian, for this project was unfortunate. Major Fujiwara at Singapore proved to be a tactless leader; the two Indian lawyers chosen to head the movement in that city soon became difficult to handle[94] when they saw that Japan was not disinterestedly promoting the cause of India's freedom; and the first Indian Independence League president on the peninsula, N. Raghavan, became involved in a financial scandal over the use of League funds. It was not until the magnetic Netaji, S. C. Bose, arrived at Singapore in July 1943 that the movement really got under way. Four days after his arrival, Bose was named commander in chief of the Indian National Army (INA), and three months later he founded the Provisional Government of Azad Hind, which was an autonomous body in the eyes of many Southeast Asian Indians but in fact was a closely integrated part of Japan's policy in Asia.

Two of the three INA divisions which Bose recruited in Malaya saw action. The first division was moved up to Burma during 1944 to aid the Japanese offensive in Manipur, and a large part of the second division was used in the later Burma campaign. During the early stages, relations between Bose and the Japanese were apparently close, but they became progressively strained as the Japanese experienced military reverses. However, even after Bose reestablished his headquarters at Singapore following the failure of his "march on Delhi," he retained the façade of an independent command, for he still displayed money-raising capacities.

Even today it is difficult to determine what percentage of Southeast Asian Indians joined or contributed to the Azad Hind movement out of nationalist loyalties, the hope of earning a livelihood or of escaping the Kempetai, or because of plain extortion. Bose's speaking tours of Malaya brought in considerable donations, especially from women, whom he charmed into giving him their jewelry for the cause.[95] Recruits for the INA came chiefly from among unemployed Indian estate laborers. As of June 1945, there were nine IIL branches in Malaya, including the Singapore headquarters. That some Indians resisted the movement was proved by the existence of at least one camp for recalcitrants, called an agricultural settlement, and the presence of a few Indians among the Chinese-led anti-Japanese guerrillas. Nevertheless, it is believed that a good deal of real patriotism was stirred up by Bose's oratory in "a community unaccustomed to political speeches," and that Malayan Indians for the first time came to believe that they were playing a dramatic role in the history of their motherland[96]—an illusion later strengthened by

---

[94] Interviews with S. C. Goho, Mar. 2, 1947, and K. P. K. Menon, June 8, 1947.

[95] On April 1, 1954, the custodian of property, Singapore, announced that these articles as well as some other properties formerly held by the INA and IIL, totaling about Rs. 1 million in value, would be disposed of, and that consideration would be given to authentic claims of ownership.

[96] Silcock and Aziz, op. cit., pp. 22–23.

the postwar idolization of the Azad Hind in India. All the Malayan Indians with whom the writers talked after the war were agreed that the Azad Hind's great legacy to their community was the birth of political consciousness. According to two local authorities (Silcock and Aziz), they also were initiated into the use of firearms, political organization, and some techniques of collective bargaining.

The returning British in 1945 took neither a harsh nor a sentimental view of the Azad Hind. One of the first gestures made by the British Military Administration was to blow up the cenotaph memorial erected to INA heroes at Singapore, and for some time thereafter its site was covered with flowers by the local Indians on Azad Hind anniversaries. But on the whole, the British felt that the rank and file of Azad Hind adherents were those who had joined under pressure, and their quiet absorption into civilian life was permitted. Only about 54 Malayan Indians were formally indicted on charges of collaboration with the Japanese, and for their defense five lawyers were dispatched from India. After some months of incarceration, they too were freed to resume their prewar occupations, and only in a negative sense did the stigma of the Azad Hind linger on. Indians were not represented in the same way as were other communities on the advisory boards set up by the civilian administration after it again took up the reins of government in April 1946.

The most noteworthy feature of the Malayan Indians' new-found political consciousness was its orientation toward India, not Malaya. A regrettable consequence of their greater absorption in India's political struggle was the appearance in Malaya of the religious hatred that plagued the homeland. Shortly after the Japanese surrender, there occurred in Malaya for the first time Hindu-Muslim riots at Penang and later at Singapore. Fortunately such violence was short-lived and confined to isolated instances; moreover, it contained an admixture of hooliganism and retaliation for individual wartime grievances. Many Indians claimed, and the C.I.D. investigator confirmed, that these disturbances were not bona fide communal riots,[97] but they did show that antagonism among the local Indians went deeper than in prewar days. It was not long after the war ended that Hindu, Muslim, and even Christian Indians began busily organizing themselves into separate bodies for the avowed purpose of safeguarding their own special interests.

In the first postwar years, Indians on the peninsula were affected by two local developments. One was the rapidly growing domination of organized labor by Chinese Communists, and the other was the offer of citizenship in the Malayan Union. Both served to increase divisions among an already divided community, whose status has further declined in consequence.

Even before the war, the Klang strike of Indian rubber tappers had disclosed a close control of the existing Indian labor organizations by the Ma-

[97] *Straits Times,* June 23, 1946.

layan Communist Party. And this relationship was reinforced by Chinese Communist leadership of the anti-Japanese resistance movement, in which some Indians participated. In September 1945, an Indian mass meeting at Ipoh discussed the Malayan Communist Party's eight proposals for Malaya's future government,[98] and the next month saw the formation at Singapore of a Communist-inspired Indian Democratic League, which reportedly received support in funds and arms from the Malayan Communist Party. Later a small Indian Communist Party was organized at Singapore, under Mahadev Singh, whose activities were publicized in its newspaper, *Voice of the People*. This new body was believed to be affiliated with the Communist Party of China, through the Malayan Communist Party, rather than with the Communist Party of India. Malayan Communist Party agents concentrated their proselytizing zeal among former members of the Indian Independence Leagues and among a group of dissident Sikhs living in Kelantan and southern Thailand. Chinese Communists apparently had no trouble in controlling organized Indian laborers, despite the latter's numerical preponderance and the assignment of a few high posts to Indian leaders. According to the author of an alleged Malayan Communist Party document seized by the British in January 1949, it was this domination rather than the indoctrination and integration of Indian labor into the movement that was a major cause of the Communist revolt's initial failure.[99] This same docility on the part of the rank and file of Indian labor, however, made easier the task of their later leaders, such as P. Ramani and P. P. Narayanan, who were able to guide the reorganized trade unions into membership in the International Confederation of Free Trade Unions.

In part it was to counteract the growing influence of communism among Malayan Indians that the Malayan Indian Congress (MIC) was formed in August 1946. But probably a more important influence was Nehru's visit to Malaya in March 1946, which inspired the local Indians to form a party modeled after that of India's Congress. A third factor was the need for Indians to take some unified stand in regard to the citizenship proposals that were the burning issue in Malaya throughout 1946. As usual, it was among former IIL members that John Thivy was able to find most of his recruits for the MIC, which from the outset claimed to speak for the entire local-born Indian community. Nehru had flatly told Malaya's Indians that in the future they must choose between being nationals of India or of Malaya, and that if they claimed the privileges of Malayan citizenship they could not simultaneously claim those of India. At the same time, Nehru opened new and attractive vistas. Singapore, he said, would become the site of a new Asian unity, he spoke of the ever growing bonds between the Indian and Chinese peoples,

[98] *Malayan Tribune* (Penang), Sept. 22, 1945.   [99] *Straits Times*, Mar. 4, 1949.

and he pledged that when India became free she would use every ounce of her strength to free all subject nations. Although India was not then in a position to defend her children overseas, he added, the time would soon come when her arms would be long enough to protect them. In the meantime, because of Malaya's cosmopolitan make-up, Indians must co-operate with other sections of the country for the sake of India's future.

Nehru's visit, which aroused great enthusiasm among both the Indians and the Chinese of Malaya did not "clear the air" as many thought it had.[100] Though he had come out strongly against dual nationality as he also did in Burma, Nehru's promise of future protection reinforced the local Indians' tendency to look to India rather than to themselves for their own advancement as a community. And the picture he painted of sovereign India's role in the world made their identification with it far more attractive than that with Malaya, whose citizenship was not tantamount to nationality, did not convey any specified privileges, and was being made increasingly difficult to obtain.

From its inaugural meeting, the MIC reflected this confused orientation. The conference was opened by a prominent member of Bengal's Congress Party; the 600 Malayan Indian delegates present unanimously expressed sympathy with their compatriots at home; they condemned the anti-Indian policies of the South African government; and they gave verbal support to the independence struggles of the Indonesian, Burmese, and Vietnamese peoples.[101] Turning to local issues, the conference asked the government of India to maintain its ban on the emigration of unskilled labor to Malaya "until conditions should become more settled," and to support the right of local Indians to freedom of speech, assembly, and organization. Though the newborn MIC announced that it would co-operate with all other communities in establishing a free and independent Malaya, it passed resolutions that reflected its paramount concern with communal interests. These called for the intensive propagation of the Hindi language, a truly national education, and a policy that would secure for Malayan Indians "their due share" of the country's wealth.

Six months later the MIC convened its second congress, this time to replace the vague resolutions passed at its first meeting by a specific stand regarding the citizenship question. (In the interval, protracted and secret negotiations between the British and the United Malays National Organization had resulted in citizenship proposals definitely less advantageous to non-Malays than those of the existing Malayan Union.) At this meeting, the MIC decided to join the coalition which had just become the Council for Joint Action (CJA) for the purpose of boycotting the new federal constitution. The CJA's counter-

100 See the *Hindustan Times*, Mar. 24, 1947.
101 Associated Press despatch, Kuala Lumpur, Aug. 8, 1946.

proposal envisaged a democratic and self-governing Malaya that included Singapore and in which universal suffrage would be enjoyed by all Chinese and Indians who had lived in the country for eight years or more and who would pledge their exclusive loyalty to Malaya. Many Indians objected to this last qualification, just as they had opposed the requirement for citizenship contained in the federal constitution that they declare Malaya to be their permanent residence. As British subjects, some of them claimed, they felt that their ultimate return to Mother India to die had not prevented members of their community from becoming loyal public servants. Thus in joining the CJA, the MIC from the outset not only alienated a large segment of its potential and actual membership, but also later found itself aligned with left-wing groups that came increasingly under Chinese Communist domination.

If the eyes of the MIC were focused on India and on its own communal welfare, those of the Pan-Malayan Muslim Indian League were similarly oriented toward Pakistan and Muslim interests. Immediately after the British reoccupation of Malaya, the Indian Muslims of Singapore formed a provisional committee frankly for self-protection.[102] And a month before the MIC was set up, a similar organization for Indian Muslims was formed in Selangor. Holding its first session at Penang in January 1947, to formulate its own attitude toward the new constitutional proposals, the meeting was chaired by a prominent Pakistani sent from the homeland in place of Jinnah, who had been unable to accept an invitation to attend. M. A. Cassim, who represented Indian Muslims on the Penang Settlement Council, told the assembled delegates that their community's primary concern was to be treated as a group of sufficient importance to merit separate political representation.[103] This stand inevitably precluded co-operation with the CJA in opposing the new constitution, and it also ruled out making common cause with the community's coreligionists, the Malays. In March 1947, the writers were told by a prominent member of the CJA that the Indian Muslims tended to look down upon the Malays, whose sultans they tolerated only as religious figureheads, and that their pan-Malayan feelings were confined to the name of their organization.[104] As time passed, the Pan-Malayan Muslim Indian League went into political eclipse, though local branches survived as individual units. It was not until September 1953 that the idea of a united organization was revived and the Malayan Pakistani League was founded in the Federation.

S. M. Shafi of Kuala Lumpur, who was elected president of the new league, urged all Pakistanis in the peninsula to regard Malaya as their home and themselves as Malayans, and to co-operate with other communities in the country. But at the same time he sounded a strongly communal note when

---

102 *Straits Times*, Sept. 12, 1945.   103 *Ibid.*, Jan. 24, 1947.
104 Interview with John Eber, Mar. 8, 1947.

he said that the League would act as the spokesman of Pakistanis in Malaya in all matters affecting their interests, and would seek representation on the Federal, State, and Settlement councils.[105]

Although the Malayan Indian Congress actively, and the Malayan Muslim Indian League passively, opposed the federal constitution at the time it went into force, individual Indians proved willing to co-operate with the Anglo-Malay bloc. On the Cheeseman Committee, set up late in 1946 to hear and evaluate criticism of the new constitutional proposals, there were two Indian members (Doraisamy Ayer and C. P. R. Menon), and on the nominated Federal Legislative Council, which came into being in February 1948, five seats were reserved for Indians—some of whom subsequently made outstanding contributions to the discussions of that body. The obviously growing domination of Indian trade unions and of the CJA by Chinese Communists was alienating many conservative Indians, who were the more willing to go along with the government, out of either opportunism or conviction. And even within the MIC important elements were opposing its increasingly radical trend.

If the Malayan Indian Congress was failing to give a unified leadership to the Hindu community on the mainland, at Singapore it met with a clear-cut reverse. In 1947, it was announced that for the first time in history British subjects resident at Singapore would elect some members to its Legislative Council. The then president of the Malayan Indian Congress, Budh Singh, lost no time in opposing Indian participation, and called on Singapore Indians to boycott the election, which, he claimed, was not a local but a major issue.[106] Since the electorate was confined to British subjects over twenty-one years of age, regardless of sex and of literacy status, Indians might well be tempted to vote, for these qualifications gave them an immense advantage over the far more numerous Chinese. And indeed this proved to be the case. Although only some 23,000 out of a potential electorate of over 200,000 bothered to register as voters, almost half of them were Indians.[107] Nearly 10,000 Indians registered as compared with 5,000-odd Chinese, in a city where about a third of the total population of about 1 million were classed as alien immigrants and where about 400,000 were under the age of twenty-one. In vain did Budh Singh come to Singapore to intensify his boycott by threatening to expel from the MIC any Indians who became candidates for election and, through the Malayan Democratic Union, to protest to Nehru against their disloyalty. Not only did Singapore Indians register in large numbers, but three of the six Councillors elected were Indians, not one of whom had been born in Singapore. In every election since held at Singapore, Indians have given evidence

[105] *Straits Times*, September 28, 1953.   [106] *Ibid.*, Sept. 19, 1947.
[107] *Ibid.*, Mar. 11, 1948.

of a political acumen and a predominance far superior to their numbers, and this has been made possible by the noncommunal character of Singapore politics.

This setback for the MIC at Singapore, coming one month after its failure to prevent Indian participation in the Federal Council, was followed very soon by the outbreak of the Communist revolt. Though it neither dissolved itself, as did the Malayan Democratic Union, nor went underground, as did the Malayan Communist Party, the MIC was so shaken by the new turn of events that, in July 1948, it announced a voluntary suspension of all political activity in Malaya until the "emergency" was over. Simultaneously it condemned the current violence and called upon all Indians to refrain from lawlessness and subversive activities. Either in response to this appeal or out of apathy or caution, Malayan Indians as a whole seem not to have taken any active part in the revolt. But the dynamism inherent in the MIC could not long remain in suspense, and by 1949 it brought a recrudescence of political agitation and internal dissension.

In March 1949 the MIC joined with the recently formed Malayan Chinese Association (MCA) in pressing for a revision of the citizenship clauses in the federal constitution. Advocating the replacement of citizenship by a Malayan nationality, the MIC in a rather remarkable resolution urged a trusteeship status for Malaya and a "political and educational program designed to bring self-government in a reasonably short time."[108] Taking no chances on the interval period, the MIC insisted that for the present the status of local Indians as nationals of India should be safeguarded.[109] But it was the Communities Liaison Committee, formed early in 1949, that became the torchbearer for liberalization of Malayan citizenship, and no Indians were appointed to it.[110] Thanks to its persuasiveness, each of the nine Malay states in the Federation finally consented to a change being made. And in September 1952 the bars were let down to the point where second-generation Indians on the mainland—about 30 percent of all Indians living there—became eligible for a citizenship that was now to be tantamount to a Malayan nationality. Premier Nehru told India's House of the People that the total number of Indians who had acquired Malayan citizenship by the end of 1952 was estimated to be 200,000.[111]

In 1951 still another attempt was made to unify the three existing Indian organizations in Singapore and the Federation which claimed an all-Malayan basis—the Malayan Indian Congress, the Malayan Indian Association, and the Federation of Indian Organizations. Creation of the last-mentioned body

108 *Ibid.*, Apr. 20, 1949.   109 *Ibid.*, Mar. 21, 1949.
110 It consisted of 7 Malays, 5 Chinese, 1 European, and 1 Ceylonese.
111 *Eastern World*, June 1953.

in 1950 had been frankly inspired by the success which the UMNO and the MCA had had in promoting unity within the other two major communities in the country, and its organizers felt that the time had come for some comparable organization to speak with a strong voice for all the Indians living in Malaya. Although the extreme radicalism which had been the most corrosive element in earlier moves to unite Malayan Indians was now in abeyance, the community was still deeply divided in its orientation and suffered from a plethora of would-be leaders. Each of the three organizations mentioned above claimed that neither of the others had any right to speak for the entire community, and that it would join no league or federation that included both the domiciled and floating Indian population.

In May 1951, 15 representatives of the three all-Malayan Indian organizations met and agreed to merge them, but almost at once trouble arose. Certain officers of these organizations claimed that no mandate to commit them had been given to the so-called representatives. Agreement was also lacking as to qualifications for membership in the proposed union, and as to whether or not it should have political objectives. The MIC, which at first had agreed to the merger and which could not claim to include in its membership a majority of the Indian community, soon laid down conditions unacceptable to the others—chiefly by insisting upon their primary loyalty to Malaya. And the whole unification effort foundered when, in September 1951, the MIC came out in support of the Independence of Malaya Party (IMP). The fact that the MIC later became for a time the backbone of the IMP's small membership —probably not over two or three thousand—may well have been chiefly responsible for that organization's lack of success in establishing an intercommunal organization on the mainland.

Certainly the successes registered in Malaya's recent municipal elections by the UMNO-MCA alliance had acted as an irritant rather than as a stimulant to unification among the Indians, who resented their exclusion from it. This resentment boiled over in October 1953 when two members of the alliance were named to the federal "cabinet" and not a single Indian was offered a portfolio. (In 1951 a ministerial post had indeed been offered to the labor leader, P. Ramani, but he had refused it then for personal reasons.) Five out of the six Indian Legislative Councillors promptly resigned without any prior representation of their grievances to the High Commissioner and apparently without seriously weighing the probable consequences of their hasty action. Many Malayans sympathized with what might well have been interpreted as a slight to the Indian community, but few could condone what appeared to be an overriding communal loyalty on the part of at least two of the Councillors—those who had been named to represent the intercommunal trade unions. One of these, Ramani, defended his action by saying that the Indians as a minority group must stand up for their rights in the same way as had the Malays and Chinese. In their joint letter of resignation, the 5 Councillors put it more emotionally:

This attitude of the government is bound to create the feeling here and elsewhere that the Indian community is no longer regarded by the government as of any political significance, now or in the future. We have no alternative but to step back to the side of our countrymen and share with them the burden of their economic and political unimportance.[112]

In late January 1954 the British moved to appease injured Indian feelings by appointing a member of that community to a newly created ministerial post in the Federation. But the damage of heightening Indian communal feeling had already been done. In December 1953, R. Jumabhoy[113] attacked the new immigration law as anti-Indian and suggested to Singapore's Legislative Councillors that each community should be equally represented in a self-governing Singapore.[114] And in a memorandum submitted that same month to the Rendel Commission on constitutional development, the MIC advocated special safeguards for minority interests along the same lines, and also supported the eventual fusion of Chinese-dominated Singapore with the Federation, which had a larger Indian minority.[115]

In the Federation, though it continued to advocate reserved seats for the Indian community, the MIC surprisingly found itself in agreement with the Alliance in pressing for federal elections by late 1954. Indeed the position of the Indians under the new federal constitution promised to be a sorry one: in the proposed Council only one seat was reserved for the Indian community in general and one for the Indian Chamber of Commerce. According to so well informed a man as Ramani, it was very doubtful if even one Indian could get himself elected to its membership. The *Straits Times,* in an editorial on June 3, 1954, regretted "that Indian representation is a problem which has largely escaped attention and that 52 elected members with not an Indian among them would be a poor advertisement for Malayanization."

Like the Chinese, but for different reasons, the Indians have come to feel that the British in Malaya are against them. As for the Chinese, they believe that the government is actively discriminating against them, whereas the Indians are hurt by being ignored. At the root of their failure to achieve solidarity and to play a major role as a community is the perennial reluctance of Indians to break their ties with India, which are stronger than those uniting the other immigrants in Malaya to their homelands. How unwilling they have been to hitch their wagon to the Malayan star is shown by the fact that only 7 percent of the 300,000 certificates of federal citizenship issued up to April

112 Quoted in the *Christian Science Monitor,* Oct. 29, 1953.
113 See pp. 109–110.
114 *Straits Times,* Dec. 17, 1953.
115 *Straits Budget,* Dec. 17, 1953.

1951 went to Indian applicants. It was to better themselves that Indians came to Malaya, and the great majority remain there only so long as it is in their interest to do so. In 1951 the rubber boom brought thousands of Indians to the country, but a year later they departed in even larger numbers when the enforcement of the manpower regulations threatened them with military conscription. This transiency based obviously on self-interest naturally makes the Indians unpopular with other communities. Although it is true that some Indians—a minority—have become permanently settled in the country, even they have frittered away their energies in dissensions among themselves and with the immigrant contingent. Also three times politically they have bet on the wrong local horse—first the Azad Hind, then the CJA, and finally the IMP. They have never, however, either before or after these mistakes, developed strong organizations or used their bargaining power as a community in the same way as have the Chinese. Individual Indians have achieved deserved prominence in local public service, but as an ethnic group the Indians have seemed content to coast along on such privileges as may come their way as a by-product of the more creative and shrewd activity of the Chinese.

The Economic Stake: Investments and Banking

In Malaya it has been the Indians, both chettyars and Sikhs, who have been the country's major moneylenders. As of 1940, there were about 50 chettyar firms in Singapore, with a total capital estimated at Str. $30–40 million, and thousands of minor Sikh moneylenders were operating both in Singapore and on the peninsula.

Since the war, one of the main preoccupations of Malaya's chettyars has been the settlement of transactions conducted in their name during the Japanese occupation. In 1942–43, when money was very tight in Malaya, their agents forced debtors to pay or be brought to court. Inevitably this aroused great bitterness, which the chettyars later tried to assuage by explaining that, under great pressure from the Japanese-sponsored Azad Hind for huge contributions, they had no choice but to press debtors for payment. After the war, the agent of the government of India claimed that the chettyars were the group of Malayan Indians most severely hit by the war.[116] But they still owned 175,000 acres of rubber plantations and had interests in the country valued at a total of Rs. 20 crores. Moreover, they were frequently reproached both before and after the war for their lack of public spirit, as evidenced by paltry contributions or none at all to war funds or charities. A spokesman for the chettyars pointed out with some justice that his community, like every other foreign group in the country, was there to make money, and he cited as chettyar contributions to the public welfare a recent gift of Str. $9,500 to

116 *Straits Times,* June 5, 1946.

charities and a silver cup for the best exhibit at Singapore's flower show.[117]

In March 1946 the chettyars of India petitioned the British Secretary for Colonies for permission to repudiate all transactions carried out by their agents or partners during the Japanese occupation.[118] Realizing that, in the absence of any prewar legislation invalidating business deals carried out during a period of enemy occupation, any retroactive law would undermine the financial stability of many Malayans, the government hesitated. It was not until 1949 that a decision—adverse to the chettyars—was made, and according to Kondapi,[119] it involved them in such enormous losses that many of them were anxious to liquidate their interests in Malaya and return to India.

A few years later, Indian financiers in Malaya received another blow. In April 1952, there was promulgated a stringent Moneylenders Ordinance which affected both the 800 chettyar firms and the Sikh moneylenders, estimated to number at that time about 10,000 in the Federation alone. Both groups, in protest, stopped their business operations. In August 1952 the chettyars in the Federation were said to be planning to open a bank with some of their capital which had been lying idle since the ordinance came into force. Owing at least in part to this strong chettyar reaction, the government was reported a year later to be drafting amendments to the Moneylenders Ordinance.

The Economic Stake: Trade and Industry

Indian business interests in Malaya, which had steadily increased over a seventy-five-year period preceding World War II, received a setback during the six months of British military administration that followed the Japanese surrender. The disabilities under which Indian traders worked during that regime were passionately voiced by R. Jumabhoy, president of the Singapore Indian Chamber of Commerce.[120] His general complaint was the same as that of his compatriots in Burma—regulations were imposed by the military authorities that operated in such a way as to favor unduly prewar British firms. Speaking in the name of Singapore Indian merchants, he protested against the retention of official controls eight months after the war had ended, and gave instances of how such measures were discriminating against Indian interests.[121]

As to tin, he contrasted the freedom enjoyed by local exporters before the war with the monopoly of tin exports given just after it to the Tin Buying

[117] *Ibid.*, Feb. 6, 1947. As recently as March 1954, the Federal Member for education called upon the chettyars to cease holding themselves aloof and to share in the social and political life of Malaya.
[118] *Ibid.*, Mar. 6, 11, 1946.
[119] *Op. cit.*, p. 304.
[120] Jumabhoy had been one of the Indians fortunate enough to escape from Malaya during the war and therefore to avoid involvement in the Azad Hind fiasco.
[121] *Straits Times*, Mar. 3, 1946.

Unit set up by the British Military Administration. Although India had been allotted a quota of Malaya's tin output under the world control scheme, Malaya's Indian tin exporters who had handled such shipments in prewar days were now unable to resume operations, for all the tin shipped to India was sent through the British Straits Trading Company and Eastern Smelting Company. Coconut oil was another commodity that had been shipped to India in large quantities before the war and could no longer be handled by local Indian merchants. Turning to imports, Jumabhoy stated that although the government forbade the re-export of textiles received from India, it permitted the re-export of a fourth of the textiles received from Hong Kong. Moreover, Chinese traders, he charged, were evading the ban and exporting Indian piece-goods along with those from Hong Kong.

A year later Jumabhoy returned to the charge, claiming to find little improvement in the situation even though civil administration had replaced the military in April 1946: controls on the export of certain commodities had been relaxed, but they were still maintained with respect to shipments to India. He asserted that no uniform policy was being pursued, that shipping space for India was inadequate, that the government should and could give fair treatment to all firms and cease allowing monopolies by British houses, and that the Chinese evaded regulations while the Indians remained law-abiding and were further handicapped by having their capital frozen.[122]

Another grievance which he expressed was the failure to give representation to the Singapore Indian Chamber of Commerce on public bodies—a privilege enjoyed by both its British and Chinese counterparts. To obviate any excuse that none of the three existing Indian commercial bodies in Singapore (the South Indian, Chettyars, and Indian Chambers of Commerce) could properly represent the city's entire Indian mercantile community, he took the initiative in trying to form a Federation of Indian Chambers in April 1947. But like so many similar Indian efforts in the political field, this attempt to achieve unity in the commercial sphere seems to have come to nought, owing to the insistence of the Singapore Indian Chamber—in typical Indian fashion —that it alone had the right to speak for all its colleagues.[123]

In 1949, however, a marked improvement in the position of Malaya's Indian traders became apparent. In that year, imports from India increased phenomenally and Malayan exports to that country also picked up. By 1951, Indo-Malayan trade had reached a record value of Str. $322 million, Malaya exporting to India goods valued at $116 million and importing $206 million worth from that country. Although the trade balance was decidedly favorable to India, thanks to its piece-goods export, Malayan exports to India had also risen considerably. In May of that year, the fourth Indian bank in Malaya was

[122] *Ibid.*, May 13, 1947.   [123] *Ibid.*, July 5, 1947.

established to deal with the growing volume of Indian business in the country. When, in the spring of 1952, Indians were accused of running away from Malaya in order to avoid military conscription, the secretary of the Penang Indian Chamber said that this was certainly not true of Indian traders. Far from selling out their Malayan interests and transferring their capital to India, they were becoming more prosperous and more settled in the country. Said the secretary: ". . . more Indian firms have been established in Malaya in recent years, and local traders are likely to adopt Malaya as their second home."[124] When India's Trade Commissioner left the country in May 1952, he spoke of his past three years in Malaya as "an historic period of phenomenal expansion" in the trade relations between the two countries.[125] If the immigrant-laborer element in the Indian community was shrinking in numbers, the growing prosperity of the Indian merchants was rooting them more firmly in Malaya.

The Economic Stake: Labor and Occupations

As of 1937, about 244,000 Indians worked on Malayan rubber estates, 44,000 in government departments, over 40,000 in trade, upwards of 25,000 in transport and communications, 9,000 in factories, 8,700 in mines and some 4,000 in the police—making a total of 370,000 employed in the foregoing categories plus an undetermined number in various other occupations. Generally speaking, south Indians were employed on rubber estates, while north Indians were more numerous in business and the professions.

Indian laborers showed no tendency to organize themselves until the eve of World War II, and even then the majority of associations they formed bore little resemblance to orthodox trade unions. Their basis was caste, geographical origin, or occupation, and their objectives usually were cultural, social, or recreational. According to two British trade unionists who studied these organizations, "there was no purely Indian association which could easily and rapidly have developed into a trades union, and Indians as a whole do not appear to have appreciated the value of such organizations to anything like the same extent as the Chinese."[126]

Obviously the reason why prewar Indian laborers failed to organize for their own advancement was not so much the caste and language divisions among them and their mutual isolation as it was the regulations formulated by the governments of Malaya and India concerning immigration, employment, and working and living conditions. The Malayan Labor Department hovered paternalistically over the Indian laborer throughout his sojourn in

124 *Ibid.,* June 29, 1952.
125 *Ibid.,* May 12, 1952.
126 S. S. Awbery and F. W. Dalley, *Report on Labor and Trades-Union Organizations* (Kuala Lumpur, 1948).

Malaya, occupying itself with his wages, housing, medical care, working hours, and repatriation. But most of the improvements brought about in the status of Malaya's Indian workers were effected because of the intervention of the government of India. After that government had placed a ban on the emigration of unskilled Indian laborers to Malaya in 1938, the rubber boom of the years just before the war caught employers in Malaya short-handed. As a result, Indian and other laborers had the chance to win better working conditions largely through their own efforts. About the same time, a group of Indian middle-class intellectuals, who had formed themselves into the Central Indian Association of Malaya (CIAM) in 1936,[127] began to take up the cause of their less fortunate compatriots. It was they who gave Malayan Indian labor its first union organization and oriented its new-found strength toward the same political objectives as those of the radical Chinese labor groups.

The end of the war found Malaya in a condition ripe for labor organization and agitation. Food had been scarce for three and a half years, and there was widespread malnutrition; prices were greatly inflated, and the returning British had declared the Japanese-issued currency worthless; above all, thousands of persons were displaced from their normal habitats. Indian rubber tappers who had survived forced labor on the Thailand Death Railway, numbering some 42,000, were brought back to Malaya by the British Military Administration. At first they were placed in relief camps, but by the end of 1946 they were returned to the plantations where they had previously worked. In that year there were 150,093 Indians employed on more than 2,400 estates, exceeding the number of Chinese so employed by 80,000 and constituting three times the number of Malay and Javanese tappers together. But when it came to industry the racial predominance was reversed; there, 4,613 Indians were employed in mining as against 13,478 Chinese, and 3,497 in factories, as compared with 16,256 Chinese. Indians, who in the 1930's had formed over half of Malaya's labor force, now accounted for less than 50 percent, but proportionately their prewar predominance in the rubber industry and their inferiority in industrial employment remained unchanged. The wage differential between Chinese and Indian workers also was maintained. Tougher, more efficient, willing to labor longer and harder on a piece-work basis, and not hindered by intergovernmental arrangements, the Chinese laborers have always demanded and received higher pay than the Indians. And all protests by Indians in the postwar period against this disparity have proved unavailing.[128]

The most notable change that has occurred in postwar labor conditions in Malaya is not so much the diminished number of Indian workers as the increased use of Malay labor on estates and in factories. Before the war there

[127] See p. 98.
[128] Straits Times, Apr. 28, 1947; Kondapi, op. cit., p. 100.

were only about 25,000 Malays so employed, but by 1947 the number had risen to over 78,000. And to an increasing extent Malays were filling jobs previously held by the Indians and Chinese, whose ranks were not being swelled by fresh immigration and who were tending to enter other fields. Many former Indian estate laborers have taken up land near their old places of work, where they can combine farming with occasional rubber tapping.

Probably a major cause of this transition by Indian labor has been the low wages paid to tappers and the high price and scarcity of rice, especially during the first postwar years. During its six months of power, from September 1945 through March 1946, the British Military Administration tried to reimpose 1941 price and wage regulations. Because it was unable at the same time to provide enough food and consumer goods, black markets developed rapidly, and with them, inflation. Official wages, in most instances, had risen only 50 percent as much as had the general price level. After the civil administration was reinstated in April 1946, basic wages were raised slightly and an allowance was added; but as the cost of living had risen from 400 to 500 percent above the prewar level, the workers felt little relief. A scanty rice ration made matters worse, for the conservative Indians would not change their eating habits and were unable to afford black-market prices for their rice. The inevitable result was a very rapid increase in labor organization and agitation.

What was perhaps not so inevitable was the rapidity with which Chinese extremists asserted an almost undisputed leadership over Indian labor. The combination of transiency in the country, geographical dispersal, and government paternalism goes far to explain why Indian labor in Malaya has produced so few able leaders. The Labor government in Britain, committed to the promotion of trades unions in colonial areas, sent a labor expert to Malaya soon after the war to aid in the formation of unions there and to build up conciliation machinery to settle labor disputes. But this expert did not always see eye to eye with local officials or employers, who in some cases preferred strong-arm methods when dealing with troublesome union organizers, and later he was at loggerheads with the second trades-union adviser sent out from Britain. Into this melee stepped the Malayan Communist Party, which swiftly built up pyramidal labor unions into two large federations. Though the majority of their members were Indians, as were some of the top-ranking officials, policy was set for these federations by the Chinese Communists. This was disclosed upon the collapse of the whole structure following the disappearance of their leaders underground when the Malayan Communist Party broke into open revolt in 1948.

Despite their unsavory connection with the Malayan Communist Party, the rank and file of Indian labor was regarded as more sinned against than sinning. However, Ganapathy, former head of the Pan-Malayan Federation of

Trades Unions, was hanged in May 1949; his successor, Veeranasan, was shot dead by the police; and still another Indian union leader, Sambasivam, was sentenced to death. And as of September 1949, there were about 800 Indians held in detention camps, the majority of whom had not yet been brought to trial. Kondapi insisted, however, that it was "officially admitted that the number of Indians participating in terrorist activities is less than 1 percent."[129] A document allegedly of Malayan Communist Party authorship, seized by the police in 1949, throws some light on the position of Indian labor vis-à-vis the Chinese Communists:

Indian laborers in general do not understand what the object of our present struggle is. Some are afraid that if their factories are destroyed they will be unable to get work and become homeless.

And another Communist writer bewailed his party's underestimation of the importance of winning Indian workers to its cause.[130]

A year after the revolt broke out, we find Indians once again forming the bulk of the reorganized but far smaller trade-union movement in Malaya. As of July 1949, Indians represented 62.5 percent of the total membership of all Malayan trade unions.[131] And in the Malayan Trades Union Council, founded at Kuala Lumpur in March 1950, more than half of its 43,000 members and most of its leadership from the outset was south Indian.[132] This organization has avoided political activities and has shown more skill than any of its predecessors in wage bargaining, particularly as regards the pay of rubber tappers. Membership in the Council has steadily increased, as has its prestige, largely due to the capable leadership given by its Indian president, P. P. Narayanan, who has linked any real improvement in the workers' status to the eradication of terrorism.[133] More recently Narayanan has tended to voice political sentiments that include accusing the British of having encouraged racial tensions in Malaya, and to advocate its rapid transformation into an independent socialist state.[134]

Cultural Activities and Social Welfare

In analyzing the census of Malaya which he organized in 1931, C. A. Vlieland found the local Indian laborers largely illiterate. "The percentage of literacy of this class," he wrote, "is far below that of any other section of British Malaya . . . [it is] a section of the community which the Malayan education system is powerless to touch."[135] In less euphemistic terms, the pre-

[129] Op. cit., p. 113.
[131] Kondapi, op. cit., p. 114.
[133] Straits Times, Mar. 28, 1952.
[135] Vlieland, op. cit., p. 91.
[130] Straits Times, Mar. 4, 1949.
[132] The Times, London (weekly edition), June 7, 1950.
[134] New York Herald Tribune, Apr. 7, 1953.

war colonial government of Malaya accepted no responsibility for the education of non-Malay races beyond some small grants-in-aid and the requirement that employers in specified cases must provide a modicum of instruction to the children of their laborers.

It was not until a few years before the war that Indian voices were raised in protest against this situation. The CIAM was the first to complain that Tamil education in Malaya had been grossly neglected and to demand that the government assume more responsibility in this regard. Its president, N. Raghavan, late in 1940 bewailed that "our 750,000 Indians in Malaya have to await the pleasure and convenience of a none-too-sympathetic government to receive an education."[136] The problem, he said, was both chronic and acute; Indians had no proper schools, not enough teachers, and no policy, and the vast majority of Tamil schools were such in name only. In the Federated and Unfederated Malay States there were a few government Tamil schools, but none at all in the Straits Settlements. The government, he went on to complain, enforced the educational provisions of the Labor Code[137] only against estate employers, but made no effort at all for its own employees or those of urban employers. As taxpayers, he believed, Indians had the right to free education provided by the government, but while 30 percent of its budget was spent on the Malays and 3 percent on the Chinese, only 1½ percent was allocated to Indian education. But the Indian community itself failed to respond adequately to the CIAM's appeal in November 1940 for enough funds to build a central Indian high school.

On the eve of World War II there were 628 Indian vernacular schools in Malaya, attended by 27,539 pupils. Small as this number was, it represented a quantitative improvement over the situation in 1931, when there were only 10,000 students attending Indian schools in the country.[138] Any comparable improvement in the quality of these schools depended upon getting more and better Indian teachers. For the hard and useful work he did, the Tamil rural teacher received a princely salary ranging from Str. $10 to $30 a month and he enjoyed none of the housing or other privileges accorded to the Asian estate staff. Tamil teachers in government schools had a few more amenities.

Many basic difficulties explain the uphill struggle of Indian education in Malaya. In rural areas, parents preferred that their children earn money rather than attend school. Estate managers, with few exceptions, had no real interest in the education of their coolies' children and undertook it simply because the law required it. Teachers were overworked, underpaid, and largely untrained, and enjoyed neither prestige nor authority. Also, perhaps because of

136 *Straits Times,* Nov. 4, 1940.
137 Where there are 10 children or more between the ages of seven and fourteen in the place of employment, an estate manager at his own expense must provide a school with trained teachers.
138 *Ibid.,* May 7, 1941.

the instability of the local Indian population, Indian schools have lacked the wealthy patronage that in Malaya has been a great boon to Chinese education. And finally, it was not until 1912 that the government began to assist Indian schools and then only with minuscule grants-in-aid. The 1930–40 decade saw the first real improvement in Malayan Indian education, as described in the following testimony by an inspector of Indian schools in 1941:

No longer is the Tamil or Telugu school a mockery, just a hole in the corner where a number of dirty undisciplined children swarm on the floor while a so-called teacher sits back on a chair and, if he can read, has a book. Such schools, called superior creches, still exist but they are becoming very rare. The school building, furniture, books and general equipment have greatly improved. . . . These things have not developed of themselves. Little could have been done without the support of estate managers, their encouragement especially in such matters as attendance, and provision of good buildings has been indispensable. There has been hard work on the part of Indian Inspectors and improvement in the quality of teachers. . . .[139]

Out of 415 Indian teachers employed in 1931, only 64 were trained; as of 1941 there were 235 teachers who had been educated at the six centers established during the preceding decade for the training of Indian teachers. Moreover, by 1941 most of them were full-time teachers, whereas ten years before, the majority had combined teaching with a variety of other jobs. Gardening, crafts, hygiene, and other courses had been added to the curriculum, and there was a notable increase in the number of pupils in the higher grades. As of 1931, four-fifths of the students in Indian schools were in the first two Standards; ten years later this proportion had been reduced to three-fifths and an extra grade—Standard VII—had been added.

The Japanese occupation marked a setback for the education of all communities in Malaya, and Indian estate schools declined notably in number. This trend continued during the first postwar years, and by the end of 1946 the number of registered estate schools had shrunk to 951 although the government had increased its allocations for Tamil education to one-sixth of the total education budget.[140] Early in 1947, the government began gradually taking over control of the estate schools and proposed to increase the number of trained teachers for them.[141] A major difficulty was that the parents of estate children were more reluctant than ever to dispense with their earning capacity and permit them to attend school. And the Education Department, appreciating the hardships caused by inflation for the laboring class, did not have the heart to compel attendance. As of 1951, there were only 869 Indian

[139] *Ibid.*, Nov. 17, 1941.
[140] Kondapi, *op. cit.*, pp. 145, 150.
[141] Interview with H. R. Cheeseman, then director of education for the Malayan Union, Mar. 13, 1947.

schools in the Federation, as compared with 1,246 Chinese and 1,682 Malay schools, and their caliber remained poor. An unofficial mission from Madras which visited Malaya in 1948 deplored the low standard of Indian education in the country, and estimated that 75 percent of the Indian teaching staff was inadequately trained.

Voluntary contributions from the Indian community have remained small, despite a greater interest in education on the part of a number of Indian organizations. The Malayan Indian Congress at its formative session stated as one of its major objectives an intensive propagation of the Hindustani language and national education.[142] At about the same time, the newly organized branch at Taiping of the Indian Laborers Association started classes in Hindu and English for estate laborers and their children, and paid a teacher to visit specified estates once a week.[143] In Penang the Indian Education Committee awarded 20 scholarships as a memorial to Gandhi in 1949. Considerable interest was shown, too, in adult education for Indians.

Basically it was the varying prosperity of the Indian community that determined the quality of the education it received, and consequently it followed a sharp geographical division. Singapore offered the best educational facilities for Indians because it had the most prosperous Indian merchants and professional men, whereas the majority of the Indians in the Federation were estate laborers. The 1947 Social Survey of Singapore showed that, though the Indians there numbered only about 50,000, they had the highest proportion of children of school age—both boys and girls—receiving a formal education. And they were also the only large community in which the majority of children attended English schools.[144] In the lower age groups (up to thirty), Indian males showed slightly higher literacy rates than either the Chinese or Malays, and the rates for Indian females in the same age group were comparable with those of the Chinese and higher than those of the Malays.[145]

The Neilson Plan, launched in 1947, promised to revolutionize education in Singapore by offering for the first time free primary education to all children regardless of race or sex. Initially this was to be given in sections based on the mother tongues of the pupils, English being taught in the postprimary grades. But the implementation of this plan proceeded so slowly that a supplementary five-year scheme, called the Frisby Plan, was put into force at the end of 1949. It called for the building of a specified number of new English schools annually and, as regards Indian primary education, the importation of vernacular teachers from India to supervise the Tamil curriculum. The guiding principle was that pupils should learn their mother tongue while at

[142] *Straits Times*, Aug. 6, 1946.
[143] *Straits Budget*, Sept. 5, 1946.
[144] Singapore Department of Social Welfare, *A Social Survey of Singapore* (Singapore, 1948), p. 106.
[145] Smith, *op. cit.*, p. 85.

the same time receiving their basic instruction in English. This plan was highly satisfactory to Indian parents who wanted their children both to learn their home language and to receive an English education, and who had up to that time found it very difficult to give them both. This dilemma was well expressed by Dr. N. K. Menon, a prominent Indian of Penang:

Without a good English education, the future in Malaya for the Indian community is hopeless in every walk of life. An increased number of Indian children are going to English schools, but it is a source of distress to their parents that they are illiterate in their mother tongue.[146]

In the Federation the problem has not yet received so hopeful a solution. While the federal government sought guidance for its educational policy regarding the Malays in the Barnes Report and for the Chinese in the Fenn-Wu Report, it apparently did not consider Indian education, as such, important enough to merit a separate study. The Barnes Plan, however, affected the Indians, for it proposed a fundamental change in the Federation's entire educational policy. Barnes proposed to abolish the free Malay schools and substitute for them national schools. These schools would give free primary education to all children between the ages of six and twelve in both the Malay and English languages; following completion of this course there would be two more years of free instruction that would have a vocational and practical emphasis. The existing English schools were to dispense only secondary education, teaching exclusively in English and preparing their graduates to enter either the University of Malaya or the Teachers Training College. As this program made no provision for either Indian or Chinese languages, an outcry was raised by the Indian community, which seemed to astonish the authorities. At Kuala Lumpur, 35 Indian educators met to discuss and to condemn the Barnes Plan and to ask that its implementation be postponed. Their disapproval was based on fear lest the proposed national schools destroy the cultural heritage of Malayan Indians and also on the ground that learning two unfamiliar languages simultaneously would place too great a strain on a child of six. Those Indian educators advocated using the child's vernacular in the first grades and only later adding Malay and English.[147] Adverse Indian, as well as Chinese, reaction to the Barnes Plan was such that it was referred to a special committee for further study, and as of early 1954 no national school had yet been set up in the Federation.

As to higher education, the quality of Indian primary and secondary instruction in Malaya has been so poor that Indian pupils attending the University of Malaya have been conspicuously few. It is typical of the authorities' attitude toward the problem that no proposal was initially made to establish a

[146] *Straits Times,* Nov. 15, 1947.

[147] See article by Dr. V. D. Kuppusamy, headmaster of a Chinese school at Kampar, in the *Straits Times,* June 27, 1951.

chair of Indian studies along with those proposed for Malay and Chinese culture. When the Carr-Saunders Commission was studying the question of higher education for Malaya in 1947, two outstanding Singapore Indian associations made virtually identical recommendations to it. Both the Indo-Malayan Association and the Indian Chamber of Commerce proposed that in the University the medium of instruction should be English; Singapore should be the site of the University; the staff should be locally recruited and sent to the United Kingdom for training; and the curriculum should include courses in law, engineering, political science, and oriental languages, including Tamil or Hindustani.[148]

In 1953, as a side effect of the Chinese move to found their own university at Singapore, the government began showing more concern for Indian higher education. Professor Nilakantha Sastri of the University of Madras was officially invited to Singapore for the purpose of advising the authorities of the University of Malaya on the establishment therein of a department of Indian studies. The Chinese, in an effort to propitiate other communities in Malaya, have likewise announced their intention of eventually setting up departments of Indian and Malay studies, in their projected Nanyang University.

Intergovernmental Relations

It has already been noted that Malaya's greater distance and its earlier administrative separation from India, as well as the lack of a strong nationalist movement within the country, inevitably caused its prewar relations with that subcontinent to vary markedly from those of Burma. The main postwar questions to be studied are in what ways, if any, the policy of sovereign India differs from that of its British predecessors, and whether the intervention of independent India in the affairs of Malayan Indians has been spontaneous or solicited, and to what extent.

After the Japanese surrender, while India was still under British rule but increasingly subject to internal nationalist pressures, its government intervened strongly and consistently on behalf of the Malayan Indians. No sooner had the British reoccupied Malaya than missions were dispatched from India to give medical and other relief to destitute Indians and to aid those charged with Azad Hind activities, and funds were sent for the repatriation of Indians stranded in the Malaysian area. The report submitted by the government of India's representative in Malaya (S. K. Chettur) late in 1945 on the status of local Indians met with no favor in the eyes of some members of that community. In January 1946 the Selangor Indian Labor Union passed a vote of no confidence in him,[149] and the following September other voices were

---

[148] *Straits Times*, May 18, April 20, 1947.   [149] *Straits Times*, Jan. 28, 1946.

raised to ask that he be replaced. Far from acceding to such demands, the government of India in May 1947 extended the scope of its representative's official responsibility to include Hong Kong and British North Borneo. Later, however, Chettur was replaced by a Malaya-born Indian, John Thivy.

The announced purpose of Nehru's visit to Malaya in March 1946 was to "give psychological relief to the Indians stranded in Malaya, to make them stand on their own feet, and to raise their morale." Probably he succeeded in the first and last of these objectives, but not in the second, though he certainly aroused their nationalist emotions. The Congress Party followed up Nehru's visit with an invitation to Malayan Indians to attend its next session, and seven of them went to the Meerut meeting in August 1946. A circular sent by the Congress committee told Malayan Indians that—

the time has come when overseas Indians should be in close touch, not only with India but also with each other. With this end in view, it is contemplated to hold a conference of overseas Indians somewhere in India at the time of the Congress's next sessions.[150]

This patent encouragement of the nationalism of overseas Indians diminished after India achieved independence, but the government of India has not been able to resist periodic and gratuitous intervention in Malayan affairs. Some time after proposals for the Federation constitution were published, the Indian government late in 1947 pleaded for an amendment to the citizenship clause that would be more favorable to Malayan Indians.[151] In March 1948, India turned a deaf ear to the MIC's protest against Indian participation in the Singapore elections. Four months later the government of India asked the British authorities in Malaya to improve living conditions for Indian laborers as the most effective way of preventing their participation in the Communist revolt.[152] And when Ganapathy, the former president of the Pan-Malayan Federation of Trade Unions, was condemned to death in 1949 for the unlawful possession of firearms, the Indian government asked for clemency.[153] In August 1952 a 5-man "good will" mission from India visited the Federation to find out how far the new Moneylenders Ordinance would adversely affect chettyar interests in Malaya. Obviously the government of India was taking a stronger and less tactful stand when dealing with a colonial rather than a national administration. Its representations to the Malayan government were apparently undertaken on its own initiative and were not always identical with the wishes of local Indians, and they were consistently unsuccessful.

Actually, there are no major problems to be resolved between India and Malaya and, consequently, no real tension between them. Only a small por-

150 *Straits Budget,* Aug. 14, 1946.   151 Kondapi, *op. cit.,* p. 418.
152 *Ibid.,* p. 114.   153 *Straits Times,* May 6, 1949.

tion of the employer group in Malaya actively advocates a return to the old days of unrestricted Indian immigration. Indian workers in Malaya form the backbone of the trade-union movement that has been reorganized under British aegis. The minority of the local Indian community that has decided to make Malaya its permanent home appears to have settled down to become industrious citizens, if not active in civic affairs.

The tapering off of India's interest in Malaya's Indians has been due partly to realization of the foregoing developments, partly to the winning of Indian independence (which diminished its need for their support), and partly to the lack of success that attended all its attempts at intervention. Only the Indian Communist Party seemed to remain aggressive in consistently picturing the current strife in Malaya as a nationalist revolt. It campaigned actively against the recruitment of Gurkha troops for service in the "gestapo-like state," and this propaganda found some support from non-Communist politicians in India. One important source of Indian misinformation about the Communist revolt in Malaya has been the biased views expressed by former detainees under the Emergency Regulations, who had been repatriated to India. When Dato Onn bin Jaafar visited Delhi and Karachi in April 1952 he tried to dispel such misconceptions. And some Malayan Indians who more recently returned from a visit to their homeland urged the British administration to invite outstanding Indian journalists to Malaya so that they might get a more realistic view of the situation.[154] Twenty-six students from the University of Malaya who visited India in the summer of 1953 reported that their counterparts in Indian universities were "extremely ignorant" of Malayan affairs and still believed that Malaya was in the throes of a national struggle started by the people.[155] They felt that a solution might lie in the Malayan government's awarding scholarships in the University of Malaya to Indian students.

Werner Levi has pointed out that Nehru himself has undergone a change of heart in regard to Malaya.[156] From his early advocacy of freedom for the remaining British possessions in the Far East, Nehru has shifted to making it contingent upon a prior restoration of peace and order in Malaya. Because of his growing appreciation of the difficulties created by Malaya's special demographic problems and of the opportunities which Britain's withdrawal would create for the Communists there, some factions in India have charged him with kowtowing to imperialists. According to Levi, Britain's project of creating a dominion out of its Malaysian possessions has been proceeding under regular consultation with the Indian government and in consonance with its wishes.

[154] *Ibid.*, Sept. 12, 1952.   [155] Reuter despatch, Singapore, Sept. 23, 1953.
[156] *Op. cit.*, p. 117.

INDONESIA

Population and Immigration

Indonesia's most recent census, now a quarter-century old, showed that there were then (1930) in the archipelago 27,684 Indians, of whom 12,654 were born in the Indies and among whom the men outnumbered the women by a ratio of 2 to 1. Indians were chiefly concentrated in Java and Sumatra, particularly in the former island where they numbered 25,638, and the remaining 2,000 or so were scattered widely throughout the outer provinces. On Java, most of the Indians were small shopkeepers, while on Sumatra many were to be found in the plantation areas of Deli as coolies, drivers of motor vehicles, cattlemen, and night watchmen. The majority of Indonesian Indians came from the coastal districts of Coromandel and Malabar, and as most of them were Muslims there was a common religious bond between them and the Indonesian people.

When the British came to receive the surrender of Japanese forces in the Indies in September 1945, they brought with them Indian troops. Subsequent use of these units in action against the Indonesian independence movement was the object of considerable protest in India. After the British evacuated their forces from the archipelago in November 1946, some Indians may have remained behind, for the Republic later received complaints about the behavior of certain Pakistani soldiers serving in the nationalist army. As the complaints concerned Pakistani attacks on the life and property of resident Hindus, and "as the Pakistani were good soldiers and good Muslims, the Republicans are finding it hard to deal with them."[157] In August 1953, 25 Pakistanis who had fought in the International Brigade of the Republican army were repatriated after being formally thanked for their contributions to Indonesian independence.[158]

Not only was the Indian population never large in Indonesia but it has apparently decreased in the postwar period. Newcomers, such as soldiers, have been more than offset by Indians leaving the country. In 1945 some 3,000 Indians living in Medan, "who were being persecuted by the local bandits," wanted to return to India and were aided to do so by the government of India.

As of early 1954, Indonesia's restriction of immigration had not yet been formalized by law, but a multitude of regulations were in force. The average annual number of all immigrants has been limited to 8,000 and formalities have been so complicated as to discourage all but the most persistent. Before an entry permit is granted, sanctions must be obtained from the Ministry having jurisdiction over the candidate's place of future employment, from the Manpower Placement Office, from the local civil service, and from the At-

---

[157] Kondapi, *op. cit.*, p. 348.   [158] Antara despatch, Djakarta, Aug. 13, 1953.

torney General's office. Priority, it was officially said, would be given to foreigners who had previously resided in Indonesia and those whose services were needed by the country. Prospective immigrants were divided into 8 groups—each of which was allocated a quota of 1,000, including wives and children—according to the country of their origin, and applicants from India, Pakistan, Burma, and Ceylon made up the second of these categories.

Before Indonesia became independent, a very liberal immigration policy was foreshadowed—probably for political propaganda purposes. On September 4, 1949, the then Foreign Minister of the Republic, Hadji Agus Salim, made a general statement to the effect that when Indonesia was fully sovereign, it would be capable of absorbing Asians from adjacent lands who might otherwise envy Australia's open spaces.[159] In practice, however, independent Indonesia has not only not welcomed unrestricted immigration, but has officially announced (in April 1953) that the "open door" policy of the Dutch era has been given up. As regards Indians, doctors are virtually the only group whose immigration has been actively encouraged.

The Economic Stake

In prewar Java the majority of Indians were retail merchants, whereas in Sumatra they were chiefly skilled and unskilled laborers. Recent reports indicate no change in these occupations, but only a diminution in the number of Indians living in Sumatra.

A few years ago, India made a move to increase its commerce with Indonesia. In September 1950, the imminent arrival at Djakarta of an Indian trade commission headed by the president of Tata Industries was announced. An agreement between the two countries was reached, providing for annual trade of about Rs. 46 million each way. This represented a threefold increase in Indo-Indonesian commerce over 1949–50, and involved the exchange of Indian manufactured goods for such Indonesian commodities as tin and copra.[160]

In April 1954, the newly arrived Indian ambassador at a meeting organized by the Indian Association of Djakarta, urged Indian merchants in Indonesia to bring Indonesians into their enterprises. This would permit Indonesians to benefit by Indian experience in commerce and would also assure "our Indonesian friends . . . that the Indian business community is doing something worthwhile in strengthening Indonesia's economic position."[161]

Intergovernmental Relations

From its earliest days, the Indonesia Republic has sought the friendship of India, and Nehru has responded in kind. In 1946 Premier Sjahrir offered rice

159 Kondapi, *op. cit.,* p. 505.
160 *Economic Survey of Asia and the Far East—1950,* p. 295.
161 *Times of Indonesia,* Apr. 9, 1954.

to alleviate famine conditions in south India, and though not much of the proffered tonnage was actually shipped the gesture was well-timed and was deeply appreciated by India. Again in September 1952, the Indonesian Cabinet voted to contribute food valued at U.S. $6,000 to famine victims in India. And in August 1953, the Indonesian Red Cross announced the shipment of 80 tons of food to hungry Indians.

India has given more than a *quid pro quo* in the form of political and moral support for the Indonesian Republic. Both in the United Nations Security Council, late in 1946, and at the special conference on Indonesia called at New Delhi in January 1949, India actively championed Indonesian independence from the Dutch. In February 1954, an India-Indonesian Friendship Center was inaugurated at New Delhi "to bring the two countries more closely together."

President Sukarno made his first visit to any foreign country in January 1950 when he went to India. There he reportedly asked for India's support of Indonesia's claim to Irian (Western New Guinea). The following June, Nehru returned his visit and was given an enthusiastic welcome by the Indonesians. Pressed for some commitment on the Irian question, he said at a press conference at Djakarta: "Generally it seems to me that historical and geographical approaches give weight to Indonesia's claim to include West New Guinea in Indonesia," but he obviously preferred to discuss in wider terms the problem of ridding Asia of its last colonial remnants.[162] Moreover, he stressed Asia's need to look after its own peoples' welfare before its governments could attempt to tackle the world's vast problems.

Though the Indonesians were disappointed by Nehru's tepid expressions as to Irian, and some were offended at what they interpreted as his indifference to other Indonesian aspirations, they were impressed by his broad international outlook and his concern for raising mass living standards. This ideological compatibility with Indonesia's leaders found common expression in foreign policy—with one outstanding exception. In adopting an "independent" course as between the two world power blocs and standing for an end to colonialism everywhere, Indonesia saw eye to eye with India. Notably on the Korean conflict and the Tunisian question, Indonesia lined up with India. According to the present Indonesian ambassador to New Delhi, emergence of the Asian-African group in the United Nations was largely due to the efforts of India and Indonesia.[163] At the Asian premiers' conference at Colombo in April 1954, Premier Ali—partly for internal political reasons, to be sure—followed India's lead in opposing a forthright denunciation of Communist aggression. Their paths diverged, however, when it came to the Japanese peace treaty. In the hope of getting reparations from Japan for the war-

[162] Levi, *op. cit.*, pp. 114 *et seq.; Report on Indonesia*, June 16, 1950.
[163] *Times of Indonesia*, Feb. 9, 1954.

time damage done his country, Indonesia's Foreign Minister signed the treaty. But so strong has been the feeling in Indonesia that he thereby impaired its "independent" foreign policy and its solidarity with India, that the government has never dared submit the treaty to the Indonesian Parliament for ratification.

THAILAND

Population and Immigration

Prewar estimates of the number of Indians then in Thailand varied widely. A reasonable figure appeared to be around 5,000, of whom approximately 3,000 lived in Bangkok. Though there were some permanent residents, the average Indian in Thailand was a young male immigrant who regarded India as his home, to which he expected to return sooner or later.

Since the war, there appear to have been no significant shifts in either the number or the concentration of Thailand's Indian community. A ruling made by the local authorities in 1949, requiring Indian immigrants to name a guarantor, aroused the government of India to protest.[164] Its representations, however, seem to have been unavailing, for in August 1950 the Indian Legation at Bangkok notified its nationals that they must conform to Thai law and obtain an alien-registration card. Failure to do so, it was pointed out, would entail deportation.[165] The Thai government had informed the Legation that, despite repeated notification, there still remained many unregistered Indians; as a special favor, the deadline for registration by Indians was extended through December 31, 1950.

Political Activities

Such political consciousness as the Thai Indians have developed was a phenomenon of wartime and the early postwar years, and was oriented toward the mother country. In prewar days, there existed two Indian organizations in Thailand—the Indian Association, founded in 1928, and the Thai Bharat Cultural Lodge, established in 1940. Neither of them was a political organization, in part because of lack of interest and also because the Thai government would have discouraged any political activities on their part.

There was no local branch of the Congress in Thailand, despite the presence there of several ardent nationalists from India. One of these was Giasi P. Singh, who came to Bangkok in 1933, and another was Amon Singh. The Japanese invasion of Thailand found these revolutionaries eager to organize their compatriots into what eventually became the Thai branch of the Indian Independence League (IIL). A third Indian who achieved prominence in

[164] Kondapi, *op. cit.*, p. 203.   [165] *Standard*, Bangkok, Aug. 19, 1950.

the early days of the Japanese occupation was Swami Satyandanda Puri, who had been sent to the country in 1932 by Tagore at the request of the Thai royal family, desirous of having there an unofficial cultural ambassador from India. In 1940 he founded the Thai Bharat Cultural Lodge, and in 1941 the Indian National Council for the Freedom of India. For some time the latter organization remained separate from the IIL.

More active than the Indian National Council, the IIL sent some of its members to Malaya in 1941 to do propaganda work among soldiers of the British Indian army. G. P. Singh followed shortly after the fall of Singapore and helped to form branches of the League in Malaya. Toward the end of March 1942 both he and Swami Puri were killed in a plane accident while en route to Tokyo, and two months later the IIL and the Indian National Council were merged. Never so important in Thailand as in Malaya or Burma, the local IIL nevertheless pressured Bangkok's Indian merchants into becoming members and contributing funds. Many of them reportedly became Thai citizens at that time in order to escape IIL extortion.

In 1943 a third Indian organization, the Balak Sena (Indian Youth Movement) was founded at Bangkok. This was patterned after the Boy Scout movement; it aimed to teach local Indian youths self-help, a national spirit, and good civic principles, and its slogan was "Down with Communal Splits and Tensions." Unlike the Indian political organizations, it survived the war, and by September 1946 boasted a membership of 200, including Sikhs, Muslims, and Hindus. While it carried on some social work, such as caring for the orphans of Indian workers on the Death Railway, it became politically minded as India progressed toward independence.[166]

India's accession to sovereignty in August 1947 apparently fulfilled the aspirations of Thai Indians, who gradually ceased all political agitation in south Thailand and even the celebration of Azad Hind anniversaries in Bangkok. In December 1946 the arrival at Bangkok of India's first consul to Thailand, Bhagwat Dayal, gave the local Indians a focal point for their nationalist sentiments. During his five-year stay in the country, Dayal proved to be an exceptionally popular diplomat, rising in rank to minister with the consulate's elevation to a legation in September 1947. He constantly stressed Thai-Indian amity, as well as cultural and commercial ties.

The local Indian community has been praised on more than one occasion for promoting trade between India and Thailand and for being law-abiding residents. Failure on the part of many Indians to register as aliens seemingly has been the only complaint lodged against them. By comparison with the traits of the Chinese, the rather negative virtues of the Indians apparently loom large in Thai eyes. In September 1952, however, a letter was written to the local press[167] by the secretary of Bangkok's Indian Chamber of Com-

[166] Bangkok Post, Sept. 30, 1946.   [167] Ibid., Sept. 10, 1952.

merce protesting against the slurs which he said Radio Bangkok had been casting on his compatriots in regard to the smallness of their donations to public charities.

The Economic Stake

Of Thailand's Indian residents, the majority have always been merchants. As in other Southeast Asian countries, it took some time after the Japanese surrender to resume profitable trading. In the case of Thailand, which the British regarded as enemy territory, it was not until July 1946 that private trade was restored between that country and India. Two months later, the Indian Chamber of Commerce at Bangkok was able to hold its first postwar meeting. In December 1946 the government of India authorized a Bangkok Indian syndicate, formed by the four chief prewar Indian rice exporters, to be responsible for all rice shipments from Thailand to India.[168] Throughout the postwar period, rice has been the major Thai export to India and textiles have been the chief import from that country. In June 1954, a trade mission sponsored by private commercial groups in Bangkok but backed by the Thai government went to India to discuss ways of expanding trade between the two countries. Following abrogation of the early postwar British-Thai agreements (which had included India), the Bangkok authorities were seeking a new basis for trade with India, but the timing was not propitious. The Indo-Burmese agreement of March 1954 promised to fill amply India's need for rice—the commodity which had always been the chief item of its trade with Thailand—and Thai teak could not hope to compete with its Burmese counterpart because of the preferential treatment given the latter in the Indian market.

Cultural Activities

In September 1946 Nehru addressed a letter of advice to his compatriots in Thailand, in which he urged them "to forget their petty quarrels and remember that they represented India wherever they may be."[169] They were also told to hold together, to help each other, and to start national schools for their children, who would thereby be trained "for service of the India which may come sooner than most people expect." At that time there were only three Indian schools in Bangkok, one each for the Sikh, Muslim, and Hindu communities. It took time and Gandhi's assassination for the Thai Indians to decide to found such a school, that would be a memorial to the Mahatma and open to the children of all communities. By September 1952, the Vidyalaya School had grown to have 200 students—a third of whom were Thai and all of whom were in primary grades.[170]

[168] *The Burman*, Dec. 17, 1946.   [169] *Bangkok Post*, Sept. 4, 1946.
[170] *Ibid.*, Sept. 15, 1952.

Quicker to react to Nehru's suggestion was the Thai Bharat Lodge, which had been founded before the war to promote cultural unity between India and Thailand. In September 1946 the lodge started classes in Thai, Hindustani, and Sanskrit. Cultural exchange, however, has been fostered also at the governmental level. In September 1947, a Thai version of the Tripitaka was formally presented to India, and in January 1952 an exhibition of Indian art was held under official auspices at Bangkok. India has received many Thai for training in specialized fields, and the Thai community in India, composed chiefly of students, has grown markedly in recent years.[171]

Intergovernmental Relations

The Thai Indian community is so small compared with those in Burma and Malaya that it has received little attention from Delhi. Nehru did not trouble to visit Bangkok either when he went to Malaya in 1946 or to Indonesia in 1950. Prominent visitors from India have periodically appeared in Thailand during the past few years, but in most cases they have simply stopped over en route to somewhere else.

In 1946 Thailand borrowed Rs. 50 millions from India, and this loan has been repaid. In 1947 India raised its diplomatic mission in Thailand to legation status and opened a consulate at Songkhla. In 1949 Thailand first refused to attend the conference India called on Indonesia, but later agreed to send an observer. In 1951 the Royal Thai Air Force was invited by the Indian government to spend ten days in India, and in June 1952 the Indian Navy returned the visit. In the spring of 1954, Thailand's decision to ask the United Nations to send observers to study the possible dangers to Thai sovereignty arising from the war in Indochina was opposed by India. Reportedly India suspected that Bangkok's move had been inspired by the United States and that it had been deliberately timed to "undo the good work being done at Geneva."[172]

Relations between the two countries, though perfunctory, have in general been good, especially on the cultural side. India's chief interest in Thailand has been its rice, and Thailand has charged ever higher prices for quantities of rice smaller than India has asked for. In international relations their paths have diverged sharply, though amicably, for there are no direct issues between them at stake. Since early 1950, Thailand has aligned itself definitely with the Western bloc of powers, while India has remained the leading Asian exponent of a "third-force" policy. A sign of the 1954 political climate in Southeast Asia, however, was the fact that the Thai premier was not sent an invitation to attend the Ceylon meeting of Asian prime ministers on the Indochina crisis in April of that year.

---

[171] *Standard,* June 2, 1951.
[172] United Press despatch, New Delhi, *Bangkok Post,* June 3, 1954.

INDOCHINA

Population and Immigration

As in many other Southeast Asian countries which have a small Indian population, statistics about them are hard to obtain in Indochina, where Indians are lumped with other categories of alien Asians. In prewar days, it was believed that they numbered about 6,000 there, concentrated largely in Cochin China and to a lesser extent in Cambodia. Probably half of the Indian component came from France's colonies in India; the remainder comprised Muslims from North India, chettyars from South India, and a handful of Parsees from the Bombay area.

No census has been taken in Indochina since the war, but the figure of 1,000 given by Kondapi[173] as the Indian population there in 1949 seems an underestimate. According to him Indochina's Indians were undisturbed during the war and no restrictions were placed upon their movements.

In 1948 the French levied on Indians a "personal tax" in the form of an immigration fee. Indian resentment was aroused less by the sum involved than by the fact that its imposition was accompanied by a requirement that Indian immigrants be fingerprinted. As a result of forceful protests from the government of India, this tax was withdrawn.[174]

Political Activities

The Indian community in Indochina has suffered from an unpopularity due not to its size but to its composition and activities. As was the case with their compatriots in Burma, who thronged in after the British came, the arrival of Indians in Indochina in the wake of the French early identified them with the country's conquerors. Since almost half of the local Indians came from France's "Old Colonies" in India, they were French citizens and therefore eligible for posts not available to the Vietnamese until many years later.

Another important segment of the Indian minority in Indochina was made up of chettyars, whose moneylending tactics aroused the same resentment there that they did in Burma. The French, for their part, claimed that the chettyars caused political disturbances in the country and ordered the deportation of five of their number. Though that order was subsequently rescinded, it aroused considerable chettyar resentment and apprehension.

It was around such dissident elements that the Indian Independence League was formed by the Japanese in Indochina during the war. However, the local Indians were neither sufficiently numerous nor wealthy enough for it to become an outstanding branch of the Azad Hind movement. Such importance as it attained derived from the presence in Indochina of highly

[173] Op. cit., p. 348.   [174] Ibid., pp. 175, 203.

placed Japanese officers who, from time to time, summoned there Indians prominent in the movement elsewhere in Southeast Asia. Six months after the Japanese surrender, the British at Hanoi arrested six Indian National Army leaders, including the Foreign Minister of the Azad Hind (Major-General Chatterjee) who had fled north with a few companions late in August 1945 in the hope of escaping into southern China.[175]

The Republic of Viet Nam, after its establishment at Hanoi in September 1945, made several efforts to enlist the support of local Indians. In October 1945 the following appeal was made in the name of the "Fighting Committee of the Revolutionary Peoples of Southern Indochina" to Indians in the British army of occupation: "Your fellow-countrymen are fighting for liberty as we are; our ideals are the same and we must love each other. We must not be divided by anyone."[176]

After the outbreak of hostilities in Tonkin, in December 1946, Radio Viet Minh claimed that some Indian residents of Hanoi had freely elected to fight with the forces of the Republic and that the Indians of Saigon-Cholon had sent 40,000 piastres to Ho Chi Minh along with a "touching letter of solidarity."[177] A Reuter despatch from Hanoi[178] confirmed that at least some of that city's 400 Indians were reluctant to be evacuated "because the Vietnamese had shown no hostility towards them." However, Nehru stated the following month that, although three Indians had been killed during the December outbreak at Hanoi, "no Indians are fighting in Indochina as far as the Indian government is aware."[179]

The Economic Stake

From the economic viewpoint, by far the most important members of Indochina's Indian community have been the chettyars. Concentrated chiefly in Cochin China, where they were organized into 120 firms, they have possessed a big stake in the export trade and at one time owned a fourth of that colony's riceland. Their unpopularity grew to such proportions, as the result of mortgage foreclosures during the depression, that the French authorities established their own credit facilities in Cochin China and even threatened some of the chettyars with deportation. Seeing the handwriting on the wall, the chettyars—before World War II—reportedly transferred 65 percent of their capital out of the country.[180] Nevertheless, their remaining investments throughout Indochina were estimated in 1947 to amount to Rs. 2.14 crores.[181]

[175] *Democracy*, Bangkok, Jan. 8, 1946.
[176] *Straits Times*, Oct. 24, 1945.
[177] Radio of the Viet Nam Republic, Mar. 15, 1947.
[178] Jan. 27, 1947.
[179] *The Burman*, Feb. 16, 1947.
[180] *Asiatic Review*, November 1937; *Indian Review*, November 1940.
[181] Kondapi, *op. cit.*, p. 348.

There has been a fairly clear-cut occupational division among Indians in Indochina. Roughly half of them are French citizens and therefore eligible for government service, and for the most part they are employed as clerks, postmen, policemen, registrars, and the like. South Indian chettyars have plied their usual business as moneylenders; the north Indians, shopkeeping; and almost all the Parsees have been engaged in trade.

Indian merchants in Vietnam have suffered from strict French controls and the trade paralysis resulting from postwar hostilities in that country just as have the Chinese. But reportedly they have not been as successful as the Chinese in profitably provisioning both antagonists in the conflict, although in Tonkin they are said to have captured a few of the lesser trade plums.

Intergovernmental Relations

Even before the outbreak of Franco-Vietnamese hostilities in December 1946, Ho Chi Minh sent Mai the Chau as his special envoy to India, with both a general and a specific assignment. He was to contact Indian leaders and to win their sympathy for the Republic's cause and their condemnation of French policy in Indochina. Another of his tasks was to try to block the work of the French Purchasing Mission at New Delhi, and to prevent the repair of French planes and the refuelling of French ships plying between France and Indochina.[182]

India impartially received delegates to the Asian Relations Conference of March 1947 from both Republican and French-held territories in Indochina. Chau, as the Republic's representative, got an enthusiastic welcome from the assembled conference whereas the French-sponsored delegates were politely ignored. Chau expressed his hope that a strong and independent India would be not only the effective advocate for Asia's oppressed peoples but also the torchbearer of all the colonial and semicolonial peoples of the world. Later he toured India, making somewhat more specific appeals for the Viet Nam Republic.[183] In October 1947, according to a Reuter despatch from Saigon,[184] Ho addressed a message to Nehru, asking him to raise the Viet Nam question in the Security Council and to "immediately appoint a commission of outstanding Indian leaders to visit Viet Nam in order to study actual conditions on the spot." And in the early months of 1948 a prominent member of the Viet Minh, Phan ngoc Thanh, went to India and held meetings with Indian political leaders and big industrialists.[185]

Bao Dai, for his part, made two attempts to enlist Indian support, after he had reached agreement with the French whereby his government could send some diplomatic missions abroad. As his second envoy he selected a former

[182] Radio of the Viet Nam Republic, Apr. 23, 1947.
[183] *Sunday Standard,* Bombay, June 29, 1947.
[184] Oct. 12, 1947.
[185] *Vietnam American Friendship Association Bulletin,* New York, Apr. 7, 1948.

high official of the Republic, Nguyen duy Thanh, as the person best qualified to win recognition for the Bao Dai regime and to convince the Indians that the Viet Minh were working against and not for Asia's freedom.[186] India granted Thanh a visa but made it clear that he could not be received officially at New Delhi.

None of these envoys of either side succeeded in his mission. Indian public opinion continued to favor the Viet Nam Republic as champion of Vietnamese independence but Nehru became progressively more cautious. In October 1946 he had sent the greetings and good wishes of the Indian people to Ho.[187] Two months later, after hostilities broke out at Hanoi, Nehru broadcast a message to the French people warning them that the use of armed might was reducing their country's prestige in Asia:

Our hearts are with the people of Indochina. The attempt of France to crush the spirit of freedom in Indochina has deeply moved the Indian people . . . Though it is difficult for Indians to know the true facts of the conflict, one thing is patent —that foreign armed forces are trying to crush Vietnam.[188]

At the same time Nehru recognized the international aspects of the problem far more than did many of his compatriots who were pressing for vigorous intervention on behalf of the Republic. When Sarat Chandra Bose, in cooperation with the Burman, Boh Lat Yaing, tried to raise a volunteer brigade to fight against the French in Viet Nam, Nehru was unwilling to supply the transport facilities requested, though he agreed to the dispatch of an Indian medical mission to Indochina.[189] Gandhi sent a message of "full sympathy for the cause for which the people of Vietnam are fighting,"[190] and Kripalani, then president of the Indian Congress, expressed a similar sentiment.[191] At Calcutta, a demonstration by Indian students in favor of the Viet Nam Republic turned into a riot, and public meetings commemorating Viet Nam Day, were held by youth and labor groups in many parts of India.[192] In November 1949, Indian officials in London managed to circumvent Nehru's policy, and showed their sympathy with the Viet Nam Republic by leaking a report from India's consul at Saigon that asserted Ho, not Bao Dai, enjoyed his people's support. Six months earlier, the Deputy Minister for External Affairs upon his return to India had been virtually forced to retract a statement he had made at Saigon that was regarded by his compatriots as too favorable to Bao Dai.[193]

Nevertheless, Nehru's prudent policy triumphed. "Aside from a few mani-

[186] New York Times, Aug. 1, 1950.   [187] The Burman, Oct. 16, 1946.
[188] United Press despatch, London, Jan. 8, 1947.   [189] Hindustan Times, Mar. 21, 1947.
[190] Reuter despatch, New Delhi, Apr. 8, 1947.   [191] Ibid., Jan. 4, 1947.
[192] Ibid., Calcutta, Jan. 22, 1947; Indian Express, June 21, 1947.
[193] Levi, op. cit., p. 118.

festations and a boycott lasting a few days of French ships by stevedores in India and a limitation of French plane traffic, India did nothing concrete and remained very cautious."[194] At the Colombo conference of January 1950, Nehru succeeded in preventing the assembled Commonwealth ministers from taking positive action in favor of Bao Dai, but he did not persuade them that they should follow his own noncommittal attitude. Nehru continued to insist that India's position in this respect was not a negative one. He told a reporter[195] that, in general, he condemned the French approach in Indochina as in Morocco, and hoped for a negotiated settlement between Bao Dai on the one hand, and Ho on the other. India, he claimed, had not intervened in the struggle directly because she felt that nothing constructive could be accomplished thereby until the Vietnamese people themselves chose their own regime. Nehru's general attitude toward France could not but be influenced by the unresolved differences in regard to the fate of the French colonies in India.

In July 1951, Radio Viet Minh gave considerable publicity[196] to a proposal made by the French journalist, Claude Bourdet,[197] for a Sino-Indian mediation of the Indochina conflict. When this theme was again taken up by Bourdet in March 1952, India's Foreign Minister and her ambassador to France both felt called upon to deny that India contemplated taking any such role.

In the spring of 1954 the American proposal for a Southeast Asia collective security pact and the crisis reached in the Indochina war once more aroused Nehru to action. Wishing to present a united Asian front to negotiators at the conference on Korea and Indochina to be held at Geneva in late April, he convened a meeting at Colombo of the premiers of Ceylon, Pakistan, Burma, and Indonesia. To them he outlined a 5-point plan which called for (1) an immediate cease-fire in Indochina, (2) direct negotiations between the forces fighting in Indochina, (3) French pledges of immediate independence for the Associated States, (4) a cessation of all military aid to both parties in the conflict, and (5) establishment of a climate of peace prior to the Geneva talks.[198] Only on the first and third points was Nehru able to carry his colleagues with him. To all appearances at the time, the conference was a failure as regards either achieving a united Asian front or, consequently, influencing the course of the Geneva negotiations.

Nevertheless, Nehru (working closely with Britain) exerted considerable influence at Geneva. Though India was not officially represented at that con-

---

194 Philippe Devillers, *Histoire du Vietnam* (Paris, 1952), p. 379.
195 Sol Sanders; *Bangkok Post*, Mar. 26, 1951.
196 *Le Monde*, July 25, 1951.
197 *L'Observateur*, Paris, July 5, 1951.
198 *Christian Science Monitor*, Apr. 24, 1954.

ference, its delegate to the United Nations, Krishna Menon, was active in holding informal talks with the principal delegates. It is widely believed that he convinced the Russians that Soviet support for the Viet Minh's refusal to evacuate its troops from Laos and Cambodia would mean for the Communists a loss of the friendship of the independent nations of south Asia.[199] Later, in July 1954, Nehru enthusiastically hailed the cease-fire agreement, which he had been among the first to advocate, and expressed India's willingness to serve as chairman of the 3-nation supervisory commission for the Indochina truce.

[199] United Press despatch, London, *Christian Science Monitor*, June 2, 1954.

Chapter Three

INDIGENOUS MINORITIES

THE EURASIANS

A EURASIAN problem exists wherever Europeans have maintained control of a Southeast Asian country and not where they long ago lost or never had dominion over it. Eurasians of Portuguese descent tend to merge with the major community, as do those of Thailand, for their white blood has never won special privileges for them or awakened unfulfilled aspirations in them.

Throughout the colonial areas, Eurasians have faced the same handicaps, reacted to them in identical fashion, and displayed similar communal characteristics. Though the size of their communities varies from country to country, all of them are very small in relation to the dominant people. Everywhere Eurasians are city dwellers and are employed in white-collar occupations. The unemployment from which they were beginning to suffer before the war has become more pronounced, owing to increased competition from educated Asians and to the Eurasians' insistence on maintaining European standards of living.[1]

Whereas the policy of the Western governments toward Eurasians has ranged from one of encouragement (as in the Indies) to a belated and spotty legal protection (as in Indochina), the Eurasians everywhere have been loyal to them. And this loyalty bears little relation to the educational and economic opportunities which these governments have grudgingly and slowly accorded them. Socially and, to a lesser extent, professionally they have been snubbed, and only a handful among them has been able to surmount the obstacles which the color bar has placed in their way. Though they are a stable and largely homogeneous element in each colony and cling to their European ancestry, these common bonds have not brought unity or strength to them as a community.

Primarily responsible for this weakness has been the attitude of Europeans and, secondarily, that of Asians toward them. To the irresponsibility of their European fathers are added the barriers erected by the European community as a whole against their progress as a group. While the Eurasians consider themselves Europeans, the Europeans regard them neither as compatriots nor

[1] In Malaya, Criminal Investigation Department officers have charged that more unemployed Singapore Eurasians were operating as gangsters than at any time before the war (*Straits Times*, June 7, 1951).

as natives, but as something apart from either. European clubs and some hotels have been closed to them, and there have been instances where a European has lost his job by marrying a Eurasian. The arrival of large numbers of European women in Southeast Asia, especially during the interwar period, increased the social ostracism of the Eurasians and also prevented any sizable increase in their community. Refused admittance to the ruling class, and refusing to be merged with the majority people, these small groups of half-castes move in a vacuum between the two. The only Europeans who have consistently welcomed them are the Catholic missionaries, whose institutions provide them with shelter and some education. Perforce, the Eurasians have developed certain traditions and customs, but they lack a culture of their own, aping that of the Europeans above them and looking down on the Asian civilization that surrounds them. While they have received less from the Europeans than they feel is their due, they have enjoyed in Asian eyes a privileged position as regards employment and standard of living.

Just as the Eurasians have felt rejected by their European kinsmen, so the pure-blooded Asians have felt spurned by their Eurasian relatives. To them it is inexplicable that a group whose members have received such shabby treatment from their European fathers should despise the Asian mothers who reared them. The contrast between the product of Chinese mixed marriages and those of Europeans is indeed striking. Not only has the Chinese father contributed a physical stamina lacking in Southeast Asians, but he has assumed responsibility for and pride in his children by indigenous mothers. And the children in turn not only have felt proud of their Chinese heritage but are not ashamed of their Southeast Asian blood. They have added an element of strength to the countries where they live, whereas the Eurasians are a rootless, frustrated, and divided minority—foreigners in the land of their birth, yet unable to move elsewhere.

During the war, both Japanese policy and adverse economic conditions caused a further deterioration in the Eurasian position. Those who had clearly identified themselves with Europeans, either in the armed forces or in government service, were subjected to harsh treatment in concentration camps. Inevitably Eurasians who had worked for Europeans were out of jobs and suffered acutely from unemployment. The rank and file were grist to the mill of Japan's forced-labor organizations and, in food-shortage areas like Malaya, had no alternative but starvation if they resisted Japanese pressure to form agricultural colonies. Both for propaganda purposes and to get better cooperation from the Eurasians, Japan courted some Eurasian leaders, who for the sake of their community's survival had to make a show of accepting loyally. Collaboration with the Japanese could hardly have been spontaneous, for it ran against the very grain of their cultural traditions, which were wholly European. Cut off from their association with European life and prestige and undergoing great physical hardships, the Eurasians also had to witness passively their former positions being taken over by the native majority in each country of Southeast Asia.

The contemporary Eurasian dilemma was well expressed to James Michener by a member of that community in Singapore:

I can neither go up nor down. I am the man ordained by God always to be a clerk in some English shop. They don't have to pay me much for I can't leave. There's no other job I could get. And they don't have to promote me because everyone knows I am not really to be trusted. What am I? I am a Eurasian. I can never be a European as long as Englishmen despise anyone with even a drop of color. I can never be an Asian as long as my parents bring me up to imitate the white man. . . . My religion is a great solace to me . . . and I have always felt myself a brother with all Catholics across the world.[2]

The plight of this "marginal man" has been made worse, first by the Japanese who caused him to suffer for his white blood during the war, and later by Asian nationalists who are not unnaturally mindful of their own and resentful of the Eurasian sense of superiority. While they are willing to accept and even welcome Eurasians who identify themselves with their Asian brethren, they are not going to tolerate a privileged status for the great bulk of Eurasians who continue to think of themselves as Europeans. Eurasians living in areas that are still under colonial rule have been able to continue as a group apart, but the leaders of their community foresee the day when they must decide between various and—to them—distasteful alternatives.

Clearly, it is impossible for them to continue as a separate ethnic minority. Their number has never been large, and even with the additions to it that are coming from the white troops fighting in the area, the rate of its natural increase is very low compared with that of the Asians. Their mastery of the prevailing European language, which was their greatest asset for employment in colonial days, is no longer the advantage it once was, and many of them can speak only haltingly the native tongue which has now become the official one. Most of them have been too poor and many of them too apathetic to acquire the education and training necessary to qualify for the top jobs in which they could not easily be replaced. And they are becoming increasingly expendable as opportunities increase for the dominant people to take over the posts they held.

The idea of a homeland for Eurasians has long attracted many of them, and the example of the Jews in Israel gave it renewed impetus. But in their attempts to colonize New Guinea, the Eurasians have shown none of the Jews' aptitude for transforming themselves into an agricultural people, nor have they the capital and perseverance required. Some have thought of emigrating to Brazil, one of the few countries still open to limited immigration and tolerant

2 *Straits Budget*, May 3, 1951.

of racial mixtures. But it is to the country of their European ancestors that they instinctively turn, though the great majority of them have never been there and know nothing about the difficult conditions in postwar Europe. Thousands have used all their savings to go "home," and the results have been unfortunate both for them and the European country involved. Only the Netherlands government has assumed much responsibility for the survival and welfare of its citizens of mixed blood.

Obviously the only practical solution is for the Eurasians to stay in the land of their birth and adjust themselves to becoming an integral part of it. But thus far, in no country of Southeast Asia has a majority of its Eurasians accepted the inevitability of making this decision. Probably it is impossible for most of the adult Eurasians to do so, and it will lie with the youth of that community and also with the nationalist leaders of Southeast Asia to show the flexibility and spirit of compromise necessary to effect this transition.

Indonesia

Three and a half centuries of Dutch rule produced in the Indies the largest single group of Eurasians to be found anywhere in Southeast Asia. And thanks to a change in Dutch policy, dating from the middle of the nineteenth century, their status was superior to that of other Eurasians in the area.

In 1848, strong protests were voiced by Indies-born Hollanders and Eurasians living in Batavia against the preferential position then enjoyed by Netherlands-born Dutchmen as regards employment.[3] Up to this time, the poor education of the Eurasians had prevented their acquiring jobs above the lowest clerical level and hurt their social assimilation to the Dutch, though they retained the European name of their father and adhered to his Christian religion. Humble though their status was, the size of the community was sufficiently large to make the authorities heed their complaints, and by the laws of 1854 and 1892 all descendants of Europeans on the father's side—that is, the very great majority of the Eurasian community—came to be legally classed as Europeans.

The gradual improvement in the educational facilities open to them which followed this betterment of their legal status became rapid under the "ethical policy" instituted in 1902. In proportion as they were given access to institutions of higher learning, they moved up in the economic and social scale. They not only overran the administrative services, but also entered the professional field. Before World War II the heads of four of the eight government departments and the commander in chief of the NEI Army were Indo-Europeans. "Only in commerce did some prejudice continue against them on the ground that they lacked drive and initiative."[4]

[3] C. Fisher, "Eurasian Resettlement in Indonesia," *Eastern World*, October 1951.
[4] Fisher, *op. cit.*

In the interwar period, according to C. Fisher, perhaps 5 percent of the Eurasians held posts that would have been considered good by European standards, a further 25 percent had jobs that would not have been considered beneath the dignity of Europeans, and the rest were in the lower white-collar and skilled-labor categories.[5] Thus, while only a small proportion of the Eurasians were on a par with the Netherlands-born Dutch in the higher eche-lons, the bulk of their community occupied posts which educated Indonesians felt themselves qualified to hold. By giving the Eurasians a large-enough stake in the regime to assure their loyalty, the Dutch alienated the far-more-numerous Indonesians and embittered relations between the two indigenous populations. The retrenchment necessitated by the world depression of the early 1930's compelled the Dutch to yield some ground to nationalist demands in replacing many Eurasians by members of the growing and progressively aggrieved Indonesian elite. This inevitably increased the tension between the two communities, now in open competition with each other.

As early as 1912 the Eurasians organized an Indo-European League (Indo-Europeesch Verbond), partly so as to be able to protest more effectively against the quotas established for their community in the Dutch navy and the staffs of some private business concerns. Though this organization developed mainly along social lines, it was later given representation in the Volksraad. Its politico-economic aspects developed during the interwar period in propor-tion as its members felt their privileged position to be threatened by the Indo-nesians, more of whom each day were becoming competent to do the same work for less pay. Though a small minority of Eurasians were able to obtain an education in Holland, which reinforced their tendency to think of them-selves as Netherlanders, the majority could not afford this luxury and some among them began wanting a homeland of their own. A Eurasian agricul-tural colony in New Guinea was actually attempted but it soon failed, al-legedly because of hasty and inadequate preparation. In any case, the post-depression position of the Eurasians improved so markedly that such schemes came to seem less desirable. According to Fisher, their economic status and prospects in the years just before World War II were probably better than ever before and their solidarity with the Indies-born Dutch was steadily growing.

The defeat of Japan in August 1945 brought little improvement to South-east Asia's Eurasians and least of all to those of Indonesia, whose status had been higher and whose numbers had been greater than in any other country of the area before the war. For months after the war ended, the majority of

[5] In 1930, of the employed "Europeans" born in Indonesia, 47.3 percent were in the civil service and in various transport and communications departments. Only 10.4 percent were in independent occupations and 59 percent of these were women (P. W. van der Veur, "The Eurasians of Indonesia: Castaways of Colonialism," *Pacific Affairs*, June 1954).

Eurasian internees had to remain in their camps behind Republican lines and to suffer all the uncertainties felt by hostages throughout a protracted struggle. During the guerrilla phase of the Dutch-Indonesian conflict and particularly the two Dutch police actions, many Eurasians lost their lives and more their possessions. Although no accurate figures have been published, it has been estimated that at least 20,000 Eurasians died during the war and the four years that followed it.[6] Some of them died in Japanese concentration camps, some were murdered by irresponsible Indonesian elements, and still others suffered fortuitously, but the memory of this period of violence and terror will long remain green and has already made adjustment to the transfer of sovereignty in December 1949 very difficult for the Eurasians.

By the Hague Agreement of August 1949, Eurasians—then estimated to number about 100,000—were given two years in which to make up their minds about the future. If, by December 27, 1951, they failed to declare for Indonesian citizenship, they were to be regarded as Dutch nationals. If they opted for Netherlands citizenship, this would lay a very heavy burden on the Dutch government, especially if they tried to live in Holland. According to P. W. van der Veur, official Dutch circles in 1949 expected that most of the Eurasians would choose Dutch citizenship. And even if they remained in Indonesia as Dutchmen, the Netherlands still felt a responsibility since they would then suffer from nationalistic restrictions imposed on the employment of foreigners. The Dutch could not very well deny Eurasian members of the NEI army (KNIL) their right to be sent to Holland, but in view of the difficulties they would surely experience in adjusting to life there, it was naturally hoped that they would accept transfer to the Indonesian army. There was also a revival of the scheme of a Eurasian "homeland" in New Guinea. As early as 1945, exaggerated reports of that island's potentialities for the oil industry had drawn some hundreds of Eurasians as settlers. By mid-1948, somewhat under 3,000 had migrated there despite Dutch counsels of caution and uniformly discouraging reports from New Guinea. In January 1950, 600 unsuccessful settlers, the majority of whom were Eurasians, cabled an appeal for refuge in Surabaja, but a few days later 200 more would-be colonists sailed from Makassar to New Guinea.[7] As the Eurasians were predominantly urban and belonged to the white-collar class, they lacked the training, stamina, and funds to colonize New Guinea. As recently as September 1953, when there were about 8,000 Eurasians there, a Dutch Labor M.P. writing in *Het Parool* warned his government against employing more Eurasians as civil servants in western New Guinea, on the ground that they were "not constructive" in their work and were "the cause of many difficulties."[8] There has also been a smaller-scale Eurasian emigration to Surinam and Brazil.

[6] *Burmese Review*, Nov. 13, 1950.   [7] *Report on Indonesia*, Feb. 1, 1950.
[8] Antara despatch, Amsterdam, *Times of Indonesia*, Sept. 21, 1953.

The easiest way out, and one persistently urged by the prewar Indo-European League (which later became the GIKI) and postwar Federasi Penghapus Minoritet and Partai Indo-Nasional, was for the Eurasians to give their allegiance to the new Republic. Perforce the majority would have to remain in Indonesia, and so had a long-term interest in identifying themselves with the new state. The Indonesians promised all minority groups freedom and protection under the law, appealed to the Eurasians to become loyal citizens, and allotted them representation in Parliament, though not in proportion to their numbers or importance. Yet by March 1954, only 20,000 Eurasians had elected to become Indonesian citizens.[9] Thus, it is evident that the great majority of the Eurasians have not been able to bring themselves to accept being merged with a people whom they have always considered inferior, and losing their separate identity as a group which they have long sought to maintain. In actual practice, most Eurasians who are at the lowest economic level would find little real difference in living as Indonesians; the handful of highly qualified Eurasians would always find posts in a country where it will take many years to train Indonesians to fill them. But the remaining middle group regards the prospect of becoming Indonesian as retrogression both economically and psychologically. Some have even refused to acknowledge their Indonesian blood, most of them feel more Dutch than the Dutch themselves, and virtually all insist on being foreigners in their own country. When the time for decision came, an overwhelming majority—about 89 percent of the total Eurasian population —chose to retain their Dutch citizenship even though most of them had never been out of Indonesia.

Various circumstances were responsible for the unfortunate attitude adopted by the Eurasians in December 1951—the Westerling affair, transformation of the federal governmental structure into the unitary Republic of Indonesia, and a law passed by the Dutch Parliament in 1950 guaranteeing the salaries of civil servants of Dutch nationality who were employed by the Indonesian government.[10] More fundamental was the failure of the Dutch government at this time to grasp the Eurasian viewpoint and to guide it toward a more realistic acceptance of the situation. Moreover, the Indonesian government's suspicion of, and discrimination against, the Eurasian group as a whole did nothing to allay Eurasian fears, which were focused on the educational and agrarian questions. The Eurasians wanted to be assured that schools would be available to them wherein they could retain their Dutch culture and that the agrarian law of 1875 would be revised in such a way as to enable them to acquire titles to land.

The unresolved problems posed by Eurasian intransigency regarding Indonesian citizenship and by the increasing number of Eurasians leaving for the Netherlands impelled the Dutch government in 1952 to appoint a commission

[9] *Times of Indonesia*, Mar. 15, 1954.   [10] See article by P. W. van der Veur, *op. cit.*

headed by P. H. Werner, secretary-general of the Ministry of Social Affairs, to investigate the situation and recommend a course of action. Among other things it was to report as to the advisability of bringing poorer Eurasians to Holland, to inform them of the slim chance they had of getting employment there, to study job openings for them in Indonesia, and generally to see what could be done to improve their status.

For purposes of broad classification, the Werner Commission divided the Eurasians into two groups—the occidental element, who had a Western education and economic level, and close ties with the Netherlands; and the oriental element, who were more rooted in Indonesia by their customs and culture. The Commission's report, issued in October 1952, estimated that of the 100,000-odd Dutch citizens then in Indonesia, some 97,000 were Eurasians. Of these, only 20,000 or about 16 percent of the total had acquired Indonesian citizenship; approximately 7,000 were employed in the Indonesian government service; some 70,000 were working in private enterprise; and 7,500 or so were carrying on their own businesses. The remaining 10,000 comprised small traders, those engaged in miscellaneous occupations, and the destitute.

It was found that the number of Eurasians in government service was declining daily. According to unofficial sources, it had decreased from 16,000 at the end of 1951—the deadline for the citizenship decision—to 7,111 in the summer of 1952. These were chiefly technicians, but 2,000 of them who held subordinate posts were to be replaced by Indonesians during the ensuing five years. Those persons, along with the remaining 5,000 Eurasians and their families, would obviously require help from the Netherlands government.

Of the approximately 100,000 Dutch citizens still in Indonesia, 44,000 had the right—the Commission believed—to free transport to Holland. Its report estimated that there were some 5,000 destitute and aged, and approximately 17,000 living on pensions which, under postwar inflationary conditions, had become inadequate for their needs. Currently the Dutch government was spending about 600,000 Rp. monthly for their support and welfare and that of the destitute and unemployable. With the growing scarcity of white-collar employment available to non-Indonesians, many Eurasians of that class had been forced to accept unskilled jobs at very low pay, and even these were hard to obtain. In such cases, the Netherlands government supplemented their earnings, but this had encouraged employers in some instances to offer lower than a living wage. Though there was a marked reluctance on the part of all employers, even Dutch firms, to give jobs to Eurasians, the Commission found that the latter were not taking advantage of their ample opportunities to train themselves for higher positions. In contrast to the many Indonesians and Chinese who were attending night schools, most Eurasians were not trying to supplement their meager education so as to qualify for posts in which they could not be readily replaced. Stress was placed by the Commission on the need for better training of Eurasian youth.

Among the conclusions to which the Commission came, the following were the most important:

1. Impoverished Dutch citizens living in Indonesia must be prevented from going to Holland, where they would find it hard to adapt themselves and earn a living. But none who had the means to go there to live should be barred from doing so.

2. Since the great majority of Eurasians should remain in Indonesia, the Dutch government must help them to equip themselves educationally and psychologically for living there as a self-supporting and integral part of the Indonesian community.

3. Relief for the destitute and unemployable would have to be financed by the Netherlands government, which should also formulate the policy for its dispensation but leave its execution in the hands of religious and other private charitable institutions.

Unfortunately the Commission did not also suggest practical ways in which its recommendations could be implemented, nor did it discuss the whole problem with the Indonesian authorities. Moreover, according to Paul van der Veur, there are indications that governmental policy, not scholarly research, dictated the recommendations of the report and that the problem in its entirety had not yet been adequately studied. But an important general principle, to which the Commission subscribed, was that the Netherlands government was morally bound to assume responsibility for Eurasian affairs, whether in Holland or in Indonesia. This commendable assumption of responsibility vis-à-vis the Eurasians has taken the form of substantial relief measures for those still living in Indonesia. And for the Eurasians now resident in Holland (who by early 1954 numbered some 100,000), the Dutch government has provided housing and employment opportunities, and has also tried belatedly to remedy its former discrimination against them in regard to payment for wartime damages and salary losses.

Malaya

When Raffles landed at Singapore in 1819, he brought ashore with him a small group of Anglo-Indians who were serving in the East India Company. There existed already in Malacca and also in Penang a small colony of Eurasians who were the descendants of early Portuguese and Dutch conquistadores and traders. Eurasian groups still live in those Straits ports, but long ago a number of their more enterprising members began to migrate to faster-developing Singapore, where they now form the largest Eurasian community in Malaya.

Throughout their history in Malaya, Eurasians have suffered from prejudice and disabilities. Their petitions to the British Parliament early in the nineteenth century resulted in 1831 in an Act which enabled others than covenanted servants of the East India Company to be eligible for appointment as Justices of the Peace. But even after they could be employed by the company, they still had to surmount the color bar. Despite this handicap some Eurasians distinguished themselves as lawyers, engineers, and journalists and also in cultural fields. From 1885 to 1909, the Queen's Scholarships were awarded almost every year to Eurasians, and Eurasian teachers did outstanding work, especially in improving education for girls in Malaya. With the opening of new opportunities, their economic and political status improved. During the interwar period they were represented on Singapore's Legislative Council, Municipal Commission, and Rural Board. Although the Malayan civil and legal services remained closed to them on the mainland, they entered the Straits Settlements civil and legal services and also the Malayan medical service. Their social status, however, did not show an analogous improvement, though the Eurasians clung to their British names, spoke English as their mother tongue, and were practically all Christians.

In Malaya, a crucial aspect of the Eurasian problem has been military service. In 1883 the Eurasians, along with the local Europeans, joined the Volunteer Corps when it was first formed. Gradually, however, the Eurasians disappeared from this mixed unit. Again they joined up when the Singapore Volunteers Infantry was recruited in 1901, but its Eurasian company was disbanded eight years later. During World War I the Eurasians demanded the formation of another Volunteer Corps, but permission was not granted until four months before the armistice. Though this corps survived until the fall of Singapore in February 1942, it was not until ten months after the Second World War broke out in Europe that Eurasians—after months of agitation— were allowed to enlist in the British army. And soon a new grievance cropped up in the pay differential between European and Eurasian volunteers. In spite of strong Eurasian pressure, the government refused to reconsider its policy, and the sense of injustice thus engendered carried over into the early post war period to become part of what was then known as the Back Pay Controversy.

Eurasian attempts at self-government as a community were uniformly unsuccessful in Malaya. Some of these associations antedated World War I, but they were almost all of a recreational nature, and by 1938 only 20 percent of the community, split into many groups, belonged to any of them.[11] A *Eurasian Review* started at Penang in the early 1930's had to cease publication for lack of support two years before World War II broke out. As to the presence of a Eurasian (Dr. J. E. Smith) on the Singapore Legislative Council, opinion in the community was divided: some thought that he had enhanced Eurasian

[11] *Straits Times*, Dec. 21, 1938.

self-confidence, and others claimed that he dared not defend his people's rights and interests "for fear of reprisals in the employment market."[12]

This question of employment had become increasingly acute during the interwar period. In the late nineteenth century, about 74 percent of the clerks in the Straits Settlements government and municipal services were Eurasians, but by 1939 this proportion had declined to approximately 25 percent because of their progressive replacement by Chinese.[13] A major handicap was the poor quality of education available to Eurasians. The government took no responsibility for their schooling, and what little formal instruction they received came from mission schools. Poverty prevented their getting training for high posts, and their one great asset as regarded employment over other non-Europeans was their fluency in the English language. Unwilling to accept humbly paid jobs because they felt an inner compulsion to live according to European standards, and unable to obtain the top posts and to enter British society, the Eurasians were fighting a losing battle even to retain what they had.

Recognition on the part of some farseeing Eurasians that the salvation of their community lay only with themselves led to the organization in February 1940 of the first all-Malayan Eurasian conference. The hope was then expressed that the new organization which materialized from this meeting might be the turning point for a group which overmuch brooding on its handicaps had reduced to inactivity. Unfortunately there was no widespread realization of the need for concerted action. A year after its formation this Eurasian assembly had only 800 members, of whom about 80 percent were too apathetic to attend meetings and were content simply to pay their Str. $2 annual dues.[14]

Since World War II, Eurasians in Malaya have achieved a political prominence justified neither by their numbers—a little under 20,000—nor their unity. In most instances the government has taken the initiative by appointing Eurasians to public bodies disproportionately to the size of their community as compared with that of the Indians. In some cases, individual Eurasians have proved to be outstanding leaders. But the Eurasians as a group have shown no more strength or cohesion than they did in prewar days, despite the revival of the All-Malayan Eurasian Union soon after the war's end.

In 1946 two Eurasians were appointed to the Cheeseman Committee set up to consider criticism of the proposed federal constitution, and later one Eurasian was appointed to the Federal Legislative Council. There were 1,800 Eurasians on Singapore's electoral rolls, as compared with 3,148 Malays, 10,000 Indians, and 5,391 Chinese. Yet no Eurasian was elected to the Singapore Legislative Council in March 1948, and the government had to name a Eurasian as one of its appointive members. As of June 1951, there were two Eurasians on the Singapore Legislative Council, one of whom—an outstanding

[12] *Ibid.*, Mar. 6, 1939.   [13] *Ibid.*, Jan. 26, 1939.   [14] *Ibid.*, Mar. 20, 1941.

leader of that community, Dr. Paglar—had been given the honorific title of Dato by the Sultan of Johore.

Aside from the Eurasians who have been government appointees, there are a few communal leaders who have been associated with the country's postwar radical movements. John Eber, a lawyer who belongs to one of Singapore's prominent Eurasian families, was the brains behind the Malayan Democratic Union, which was the first intercommunal political organization born in the country to advocate freedom for a democratically constituted Malaya. In January 1951 he was arrested on charges of subversive activities, but was never brought to trial. He was finally released in February 1953, at which time it was reported that no formal charges had ever been brought against him. On the peninsula, the Eurasian Union, too, has inclined toward a fairly radical solution for Malaya's future. In September 1951 its president welcomed the creation of the Independence of Malaya Party, the aims of which included Malaya's independence within seven years and the creation of an intercommunal Malayan nationality. But the great majority of Eurasians apparently remain inarticulate and divided, and they continue to cling to their British traditions and aloofness from other communities. Only briefly and on a very small scale did some of them show any interest in the establishment of a Eurasian homeland in New Guinea, as promoted in 1945 by some Indo-Europeans.

So long as Malaya remains a British colony, the Eurasians can persevere in their ostrich-like attitude and refuse to see the future that threatens them. A glance at the 1947 census figures, however, would show them how slow is their rate of growth—19.8 percent in the preceding sixteen years—in comparison with the great numerical increases registered by the other domiciled communities. The object lesson furnished by the plight of Eurasians in the new national states of southern Asia seems to have been lost on them, and they continue to rely on official British support rather than to capitalize on their potentialities.

Burma

Because Burma was administered as a part of India until 1937, the status of Eurasians mirrored the unhappy lot of their community in the latter country. And for the same reasons, the Eurasians in Burma comprised both Anglo-Indians and Anglo-Burmans.

Under British rule they enjoyed what Burmans considered to be a privileged status economically. Their familiarity with British ways and grasp of the English language enabled them from the outset to hold administrative and technical posts for which Burmans were considered unqualified. But as in Indonesia, the growth of an educated and increasingly nationalistic Burmese elite, in conjunction with the world depression, displaced an important segment of the Eurasians from their jobs. While a few individuals had become prominent in the professions, the great majority of wage-earning Eurasians were clerks in the civil service or in the police.[15] And the increasing competition for employment in the middle and lower administrative categories, as well as that of skilled labor, was beginning to be felt before World War II, particularly after 1937 when there was a strong Burmese demand for Burmanization of all civil-service positions and of technical jobs in foreign-owned companies operating in Burma. As in Malaya, a few Eurasian organizations existed, but their membership included only a fraction of the whole community, and their objectives were almost wholly social and recreational.

In the period between the Japanese surrender and Burma's acquisition of independence, Burmese nationalists courted the Eurasians as they did all the indigenous minorities, and urged them to unite with Burmans in the fight for freedom. In December 1946, Aung San delivered a speech to the Anglo-Burman Council in which he alternately wooed and warned them.[16] He first apologized for not having been able to do more to alleviate their wartime sufferings. While he was pleased to learn that members of the Anglo-Burman Council regarded themselves as nationals of Burma, they must prove this by actions as well as words and must "awaken to a new sense of values." If they truly identified themselves with Burma, he promised that they need have no apprehensions regarding their status once the country became independent.

After Aung San's assassination in July 1947, his successor took pains to renew this assurance. In September, a special communiqué was addressed to the Anglo-Burman community in which its members were told that the government regarded them as valued nationals of Burma, whose services would be utilized without discrimination.[17] But not all of the community was convinced, and the post-independence period proved to be a trying time for them.

As elsewhere in Southeast Asia, Burma's Eurasians were divided between those who wanted a separate communal status, either inside the country or abroad, and those who were willing to identify themselves with the Burmans. This division cut across the five existing Eurasian organizations,[18] and these did not by any means include even a majority of the whole community. In 1946 several new organizations were formed with the aim of either appealing to those not already included or of merging existing associations. A new group, piquantly named the League of Peace Promoters of Burma and claiming a membership of 3,000 (no dues were required), late in 1946 proposed to unite with the Anglo-Burman Council, but nothing further was heard of this suggestion. In June 1946, the Burma Union came out strongly in favor of merging Eurasians with the Burmans, and a few months later the Anglo-Burman Council followed suit.[19]

[15] Christian, op. cit., p. 17.   [16] The Burman, Dec. 11, 1946.
[17] Ibid., Sept. 28, 1947.
[18] The Anglo-Burman Union, the "Gedhawk" youth group, the Burma Union, the Burma League, and the Anglo-Burman Council.   [19] The Burman, June 27, 1946.

Those Eurasians who chose to be Burma nationals decided in November 1946 to form an Anglo-Burman Congress, to claim the rights of Burmese citizenship, and to put up candidates for election to the forthcoming Constituent Assembly. In April 1947, four members of that community were elected without opposition.[20] After Burma became independent in January 1948, this element showed an activity it had never before displayed, both in its own communal organizations and in support of the government.[21]

Another, less articulate, segment of the Eurasians could not accept the changed conditions, notably those who personally suffered from the disorders of the post-independence period and a larger group who continued to think of themselves as British. As early as June 1946, a prominent Anglo-Burman (C. H. Campagnac) proposed setting up a model town for his community, or starting agricultural colonies in the Shan States for the benefit of unemployed Anglo-Burmans. Both proposals were voted down by a majority of the local Eurasians on the ground that such solutions "would continue to isolate the community and protract the problem facing it."[22] Later an Anglo-Indian (Colonel Fleury) announced that he had been investigating Brazil as a home for Burma's Eurasians. Though he frankly admitted the discouraging features involved, he thought that "opportunities existed there for the adventurous."[23]

But it was Britain, not Brazil, that chiefly attracted such Eurasians as could not or would not live in sovereign Burma. Many of these, born in Burma with no more than a diluted drop of British blood, educated in English schools and employed all their lives in some obscure post in Burma, yet called the England they had never seen "home." The main exodus of this group occurred as a consequence of the severe internal disturbances of 1949, in which Eurasians suffered material losses along with the other communities but from which they acquired a greater fear for the future. Most of those who then left the country had to spend all their savings in buying passage to Britain and for food and lodging during the long, lonely months in which they wandered from one employment agency to another. Postwar England proved to be a great shock for them, as they had expected to be received there with open arms. Adjustment to the climate and food was difficult for them, no shortage of skilled workers existed, and jobs could be obtained only by the handful of highly qualified men among them. Some Anglo-Burmans who had held fairly good posts in the Burma railroads, police, or customs were reduced to taking jobs as laborers or factory hands. A Burman reported from London, in the fall of 1952, that these Anglo-Burmans were marooned, unhappy, and all wanting to go back to a Burma which for the first time they were now calling "home."[24]

[20] *Burmese Review,* Apr. 7, 1947.   [21] *The Burman,* Jan. 30, 1950.
[22] *Ibid.,* June 27, 1946.   [23] *Ibid.,* Feb. 11, 1947.
[24] *Ibid.,* Sept. 13, 1952.

Indochina

The economic as well as social handicaps under which the Eurasians of Indochina long labored were typical of colonial countries throughout Southeast Asia, with one important difference. From the early days of the French civil administration, the French Indian citizens in Indochina competed with Eurasians at clerical and technical levels, thus creating a situation unique in the area. This phenomenon caused Indochinese Eurasians to concentrate on the acquisition of French citizenship in an effort to improve their status.

In November 1912 a first step was made toward this goal when a relevant Metropolitan French law was made applicable to Indochina. Eurasians were thereby authorized to produce legal evidence of their French paternity and in this way to qualify for citizenship. Though this was an important concession in principle, it proved to be of little practical advantage to them. Many Eurasians could not produce the required evidence and most of them were in no position to bear the expense of the long and costly procedure involved. For the next sixteen years their status remained largely as before. The law classed those not legitimatized by their fathers either as French subjects or protégés; they did their military service as native Indochinese; and it was on the same terms as Vietnamese, Cambodians, and Laotians that they were admitted into the administration. The difficulties they encountered in attending French schools prevented their acquiring an education that might have broken down their ostracism by French society.

In 1926 the Hanoi Court of Appeal took the significant step of reversing previous decisions by declaring the Franco-Annamite to be a French citizen. Two years later this decision was confirmed by decree, and this effected a marked improvement in the status of the Eurasian community. Thereafter they were admitted into schools and professions as French citizens. However, they still were not socially accepted as French, and in the administration and army their pay and promotion opportunities were inferior to those of citizens born in France.

During the war the Eurasians of Indochina did not meet with so many physical hardships as did their confrères in other parts of Southeast Asia, because the French administration remained intact until the Japanese coup of March 1945. However, they did experience some discrimination at the hands of the Vichy regime, which progressively reduced the pay of government servants who were French citizens of Asian origin. It was not until early 1949 that two decrees abrogated this wartime legislation, and even now their local application has not been extended to Eurasians unable to produce evidence that they had at least two French ancestors. This continued discrimination has provided Indochina's Eurasians with the basis for their claim to be treated as a separate ethnic minority.

In August 1950, a mission of eight Indochinese Eurasians headed by William Bazé presented this claim in person to M. Coste-Floret, then Minister for Overseas France. Speaking for the "100,000 Eurasians of Indochina"— this number was generally regarded as a gross exaggeration—they also asked for special representation in France, particularly in the Assembly of the French Union.[25] They told the Minister that 95 percent of the Eurasian community did not want to leave Indochina, where they had their families and special traditions, and that a proposal to transfer them to some other part of the French empire had aroused their strong opposition. Coste-Floret informed them that as French citizens they were not eligible for separate political representation in France, but though he was not willing to consider them an ethnic minority he did admit that they had *"un particularisme régional très marqué."*

To what extent the group for which Bazé was the spokesman represented the whole community it is impossible to say. In substantiation of Bazé's assertion that his fellow Eurasians, even the most wretched, regarded France as their motherland could be cited Vietnamese nationalist reprisals against that community and efforts to enlist the loyalty of Eurasian youth. The Vietnamese, like other Southeast Asian nationalists, were naturally pressing Eurasians to become citizens of the country, and the French authorities seemed to be doing nothing at all to offset this appeal. Actually the only local agency that maintained the Eurasians' cultural ties with France were the French Catholic missionaries, who continued to give Eurasian children shelter in their orphanages and a French education. As of 1952 there were also about 500 Indochinese Eurasian children at school in France.

Leaders who urge the perpetuation of a separate communal status for Eurasians in Indochina want the government to improve the status of Eurasian officials, subsidize the education of Eurasian youth in the country, and increase the opportunities for the Eurasian elite to receive higher training in France. They maintain that this would be a cheap price to pay for rewarding and encouraging the loyalty of a group that can perpetuate French culture in Indochina and serve as the logical link between France and independent Vietnam. Probably so long as France remains in Indochina, the Eurasians will insist on their French culture and apartness from the other indigenous communities, and it is significant that Viet Minh propaganda has never cited Eurasians as among the native supporters of the Republic.

Thailand

By comparison with neighboring colonial countries, Thailand has no Eurasian problem. First-generation Eurasians have long been given the option of registering as Europeans if they so wish, but few of them have cared to do so. Eurasian girls who married Europeans automatically have identified themselves with their husbands' community; Eurasian boys have generally been

[25] Bazé, W. "Les 100,000 Eurasiens d'Indochine," *France-Asie,* August 1952.

absorbed into Thai society and by the third generation are legally considered to be Thai. Indeed the Eurasians have had every reason to identify themselves with the people of a sovereign country, who accept them tolerantly provided that they do not stress unduly their European blood. In a state like Thailand, the Eurasians have everything to gain and nothing to lose by throwing in their lot with the majority community.

THE ARAKANESE

Arakan's minority problems have been further complicated by its isolation from the rest of Burma and, since 1947, its common land frontier with newly created Pakistan. And the state of confusion that already existed before the war was intensified from 1942 to 1945 by the Japanese occupation and by military operations in the Arakan division.

In southern Arakan there is no minority problem, properly speaking, for the Burmese Buddhists living there are neither culturally nor ethnically different from the inhabitants of Burma proper. But the memory of an independent kingdom of Arakan that flourished in the eighteenth century is still green among them and has fostered a regionalism that probably could never have developed if better communications with the rest of Burma had been established across the high hills of the Arakan Yoma or along the coast. Local legend promises that the return to Arakan of the Mahamuni image, carried off to Mandalay centuries ago, will bring about the restoration of the kingdom of Arakan. Sentimental traditions of this kind were strong even before the war, but wartime and postwar events have fortified them. Furthermore, nothing has been done to lessen Arakan's isolation, which makes the Arakanese feel neglected economically and culturally, and permits officials from Rangoon to administer the division with a free and not always capable or disinterested hand.

Before the war, the existence of a land frontier with India had already given rise to a problem that later, with the establishment of Pakistan, became much more serious. As a result of the fact that movement across this frontier between Chittagong and Akyab district was quick, easy, and cheap, the Indian community in Arakan has taken on a special character. This was reflected by the 1931 census, which showed that about 97 percent of the Arakanese Indians were concentrated in Akyab district, although Indians accounted for only 217,801 of Arakan division's total population of 1,008,548. Of the Indian community in Akyab (which was predominantly Chittagonian), 167,-000 were born in Burma and 44,000 outside. Women constituted 48.5 percent of the local-born Indians and 13.6 percent of the India-born. This great deficiency of women in the latter component indicated the highly immigrant and unsettled nature of that element, whereas the approximation to sex equilibrium in the former group was the mark of its more stable character.

Unlike the Indian immigrants generally in other parts of Burma, who commonly spent periods of about three years in the country without returning home, the bulk of the Chittagonians in Arakan, who came to reap the paddy crop, went back to Chittagong when the harvest was finished. Before the war, this Chittagonian penetration of Arakan was steadily continuing and was resented not only by the Arakanese proper but by the settled Chittagonians as well. For neither of the latter groups could compete with the cheap labor supplied by the seasonal immigrants, whose standards of living were lower and whose industriousness was greater. Just before World War II, the view was expressed to the Baxter Committee on Indian Immigration[26] that migrants from Chittagong should be restricted, on the ground that, if cheap Chittagonian labor should be less readily available, the settled population could play a larger role in harvesting the paddy crop.

During the war, Arakanese economy suffered from the elimination of its exports to India, requisitioning of livestock and rice by the Japanese, and bombings by Allied airmen. Some effort was made by the Japanese to maintain paddy production in the Kaladan valley, Arakan's granary, but its output went to their troops, so that the local people were reduced to subsistence levels. By 1943 the elected Arakanese headmen had been replaced by Japanese-appointed officials, and there was a general breakdown of the whole civil administration. By October of that year a Japanese-trained Arakan Defense Force was reported by Tokyo to have been formed, but it was only semi-equipped, with a motley array of weapons, and was used more for guiding than for fighting. During the British campaign of 1943, the Arakanese were not unfriendly, apart from their dislike of the presence of Indian troops, and the subsequent arrival of some of Bose's followers reportedly diverted some of this anti-Indian sentiment to them.

Late in the war some Arakanese organized a resistance movement which carried on propaganda aimed at denying provisions and labor to the Japanese, and in early December 1944 two British officers joined the movement as military advisers. While the Japanese obviously failed to win active Arakanese support because of the economic distress, forced labor, and upheaval in village administration which their occupation had brought, neither did the Arakanese want the British back. Allied bombing caused resentment and a big exodus of Akyab's population in mid-1944, and Arakanese Buddhists were said to be afraid of "reprisals" from the returning British. The Japanese surrender left great stocks of arms in Arakan and a considerable number of Arakanese able to use them. The war had intensified Arakan's isolation and therefore its regionalism, and in the next few years there was very little exchange of information about what was transpiring both there and in Burma proper.

On June 24, 1945, the Arakanese of Rangoon held a meeting there which

26 See also p. 73.

was attended by only 15 persons, among whom, however, were two stormy petrels of prewar days. An irredentist note was sounded with the proposal that the Burmese government should see that the portions of Arakan "annexed" by India were returned and that the rights of Arakanese living in Chittagong were safeguarded. A separate assembly for Arakan within a federal framework for Burma was also advocated, and the demand for return of the Mahamuni image was revived. So, even as the war was ending, the stage was set for the troubles that have since plagued Arakan.

Two separatist movements developed successively in different parts of the area, and came to involve Burma's relations with Pakistan. Then first the Red Flag Communists and later the White Flag Communists found the troubled waters of Arakan an excellent place in which to fish. At the same time, intensive rice smuggling between Arakan and Pakistan was accompanied by a rapid growth in crime throughout the division. Burmese officials sent from Rangoon proved to be generally unpopular administrators, and the central government could only periodically dispatch troops to quell the disturbances. Not only did both the civilian and military elements sent to Arakan by the Burmese government fail to straighten out the situation, but they actually contributed to its worsening.

The separatist movement that developed among Arakanese Buddhists was an outgrowth of the Pacific war, for no formal demand for separate status had been made by the Arakanese at the time of Burma's separation from India in 1937. Late in 1946 the revolt broke out, led by a local monk, U Seinda, who had distinguished himself as a leader of the anti-Japanese resistance movement. The number of his wartime followers was now swelled by Arakanese who had grievances against the highhanded action of some Burmese officials in the area and others who resented the growing influx of Muslim immigrants from Chittagong. In part because the government believed that U Seinda was misinformed regarding the imminent British withdrawal from Burma and that his revolt was a prolongation of his patriotic activities during the war, and in part because of its admitted inability to maintain law and order in Arakan,[27] amnesty on generous terms was offered to the rebels. U Seinda was arrested but almost immediately released, and trouble soon broke out again. Neither he nor his followers would surrender their arms or give up political agitation; crime and violence grew apace, and in April 1947 U Seinda was rearrested. This simply aggravated the unrest, and the following month the government had to send 2,000 troops to Arakan. Reassuring bulletins were issued, announcing that the situation was in hand, that the prevalent crime was at the root of Arakan's troubles, and that there was no genuine demand for partition.[28] No mention was made of a petition for regional autonomy submitted shortly before to the Frontier Areas Commission by the Arakanese separatists.

[27] Reuter despatch, Dec. 12, 1946.   [28] *The Burman*, May 17, 1947.

When Bogyoke Aung San visited Arakan, local youths displayed posters demanding statehood for the area, more pay for teachers, and the establishment of an intermediate college in the area.

In mid-1947 Thakin Soe, leader of the Red Flag Communists, began exploiting the Arakanese situation. Directives were reportedly issued to his two local lieutenants, Bonpauk Tha Gyaw and Aung Lin, to align themselves with the dissidents and bandits in order to foment further disorders. This new element stimulated a visit to Arakan, late in the year, by the deputy premier and some high-ranking members of the AFPFL, and at the same time a campaign by the military and police "to wipe out nests of dacoits." In November, the government dispatched one of its ablest civil servants, Khin Maung Pyu, to take charge of Arakan division. Still the unrest continued. In December 100 students at Akyab held a "protest meeting," and the arrest of 10 of their number increased Arakanese hostility toward the Burmese officials responsible. In March 1948, the government appointed a commission, under Nyo Tun, charged with inquiring into the "causes of dissatisfaction on the part of the people of Arakan towards the Union Government." The appointment of this body coincided with the start of the White Flag Communist revolt in Burma proper, followed by that of most of the White PVO's, and both groups soon added to the confusion and violence in Arakan.

In the meantime northern Arakan had become the scene of even more serious trouble. The postwar illegal immigration of Chittagonians into that area was on a vast scale, and in the Maungdaw and Buthidaung areas they replaced the Arakanese, who had had to withdraw because of wartime bombings.[29] The newcomers were called Mujahids (crusaders), in contrast to the Rwangya or settled Chittagonian population, and though there were economic differences between them, both groups were Muslims and together came to outnumber the Arakanese Buddhists.[30] The Muslims of northern Arakan not only were smuggling huge quantities of rice into Pakistan but were beginning to press for annexation of the area to that country.

As early as May 1946, the Mujahids voiced their desire for separation from the Buddhist Arakanese and Burmans, and appealed to Jinnah for help. Two months later the North Arakan Muslim League was formed in Akyab district, under the presidency of Moulvi Lookman Sahib, and its members immediately passed a resolution formally asking for union with their fellow Muslims across the border. The Rwangya element was reportedly not in favor of this move; the Arakanese branch of the AFPFL actively opposed it; and Jinnah himself later assured Aung San that he had discouraged Mujahid

[29] *Burmese Review*, Jan. 13, 1947.

[30] According to the *New York Times*, Mar. 21, 1952, there were at that time 400,000–500,000 Muslims and a substantially smaller number of Buddhists in Arakan.

aspirations.[81] Among the Burmese, all this produced a minor irredentist re-action. U Saw, the wartime premier, reportedly said that if any change was to be made, "the only right thing is for Chittagong to go back to Burma . . . it once belonged to Burma, as did Assam and Manipur."[32]

Discouraged by this setback, the Mujahids remained quiescent politically for some time, even after Pakistan became an independent state in August 1947. But late in 1948 reports began to filter through to Rangoon of serious communal differences between the Mujahids and the Arakanese Buddhists, and government forces were said to be fighting the former in the Buthidaung-Maungdaw area. At the same time certain events occurred that caused the Arakan situation to worsen: some newspapers in Pakistan hinted at persecution of Arakanese Muslims by the Burma government.[33] Early in 1949, the Karen revolt forced the government to withdraw most of its troops from Arakan and, as a result of rebel victories, U Seinda escaped from his Tharrawaddy jail and made his way back to Arakan. There an alliance was formed between the White PVO's, Communist elements, and Arakanese dissidents. Although the hard-pressed government could not prevent this, in August it set up still another commission to study the relations between the Mujahids and Arakanese Buddhists, thus indicating its willingness now to consider partitioning Akyab district so as to separate the stronger elements in each section.[34]

For some months the government was so preoccupied with quelling the multiple revolts in Burma proper that it could pay only fitful attention to the problems of distant Arakan. The Minister for Minorities, himself an Arakanese Muslim, worked valiantly to bring about peace, and early in 1950 Premier Nu visited the troubled area in company with the Pakistani ambassador. Nu called the Mujahids "bad citizens of the Union" but recognized that the outcome of their revolt would depend upon putting down that of the Communists, with which it was now firmly linked.[35] No progress toward the restoration of order was made by the end of 1950, and the combined strength of the armed rebel forces then operating in Arakan was believed to number over 3,000.[36] In 1951 Arakan remained so troubled that elections to the new Parliament could be held in only a few places.

By early 1952 the struggle in Arakan, where banditry remained a major element, was taking on a religious as well as a political form. At that time charges long made in the Rangoon press as to the alleged maltreatment of Arakanese Buddhists in Pakistan were revived. Since Pakistan's attainment of independence, the East Pakistanis were said to have become aggressive toward the Arakanese Buddhists living in their midst by attempting to convert them

31 *The Burman*, Jan. 10, 1947. "Asmi," writing in *The Guardian* for August 1954, claimed that the British had made a wartime promise of semi-autonomy to the Muslim districts of Arakan.
32 *The Statesman*, Calcutta, Dec. 22, 1946.   33 *Burmese Review*, Dec. 20, 1948.
34 *Ibid.*, Aug. 8, 1949.   35 *Ibid.*, Mar. 13, 1950.   36 *The Burman*, May 7, 1950.

forcibly to Islam and to displace them from the fertile areas they had long occupied. And rumors persisted, despite denials both by high Pakistan officials and the Burmese government, that the Mujahids in Arakan were receiving arms and funds from Pakistan. While the Pakistani support given the Mujahids was most probably unofficial, there is little doubt but that the Mujahid leaders frequently crossed over into Pakistan either in search of arms or of a place in which to cache their plunder. It was perhaps such rumors of foreign Muslim support that caused the rift in June 1952 between U Seinda and the Mujahid chief, Cassim,[37] who had at one time been a follower of the Arakanese Buddist leader in their joint opposition to the Burmese government. (The role played by the Communists at this juncture was confusing, for until U Seinda turned on the Mujahids they had remained his allies. Their refusal to join Arakanese Buddhist dissidents in attacking the Mujahids lent substance to a report that the riots of February 1952 in East Pakistan had been Communist-inspired.)

Belief that the Pakistan Muslims were persecuting Arakanese Buddhists gained ground in Burma to such an extent that some of the government forces, who had been sent to fight the Communists and other rebels in the area, reportedly sold their arms to the Arakanese Buddhists and returned home. A Pakistani countercontention that the Mujahids were simply acting in self-defense further aroused Burmese ire, and the Mujahids' addiction to banditry made it comparatively easy for the Burmese government to discredit this Pakistani excuse. U Pe Khin, Burma's ambassador to Pakistan, in December 1952 described as "utter nonsense" the Mujahid's attempt to give "their nefarious actions high-sounding names."[38] Said he: "They are placing the indigenous Muslims of Burma in an awkward position ... and terrorizing those who do not side with them." Refuting reports that the Arakanese Buddhists were oppressing the Mujahids as Muslims, he asked, "How could a small minority of 2,000 Buddhists persecute them when Muslims in those areas are in an absolute majority?"

No matter what motives the Burmese government might attribute to the Mujahids, it seemed quite incapable of coping with them or with any of the other revolts that were troubling Arakan. Even the troops which it sent to put down the rebels hardly distinguished themselves from the latter as regards looting and kidnapping prosperous Arakanese. Under such circumstances it was only natural that the local demand for separate status should grow apace. Twelve of the 23 Arakanese elected to Parliament in 1951 were advocates of regional autonomy. In opposition to those Arakanese members of Parliament

[37] Reported by the Pakistani embassy at Rangoon to have been killed in East Pakistan in early 1954. Later, Cassim was said to have been arrested by the Pakistan government. Reportedly he had been supplied with arms by some Pakistanis who regarded him as a hero because he provided rice which they badly needed.

[38] Associated Press despatch, Dacca, Pakistan, Dec. 17, 1952.

who adhered to the AFPFL, they formed the Independent Arakanese Parliamentary Group (IAPG, a name later changed to that of the Arakan United National Organization), and moved a resolution in the House of Nationalities that the Arakanese no longer be classified as a minority.[39]

Arakan's marked regionalism and isolation, and its semi-feudal setup, go far to explain the electoral victory of the IAPG at a time when the AFPFL was winning resounding victories elsewhere in Burma. The AFPFL's failure to rebuild Arakan's war-damaged economy or remedy its isolation from the rest of Burma were skillfully utilized by the Parliamentary opposition, which was made up almost exclusively of an Akyab family group consisting of U Kyaw Min and his relatives. Arakanese in general and the people of Akyab in particular were proud of well-educated Kyaw Min, who had made a success in business after retiring from the Indian Civil Service. Although the Kyaw Min group had no positive program, it effectively stressed the facts that rice —Arakan's sole important product—was rotting in godowns for lack of transport, that the local merchant class was being ruined by the government's drive to eliminate middlemen, and that agricultural loans were totally inadequate to the farmers' needs. Politically, too, the AFPFL was vulnerable to the charge that it had appointed often-incompetent party members to high administrative posts formerly held by capable career civil servants. As a result, a majority of the Parliamentarians elected in 1951 were opponents of the AFPFL.

Yet there still exist in Arakan strong forces hostile to the IAPG and potentially favorable to Burma's dominant party. Two of Arakan's three districts, Sandoway and Kyaukpyu, have been traditionally resentful of Akyab's domination and "snobbishness," and consequently are opposed automatically to the IAPG as a manifestation of that Buddhist district's feeling of superiority to the Muslim north. Kyaukpyu would like to have administrative separation from Akyab and to set itself up as a "four-township island."[40] And in Maungdaw and Buthidaung, even those Muslims who do not advocate merging with Pakistan prefer control by the Union government to domination by the leaders of Akyab. Members of the leading family of this area—that of Sultan Ahmed —were elected to Parliament as independents and have disassociated themselves with the Arakan AFPFL, but in practice they support the present administration.

On the economic plane, too, there is suspicion of an IAPG-controlled Arakan. Kyaw Min and his group are prosperous landowners and capitalists, high government officials, and professional men. And the small rice farmer in Akyab, as elsewhere in the division, has good reason to fear that he might be oppressed should the IAPG win its campaign for an autonomous Arakan state.

By 1953, Premier Nu realized that he must personally intervene in Arakan

[39] *The Burman*, Sept. 11, 1952.
[40] Ba Chan, "Report on Arakan," *The Guardian*, November 1953.

to encourage the favorable elements in an otherwise adverse political situation. Touring the country, he preached the virtues of unity and the objectives of his welfare state. On a more practical level, he tried to end the rifts that had caused serious disintegration of the Arakan AFPFL. He also removed political appointees from the posts of deputy commissioner, and promised satisfaction for the population's demand for better economic and social conditions. The government has pledged the replacement of Akyab's dilapidated hospital by a bigger, modern structure, has opened a school at Kyaukpyu, and has initiated a housing program for the division. More important, it has drawn up plans for improvement of the communications system, now confined to a fitful coastal shipping service—recently nationalized—and an expensive airline.

If the AFPFL can soon allay the perennial Arakanese sense of grievance at being neglected and isolated by the central government, the centrifugal tendency represented by the IAPG may be offset and the Union correspondingly strengthened.

THE MALAYS OF SOUTH THAILAND

Muslim Malays—the largest indigenous minority in Thailand—number some half a million and form about 85 percent of the population in the southernmost provinces of Patani, Satul, Yala, and Naradhivas. Their situation is largely analogous to that of many residents of north Arakan. Here are two Muslim peoples, highly conscious of their minority status vis-à-vis the Buddhist majority in the countries where they live, and of the presence of their coreligionists in adjacent states. Among the Islamic peoples across the frontier also live Buddhist minorities, who are closely related, respectively, to the southern Arakanese and northern Thai. In both cases these border areas are the centers of a lucrative transfrontier smuggling trade and the scene of crime and violence that have religious, political and economic aspects. In addition, the Malays of Thailand are strongly conscious of the vanished grandeur and prosperity that marked Patani in the fourteenth century, and have felt cut off from their fellow Malays to the south ever since the area in which they live was made a part of Thailand in 1832.

In the late nineteenth and early twentieth centuries, some British officials in Malaya wanted to reunite the whole Malay community of the peninsula under their rule. London refused to support such a move, however, for this was the period of intense Anglo-French rivalry for control of continental Southeast Asia, and Britain felt that it must maintain a friendly Thailand to serve as buffer against French expansion from Indochina. Failing to get British support, the Malays of Thailand seem to have resigned themselves to the status quo, until the coup d'état of 1932 brought to power at Bangkok a constitutional regime that was soon to cause a change in their lives.

At first the new Thai leaders were careful, as are all who seek the consolidation of freshly acquired power, not to offend the ethnic minorities. When a new civil and commercial code for Buddhist Thailand was drafted in 1934, special exemptions in regard to marriage and inheritance were authorized for the country's Muslim population. But in the wave of chauvinistic nationalism that swept the country after Pibul became premier in 1938, the Malay Muslims were subjected to increasing pressures. Efforts to Siamize them included compelling them to adopt Thai dress, language, and customs, and in 1941 their exemption from the enforcement of Buddhist law relating to marriage and inheritance was withdrawn despite their strong objections. During the war, the Japanese presented the northern states of Malaya to Thailand to administer, but after the defeat of Japan the Bangkok government hastily handed its ill-gotten gains back to the British, and the Muslim Malays were once again divided by a political frontier.

The replacement of Pibul by a Free Thai government, beginning in July 1944, was followed by a relaxation of some of the most objectionable features of his long dictatorship. And when the new Thai constitution was promulgated in June 1946, the prewar exemptions were restored for Muslims as substantiation of its guaranty of religious freedom. The administration received counsel on Malay Muslim affairs from the Islamic adviser (the Chularajmontri), a Central Islamic Committee, and provincial Muslim subcommittees. But Bangkok was a long way from the southern provinces and exercised little control over the Thai officials stationed there. Moreover, those provinces bordered on Malaya where, for the first time, a nationalist movement had come into being. And the Malay nationalists developed an irredentist concern for their fellow Muslims in Thailand.

At the same time the prevailing food shortage in Malaya stimulated a vast rice-smuggling traffic across the frontier, which led to such a growth of crime and to such venality on the part of the local Thai administrators, police, and armed forces that the whole area began to suffer not only insecurity but also a shortage of rice and a marked rise in the cost of living. Geographical and political barriers did not coincide there, and the terrain of south Thailand proved to be an ideal place of refuge for bandits and political dissidents who were able to get shelter and supplies and to plan fresh forays into Malaya. To add to the confusion, a group of Indians—chiefly Sikhs—who had been active in the wartime Indian Independence Leagues found the south Thai rail center of Haad Yai a good place in which to hide and to continue working for the freedom of India in concert with the Communist parties of their homeland and of China.

As early as the spring of 1946, British army officers asked the Thai to help them in cleaning up the whole area. But the Bangkok government still resented the harsh terms of the Anglo-Thai treaty signed the preceding January 1, its officials were making too much money in the southern provinces, and in any case it was felt that police operations in the area would be excessively costly and difficult. They were even less inclined to co-operate with the British when it became apparent that there was growing support in Malaya for re-uniting the Thai Malay provinces with that country. A movement to liberate fellow Muslims from the Thai Buddhist "yoke" developed in Kelantan, where the son of Patani's last raja lived in exile. He claimed that he received daily complaints from his "subjects" of persecution by corrupt and oppressive Thai officials.[41] Specifically they complained of being forced to worship idols (probably Buddha images), being assigned mosque officials not of their own choosing, and being ruled by Buddhist, not Koranic, law—despite Bangkok's pledges to the contrary.

The grievances voiced by Thai Malays would probably never have moved the Thai government to action had it not been for the fear that Britain might use them as an excuse to annex the southern provinces. King Ananda led off the appeasement move in May 1946 by donating 20,000 baht to promote Is-lamic religious and educational welfare there.[42] At about the same time an official delegation headed by the Minister of Justice and composed of Malay leaders from Bangkok was sent to investigate local complaints on the spot. Im-provements in their status were promised in consequence, but the Malays re-mained skeptical. Possibly nothing further would have been heard of this in-vestigation had it not been for the arrest, on July 25, of two former members of the National Assembly by the Thai police at Yala. It was alleged that these men were plotting to encourage a separatist movement in the south, with the aid of sympathizers in Kelantan.

A faint echo of the Thai Malays' grievances was heard from their counter-parts in Kedah—the 15,000 or so Buddhist Thai[43] living in that Muslim state of Malaya. Feeling themselves discriminated against by the Kedah authorities, this small minority asked for the appointment of a Thai official who would look after their interests.[44] Unfortunately this group had acquired a bad repu-tation during the war when certain of its members had joined with the Thai army deserters to form robber bands that raided across the border. However, there was another element among them which had organized an anti-Japanese guerrilla unit, to whose valor a British officer of Force 136 has paid tribute.[45] It was this latter, law-abiding element which early in 1947 formed itself into a Kedah-Siamese Association, whose aim was to give physical and moral help to the wayward and destitute members of its community. Nothing further was heard of the Thai in Kedah until August 1949, when a Malay member of the State Council urged the appointment of a Thai affairs officer to promote the welfare of that impoverished, disease-ridden, and neglected community.[46]

41 *Straits Times*, Feb. 5, 1947.   42 *Democracy*, Bangkok, May 23, 1946.
43 Called Samsams or Ulu Siamese.   44 *Straits Times*, Jan. 7, 1947.
45 *Bangkok Post*, Jan. 8, 1947.   46 *Ibid.*, Aug. 17, 1949.

In March 1953 the sultan of Kedah announced a recrudescence of banditry among his Thai subjects.[47] Surprisingly enough, the Bangkok authorities seem not to have concerned themselves, either at this time or previously, regarding conditions among their compatriots living in Kedah.

As to the Malays in south Thailand, their status continued to deteriorate. Ferment in this dissident area increased in the spring of 1948 after the Communist revolt broke out in Malaya and after Pibul had again become premier of Thailand. A coup d'état at Bangkok in November 1947, which paved the way for Pibul's return to power five months later, had immediate repercussions in south Thailand. The Chularajmontri, who was identified with the ousted government, fled to Singapore, leaving his community with no official head. Into this void stepped Haji Sulong, a local leader of the Malay Muslims. To the new administration he submitted a petition for the following concessions: the appointment of a high commissioner to govern the southern provinces, with powers similar to those of a mufti; complete religious freedom; the use of Malay along with Thai as the region's official language; the selection of Muslims to fill 80 percent of the area's administrative posts; and the transfer to Islamic organizations of authority over religious affairs, including the power to assess special taxes, such as the zakat, or religious tithe.

Haji Sulong and four of his followers were soon arrested, in January 1948, and charged with treason. These arrests touched off the simmering discontent in south Thailand, and the flames were allegedly fanned by agitators from Kelantan. In May a revolt broke out in Naradhivas province, but it was so poorly organized that the Thai police had no difficulty in crushing it. Its suppression, however, cost many lives—variously estimated from tens to hundreds—and resulted in the flight of some 2,000 persons to Malaya. This exodus seems to have made the Bangkok authorities aware of the ominous nature of the situation, for they sent another committee to investigate and, in June, transferred the scene of the Sulong trial to Nakorn Srithammaraj. Months passed before the committee made its report and, in the meantime, members of Parliament from the area periodically reminded the government that their constituents still suffered from rice shortages and maladministration. The Malay press across the border agitated for the incorporation of the four Thai Malay provinces into the Federation of Malaya, which came into being in February 1948. And the Patani Muslims petitioned Britain to withhold recognition of the new government in Bangkok pending redress of their grievances.

Premier Attlee, who was extremely eager to increase Thai rice exports, was not willing to risk offending whatever government ruled Thailand, and he contented himself with "making it understood in Bangkok that Whitehall expects a just solution of Patani's case."[48] Naturally this did not satisfy either

---

[47] *Ibid.*, Mar. 7, 1953.
[48] B. Whittingham-Jones, "Patani Appeals to UNO," *Eastern World,* April 1948.

the Malays of Thailand or those of Malaya, and at Singapore there was formed an organization called the GAMPAR, which aimed at helping the Thai Malays to break away and join the Federation of Malaya.[49] Discovery of the existence of this organization, through a raid by the Singapore police in November 1948, frightened the moderate Malays among Malaya's nationalists and embarrassed the British, who hastily told Bangkok that they considered the whole movement illegal. As an unfortunate by-product, it provoked reprisals by the Thai police on the Malays of the southern provinces, who protested bitterly that their movement for autonomy was authentically indigenous and had not been "made in Malaya."[50]

In the meantime, progress had been made toward closer Thai-British co-operation in policing the border area, and, in January 1949, Songkhla was the scene of the first major postwar meeting between high-ranking British and Thai officials to draw up a plan for joint action. It was to the Thais' interest to win British co-operation in checking Malayan support for the secessionist movement in the south and in suppressing the area's smugglers and terrorists. In turn, the British now needed Bangkok's help in preventing Communist insurgents from escaping to immunity in south Thailand; moreover, their dependence on Thai rice to feed Malaya's population had not diminished.

In consequence of their mutual needs, Anglo-Thai co-operation in the region increased, but reports as to its effectiveness differed. Some British claimed that the indolent and venal Thai police, poorly paid and equipped, were doing virtually nothing to stop the insurgents from crossing the border or smuggling arms and provisions to their companions in Malaya. Others more optimistically pointed out that there had been at least some reduction in rice smuggling and that south Thailand no longer served as a major training ground and refuge for Malaya's bandits. (A renewal of bandit Communist activity and of the movement of contraband in 1953 somewhat modified this hopeful viewpoint.) In any case, improved co-operation at high levels and between the Malayan and Thai forces in the frontier area helped to temper the resentment often expressed in the Malayan press in regard to the high prices Thailand was charging for its rice and the indulgence with which this former wartime ally of the Japanese was being treated. And on the Thai side, joint action with the British was used by the government to justify asking for huge appropriations for military and police units stationed in the southern provinces, whose presence there certainly served to quell the local autonomy movement.

Late in February 1949, the long-drawn-out trial of Haji Sulong and his fellow defendants ended in a fairly mild sentence. The court dismissed charges that they had plotted against the government and had collected funds for a secessionist movement, but it sentenced them to three years' imprison-

[49] *Bangkok Post*, Dec. 13, 18, 1948.   [50] *Ibid.*, Dec. 14, 1948.

ment for libeling the government in pamphlets they had distributed to the local population. Shortly afterward, the government issued a communiqué refuting allegations of its harsh treatment of Thai Malays and listing the reforms which, it claimed, were being implemented according to the recommendations made by the investigating committee in 1948.[51] These reforms included greater care in the selection of administrative officials, with preference being given to candidates versed in Muslim law and culture; replacement of Buddhist by Muslim holidays for government offices; permission to Malay officials to wear their national dress; subsidies for the building and upkeep of mosques; the application of Islamic law in regard to marriage and inheritance; provision in schools for the teaching of Malay on the same basis as Thai; the establishment of a Malay college at Bangkok; and special concessions regarding the religious requirements of Malays conscripted for military service. It also stressed that a new Islamic adviser had been appointed and that Thailand's newest constitution granted complete freedom to minorities.

Thai Malays, however, were quick to note the omissions in this impressive list. They pointed out that Sulong and his companions were still in prison; that Muslim marriages still had to be registered with the civil rather than with the religious authorities; and that the proposed Muslim college should be located not in Bangkok but in the south. And as the time went on they continued to complain that such concessions as had been made on paper were never implemented—the number of Malay officials had not grown perceptibly, political and religious liberties were far from complete, and in brief, that they were no nearer autonomy than they had been before. The Thai countered by claiming that they possessed evidence of Communist support for the secessionists on both sides of the frontier, and the Thai governor of Yala told the press that Kelantan Malays were again stirring up unrest among their coreligionists in south Thailand.[52]

To offset reports circulating in Malaya about the harsh treatment of the Malays by the Thai police, the Bangkok government invited six Malayan journalists to visit the southern provinces and investigate the situation for themselves. As it turned out, this gesture backfired, for the journalists upon their return to Malaya claimed that though they had been closely shadowed by the Thai police they had seen evidence of both active and passive Malay unrest in south Thailand. On the active side, they said that preparations for a mass revolt were being more carefully made than they had been in 1948, and that its objective was restoration of the kingdom of Patani under its own ruler. As to passive resistance, they found the local Malays continuing to wear their national dress and refusing to learn the Thai language. However, some of the reporters admitted that there were very few Thai Malays qualified to

---

51 "Siam and Her Muslim Population," *Eastern World*, April 1949.
52 Reuter despatch, Bangkok, Oct. 16, 1949.

occupy high administrative posts, and that economic conditions in south Thailand—particularly as regarded wages and food—were generally better than those in northern Malaya. One journalist even went so far as to say that some Thai officials had effected a genuine improvement in their relations with the local Malays, and that reports of harsh treatment had been exaggerated in Malaya.[53]

Since that episode the situation has changed little, to all outward appearances. From time to time, members of Parliament from the southern provinces, supported by the Democrat (opposition) Party, have unsuccessfully introduced bills to grant amnesty to Malay political prisoners and to propose administrative reforms for the area. Among the latter was the establishment of an elected Muslim Assembly as a policy-making body, and the appointment of a Malay Council for implementation of its directives. (Inhabitants of an area served by four mosques were to elect one assemblyman.) Sponsors of these reforms pointed to the purely advisory nature of existing Islamic bodies and to the lack of any legitimate and effective machinery whereby Malay aspirations and grievances could be made known to the central government. Early in 1951, legislation embodying these proposals appeared to have a good chance of receiving a favorable vote in the Thai Parliament. But at the last moment the Chularajmontri expressed his disapproval, for an amendment tacked on to the original bill limited his term of office—currently a lifetime job—to six years.[54]

In the autumn of 1953, worsening economic conditions in south Thailand, as a result of the fall in world tin and rubber prices, once more attracted the fitful attention of Bangkok's legislators to that area.[55] Rice smuggling, it was reported, had revived along the Malayan border, and the local people's chronic suffering from the shortage and high price of rice was aggravated by growing unemployment among rubber tappers and tin miners. Among the various proposals made by national assemblymen, to which the Cabinet promised to give consideration, were an improvement in the rice-control system and the transportation network, and an increase in the area available for paddy cultivation. It is to be noted that nothing was suggested at the time about improving other than the economic aspects of life for the Thai Malays.

Early in 1954, Police General Phao was reported to have expressed a wish that more autonomy be given to the Thai Muslims.[56] But nothing concrete has yet materialized from this pious hope, for Bangkok politicians claim that giving special privileges to one minority group would necessarily entail satisfying similar demands from other minorities. In the meantime, the rice monopoly held by semiofficial "changwad companies" in the south, combined with increased smuggling of rice over the Malayan border and with the

[53] Bangkok Post, Mar. 6, 1949.
[55] Ibid., Sept. 10, 1953.
[54] Ibid., May 23, 1951.
[56] Bangkok Post, Apr. 8, 1954.

activities of Chinese Communist refugees from Malaya, continues to make the region a minor running sore in Southeast Asia.

THE AMBONESE

For centuries the Moluccas were famous as the center of the world spice trade, and in the seventeenth century Amboina was the scene of intense rivalry between the Dutch and British for control of this island group. The Dutch triumphed and the Moluccas came administratively to be a part of what was called the Great East in the prewar administration of the Netherlands East Indies.

The postwar position of the Ambonese is strikingly parallel to that of the Karens in Burma. Large elements in both communities are Christian, are loyal to their European masters, and have been the backbone of the latter's native armed forces. And recently both peoples have revolted against the newly established national governments, out of fear for their future status and for their cultural domination by the majority community. To an unknown extent the Karen and Ambonese revolts have been encouraged by European adventurers.

The South Moluccas were represented by four delegates at the conference convened by Governor General van Mook at Malino, Celebes, in July 1946 to consider the future status of the eastern islands of the Indies. By a resolution taken at this conference, the Moluccas were to form part of East Indonesia in the federal framework proposed by Dr. van Mook. Captain Julius Tahja from the South Moluccas was selected as one of seven delegates chosen to prepare proposals for constitutional reforms in the newly constructed area. The South Moluccas offered virtually a *tabula rasa* for any administrative changes, for they lacked feudal rulers and had been under direct Dutch administration, and their precolonial culture had been more completely obliterated than that of almost any other area in the archipelago.[57] During the next few years, the Dutch transferred some authority to its directly elected People's Council.[58]

At the Round Table Conference held at The Hague in the summer of 1949 to decide on the sovereignty of the Indies, the South Moluccas were represented by Drs. Nikijuluw and Warouw. These two men joined forces with Dr. Gerbrandy, leader of the die-hard Dutch colonialists, to oppose the transfer of sovereignty.[59] Despite such opposition, Indonesia became independent in December 1949, and it soon became apparent that a unitary state would shortly replace the federal structure (Republic of the United States of Indonesia) initially set up.

[57] George McT. Kahin, *Nationalism and Revolution in Indonesia* (Cornell University Press, 1952), p. 458.
[58] George McT. Kahin, "Indirect Rule in East Indonesia," *Pacific Affairs*, September 1949.
[59] *Report on Indonesia*, May 12, 1950.

East Indonesia contained most of the indigenous elements that opposed such a merger. Dr. Soumokil, its Minister of Justice, soon showed his hand by arresting some strong advocates in Celebes of union with the Republic. Also in this area were stationed most of the KNIL (troops of the former colonial government), who felt a growing concern for their status under Javanese domination, particularly after they learned that some hundreds of former Republican troops were soon to be sent to Makassar. There is some evidence, according to George Kahin,[60] that Soumokil and a few of his colleagues helped convince the KNIL men that they must act before the Republicans landed. At all events, the KNIL revolted early in April 1950, seized Makassar, and unsuccessfully opposed the Republican landing.

Soumokil fled to Amboina, the Republicans claim, in a Dutch military plane. There he again played upon the local KNIL fears for the future—this time with greater success, for he had a more fertile field in which to operate. The Ambonese were predominantly Christian and feared Javanese Muslim aggressiveness; and a great many of them were dependents of KNIL personnel, past and present, and foresaw a reduction in their incomes. Under the Dutch they had elected their own council, and it was this body which proclaimed a Republic of the South Moluccas on April 25, 1950. In its proclamation, the Council said that it had set up the South Moluccas Republic because the merging of East Indonesia into the unitary Indonesian Republic was contrary to the terms of the Hague Agreement. The newborn "state" covered 314 square miles and included the islands of Amboina, Buri, Ceram, Haruku, and Saprua; its most populous island was Amboina, whose inhabitants numbered between 70,000 and 80,000. A former Dutch Resident, J. Manuhutu, was named President of the new republic; Dr. Manusama, Defense Minister; A. Wairusal, of the former South Moluccas Council, Premier; and Dr. Soumokil, Minister of Foreign Affairs.

Despite its civilian façade, the government of the South Moluccas Republic was from the outset a military one. Small as was the area involved, its control by hostile military elements could not be tolerated by the Djakarta authorities, for the South Moluccas held a strategic position as a buffer between the main islands of Indonesia and the disputed territory of Irian (Western New Guinea). At once they dispatched Dr. Leimena, a Cabinet minister who was himself an Ambonese Christian, to negotiate a settlement with the rebels. Arriving at Amboina, he invited the local political leaders aboard his ship for a discussion of the situation. They refused to accept unless he gave a prior pledge that the sovereignty of the new republic would be respected. Naturally Leimena could not comply, and he returned to Java on May 4. A few days later, Vice-President Hatta broadcast an appeal to the people of East Indonesia

[60] *Nationalism and Revolution in Indonesia*, p. 457.

to quell the "power-hungry and military factions" creating unrest in the Moluccas.[61]

Propaganda-wise, the Indonesians wasted no time in holding the Dutch responsible for the Moluccas revolt. A communiqué of May 23 from the Ministry of Information stated that "armed units falling under the responsibility of the Netherlands government have forced some politicians to announce the proclamation of the so-called South Moluccas Republic, and they consequently made arrests and committed killings." Dr. Soumokil was identified as the key man in the situation, and it was stressed that he had recently become a naturalized Dutchman. Since the Netherlands army command was still technically in charge of the KNIL, the Indonesians demanded a clear-cut denunciation by the Dutch of the Moluccan rebels, and at the same time the right to settle the whole affair without Netherlands interference.[62]

The Dutch government was obviously in a dilemma. To begin with, it had to take into account public opinion in Holland, which favored aid to the loyal Christian Ambonese lest they suffer reprisals at the hands of the Indonesians.[63] There was also a risk that Indonesian repression of the revolt might cause the 12,000 or so Ambonese troops that were awaiting repatriation in various parts of the archipelago to follow their compatriots' lead and rise up against the Indonesian Republic. Further, there was a growing number of Ambonese in Holland[64] who were not insensible to the events transpiring in their home island. Following a cabled plea for intervention sent to the United Nations by Dr. Nikijuluw, president of the South Moluccas Association in the Netherlands, the agitation conducted by certain Ambonese in Holland grew so intense that, on June 30, 1951, the Dutch had to threaten some of their leaders with deportation.[65]

Reluctant as they were to take any decisive stand, the Dutch were finally compelled to take action in the fall of 1950, for the Indonesians, after six months of futile negotiations, had decided that the revolt must be put down by force. At first the Netherlands tried unsuccessfully through diplomatic channels and through the United Nations to dissuade Djakarta from sending an expeditionary force to Amboina. Then Premier Drees departed for the first time from the Dutch government's policy of nonintervention by cabling an appeal to Indonesia's prime minister, Natsir, to continue seeking a peaceful settlement of the revolt.[66] At this juncture, also, the United Nations Commission for Indonesia offered its services of mediation. Indonesia, however, turned down both proposals on the ground that the Amboina affair was not a

---

[61] *Report on Indonesia,* May 12, 1950.
[62] *Ibid.,* July 18, 1950.
[63] *Christian Science Monitor,* Oct. 4, 1950.
[64] As of April 1951, there were 12,500 living in camps scattered throughout the Netherlands.
[65] Reuter despatch, The Hague, June 21, 1951.
[66] *Christian Science Monitor,* Oct. 4, 1950.

dispute subject to international settlement since it had occurred after the formal transfer of sovereignty.

The landing of Indonesian troops on Amboina caused swift collapse of the civilian government of the South Moluccas Republic, though guerrilla resistance continued for some time. Some of its "ministers" fled to New Guinea, but Soumokil transferred himself and his "government" to the island of Ceram. Their precipitate departure betrayed a lack of popular support for the so-called South Moluccas Republic. According to Indonesian sources, only some 10,000, or less than one-eighth of the Ambonese, backed the revolt,[67] and there seems to have been no interest at all in it throughout the other Moluccan islands. Its failure appears to be traceable mainly to the fact that the foreign aid promised by Soumokil did not materialize.

Such encouragement as the revolt received from outside sources seems to have been on a minor and personal scale. Most Indonesians believe that certain Dutch army officers gave aid to the KNIL rebels. A free-lance Dutch journalist, Hazelhoff, who made an abortive attempt to fly to Amboina from Manila, was thought to be backed by important interests in Holland in much the same way that the British newspaperman, Campbell, who tried to help the Karen revolt in Burma, operated with funds allegedly supplied by London financiers. Hazelhoff later turned up in Washington, where his statement to the effect that the South Moluccas Republic had offered sea and air bases to the United States was officially denied on February 20, 1951. Ambonese expatriates themselves have been more persistent if equally unsuccessful. By November 1950 Dr. Nikijuluw had reached New York, where he again failed in his effort to bring about United Nations intervention, even though three months later he offered "2,000 highly trained Ambonese jungle troops" for combat in Korea.[68] And as recently as March 1952, another Ambonese claimed in Australia that the South Moluccas Republican forces were still fighting patriotically for the independence of their state.[69]

In Amboina itself, the back of the revolt was broken by late November 1950 at the cost of some 350 casualties to the Indonesian troops. After two more months, those rebels who had not either surrendered or been captured fled to Ceram. In April 1951, Indonesian troops followed them to that island and a prolonged and virtually unreported jungle war ensued. By this time, however, the revolt had become only a minor military problem. Its political importance, too, had all but evaporated, and the Indonesians were attacking its socioeconomic aspects in an enlightened fashion under the able leadership of a new governor of the Moluccas, Dr. J. Latuharhary.[70]

[67] *Report on Indonesia,* July 31, 1952.   [68] *New York Herald Tribune,* Feb. 4, 1951.
[69] Reuter despatch, Mar. 23, 1952.
[70] Dr. Latuharhary had been named to fill that office immediately after the Japanese surrender, but had been unable to take up his post because of the Dutch reoccupation of the Moluccas.

As early as November 14, 1950, Dr. Latuharhary announced that 10 million rupiahs worth of food, clothing, and medicines would be rushed from Djakarta to the war-weary, sick, and undernourished Ambonese. The lenient treatment of prisoners and the use of former rebels for the economic rehabilitation of the South Moluccas also contributed greatly to his success. Then, in mid-November, Premier Natsir visited the island to undertake the more difficult task of convincing the Ambonese that they would be welcomed as equals within the Indonesian community. Throughout 1951 other high-ranking Indonesian officials, including President Sukarno, visited the South Moluccas, and upon their return to Java they all issued glowing accounts of the physical and spiritual progress being made there. According to Dr. Rum, Christians and Muslims in Amboina were working amicably together on rehabilitation projects,[71] and Dr. Latuharhary reported the co-operation between civilian and military authorities in the Moluccas to be "excellent."[72] The governor's economic plan for the islands has already been implemented to the extent of improved communications between them and the rest of Indonesia, and the construction of six copra co-operatives. Credit should also be given to Colonel Sukawati, commander on Ceram, who initiated the cultivation of certain food crops there and who reportedly turned down a diplomatic post to continue his reconstruction work on the island.

Official Indonesian reports naturally underplayed the importance of the revolt in Amboina and dwelt chiefly on the government's moves to suppress it. On the other hand, there is no reliable evidence that might refute the official version. The revolt certainly contributed to a further deterioration in Dutch-Indonesian relations, but the main bone of contention between Djakarta and The Hague has been and still is New Guinea. The main interest of this episode for the student of Southeast Asian minorities lies in the eventual success or failure of this first attempt by independent Indonesia to integrate within its framework a community which had taken up arms in the belief that it was defending its culture and economy from domination by fellow Asians. That these fears have not been wholly allayed as yet is indicated by a report made in mid-1953 to the effect that "it is in Ambon, where Christians seem most successfully to have made their peace with their Muslim neighbors, that the greatest fear of Indonesia's becoming a Muslim state prevails."[73] Indeed, a recrudescence of Ambonese agitation may be expected whenever Islamic extremists threaten the secular nature of the Republic, or whenever Dutch-Indonesian relations undergo a drastic change.

[71] *Report on Indonesia*, Mar. 17, 1951.   [72] *Ibid.*, May 25, 1951.

[73] Winburn T. Thomas, "The Protestant Movement in Indonesia," *International Review of Missions*, July 1953.

Chapter Four

BUDDHISTS VS. BUDDHISTS

CAMBODIA

FRENCH-EDUCATED King Norodom Sihanouk ascended the Khmer throne eight months before the war broke out in the Pacific. At the age of nineteen, the last of Cambodia's absolute monarchs came to rule over a country about 181,000 square kilometers in area and sparsely settled by 3½ million people, including sizable Chinese and Vietnamese minorities. The great majority of his subjects are illiterate peasants living in scattered villages; there is virtually no indigenous middle class; and the handful of educated Khmers at the apex of this pyramid form the country's civil service. Centuries ago, Cambodia was a great military and artistic force in Southeast Asia, but its power and territory were progressively whittled away by the rising strength of Thailand to the west and of Viet Nam to the east until the French established a protectorate over the country in 1864. Safeguarded from further incursions on their flanks, steeped in memories of their glorious past, and consoled by the Hinayana Buddhism that was their faith, the gentle, artistic, and indolent Khmers long seemed content to leave political authority in the hands of their revered king and the French.

The revival of Thailand's claims to Khmer territory in the late 1930's culminated in the loss to that country of the Cambodian provinces of Battambang and Siemréap in 1941. France, weakened by her defeat in Europe, was powerless to prevent Japan from mediating the border dispute in Thailand's favor. The shock of this amputation stirred Cambodian intellectuals to political consciousness for the first time, and in 1942 this vague unrest materialized in a demonstration by some of the country's 70,000 Buddhist monks before the offices of the French Resident-Superior at Pnom-Penh. The man who had persuaded the traditionally apolitical monks to make this remarkable and isolated gesture was Son ngoc Thanh, son of a Vietnamese father and a Khmer mother, who had been brought up in Cochin China. A born orator, he was to find great scope for his talents as a political agitator during the next decade.

Cambodia suffered economically little during the war. The Allies bombed Pnom-Penh only once, and Japanese requisitioning of rice, livestock, and laborers was minimal compared with their seizures in other countries of Southeast Asia.[1] Though, in common with their neighbors, the Cambodians

[1] *Christian Science Monitor*, Feb. 4, 1946.

lost their export markets for rubber and surplus foodstuffs, most of them lived on much the same primitive level as before and were governed by the same Cambodian and French officials. It was not until the Japanese coup of March 9, 1945, which eliminated the French, that any marked change occurred. At that time a transformation did take place at the top level which was to have its repercussions in the postwar years.

On March 10, 1945, Japanese troops entered Pnom-Penh, and three days later the king declared void the treaties which had established the French protectorate and proclaimed his country independent. On March 20 a new cabinet was formed, to which was added some days later a Ministry of Foreign Affairs, the first in Cambodia's history. This portfolio was entrusted to none other than Son ngoc Thanh. After the failure of the 1942 demonstration, Thanh had fled to Bangkok, where the Japanese ambassador first gave him shelter and then sent him to Tokyo for indoctrination in Japan's program for the Greater East Asia Co-prosperity Sphere. Thanh served in the Japanese army, rising to the rank of captain, and was trained for the role the Japanese had destined him to play in Cambodia. On the eve of V-J Day, Thanh was named by the king Prime Minister, a post which had been abolished at the time King Norodom was crowned.

For the next two months little news came out of Cambodia, and developments there were overshadowed by the drama of Viet Nam. In September, the Cambodian Defense Minister, Kim Thit, came to Saigon, where he asked that French troops be sent to Pnom-Penh to end the growing unrest there. On October 9 a mixed force of French, British, and Indian troops obligingly occupied the Cambodian capital. They met with little resistance; only two French soldiers were killed, one of them in a brawl. Thanh lacked the forces to oppose the French reoccupation, and he made the tactical error of arming Vietnamese plantation workers and of letting them fly the Vietnam Republic's flag in Pnom-Penh.[2] Half-Vietnamese himself, Thanh seems not to have appreciated the chilling effect that this apparent surrender of Cambodia to its eastern neighbor would have upon the local people. On October 15, Thanh himself was captured and sent to Saigon, where he was tried by a military court on charges of high treason and sentenced to twenty years' forced labor. Later this was commuted to residence in France, where he was able to continue his law studies at the University of Poitiers, from which he received a degree in 1950.

King Norodom, who had been away from Pnom-Penh when the French troops arrived, returned to his capital on October 16. At once he made an official declaration promising co-operation with and loyalty to France, in much the same terms as he had made eloquent pledges to the Japanese a few months earlier. The swiftness with which these changes were effected caused

[2] P. Christian, "Son ngoc Thanh," *Indochine—Sud-est Asiatique,* October 1952.

some unrest, as was evidenced by a laborers' strike at Pnom-Penh on October 25. But this was short-lived, and two days later the king issued another proclamation to reassure his people that he had not forgotten their aspirations for independence and that relations with France would soon be placed on a new and more satisfactory basis.[3] In a conciliatory gesture to the rival branch of the royal family, he offered the premiership to his uncle, Prince Monireth,[4] and the latter at once opened negotiations with the French at Saigon.

On November 6, Prince Monireth returned to Pnom-Penh with French proposals—notably, one providing for autonomy for Cambodia within the French Union—that were acceptable to the king, and these were embodied in a modus vivendi signed in January 1946.[5] At the same time, the king and the French found themselves in complete agreement as regards working for the return of the provinces lost to Thailand during the war. From this time on, until 1953, the king's loyalty was above French reproach, and it was the single most important factor in smoothing over the transition period. By the fall of 1945, the king had apparently reached the conclusion that it was better for Cambodia to evolve toward autonomy under French protection than to risk falling victim to Thai irredentism or Vietnamese imperialism.

On March 7, 1946, France and Cambodia signed a provisional agreement whereby the latter was given control over specified internal affairs and the former retained direction of Cambodia's foreign policy and of matters affecting the whole Indochinese federation. Cambodian ministers and provincial governors were to have French political and technical advisers, but the number of French officials in the country was reduced from the prewar figure of 506 and they were to have no executive powers. France was favorably disposed toward the king's plan to transform the absolute monarchy into a British-type constitutional monarchy.

During an official visit to Saigon in mid-March, the king made specific proposals to French officials, which included the creation of a unicameral legislative assembly that would be elected by universal manhood suffrage.[6] Cambodia's ten-year plan for economic development, which the war had nipped in the bud, was to be implemented, and new projects were to be drawn up by a joint Franco-Cambodian committee that would encourage indigenous businessmen to replace the Chinese. Cambodia was not only willing but eager to have French technicians and capital help develop the country, and to have more Cambodians educated in France.[7] And the amity of Franco-Cambodian

[3] Radio Saigon, Oct. 27, 1945.

[4] In 1939 this prince, the elder son of King Sisowath, had been passed over in the royal succession by the French, allegedly because of his pronounced pro-Thai sympathies.

[5] A few days after the British announced their intention of withdrawing from southern Indochina in January 1946, the French hastily negotiated this modus vivendi in preparation for an unexpectedly sudden assumption of control over Cambodia. See Roger Lévy, L'Indochine et Ses Traités (Paris, 1946), p. 14.   [6] Radio Saigon, Mar. 21, 1946.

[7] Interview with Prince Monireth, L'Informateur Colonial, June 16, 1946.

relations reached honeymoon level, in December 1946, when France finally succeeded in getting the Thai to return Cambodia's "lost provinces."

Thailand and Cambodia

Thailand did not relinquish the border provinces until it had exhausted every possibility of gaining international support for their retention. To the Thai, Battambang and Siemréap were theirs by historical right and by the verdict of arms, and they still resented the French pressure exercised in the late nineteenth and early twentieth centuries to cede them. Furthermore, Khuang Aphaiwong, twice premier of Thailand, possessed vast holdings in Battambang, where his family had long been feudal lords. And Pridi Banomyong, Thailand's elder statesman and outstanding leader at that time, cherished visions of a Greater Thailand that would some day include Cambodia and Laos. But the Western Powers would not condone the wartime acquisition of territory through Japanese intervention, and a veto by France would thwart Thailand's ambition to join the United Nations. So Thai leaders reluctantly gave up the border provinces, though they did not wholly renounce their dream of hegemony.

For its part, Cambodia has not been able to forget its historical humiliation at the hands of the Thai, or more recent Thai efforts to Siamize the border provinces during the few years they were under Thailand's control. Although the Thai did much to improve the educational situation in those provinces, they made blunders in replacing Cambodian officials by their own administrators and in trying to impose their own culture on the local people.[8] Nevertheless, Bangkok has also been a religious center for Cambodian Buddhists, and would have been Cambodia's economic outlet had not political barriers intervened. Indeed, the very lack of geographical barriers between the two countries has made Thailand a logical refuge for Cambodian dissidents, and the welcome they have received there has been warm in proportion as Franco-Thai relations have been cool.

In 1940, on the eve of hostilities in the border area, a retired Cambodian official named Pock Khun moved to Bangkok, where he organized a movement among other Khmer *émigrés* for liberation of the homeland. This group, called the Khmer Issarak (Free Cambodians), received a certain degree of official recognition there after the Free Thai came to power at Bangkok in 1944. After Son ngoc Thanh was arrested in October 1945, some of his followers fled to Bangkok where they swelled the ranks of the Khmer Issarak, while another group sought refuge in Cochin China. Since most of the Issarak in Bangkok were from the disputed provinces, they received active support from Pridi. And settlement of the border dispute with France did not put an end to this friendly and protective attitude, though it did bring about a reorganiza-

[8] *Bangkok Post,* Nov. 2, 1946.

tion of the movement in which Pock Khun was replaced by new leaders—Keo Tak, Dap Chhuon, Chantarangsey, Houl, Chanto-Tres, and Leav Kéomoni. In September 1947 this group, headed by Houl, was recognized by Thailand as the "Free Cambodian Government." Thanks to the facilities placed at their disposal, the Issarak were able to buy firearms, raise money, and even publish a newspaper in Bangkok. They went so far as to carry out raids deep into Cambodian territory, in which the French claimed Thai soldiers were involved. Some of these raids were fairly successful from a military standpoint, but both in Bangkok and in the Cambodian areas where the Issarak operated, their leaders soon split up because of personal jealousies. And the tinge of banditry which they quickly acquired made them unpopular with their compatriots, who began to doubt the purity of the Issarak's patriotic motives.

The coup d'état at Bangkok in November 1947, which ousted the pro-Pridi government, dealt a severe blow to the Khmer Issarak movement in Thailand. The training camps which it had established there had to be abandoned, and their trainees dispersed along the Cambodian frontier. The new Thai government clamped down on the Issarak, and their propaganda, purchase of arms, and collection of funds had to be carried on clandestinely. After Pibul returned to power in April 1948, Houl himself was arrested, on the charge of having illegally sold an automobile![9] During the same period, negotiations were going on between eight former Issaraks, including Pock Khun, and the French which aimed at bringing back the Bangkok dissidents into the orthodox fold.[10] For all practical purposes, the Khmer Issarak movement in Thailand could be written off, at least for the next two years.

The Viet Minh and Cambodia

Even more than in the case of Thailand, Cambodia's postwar relations with the Vietnamese were not only conditioned by memories of past aggression but troubled by the presence of a Vietnamese minority in Cambodia and of a Cambodian minority in Viet Nam.

To the small Vietnamese colony in Cambodia, which dat ᷄ from the days when the empire of Annam claimed suzerain rights over that country, the French had added many more. Some of the newcomers had simply entered in the French wake to participate in the economic development that followed establishment of the French protectorate, while others had been brought in by the French to help administer a country which lacked the requisite number of qualified officials. As of 1944, there were about 250,000 Vietnamese living in Cambodia, of whom 10 percent resided in Pnom-Penh. During the war, the Japanese—perhaps for the same reasons as the French and also because their

9 *Bulletin de la France d'Outre-Mer*, May 1948.
10 *Indochine Française*, October 1947.

general policy was to foment intercommunal discord—favored this Vietnamese minority and even encouraged them to print the first Vietnamese-lan-
guage newspaper ever to appear in the Khmer capital. There is no doubt but
that these Vietnamese were among the main supporters of Son ngoc Thanh,
and after his arrest thousands of them fled from Pnom-Penh in fear of French
reprisals.[11]

Fleeing in company with these Vietnamese were about 2,000 Cambodians,
who belonged to a militia known as the Green Shirts, which had been organized in June 1945 by the Japanese as the nucleus for a future Cambodian
army. According to the Viet Minh radio at Hanoi on November 7, these
Vietnamese and Cambodian refugees—

assembled at Triton where they organized an overwhelming demonstration, in
the course of which a Committee of Independent Cambodia was formed under
the direction of the former Minister of Finance, Pak Cheoum. . . . The movement is now spreading to surrounding provinces. The Committee of Independent
Cambodia, which cooperates closely with the Republic of Vietnam, has requested
the latter to draw the world's attention to the Cambodian independence movement.

Shortly after this, the French, reoccupying the area of Cochin China in which
these refugees operated, temporarily put an end to their organized activities
there.

It was not until after the November 1947 coup at Bangkok had shattered the
Khmer Issarak movement there that the group in western Cochin China was
revitalized by the arrival of the Issarak, who no longer found Thailand tenable
as a base of operations. Despite their long-standing fear of Vietnamese aggression, the Issarak had to turn to the Viet Minh for support, and the latter responded gladly. In the early months of 1948, a plan for joint action was decided
upon, and its execution was entrusted to Nguyen thanh Son (alias Nguyen
van Tai), a member of the Viet Minh Executive Committee for Nambo. The
objectives decided upon were unification of the Khmer resistance movement;
creation of a liaison network between Thailand and south Viet Nam along
the Cambodian seacoast; and the opening of a front in southern Cambodia,
particularly in the rubber plantation area of Kompong Cham, from bases set
up along the Cochin China frontier.[12]

The active phase of Viet Minh–Issarak collaboration that followed brought
about a change in the latter group's leadership. On January 8, 1948, Dap
Chhuon became president of the new Committee for Khmer Liberation as
well as its military commander, and was charged with co-ordinating Issarak
operations with the Viet Minh's resistance to the French. But it was only in
northwestern Cambodia (Siemréap, Sisophon, Battambang, and Pursat) that

[11] Radio Hanoi, Nov. 7, 1945.
[12] "Evolution du Mouvement Khmer Issarak," *Indochine—Sud-est Asiatique,* October–November 1950.

he and his lieutenants, Keo Tak, Chantarangsey, and Sieu Heng, exercised direct authority. The southeast zone of Kandal and Kompong Cham were under the command of Son ngoc Minh, brother of Son ngoc Thanh. Their combined forces probably did not exceed 2,000 armed men, the areas they controlled were small and not contiguous, and each zone had its separate Committee of Liberation. Behind the façade of an over-all organization, disunity reigned. Each leader acted like an independent feudal lord, fought for personal power, and did not scruple to extort money and services from his "subjects." Even more detrimental to their effective action was the dissension that soon broke out between them and the Viet Minh, because of fundamentally opposed immediate objectives. The Issarak wanted money and arms but not interference from the Viet Minh, while the latter wanted to decide how such aid as it furnished should be used and eventually to gain control over the whole Issarak movement. It was at this psychological moment that King Norodom made a determined effort to end the whole revolt.

In coming to an agreement with the French, the king had insisted upon Cambodia's having armed forces of its own. As early as February 1946, he told an American journalist:

We want a Cambodian army to keep the country in good order and to safeguard our frontiers. We also desire officers and soldiers to get modern training and equipment, and we already have 32 officer cadets whose training is progressing well under the supervision of French officers.[13]

Subsequently progress toward this goal was made, but too slowly to give entire satisfaction to Khmer aspirations. As of early 1950, the Cambodian army numbered only 5,000 men, and the French were dilatory in providing them with enough arms and training for rapid expansion. In part this was due to the military priority accorded the Viet Nam front, in part to French lack of confidence in the Khmers' ability to pacify their country, and in part to the fear that some Cambodian leaders might use such forces simply to consolidate their own political power.[14] Nevertheless, by early 1949 the king felt that he had an army large enough to end the revolt by force if need be. On January 27 he declared an amnesty for repentant Issarak, accompanied by propaganda designed to reassure them as to the authenticity of Cambodia's autonomy. Previous amnesty offers and surrender appeals to the Issarak had met with little response, but this time the king spoke with more authority about the danger which collaboration with the Viet Minh represented for Cambodia's future independence.

This royal denunciation coincided with the Issarak disillusionment with their Viet Minh allies, and particularly with the latter's political commissars, who were beginning to preach openly communistic doctrines to the Issarak

---

[13] *Christian Science Monitor,* Feb. 4, 1946.
[14] *New York Times,* Mar. 25, 1950.

troops. Many of the Issarak who were sincerely attached to their king and strongly nationalistic heeded his warning. Some of them simply laid down their arms; others actually changed sides and began to fight the Viet Minh. This phenomenon first developed in the central provinces, then spread to the southwest and finally to the northwest. It culminated on July 24, 1949, when Dap Chhuon resigned as president of the Committee of Khmer Liberation. A few days after the Franco-Cambodian treaty was signed, the following November, he surrendered himself to the king in a dramatic ceremony at Angkor Thom. Negotiations with other Issarak leaders proceeded more slowly, but by the end of the year the first phase of active Viet Minh–Issarak collaboration was over.

If the Viet Minh had failed through lack of tact and caution in its initial attempt to control the Issarak movement, it had at least won a limited military success. Some of its forces were operating from bases in Cambodia, and it directly administered certain areas of the country. Recognizing their diplomatic failure, Viet Minh leaders early in 1949 set about trying to salvage what they could of the Issarak movement. A new commander, Nguyen thanh Son, was put in charge of the joint Viet Minh–Issarak forces in Cambodia and told to open a second front along the Gulf of Thailand that would permit coordinated action with the Viet Minh in Cochin China. He was also assigned the task of unifying the Issarak under Viet Minh authority, and of eliminating those who proved recalcitrant to Viet Minh directives. By mid-April, Son had united the docile Issarak in two new organizations—the United Issarak Front and the Provisional Committee of National Liberation—and at their head he placed tried-and-true Khmer Marxists, Son ngoc Minh, Changsmay, and Sieu Heng. Recalcitrant members of the old Committee of National Liberation met once more in the north in an attempt to outmaneuver the Viet Minh. They formally broke off relations with the Viet Minh, and some of them began organizing provincial and village defense units in co-operation with the royal Khmer army and the French.

Internal Politics

On the political front in Cambodia a somewhat similar struggle was going on, within the framework of Cambodia's new governmental institutions. The change-over from an absolute theocratic monarchy to parliamentary government had been very rapid. Although it had largely by-passed the bulk of the people, it had stimulated the country's small elite to new political activity and feverish ambition. An electoral law, drafted by a joint Franco-Cambodian study committee, was promulgated on May 31, 1946. The French would have preferred a more gradual transition, but—paradoxically—it was the absolute monarch who insisted upon making an abrupt break with the past.[15]

15 De Lacharrière," "Le Cambodge dans l'union Française," *Politique Etrangère,* June 1948.

By the law of May 1946, an assembly was to be elected that would advise the king in regard to the new constitution but would not have constituent powers. Eligible to vote for members of this assembly were all Cambodian males over twenty-one years of age who were not soldiers or monks and who satisfied certain residence qualifications. Considerable opposition was aroused by the last-mentioned requirement on the ground that it disenfranchised virtually all civil servants and the resident elite of Pnom-Penh.[16] On July 22 the campaign got under way for the election of 67 assemblymen from among some 200 candidates. During the course of campaigning, three political parties were formed—the Liberal, headed by Prince Norindeth; the Progressive, led by Prince Montana; and the Democrat, under Prince Youthivong. At the outset there was little to choose between the platforms each party advocated, and the main point of difference lay in the leadership. The Democrats did more propaganda work throughout the provinces than did their rivals, and they won the general support of the educated class.

As the contest developed, the three parties came to be more clearly differentiated as to aims. The Democrats, headed by such French-trained intellectuals as Prince Youthivong, Thonn Ouk, and Chheam Vam, besides favoring a maximum degree of autonomy and a minimum of French controls, advocated responsible parliamentary government, a constitutional monarchy, social reforms, and the representation of Cambodia in France's National Assembly. Prince Montana and his Progressives had a less definite platform which aimed at more gradual evolution toward autonomy. The Liberals, headed by Prince Norindeth, were frankly royalist and Buddhist in their conservative political and social program, and also urged the retention of most French controls. On September 1, 1946, Cambodia's first elections took place in a calm atmosphere; estimates as to the percentage of the electorate who voted ranged from 30 to 62 percent. The results gave a clear-cut victory to the Democrats, who won 50 seats, and marked a total defeat for the Progressives, whose leader subsequently retired from politics. In addition, 4 Liberals and 3 Independents won seats.[17]

When the Assembly convened in October 1946, the king submitted to it a draft constitution. Not unnaturally the Assembly forgot its purely advisory role and transformed itself with royal sanction into a constituent body. Because the Democrats predominated by so large a majority, the constitution that was promulgated on May 7, 1947, was in great measure their product. Its inspiration was the 1946 constitution of France, adapted to Cambodia's monarchical and Buddhist set-up, and it was bounded by the framework of existing Franco-Cambodian agreements. The new constitution stipulated that all powers emanated from the king and must be exercised in his name—a

16 *Le Monde*, Sept. 8–9, 1946.
17 *Bulletin de la France d'Outre-Mer*, Sept. 23, Oct. 7, 1946.

basic point which later became the king's justification for proroguing the Assembly. Electoral qualifications for the National Assembly remained unchanged, and for every 10,000 voters there was to be one deputy who would serve a four-year term. The Second Chamber, or Council of the Kingdom, was to be composed of 24 members—2 from the royal family and appointed by the king; 2 elected by the National Assembly; 8 chosen by a limited and indirect suffrage to represent Pnom-Penh municipality and the provincial regions; and 12 others to be selected by various professional bodies, including civil servants. In normal times, the king's powers were to be not much more extensive than those of the President of France, though his sacred person was inviolable. But during the transition period he could postpone the promulgation of a law, or modify it, and was empowered to prorogue the Assembly under conditions similar to those laid down for dissolution of France's Parliament.

During the campaign to elect Cambodia's first National Assembly in the autumn of 1947, three new parties were born. The first, Khmer Renovation, was organized by Tioulong, and was said to have the moral support of the king.[18] It published a French-language newspaper, *Khemara,* and described its program as both traditionalist and nationalist. The second party, Cambodian National Unity, was led by Kim Thit; it was composed chiefly of retired officials and had an imprecise platform advocating unity and social welfare. The third party, that of the Progressive Democrats, was founded by Prince Montana; its program was more democratic than those of the other newcomers, but it put up only 25 candidates for election. The Liberal Party remained active, especially in the provinces, and its organ, *Sereiphepap,* published strong attacks on the Democrats. In July 1947 the last-mentioned party had suffered a loss through the death of its leader, Prince Youthivong. And under his successor, Chheam Vam, the Democrats became increasingly radical, developed close affinities with the Issarak, and finally split up into many groups. At a party congress held in November 1947, a program was drawn up which called for the exercise of more powers by Cambodian officials, democratic rights for the people, and the withdrawal of Cambodian troops from fighting against the Vietnamese in Cochin China. How much this program appealed to the electorate was shown in December 1947 when the Democrats won 54 seats out of a total of 78, the Liberals 20, and the three new parties none at all.

Relations with France and Viet Nam

A major reason for the Democrats' triumph was that they expressed the growing dissatisfaction felt in Cambodia at the long delay in putting Franco-Cambodian relations on a firm and liberal basis. The constitution of 1947 did

[18] *Ibid.,* Nov. 17, 1947.

not regulate this relationship, and only in its preamble was it stated that Cambodia was an autonomous nation and a member of the French Union. (In 1948, Cambodia became the first Associated State to join the French Union, to whose Assembly at Paris it sent 5 delegates later in the year.) The modus vivendi of January 1946 had ushered in an administrative system in which Cambodian officials were given more power over specified services and French officials were relegated to the role of advisers. Yet after a year and a half of this regime, many Cambodians felt that the erstwhile powers of the French had undergone little change and that the differences between it and the prewar protectorate were purely nominal.[19] Many French officials, including those who loved Cambodia well but too paternalistically, claimed that the Cambodians were not yet ready to leave their tutelage, and to substantiate this they pointed to the undeniable decline in administrative efficiency and growth of corruption. The Black Star plot discovered in February 1947, which involved two outstanding members of the Assembly, had gone far to confirm their suspicion of the Democrat Party's sympathies for the Khmer Issarak and close links with Thailand.

In addition, there were other obstacles hampering the negotiation of a definitive treaty between Cambodia and France. A minor impediment was the Cambodians' unwillingness to have the local Chinese enjoy the same juridical rights as French citizens, and they insisted that that economically powerful minority (140,000) should be under the jurisdiction of the same courts as themselves.[20] A much more serious difficulty arose in defining Cambodia's future relationship to Viet Nam. Negotiations with Bao Dai were dragging out, and until some agreement could be reached with him, no federation could be set up that would include the non-Vietnamese states of Indochina. The Cambodians, for their part, opposed any revival of the "cumbersome, overstaffed, and costly" prewar Government-General, and before they entered into any kind of federal structure they wanted specific concessions to be made[21] that would obviate the possibility of its being used to subject Cambodia to Viet Nam. The most important of these demands aimed at assuring economic independence for Cambodia and at safeguarding the rights of the Cambodian minority in Cochin China.

In the three Cochin Chinese provinces of Rachgia, Soctrang, and Travinh, the Cambodians formed the majority population, but among the 5½ million people living in Cochin China the Cambodians numbered only some 450,000. Cambodia occasionally has asked for the restoration of the three western Cochin Chinese provinces on the grounds of historical right, but has generally recognized the unlikelihood of getting any satisfaction in this respect.

[19] *Bangkok Post,* Mar. 27, 1947.
[20] *New York Times,* Mar. 25, 1950.
[21] See open letter from Nguyen phan Long to E. Bollaert, *Du Luan* (Saigon), Apr. 2, 1947.

Cambodians have frequently complained, however, that their compatriots in Cochin China have been persecuted by the Vietnamese, and they fear that France's withdrawal from the area might seriously aggravate their plight.[22] In January 1948 there was formed in Cochin China a Cambodian Minority Party, which issued a manifesto demanding that a political representative for their community be appointed to the South Viet Nam government, that special legal institutions be created for them, and that a Bureau of Khmer Affairs be set up at Saigon.[23] In the spring of 1949, the imminent unification of the three Vietnamese countries of Cochin China, Annam, and Tonkin brought Prince Monireth to Paris and elicited protests from King Norodom and his delegates to the French Union Assembly. Disappearance of Cochin China's colonial status, they claimed, would mean an end to the political and cultural guaranties of special treatment for the Cambodian minority in that country. In March 1949, Minister Coste-Floret promised that Cambodian minority rights would be safeguarded, but later statements by the emperor's cousin, Prince Buu Loc, left the nervous Cambodians with the impression that in the future there would be only one nationality—the Vietnamese—in Cochin China.[24] And when the French finally came to terms with Bao Dai, in March 1949, the unitary state of Viet Nam was organized without prior consultation with the Cambodian government.[25]

Another facet of Vietnamese imperialism which the Cambodians had long resented was Saigon's stranglehold on Cambodia's economy. At the first Dalat conference at which Cambodia was represented, in July 1946, the head of the Cambodian delegation was promised that thenceforth Saigon would not be Cambodia's sole outlet to the sea, and that Pnom-Penh would be modernized and navigation of the Mekong so improved that ocean-going vessels would be able to reach Cambodian waters directly. In August 1947 this materialized when the first such ship reached Pnom-Penh from Singapore.[26] By 1950, 86 ocean freighters had come to the Cambodian capital and plans were well advanced for creation of a Cambodian merchant marine. At the Pau conference of the Associated States of Indochina, held in 1950, Cambodian demands for the freedom of Saigon port, a voice in its administrative council, and a share in the profits which it was making from the export of Cambodian rice and rubber, were in part satisfied. Yet the Cambodian nationalists continued to press for a further modernization of Pnom-Penh port that would permit the establishment of regular maritime services with Manila, Hong Kong, and Singapore, though the expense involved was such that it could hardly be supported by Cambodia's economy.[27] So eager has Cambodia become to

[22] *L'Aurore* (Paris), Apr. 16, 1949.
[23] *Bulletin de la France d'Outre-Mer*, January 1948.
[24] *Le Monde*, May 13, 1949.   [25] *Ibid.*, May 5, 1952.
[26] *Bulletin de la France d'Outre-Mer*, Aug. 25, 1947.
[27] J. de la Ferrière, "Le Port de Pnom-Penh," *Indochine—Sud-est Asiatique*, December 1951.

slough off the last vestiges of its dependence on Saigon that in January 1953 it began negotiations with the Thai government for the initiation of direct railroad express service between the capitals of the two countries.[28]

Cambodia's postwar economic situation presents a curious anomaly. Starting out with an undamaged economy, relative tranquillity, and surplus products in great world demand, the country has experienced a steady and growing decline in production, so that France has had to underwrite progressively larger deficits. Prominent among the difficulties has been the depredations of the Khmer Issarak; another has been the peasants' belief that the end of the French Protectorate meant that they no longer had to pay taxes; and still another has been the inefficiency and corruption of Cambodian officialdom. In mid-1949, a British reporter wrote:

Roads are seldom repaired and bridges off the main highways are beginning to sag. The government cannot impose its authority. The capital city, once clean, is sinking into dusty Oriental squalor. On two sides there is open revolt. . . . Plantations have been abandoned.[29]

Premier Yem Sambaur, who had been elected on an anticorruption ticket, canceled the outrageous contracts which his predecessor had made and tried to negotiate new ones, but no one—not even the Chinese speculators—would thereafter risk handling government contracts, and the administration had to resort to opening two gambling casinos in an effort to raise revenue. Cambodian nationalists have clung to the belief that the solution to their economic ills lay in greater independence from South Viet Nam rather than in cleaning up official corruption and streamlining the government.

Preoccupation with economic independence has been more than matched in the political field, especially after France, in the Elysée agreements of March 1949, made concessions to Bao Dai which had not yet been made to the other Associated States. In general, the Cambodians wanted complete control of their own administration, foreign relations, and army. In particular, they resented that their courts were held to be competent only in cases involving their own nationals, that French troops were still stationed in the country, and that France still controlled the movement of both Cambodians and foreigners into and out of the country. The Franco-Cambodian treaty signed November 6, 1949, formally confirmed Cambodian autonomy within the French Union, transferred more administrative functions to the Cambodians, and gave Cambodia a freer hand in the conduct of foreign relations. The Cambodians at once profited by the last-mentioned concession to send abroad ambassadors, sign agreements with the United States for economic aid in November 1950, and attend the Japanese Peace Treaty conference at San Fran-

[28] *Bangkok Post*, Jan. 16, 1953.   [29] *The Observer* (London), July 10, 1949.

cisco in September 1951.[30] But even the new treaty left unaltered Cambodia's juridical grievances, failed to allay Cambodian suspicions of Vietnamese power and ambitions, and did not resolve the country's grave economic dilemma, and it was never submitted to the National Assembly for ratification.

King vs. Opposition

Internally the political situation went from bad to worse; governments came and went without apparent cause. Lacking any tradition of parliamentary government, ministers had neither the training nor the experience nor the public spirit required to make the system work. Parties splintered, new groups were formed, and coalitions were grouped around rival personal interests. Toward the middle of 1949, opposition to the administration became systematic and open in the Assembly, and the Democrats—reportedly under orders from the Khmer Issarak—ordered members of their party to resign from the Cabinet. Only one minor Democrat did so, and he was not replaced. So the Democrat majority in the Assembly seized on this as evidence that the Constitution was being violated, and demanded a vote of confidence. Premier Yem Sambaur, a former Democrat, in a radio broadcast accused certain deputies of preparing to sell out their country, "after having sold mountains of salt, paddy, and fish." Refusing to accede to the Assembly's move for a confidence vote, he said, "It is a question of knowing whether or not the country will have to submit to the dictatorship of some party members who no longer respect the Constitution."[31] Nevertheless, a Democrat persisted in offering a motion censuring the government. But by this time the king had decided to dissolve the Assembly, and a belated vote turning down the censure motion could not save it from being prorogued on September 18, 1949.

According to the Constitution, new elections must follow within two months of the Assembly's dissolution, but the provincial chiefs whom the king consulted on this subject felt that the prevailing insecurity in the country would make any electoral campaign farcical. So the king decided to govern provisionally with the aid of the Second Chamber—a move which the Democrats at once denounced as anticonstitutional. To this the king replied that the situation was highly exceptional and that, since the Constitution emanated from himself, he was free to suspend its application in the larger interests of the state. He then assigned to his uncle, Prince Monipong, the task of creating a new government, and asked the existing political parties to formulate answers to the question as to whether he should recall the old Assembly, hold new elections, or modify the Constitution so as to legalize the existing situation.

[30] As of April 1952, Cambodia was a member of WHO, FAO, UNESCO, the Universal Postal Union, and the International Telecommunications Union.

[31] A. Surmer, "Evolution du système parlementaire Cambodgien," *Encyclopédie Coloniale,* April 1951.

Months passed while the parties debated the problem. The Democrats and Liberals naturally advocated recalling the old Assembly which they had clearly dominated, while the newer and smaller parties favored holding new elections through which they hoped to acquire more seats. As no agreement was in sight and as Prince Monipong personally preferred to call for new elections though he knew that the king felt such a course to be undesirable, he handed back his mandate on March 2, 1951. The month of April passed in continuing dissension, and a new political party—the Victorious Northeast— was formed. Democrats, Liberals, and Progressive Democrats all refused to participate in any cabinet in which they did not hold a majority of the portfolios,[32] and the king himself briefly took over the government. Finally, in May, a new "business" government was formed by Oun Chheang, who tried successfully the novel device of drafting ministers without their prior consent, "in the interests of the country at large." Almost at once the new government decided to hold elections, even against the expressed wishes of the king and of the majority parties.

The campaign began in July 1951; 496 candidates representing 8 political parties asked for the votes of an electorate then estimated to total about 700,-000.[33] On September 9 the Democrats won 53 of the Assembly's 78 seats, the Liberals 19, and the Khmer Renovation 2. Of the opposition groups, only the Victorious Northeast, which had 4 deputies elected, obtained any seat at all.[34]

No sooner had the long-standing parliamentary crisis been settled than a new and even more ominous element entered the picture—Son ngoc Thanh returned to political life. Since 1945 he had been in exile in France, but in 1951 he was allowed to go back to his country after pledging not to participate further in local politics. During his long absence, the reorganized Khmer Issarak movement under the leadership of his brother Son ngoc Minh had been integrated with the Viet Minh, and had re-established the supply route to Thailand and an auxiliary organization there. In March 1951 the Viet Minh radio announced that delegates from the Khmer and Laotian Issarak movements had agreed in a meeting to organize a joint united front that would embrace all the dissident groups throughout Indochina. Thanh's return coincided with the maturing of a situation which he felt called upon to lead, especially after thousands of his compatriots acclaimed him as their liberator and listened spellbound to his oratory.

In December 1951 he addressed a meeting in Takeo province, attended by Minister Pak Chheoum. On this occasion he advocated the same program as in 1945 and urged the people to tear up the Franco-Cambodian treaty. Cambodia would never be truly free, he told them, until the last French soldier

---

[32] *France-Indochine*, August-September 1951.   [33] *Chroniques d'Outre-Mer*, October 1951.
[34] Reuter despatch, Saigon, Oct. 13, 1951.

left the country; it was only the presence of the French that caused disorders and violence in Cambodia; and the Viet Minh had no designs on its neighbor other than to help it attain genuine independence.[35] After this demagogic outburst, Thanh returned to Pnom-Penh where he founded a newspaper in which to elaborate his views. In February 1952 this paper was suspended and Thanh was charged with fomenting disorders. Fearing arrest, he fled on March 9 to Siemréap, from which he launched radio appeals and spread tracts exhorting the people to follow him. This proving to be ineffectual, he began the next month to negotiate with the Viet Minh for support. Reportedly an agreement was reached between them on June 21, after which he apparently left for Thailand. The obscurity which surrounded his movements for the next few months led some of his opponents to believe that Thanh was less dangerous in the jungle than in Pnom-Penh, where he had been successful in winning over members of the Democrat Party and of youth groups.[36]

Thanh's activities in Pnom-Penh and his sensational flight undeniably increased political tension in Cambodia and contributed to a further deterioration in Franco-Cambodian relations. Thanks to his influence, it was widely believed, a crisis occurred in the Democrat Party in February 1952, as a result of which several Democrat ministers resigned from the government on the ground that it had become too subservient to the French.[37] At the same time the intensification of terrorist activities in the country lent weight to their plea for wider military authority, and they also pressed for a relaxation of the ties which bound Cambodia to the other Associated States and hampered its economic freedom.[38] Early in May, Cambodian pressure for a revision of the country's relations with France was highlighted by a demonstration of hundreds of Pnom-Penh youths which took place upon the return of the king from Europe and the arrival of Minister Jean Letourneau. Another student demonstration occurred at Battambang on May 19, after the publication of an official decree branding Son ngoc Thanh a rebel and a traitor.

The king, whose hand was reportedly strengthened by a French promise to revise the Cambodian treaty, at once went into action. He demanded that the Democratic Cabinet take stronger action against the dissidents, especially those sympathizing with Son ngoc Thanh. Instead, the Democrat Premier, Houy Kanthoul, used this as an excuse to arrest his party's archenemy, Yem Sambour, who was an outspoken supporter of the king and a close friend of the reformed Issarak, Dap Chhuon. King Norodom retaliated by immediately dismissing Houy Kanthoul and taking over the government himself, on the ground that the former administration had created an "almost hopeless situation." He then asked the Assembly to grant him full powers for three

[35] P. Christian, *op. cit.*
[37] *Ibid.*, Mar. 1, 1952.
[36] *Le Monde*, Mar. 20, 1952.
[38] *New York Times*, Apr. 22, 1952.

years and threatened to dissolve it if his request were voted down. In so doing, he promised to remedy the situation in two years and achieve complete independence for Cambodia in three years, after which he was prepared to have his actions judged by a popularly elected court attended by observers from six foreign countries.[39]

The king's decisive action split the Democrats.[40] One group of 28, to which the former premier, Houy Kanthoul, belonged, favored supporting the king's request. Another more extremist element composed of 24 Democrats led by the Assembly's President, Son Sann, opposed it.[41] But both groups were ignored by the new royal premier, who gave most of the portfolios to members of his family or to his entourage. The whole episode marked a new climax to the four-year-old struggle between the Democrat Party and the palace, which since the elections of September 1951 and the return of Son ngoc Thanh had taken a surprisingly acrimonious turn. The government was now composed of francophiles, royalist authoritarians, and bitter enemies of the Democrats. The move could not but please the French, for it presaged stronger Cambodian action against the dissidents, and Letourneau reportedly promised to ask Washington for more aid for Cambodia and to press for Cambodia's admission to the United Nations.

In staking his throne on the country's peaceful acceptance of his coup d'état, the king certainly showed considerable courage, though he continued to vacillate between liberalism and autocracy. His royal prestige won the gamble. On June 17 the Assembly voted to grant him the full powers he asked for, in a compromise motion that avoided an open break between it and the king. Further, a protest strike organized among students by extremist Democrats failed to come off.[42] Two days later, the king banned all meetings of a political nature as an "unnecessary waste of time at a moment when the country needs the help of all,"[43] and on June 23 he announced that he would put Cambodia on an austerity budget so as to build up the nation's forces battling the Communists. The Democrats showed some fight over this budget, which called for increased taxes, allotted 30 percent of the country's revenues (over 300 million piastres) to military expenditures, and cut down the civil service. On August 10, however, the king, after offering to reduce his own civil list by 20 percent, won an important victory, and the Assembly voted by 53 votes to 3 to accept his budget. As always, France had to grant a subsidy, which in

39 *Bangkok Post,* June 16, 1952.
40 Already the Democrats were divided into four groups—the original party; the National Rehabilitation, headed by Yem Sambaur, who had brought about the first split in the party; the Victorious Northeast, backed by Dap Chhuon; and the People's Party, a splinter from Sambaur's group which was headed by Sam Nheam.
41 United Press despatch, Pnom-Penh, June 15, 1952.
42 *Ibid.,* June 18, 1952.
43 *Ibid.,* June 20, 1952.

this case amounted to one-fifth of total expenditures (1,054,855,000 piastres).[44] But by this time, Franco-Cambodian relations had reached such a pitch of good feeling that it looked as though the Assembly might even ratify the 1949 treaty.

One of the more interesting accomplishments of the royal regime installed in June 1952 was an experiment begun in Kampot the next month, which, though smaller in scale, was similar to the somewhat earlier resettlement of about 500,000 Chinese squatters in Malaya. Because of its strategic location along the Gulf of Thailand, Kampot province had long been a major scene of Issarak activity and one of the most insecure areas in Cambodia. As in Malaya, the authorities decided to cut off the supplies, shelter, and information that the Issaraks had been receiving from the terrorized Kampot peasants by regrouping them in newly built villages situated along the main roads and protected by military posts. Though by the end of 1952 only some 30,000 individuals had been resettled, owing to the difficulties of carrying out such an operation during the rainy season when agricultural activities were at their height, the situation in Kampot had definitely improved.[45] Reprisals from the Viet Minh and the Issarak had actually aided the resettlement program by causing more and more peasants to seek the safety and amenities offered in the new villages. Again, as in Malaya, the socio-economic consequences of this transplantation of a sizable segment of the Cambodian population promised to have greater long-term significance than the more immediate military gains.

Through the summer and autumn of 1952, Son ngoc Thanh's radio had kept harping on his old theme that, so long as the French remained in Cambodia, the king was not a free agent. To disprove this, the king persuaded the French to turn over the conduct of military operations in the country's two westernmost provinces to the Cambodian army. In September 1952, Dap Chhuon was placed in charge of a new campaign against Son ngoc Thanh, and the king announced that he himself would direct it. As the year drew to an end, the military situation seemed to have improved, but student strikes in November showed that danger was reviving in that quarter. Early in January 1953 a provincial governor was murdered within twenty miles of Pnom-Penh. And the National Assembly, which had just refused to pass the budget by the December 31 deadline set by the king, also ignored a royal request to investigate the student strikes as well as the governor's assassination.

The king, who for the past month had been absorbed in mourning the death of his favorite daughter, was now roused to action by this evidence of the Assembly's renewed recalcitrance and by the discovery of an alleged plot against his government hatched by the Issarak at Bangkok. He abruptly ordered the

[44] *Le Monde*, Sept. 2, 1952.
[45] Jean Laproux, "Trente mille Cambodgiens échappent l'emprise des rebelles," *Indochine—Sud-est Asiatique*, January 1953.

arrest of about a dozen officials and members of the Democrat Party believed to be implicated in the plot, decreed a national emergency, and once more dissolved the National Assembly. Shortly after this, a new offensive against the Issarak along the Thai border was undertaken and the king announced that he would soon accept an invitation from the French government to go to Paris to discuss Cambodian affairs.[46] According to Homer Bigart,[47] the situation might look grim on paper, but nobody at Pnom-Penh seemed to be taking it seriously: the arrested Democrats passed the time pleasantly in jail by playing cards, and the leader of their party turned up as usual at the American Legation to take his English-language lessons. In March an army officer deserted with 110 men to join the rebels,[48] but this news was more than offset by reports of the impending surrender to the government of an outstanding Issarak chief, Puth Chhay, with 700 of his followers.[49] In this seesaw of adverse and favorable events, the king realized that the solution to his country's and his own political troubles lay not at home but in Paris. The Viet Minh's invasion of Laos, beginning in March, provided him with a ready-made opportunity to bring fresh pressure on the French government.

Royal Achievements

Norodom's sudden journey to Paris, undertaken without confiding its real objectives to the French authorities in Indochina, was to mark a turning point in his relations with France and consequently in his position at home. Paris officialdom was preoccupied with other matters and was misinformed as to the compulsion felt by the king to achieve personally a rapid and spectacular success in wresting concessions for his country. As a result, Norodom was treated with a casualness and a dilatoriness that he resented. Nevertheless, the sincerity with which he obstinately pressed his case did bring some appreciable results. The new protocols announced in Paris on May 9 pledged full sovereignty to Cambodia in three important fields. In military affairs the king's position as commander in chief of the army was reaffirmed and, in addition, he was given "responsibility for security and the maintenance of order" in his country. While only minor modifications were made in the economic and financial provisions of the Pau agreements of 1950, a real advance was registered in the juridical domain. Here "full judicial competence" was granted to Cambodia, though French interests, wherever directly involved, were to be safeguarded. But even such concessions fell far short of what the king considered to be the minimal requirements for overcoming the ever growing opposition to his leadership in Cambodia, led by the Democrats and

[46] Bangkok Post, Feb. 21, 1953.   [47] New York Herald-Tribune, Feb. 18, 1953.
[48] Bangkok Post, Mar. 25, 1953.   [49] Ibid., Apr. 13, 1953.

student nationalists. Moreover, even the success he had won was soon offset by France's devaluation of the piastre "under circumstances which made the king and his premier feel that they had been deliberately duped."[50]

Fearing to return home almost empty-handed, Norodom now felt that he had no other course open to him than to make an appeal to world opinion. In a lightning visit to the United States, he tried ineffectually to enlist American sympathy and governmental aid in bringing pressure on the French to grant Cambodia full independence. In a press interview at New York he played upon the West's fear lest France's failure to grant greater autonomy to Cambodia might cause his compatriots to align themselves with the Viet Minh.[51] He then stopped briefly in Japan and, perhaps as the result of a similar failure there, apparently decided as a last resort to go into voluntary exile until his demand for total independence should be met. Meanwhile, the prospect of France's soon meeting any such demand was becoming dimmer, for the Viet Minh's sudden (if partial) withdrawal from Laos early in May was lessening tension in regard to the whole area and consequently diminishing the usefulness of this leverage in bringing pressure to bear upon the French. In seeking an appropriate base abroad from which he could dramatize his plea and also possibly get help, the king logically chose Thailand, which was adjacent to Cambodia and chronically responsive to appeals from Khmer dissidents. The Thai government, embarrassed by the unheralded arrival of the Cambodian king and a suite of 34, admitted him as a political refugee and lodged him in Bangkok's most luxurious hotel. But it refused to let him head a government-in-exile or to use Thailand as his intermediary for presenting Cambodia's case to the United Nations. Thwarted once again by this lack of co-operation, the king left within a week for Battambang province, which was in the hands of Cambodian troops. He became convinced that he must make his last stand there, and he announced that he would not return to Pnom-Penh until France had met his terms.

France, then undergoing one of her prolonged intergovernment periods, was unable—even if she could decide—to take action. In view of the tense situation throughout her colonial empire, France felt that she could not yield to the king's ultimatum. Moreover, the patience of her representatives in Indochina was wearing thin, for they attributed the failure of their efforts to reach a compromise at the Inter-State Conference in February 1953 to the intransigence and ill will of the Cambodian representatives. On the other hand, the French did not want to break with the king, who wielded a great and often moderating influence over his compatriots and who reiterated his friendship for France and his willingness—if independence were granted—

[50] Krabai (nom de plume), "Quelques réflexions sur les récents évènements survenus au Cambodge," *France-Indochine,* Jan. 1, 1954.

[51] *New York Times,* Apr. 19, 1953.

that Cambodia should remain within the French Union. Some Frenchmen, long acquainted with the Khmer people, thought they detected behind the uncompromising attitude of the Cambodian negotiators inexperience in diplomacy and a fear of losing face rather than outright hostility toward France. In any case, the French were anxious to prevent the situation from further deteriorating and were particularly concerned for the safety of the 2,000 or more French civilians residing in Pnom-Penh.

Though on July 3 the newly formed Laniel government made conciliatory proposals to all the Associated States, tension in the Cambodian capital continued to rise. Students in Pnom-Penh, either spontaneously or under instructions, continued to foment strikes, threw hand grenades into schools and cafés, and paid little heed to royal exhortations to remain calm. During the first half of the month, nationalist agitation among the troops caused about 300 desertions from the Cambodian army. Some of these deserters reportedly fled to Battambang where they placed themselves directly under the king, but other desertions were instigated by supposedly loyal ex-Issarak chiefs—notably Puth Chhay, who had been charged by the king with maintaining order in the capital. (Puth Chhay's increasingly ruthless treatment of Pnom-Penh residents—whom he and his band forced at gun point to buy tickets to a "lottery" which he organized—induced the king in August to order him and his followers to leave the city.) By instigating desertions, these chiefs not only regained their independence of command but were able to sell at huge profit the guns and military equipment which their followers had received when they became part of the regular army. Such mass desertions swelled dangerously the number of rebel bands operating in and around the capital and caused a serious disintegration of the royal army, both materially and psychologically. No longer able to count on the loyalty of his armed forces and lacking the money to equip new recruits, the king appealed to the patriotism of his people to form a volunteer unpaid militia. Though the formation of this new force and the prospective mobilization of village manpower throughout Cambodia were proposed in the name of national defense, the French were inclined to believe that the king was building up support for himself in the event of a tussle with his local opponents or of a showdown with France.

As matters worked out, the king quelled local opposition by getting from the French, without recourse to armed force, virtually everything he demanded. Even after the transfer of all civil authority and services was agreed upon in principle, Norodom succeeded in overcoming French unwillingness to have this take effect immediately at Pnom-Penh without prior negotiations in Paris. Working out a compromise in the military sphere proved more difficult, and an agreement was reached only after six weeks of discussion and several threats of total breakdown. The French wanted to dispose of some Khmer troops in defending the invasion route to Laos east of the Mekong, whereas the Cambodians insisted upon withdrawing all their soldiers from under French command and using them exclusively inside the country's frontiers. To break the deadlock on this issue in mid-September, Premier Penn Nouth stated over the national radio that his country would not oppose military operations by the Viet Minh in other parts of Indochina so long as it left Cambodia alone.

As this "neutralist" declaration struck at the heart of France's policy for joint action against the common Communist threat and as it coincided with the arrival of Senator Knowland in Indochina, the reaction of France and the United States was far stronger and swifter than the Cambodians apparently anticipated. From the United States, it was reported, there came a threat to cut off all American aid, which since 1951 had amounted to over $25 million. Penn Nouth immediately sent conciliatory messages to the senator and in another broadcast explained away his earlier statement as a ruse to prove to the Cambodian people that the Viet Minh had no intention of withdrawing the 10,000 or more troops they were keeping in Cambodia and, therefore, action must be taken against them. At the same time, the premier let it be understood that Cambodia would not participate in the common fight against communism unless it was granted full independence as well as further aid from France and the United States.

By this time both France and the king had urgent reasons for quickly coming to a military agreement. For the French the approaching end of the rainy season meant a renewal of the Viet Minh offensive and a need to bolster the defenses of Laos and Cambodia. On August 30 the Laotian crown prince went in person to urge Norodom to make an agreement with France. Danger threatened the king from several quarters. New and old rebel bands were reported to be closing in on Pnom-Penh, and Son ngoc Thanh was said to have moved southward from the Thai frontier so as to join up with the Viet Minh and Issarak forces of Svongyong and Chantarangsey operating in the Tonlé Sap region.[52] Son ngoc Thanh's radio continued to advocate the establishment of a republic in Cambodia, and the Democrats had announced in midsummer that the king would have to abdicate before the year was out. In the meantime, they conducted a strong campaign against Norodom, accusing him of being a pawn of the French and a major obstacle to the achievement of national independence. Finally, on October 17, a compromise on the military issue was reached between France and Cambodia. Full command over all Cambodian territory and forces was given to the king and his government; France, in turn, received "operational" control over three Cambodian battalions stationed on the left bank of the Mekong. (It was not until May 1954 that the French agreed to repatriate all Cambodian troops currently stationed in Viet Nam.) Talks with the French on economic and financial matters were

[52] *Le Monde,* Sept. 20–21, 1953.

to begin shortly, and later Cambodia would discuss its future relations with France in Paris. On November 7 the king returned triumphantly to his capital, where he received a rousing welcome and was named by the government a "national hero." He freed 360 political prisoners, made friendly speeches about France, and publicly affirmed that Cambodia would remain within the French Union. The Viet Minh, he now said, represented the chief danger for Cambodia.[53]

No sooner had the king returned to Pnom-Penh than he was faced with a renewal of internal political dissension. In part this was due to the dormant status of the National Assembly and to the existence of two rival "governments"—the official one under Premier Penn Nouth and the unofficial "cabinet" headed by Chan Nak and formed from among those who had stayed with the king during his exile. As between the two, the king gave his support to his loyal personal adviser, Chan Nak, perhaps because he resented the popularity which Penn Nouth was enjoying in consequence of the intransigent attitude he had maintained during negotiations with the French. In part the troubled political atmosphere was caused by the undiminished hostility of many of the Democrats toward the king. The ranks of these Democrats had recently been swelled by the adherence of many ex-students, who preferred to credit Penn Nouth rather than the king with Cambodia's diplomatic victory over France and who coveted the posts currently held by protégés of the royal family. Within a week of the king's return, the resignations of Penn Nouth and two of his ministers opened the way for Norodom to appoint a new government headed by Chan Nak. This government included three Democrats, one Liberal, and one representative for each of the small parties. But no sooner had the new Cabinet taken over than conflict developed over the old issue of whether or not elections should be held for the National Assembly. The outstanding Democrat remaining in the government, Vice-Premier Son Sann, promptly resigned and Premier Chan Nak tried to follow suit, claiming that he was too old and feeble to remain premier under the circumstances. By shelving the elections issue and proclaiming the government to be merely one of transition, the king persuaded Chan Nak to stay on as premier and also to take over the Ministry of Interior. He gave the other key portfolio, that of Defense, to another devoted follower, Kim Thit, but he appointed a left-wing Democrat, Hak Mongsheng, Foreign Minister and Cambodia's sole representative at the forthcoming session of the High Council of the French Union.

In two radio broadcasts, late in November, the king took his case before the nation and threatened to abdicate if the opposition did not mend its ways. Some politicians, he complained, were belittling his role in the independence negotiations, accusing him of weakness vis-à-vis the French, and undermining his authority over the army. That the last-mentioned grievance was the most

[53] *Ibid.*, Nov. 22, 1953.

important in his eyes was shown on December 8, when the king abruptly withdrew to Siemréap. There in the most loyal of his fiefs—which Norodom has long wanted to make the royal capital—the king felt secure from a coup d'état that he apparently feared was being organized against him by the Democrats and the army. The rapidity and foresight with which the king moved, along with a belated recognition of the popularity which he had won among the elite and army by his bloodless achievement of independence, caused the opposition to backtrack. All of Cambodia's political parties hastily passed resolutions affirming their loyalty to the king, and even the Democrats denounced detractors of his courage, skill, and patriotism.[54]

Contrary to some gloomy predictions made at the time, the internal opposition not only ceased to obstruct but on a number of occasions in early 1954 actually supported the king.[55] The army showed itself grateful for having been freed by the king from French command; students became studious and disciplined as never before; and Issarak bands surrendered in unprecedented numbers. By early March 1954, it was believed that only 500 at the maximum —almost all with Son ngoc Thanh in the northwest—were still in open revolt. And even Son ngoc Thanh had offered to surrender, for he was discredited with his former allies the Democrats, abandoned by the Viet Minh in favor of his brother Son ngoc Minh, and reduced to a following of only a few hundred men. But Norodom now felt himself strong enough to reject the terms laid down by Thanh, and that erstwhile champion of an independent Cambodian republic was in consequence faced with two disagreeable alternatives—unconditional surrender or flight to a foreign country, probably Japan.

Cambodia's Prospects

Assured of comparative calm on the domestic front, Norodom was free to deal with the country's pressing economic problems, which by this time had become the major factor in determining Cambodia's future relations with France, Viet Nam, and Thailand. Norodom naturally sought independence in this field from France, but he also wanted French aid, both financial and technical. To obtain technical assistance presented no insuperable difficulties, and, after the transfer of such services as those of the merchant marine, civil aeronautics, land transportation, and labor in mid-January 1954, the Cambodians were pleased to retain in their employ some French experts in those fields. Financial aid was a more complicated question, for it involved Cambodia's relations with the other Associated States as well as with France. Cambodia's long-standing wish to sever economic ties with Viet Nam had been raised to fever pitch by certain measures taken unilaterally and contrary to

---

[54] *Le Monde*, Dec. 6–7, 1953.
[55] Krabai, "Le Cambodge vers une ère nouvelle," *France-Indochine*, April 1954.

the Pau agreements by the Vietnamese subsequent to devaluation of the piastre. Not only did the Cambodians feel that they were entitled to a proportion of the joint customs revenues larger than the 23 percent which their country had been assigned at Pau, but they particularly resented Viet Nam's contention that it could not pay immediately the almost 800 million piastres which had already accrued to Cambodia's credit from that source. If this sum had been available it would have gone far to help balance Cambodia's budget for 1954, in which the estimated revenues—amounting to about a billion piastres—would meet only about one-third of the anticipated expenditures.[56] Moreover, breaking up the customs and monetary union had other marked advantages in Cambodian eyes. Not only would the government be free to use the foreign exchange it earned for Cambodia's own development, but through patronage, the new posts that would then be created could be filled in such a way as to ensure loyalty from many of the youthful elite.

For some time it had been obvious to France and Viet Nam that the quadripartite setup devised at Pau had outlived its usefulness and that sooner or later it would become intolerable to Cambodia. So they acquiesced with good grace when Cambodia's Foreign Minister announced at a meeting of the High Council of the French Union in December 1953 that his country was withdrawing from the customs and monetary union. But to everyone's surprise, the Cambodian government immediately disavowed his action. As Premier Chan Nak had himself taken the same line as his Foreign Minister, it was hard to explain the government's about-face. One analyst of the situation believed that the unexpected alacrity with which France and Vietnam accepted Cambodia's viewpoint aroused undue suspicion on the part of the Pnom-Penh government at a time when it was in the throes of an internal political crisis.[57] Another source suggested that the premier had come suddenly to the conclusion that ending the economic union might in the long run be detrimental to Cambodian interests.[58] Cambodia had indeed been experiencing difficulty in independently finding markets for its surplus produce, and might now be looking with more favor than in the past on remaining a member of the franc zone. Then, too, a third possibility was shaping up which undoubtedly attracted Cambodia—adherence to the bloc of Buddhist countries which Thailand proposed to lead.[59] Determined as Cambodia was to acquire complete freedom of action in the political and diplomatic fields, its leaders recognized that for some time to come it could achieve only partial independence in the economic and military spheres.

In July 1953 the Cambodian premier told a Thai journalist that his country, after seceding from the quadripartite economic union, would seek interna-

[56] Reuter despatch, Saigon, Dec. 23, 1953.
[58] *Le Monde*, Dec. 8, 1953.
[57] Krabai, "Quelques réflexions . . .", cited.
[59] See p. 224.

tionalization of the Mekong River and eventually build a big port at Réam on the Gulf of Thailand; in the meantime, he said, Cambodia was considering replacing Saigon with Bangkok as the sea outlet for its foreign trade.[60] Cambodia, he added, would continue giving France preferential commercial treatment but would enter into direct trade relations with Thailand, Japan, and the United States. Six months later the Thai ambassador to Cambodia proposed at Pnom-Penh that the two countries open commercial negotiations.

In many ways, the vistas Thailand opened were tempting to the Cambodians,[61] who were above all eager to free themselves from their economic subordination to south Viet Nam. By threatening to substitute Bangkok for Saigon as the country's main outlet to the sea, the Cambodians may perhaps have hoped to exercise enough pressure on France for the latter to advance the large sums required to develop Réam port—a project which French engineers after long study had pronounced an uneconomic one. On the other hand, a commercial *rapprochement* with Thailand might involve certain drawbacks. Only the produce of Cambodia's western provinces (Battambang, Siemréap, and possibly Pursat and Kompong Chnang) to an annual maximum of 200,-000 tons of rice and 3,000 to 4,000 tons of dried fish could profitably be shipped via Thailand, and it was uncertain that Bangkok port could handle even that extra tonnage. Then, too, it was known that the Bangkok authorities did not favor Cambodia's proposal to internationalize the Mekong, since this would involve the surrender of certain Thai rights along the riverbank in the area where the Mekong formed Thailand's frontier with Indochina.[62] Nor did Viet Nam want internationalization of the river. What is more, the Vietnamese badly needed Cambodia's surplus rice and the revenues derived from the use of Saigon as port for Cambodia's foreign trade. The Pnom-Penh leaders did not want to antagonize their eastern neighbors, toward whom, moreover, they were somewhat less resentful as a result of the departure of many Vietnamese residents following the transfer of administrative services to Cambodian control.

All these factors made Cambodia hesitate to give a warm welcome to the Thai proposals, toward which Premier Chan Nak adopted a noncommittal attitude. But the Pnom-Penh government's cautious conduct in the international field did not resolve Cambodia's internal economic problems, and in May 1954 a new crisis threatened. Inflation had reached such proportions that the government was reportedly considering a drastic curtailment of administrative expenditures that would involve a 30 percent cut in officials' salaries.[63] Fearing to take a step that would surely alienate the very group that formed the background of the Democrat opposition, the government issued a com-

[60] *Bangkok Post*, Aug. 5 and 21, 1953.   [61] See p. 225 ff.
[62] *Bangkok Post*, Aug. 21, 1953.   [63] *Le Monde*, Mar. 22, 1954.

muniqué stating that it would first resort to other financial steps—getting a loan from the Bank of Issue and recuperating Cambodia's blocked customs revenues from Saigon.

Partly as a result of the Viet Minh's spring offensive in Laos, economic affairs went from bad to worse in Cambodia, while at the same time the political situation there showed definite improvement. The resignation of Chan Nak's cabinet on March 30 was unrelated to the military situation; the premier had long wanted to retire and he felt that his government had by then fulfilled the function assigned it by the king. But the composition of the next government reflected the unity and support given Norodom after the Viet Minh's invasion of Cambodian territory on April 2. Penn Nouth, who had initially refused the premiership, now agreed to govern in the king's name as head of a cabinet of 12 that included a general and 4 colonels. The expense involved in mobilizing Cambodia's manpower to meet the invasion threat inevitably added a heavy burden to an already badly unbalanced budget.

Cambodia's delegation at Geneva, in April 1954, showed the same successful obstinacy in negotiating a cease-fire for the country that King Norodom had revealed in his dealings with the French. To be sure, it was probably due largely to India's pressure on the Communist delegations that Premier Chou and the Viet Minh finally agreed to withdraw their support of the Son ngoc Minh regime and to treat Cambodia (and Laos) on a basis separate from that of Viet Nam. But it was the insistence of the Cambodians themselves, at the risk of jeopardizing Mendès-France's deadline of July 20, which won for their country two major points—that all Viet Minh–led units would evacuate Cambodia within ninety days after the armistice, and that Cambodia could exercise its sovereign right to enter into foreign alliances and to receive such foreign aid as it felt necessary for the country's security. Less successful have been Cambodia's efforts to win a wider degree of international support. Since June the king has been vainly angling for an American commitment guaranteeing Cambodia's territorial sovereignty and, in return, has indicated his country's willingness to join a Western security system for Southeast Asia. And he has also vainly pleaded for the dispatch of neutral observers to Cambodia for the purpose of ascertaining by an on-the-spot inspection that Cambodia now enjoys a degree of independence analogous to that of the Philippines, and that there is no indigenous revolt against his rule. As proof of his contention that the very great majority of the Khmer people are loyal to him, Norodom has announced his intention of integrating even the insurgents into the national community so that all will be free to participate in the elections slated to be held in 1955.

While the spotlight shifted to Geneva and attention was centered on an international solution of the whole Indochina problem, the political institutions of Cambodia remained frozen. At the time the military crisis occurred, it was not clear as to which way they would evolve. The main trend was certainly toward a consolidation of power in the king's hands. But it was not expected that the advocates of new elections or of recall of the old Assembly would long remain mute, even though experience in the 1947–52 period had shown the weaknesses of a system that permitted the legislative branch to dominate the executive. Moreover, republicanism—though in local eclipse at the moment— was expected to revive upon the return to Cambodia of students who had come under the influence of radical groups while in France. Should neighboring Viet Nam become a Communist state, it was anticipated that the monarchy in Cambodia would stand little chance of surviving.

LAOS

In many respects, the situation of Laos has been similar to that of Cambodia. Historically both countries were tributary to Thailand as well as to Vietnam until the French established protectorates over them in the late nineteenth century. Both have strongly established monarchical institutions—the dynasty of Laos dates back to the fourteenth century—and are deeply impregnated with Hinayana Buddhist culture. And both states are potentially wealthy in that they possess considerable though undeveloped natural resources upon which there is no pressure of population. Finally, both Cambodia and Laos, never restive under prewar French control, developed independence movements during the Japanese occupation which, after the war, worked closely with the Viet Nam Republic and operated from headquarters in Thailand.

Laos is the largest (83,000 square miles), least populated, and most undeveloped country of Indochina. Nearly half of its population of about one and a half million is made up of primitive tribes living in the mountainous northern provinces, which contain important mineral deposits but are agriculturally poor. Before the war, northern Laos was known as the Kingdom of Luang-Prabang, while the seven southern provinces were administered directly by the French from Vientiane. The southern provinces contain arable plains on which live the most culturally advanced elements of the population. But as their numbers were insufficient to staff the administration fully, the French brought in Vietnamese officials to supplement them. As the south offered the best opportunities for economic development, other Vietnamese and, inevitably, some Chinese followed in their wake, thereby creating in certain provinces a minority problem smaller in scale than that faced by Cambodia but analogous to it.

Again like Cambodia, Laos' use of its natural outlet to the sea through Thailand was thwarted in part by artificially created political barriers. But its isolation was more complete than that of Cambodia, for long-projected plans to link Laos with the Vietnamese countries to the east were never realized.

The country remained almost wholly undeveloped, its people were left to their own amiable and indolent devices, and the general effect was that of a delightful backwater. The French and other European residents numbered fewer than 600, they lived almost exclusively in the towns, and Franco-Laotian contacts were both minimal and friendly.

In 1941, through mediation—under Japanese pressure—of the border dispute between France and Thailand, Laos lost a slice of its western territory, but the economic loss involved was nothing like so great as was Cambodia's and it did virtually nothing to impair the traditionally close relations between Thailand and Laos. Ethnically the Laotians are a branch of the Thai, they speak the same language, and they share a common culture. Laotians cherish no bitter memories, as do the Cambodians, of the pre-French Thai administration of their country. For them, Thai sins of omission, rather than of commission, were those of neglect; Laos was a long way from Bangkok, and the Thai officials stationed in the country were not able to offer the Laotians much protection against the raids of Chinese bandits. Similarly, the gentle Laotians did not strongly reproach the French in 1941 for their failure to preserve the country intact, either from Thai irredentism or from occupation by Japanese forces.

Birth of the Issarak

Nevertheless, those two successive blows to France's prestige did leave their mark on the handful of French-educated Laotian elite. When the Vichy government directed Admiral Decoux (appointed governor general of Indochina in the summer of 1940) to collaborate with the Japanese, a handful of Laotians formed a movement which was called the Lao Issarak (Free Laotians) and some of them left the country to join the Allies either in China or Thailand. Chief among those who went to Bangkok was an intellectual idealist, Thao Oun, who proved useful to the OSS and Force 136 by suppying information to them regarding Japanese troop movements in Laos. Inside Laos, the Issarak movement did not become active until the Japanese coup of March 1945 had eliminated the French administration. At that time, some of the more anti-Japanese and pro-French Laotians joined with those French who had managed to avoid internment to form guerrilla resistance units. Other Laotian dissidents, chiefly intellectuals and princes, became active in the government, which the Japanese now largely turned over to them.

King Sisavong Vong of Luang-Prabang and his son, Crown Prince Savang, were well known for their pro-French sympathies. Probably for this reason they were slow to follow the lead given by their royal colleagues of Annam and Cambodia in proclaiming Luang-Prabang an independent kingdom within the Greater East Asia Co-prosperity Sphere. It was not until April 8 that the king declared void the treaty which had established France's protectorate; probably in reprisal for this delay, the Japanese set fire to part of the capital city two days later. To propitiate his new masters, the king sent his son and heir to Saigon where he met high-ranking Japanese military and civilian officers. But it was left to the prime minister, Prince Phetsarath,[64] to come to a working agreement with the Japanese, who gave him a fairly free hand in running the country. The Japanese, however, did make some changes, the most important of which was to unite Luang-Prabang with the seven southern provinces under one administration. And they, like the French before them, brought in Vietnamese to fill the official posts that had been vacated by Laotians reluctant to serve under the Japanese.

The French Reoccupation

The surrender of Japan in August 1945 was followed by large-scale disturbances, especially in the area around Thakhek and Savannakhet. Though the Japanese had been charged with maintaining order until the Allied forces arrived, they had very few troops stationed in Laos and in any case were not averse to seeing anti-European movements develop. The Chinese, who had been assigned the task of receiving the Japanese surrender in northern Indochina, did not reach Laos until mid-September. In the meantime a local Issarak committee, composed of Laotians and resident Vietnamese intellectuals, was formed at Vientiane under the presidency of Prince Phetsarath, which received firearms from the Japanese and took over the administration of southern Laos. Late in August a small group of French soldiers commanded by Major Fabre parachuted into Laos. With the aid of Laotian partisans they freed their compatriots, who were guarded in an internment camp by only a token Japanese force, and took up a position 18 miles outside of Vientiane. Fabre at once sent a letter to Prince Phetsarath asking him to set the time when he and his commandos could make their entry into Vientiane. Prince Phetsarath sent Fabre an evasive reply by an emissary whom Fabre persuaded to drive him into Vientiane for the purpose of having a personal talk with the Laotian premier.[65] But the prince was not to be persuaded, and he told Fabre that he could not answer for the safety of French troops and civilians, given the anti-French feeling that the Vietnamese residents were stirring up in Vientiane.

The Prince and his Issarak followers were in a serious quandary, for they wanted neither the Vietnamese nor the French to take over control of the country. To a telegram received at this time from Ho Chi Minh, in which the president of the Vietnam Republic assured Prince Phetsarath of his sympathy

[64] Prince Phetsarath, brother-in-law and cousin of the king, had been named premier of Luang-Prabang in 1941 at the same time that Admiral Decoux revived for him the title of viceroy, which had not been used for the past forty years.

[65] Surmer, André, "Aggression Vietminh contre le Royaume du Laos," Encyclopédie Coloniale, December 1953.

and support, the Laotian premier replied in friendly but vague terms. But neither was the Issarak leader pleased by the resurgence of unabashed colonialism as reflected in the actions of some of the recently liberated French. Among these was former Resident Superior Brasey, who had tactlessly dressed himself in his old uniform and presented himself to the Laotian government, announcing that he was ready to resume his old functions.[66] Then, too, a trick which Fabre—impatient at the delaying tactics of the prince—played on the Issarak was not calculated to endear him to the prince. One night Fabre had the walls of Vientiane plastered with posters carrying the name of the prince's secretary and urging the population to give an enthusiastic welcome to the French commandos when they entered Vientiane the following day. Although this ruse worked in so far as the troops' entry was concerned, Fabre later alienated the Issarak by ignoring their leadership and taking all the power at Vientiane into his own hands.

On September 8, other French parachutists entered Luang-Prabang, where, according to Issarak sources, they compelled the king to renew the protectorate agreement with France. A week later, Prince Phetsarath, from his headquarters at Vientiane, asserted that France could not resume control over Laos without a specific mandate to do so from the United Nations. This declaration was but the repetition of his Royal Proclamation of August 18, in which he said that the Japanese surrender had in no way invalidated the independence of Laos—by which he specified that he meant the whole of the country and not just Luang-Prabang. For the next month there were fruitless negotiations between the Issarak and the French, conducted against a backdrop of increasing French military activity. On September 21, French troops occupied Vientiane; three days later they removed its provincial governor, Phaya Kam Mao, from office; and on October 10 they persuaded the king to dismiss Prince Phetsarath from his post as premier. As Prince Phetsarath did not agree quickly enough to take over the leadership of the revived resistance movement (he did not do so until December 1, 1946), a "national government" was formed the next day, September 22, by the Issarak under Kam Mao. In the provisional constitution immediately adopted by this regime, all of Laos was declared to be a constitutional monarchy, in which power would be shared between the king and an elected national assembly. A few days later, the Kam Mao "government" dethroned the king on the ground that he was no longer a free agent, and on November 10 it announced that the king had agreed to abdicate and that Crown Prince Savang had recognized it as the legitimate government of Laos.

In the meantime, the military situation had become complicated by the arrival of the Chinese occupation forces and by the outbreak of fighting between the French and the Vietnamese allies of the Issarak. Early in September, the

[66] Information given the authors by Thao Oun at Bangkok, May 31, 1947.

French claimed to have intercepted a message from the Japanese commander at Hué to Ho Chi Minh, in which the latter was urged to dispatch Vietnamese troops to aid the Issarak, who were hard pressed by the French in Savannakhet, Vientiane, and Paksé provinces. The Issarak leaders, however, insisted that they never received any help from Ho, and that the only Vietnamese who supported them were those already resident in the country. Be that as it may, by mid-September fighting had broken out between the French and Vietnamese units in the central provinces, in which the Issarak did not participate and in which the Japanese—though they were technically responsible for maintaining law and order until the Chinese arrived—made no attempt to intervene.

The Chinese occupation forces, after they reached Luang-Prabang on September 22, adopted an almost equally passive attitude. They did, however, disarm and briefly arrest Major Fabre, who had been appointed the special representative of Admiral d'Argenlieu in Laos, and later temporarily obstructed the northward military advance of the French. But they never followed through on their promises of aid to the Issarak and seem generally to have acted in such a way as to prevent either side from achieving a decisive victory. Though the Chungking government may have been interested in having an independent Laos on its southern border, the Chinese occupation forces were simply concerned with getting all they could from the country. Even after the Franco-Chinese treaty of February 1946 called for their evacuation from Laos, they lingered on long enough to reap the opium harvest.

The Viet Nam Republic, for its part, was determined to prevent the French from staging as easy a comeback in Laos as they had in Cambodia. Control of Laos, they realized, would place French forces within 40 to 80 miles of the main Vietnamese cities from Hanoi to Tourane, and threaten the Republic with encirclement. To allay Laotian fears of Vietnamese imperialism and economic aggression, the Republic's propaganda repeatedly stressed the disinterested nature of its support for Laotian independence. Furthermore, it was pointed out that, despite Vietnamese aid to the Issarak, there was no Vietnamese member of the Free Laotian "government" and that the agreements between them were confined to military operations.[67] The French were convinced, however, that the Viet Nam Republic had had a hand in forcing the king's abdication, and on November 12 Admiral d'Argenlieu warned the Vietnamese that their intervention in Laotian international affairs would be severely punished.[68] For reasons of military strategy and prestige, the French were determined to reassert their control over Laos. And in view of the pro-French feeling in the north and the military weakness of the Issarak, they believed that the country could be reoccupied with few troops and little delay.

[67] *Co Dac Lap* (Hanoi), Oct. 28, 1945.
[68] Ministère des Colonies, Bulletin No. 51, Nov. 15, 1945.

This task proved to be slower and more costly than had been anticipated. After initial reverses, the French were sufficiently strengthened by reinforcements late in October to take the offensive. As the Chinese began reluctantly to withdraw, starting in February 1946, the French advanced north of Paksé, where the most serious fighting of the whole campaign took place. On March 19, they entered Savannakhet, and three days later, Thakhek was taken. Though only about 1,300 French troops and 3,000 Laotian auxiliaries were involved, Issarak resistance was crumbling fast. Guerrilla activity continued for some time, but by the end of April 1946, the great majority of the Issarak and their Vietnamese allies had crossed the Mekong and taken refuge in Thailand. Appeals for help addressed to the United States, Great Britain, and the Soviet Union were ignored, and the Issarak received real aid only from a limited number of Vietnamese and Thai. They had very little modern fighting equipment and almost no military training. Nevertheless, they had administered Laos for almost a year, and while they obviously did not get active support from the country at large, the strength and persistence of their opposition to the returning French necessitated a revision of the time-honored appraisal of the Laotians as an easygoing and politically apathetic people.

Constitutional Developments

After the French reoccupied Luang-Prabang in May 1946 they appointed a Franco-Laotian committee to draft a provisional agreement between the two countries, pending the negotiation of a treaty that would define the permanent relationship between France and Laos. This committee drew up a modus vivendi, which was signed on August 27, 1946, and which followed the same lines as the earlier provisional agreement between France and Cambodia. Laos, which now included the whole country, was to be a constitutional monarchy, with its own cabinet, responsible to a popularly elected unicameral assembly, and it would have autonomy within the French Union. As in Cambodia, French advisers were to replace the prewar Residents, and indigenous officials were placed in charge of specified government departments. An essential difference between the Cambodian and Laotian situations lay in the role of the king, for King Sisavong Vong took no initiative in granting the constitution and his powers were not curtailed thereby so drastically as were those of King Norodom. For a year after the Japanese surrender, the king's actions were highly ambiguous. As late as April 1946 he was said by the Issarak to have recognized their government and to have left to Crown Prince Savang subsequent negotiations with the French, including the signing of agreements.[69] Elderly, vacillating, and encumbered with 15 wives, King Sisavong Vong had neither the strength nor the inclination to act decisively during this critical period. Nevertheless, he continued to inspire such rever-

[69] G. Krull, "Error in Laos," *Far Eastern Survey*, June 4, 1947.

ence among his subjects that all factions contended for, and claimed they received, his support.

Later in 1946, Laotians for the first time went to the polls to elect a constituent assembly. Because of the widespread insecurity in the countryside, these elections were limited to urban centers, and even there they were hardly conclusive, because of large-scale evacuation. Notably, the population of Vientiane, which had been about 30,000 before the war, by now had been cut nearly in half by the exodus of almost all of its Vietnamese residents.[70] The constituent assembly, such as it was, made only a few minor changes in the draft constitution submitted to it. It expanded the number of King's Councillors from 5 to 9, of whom 6 were to be chosen by the king and 3 by the National Assembly, and it prolonged the length of that body's annual session from two to three months. The royal power to legislate by decree under specified circumstances, and to prolong or prorogue the Assembly, was not tampered with.

On August 25, 1947, almost exactly a year after the modus vivendi was signed, the Laotians elected 33 representatives to serve a four-year term in their first national assembly. In its inaugural session, which ran from November 26, 1947, through March 25, 1948, the deputies underwent their apprenticeship in parliamentary government. On the last day they met, the Commissioner of the French Republic paid tribute to their good will, but warned them against "a certain tendency to confuse legislative with executive powers."[71] The Assembly had transacted some business, of which the most important was the admission of Laos to the French Union. Tiao Souvannarath, who had been premier during the life of the constituent Assembly, was asked by the king to form a new government, and embryonic political parties began to emerge around outstanding personalities. The main difficulties facing the government were the perennially unfavorable economic situation, the negotiation of a treaty with France, and the enticing back to their homeland of the Free Laotian emigrés living in Thailand.

Return of the Emigrés

The last-mentioned problem was the most urgent, for the Free Laotians in Thailand numbered over 10,000 and included most of the country's tiny group of intelligentsia. From the spring of 1946 until the coup d'état of November 1947 at Bangkok, relations between the Free Laotians and the Thai government were excellent. Not only did the Pridi-backed administration have the same reasons for welcoming the Free Laotians as it had for favoring the Khmer Issarak, but the former possessed additional attractions. For one thing, early in 1946 they had renounced claims over the border area lost to Thailand

[70] *New York Times,* Mar. 26, 1950.
[71] *Bulletin d'Information de la France d'Outre-Mer,* May 1948.

in 1941, and, second, the Thai had no problem in assimilating the Free Laotian refugees such as they had in the case of the Vietnamese living in the country.

During this period the Free Laotians appeared to be better organized, more idealistic, and far more aware of the need to plan for the future than were their Cambodian counterparts.[72] Yet the seeds of dissension had already been sown among them. To begin with, there was a schism between the princes (who maintained the most elaborate protocol although living in a manner that could at best be described as modest) and the plebeian element headed by Thao Oun. Moreover, Prince Phetsarath, who was the nominal leader of the Lao Issarak, did not always see eye to eye with his two brothers, Princes Souvanna Phouma and Souvanna Vong. All of them tended to regard the main issue then at stake as the struggle between themselves and with Crown Prince Savang for the throne of Laos.

Unlike the Khmer Issarak, the Free Laotians had never broken off negotiations with the French, though they continued to organize raids across the border and guerrilla resistance inside Laos. At first the French seemed to be in no hurry to come to a settlement, and in 1946–47 there was a seven-month interval between the dispatch of successive envoys from Saigon to the Bangkok emigrés. And when they did come to negotiate, these envoys annoyed the Laotians by treating them as "charming children" not yet mature enough to know what they wanted. In reaction, the Lao Issarak asserted that they would never return until Laos became truly free, and they denounced the modus vivendi as simply perpetuating the prewar system under another name. Nevertheless, a cleavage was growing between the Issarak who insisted upon total independence for Laos and others among them who were willing to work along with the French during a transitional period. Prince Souvanna Phouma headed the latter group, while Prince Souvanna Vong[73] favored armed resistance to the French in alliance with the Viet Minh Republic.

This breach widened as the Pibul government, which had come to power at Bangkok as a result of the November 1947 coup, showed itself increasingly inhospitable to the Free Laotians. Many were having a hard time making a living, and emigrés began to return home in growing numbers. Finally, when Laos made a treaty with France (similar to the Franco-Cambodian treaty signed earlier the same year) on July 19, 1949, the backbone of the Free Laotian movement in Thailand was broken. Phaya Kam Mao and Prince

[72] By May 1947, Prince Souvanna Phouma had even drawn up a detailed project for the economic development of Laos.

[73] Born in 1912, Prince Souvanna Vong was sent by his elder brother Prince Phetsarath to France in 1930 to receive his technical education. After a few months in Paris, Souvanna Vong ceased to receive funds from his brother and had to give up his studies. Some time later he was able to resume them, thanks to the financial aid given him by Jules Bosc, a former Resident-Superior of Laos. After obtaining his degree as a mining engineer, he entered the Public Works Service in Indochina. He was stationed first at Vinh, where he met and married a Vietnamese Communist.

Souvanna Phouma proclaimed themselves satisfied that Laos had now achieved genuine independence and, in consequence, dissolved the Issarak government on October 24, 1949. An official plane sent from Saigon in November brought 25 members of the erstwhile Free Laotian government-in-exile back to Vientiane, but two of the princes—Phetsarath and Souvanna Vong—were not among them.

Prince Phetsarath, elderly and ailing, elected to stay on in Bangkok with his Thai wife, and he gradually faded from the political scene. (In May 1954 he was invited by Souvanna Phouma to return to Laos for the purpose of "settling family affairs.") But Prince Souvanna Vong, a few months before most of the Issarak returned to Laos, embarked on a course different from that taken by either of his brothers. Having been expelled from the Bangkok emigrés' movement in May 1949 for having authorized Viet Minh bands operating along the Sino-Burmese border to enter Laos,[74] Souvanna Vong returned soon afterward secretly to Indochina with a few hundred followers. After an interview with Ho Chi Minh, he set up the "Liberation Government of Laos" in north Viet Nam in August 1950. When the Viet Minh radio announced in March 1951 the formation of a united front comprising the Republic, the Khmer Issarak, and Laotian dissidents, Souvanna Vong emerged as head of a neo-Lao-Issarak movement—the Pathetlao—about which little was to be heard for the next two years.

The emigrés who returned to Vientiane in late 1949 galvanized political life in the homeland, and for the first time, parties took serious organizational form, although their programs remained largely undifferentiated. This development coincided with an intensification of Laos' chronic financial difficulties, which became acute early in 1950 after the French had announced that they would halve the subsidy which had been meeting Laotian budget deficits for the past three years. A long-standing Vietnamese grievance has been that they have always had to foot Laos' bills, and with the establishment of the Viet Nam state following Bao Dai's return to Indochina in 1949, they now needed for it all the funds at their disposal.

On February 24, 1950, Prince Boun Oum resigned as premier and Phouy Sanonikone, first president of the National Assembly, was given the task of forming a new cabinet and of coping with the grave financial situation. The budget which he presented to the Assembly early in March called for new head, land, and commercial taxes, not only to meet Laos' recurring budgetary deficit but also to pay for the perquisites of its new independence, such as the dispatch of diplomatic missions abroad. The deputies were reluctant either to increase taxes, which they claimed were already high for so undeveloped a country as Laos, or to cut expenditures, which were largely incurred to support a fantastically expensive royal family, aristocracy, and bureaucracy.[75] Yet they

[74] *Le Monde*, May 21, 1954.   [75] *New York Times*, Mar. 18, 1950.

had long demanded control over the country's foreign relations and the creation of a national army. Ultimately taxes were increased, Laos was allotted (by the Pau agreements of late 1950) 7 percent of the joint customs revenues of the Associated States, and the national army materialized sooner than was expected. For in the fall of 1950 the threatening military situation that developed in Tonkin required the transfer there of all available French troops, and it became imperative for the Laotians to organize their own armed forces.

The call to arms met with an astonishingly prompt and widespread response, and in December 1950, Laotian troops, under the command of a French officer, smashed the Viet Minh's attempt to establish a permanent base 60 miles east of Paksé. By early 1952, nearly 32,000 Laotians were under arms or undergoing military training, they had cut down guerrilla activity inside the country, and they had made Laos the most peaceful state in Indochina.[76] According to Tilman Durdin,[77] the improved military outlook stemmed from a largely satisfactory political situation, for the Laotians were more willing than either the Cambodians or Vietnamese to play the role of junior partners to the French. Realizing that they were not strong enough to stand by themselves, the Laotians had accepted limitations on their sovereignty because these were accompanied by economic aid that was indispensable to their country. Some American funds were allotted for long-term development projects, in the fields of transportation, health, and education. In the last mentioned, notable progress has already been made; 20 percent of the national budget for 1952 was devoted to the expansion of educational facilities.[78] Rural Laotians are being made aware of their country's new status in rather unusual ways: traveling troubadours who formerly sang of the exploits of ancient heroes now chant in praise of Laos' modern constitution.[79]

Largely responsible for this comparatively happy state of affairs is the Progressive Party, whose membership consists mostly of former Free Laotians. Within two years of his return from Bangkok, Prince Souvanna Phouma became premier of his country, but it had taken most of that time for the party system to take root in Laos. Elections for the 33 seats in the National Assembly were contested in August 1951 by 155 candidates belonging to five political parties. Though the opposition party, National Union of Laos, was decisively beaten in this election, no clear-cut majority was returned.[80] The Phouy Sanonikone government resigned and it was not until November 21 that a new cabinet headed by Souvanna Phouma was installed.[81] But since that time

[76] *Ibid.*, Feb. 17, 1952.

[77] *Ibid.*, Feb. 18, 1952.

[78] Primary schools in the country now number nearly 600 and are attended by more than 40,000 children, two lycées provide secondary education, a teachers' training college has been opened, and a museum has been set up at Vientiane.

[79] *Times of Indonesia*, Dec. 15, 1952.

[80] *France-Indochine*, October 1951.

[81] *Chroniques d'Outre-Mer*, December 1951.

the Souvanna Phouma government—albeit several times reshuffled—has enjoyed the Assembly's confidence, and under his leadership Laos gained admittance to various international bodies, such as FAO, WHO, and UNESCO. In August 1952 Laos applied for membership in the United Nations.

The absence of political tensions and the comparative stability of Laotian administrations permitted the government to concentrate its energies on development projects. According to the Minister of Finance, "Laos is no longer a political problem, nor yet a social one, and it is economics that are paramount."[82] Insecurity in the rural areas and adverse weather conditions in 1951–52 reduced the land under cultivation by one-tenth as compared with the area cultivated in 1950–51, when Laos already had had to import 30,000 tons of rice. The southern provinces, which had been generally self-sufficient in foodstuffs before the war, were now short of paddy, as the northern half of the country had always been. And the closing of Thailand's northeastern frontier for political reasons in 1951 had made the situation more acute by reducing imports of rice and causing its local price to rise sharply.

Early in 1952, the government announced a five-year economic plan that would cost the country some 200 million piastres annually. It aimed to improve the means of communication and the production of rice, as well as to increase the export of livestock and forest products, develop the country's hydroelectric resources, and prospect for mineral deposits.[83] Because of the small amount of capital available locally, the government admitted that it would probably have to raise a foreign loan. As regards the agricultural phase of its planning, the country was favored by the fact that most of the noncultivated arable lands in Laos belonged to the state, but it had not yet found any solution for the acute labor shortage, as the government stood firmly against the unrestricted immigration of Vietnamese and Chinese.

Such long-term difficulties as the foregoing, however, have remained largely in the realm of theory, for events in Indochina have moved rapidly since formulation of the 1952 plan. Devaluation of the piastre in May 1953 sharply increased the government's financial difficulties—the civil budget which had come to 225 million piastres in 1951 rose to an estimated 800 million for 1954. It also brought inflation to Laos, as it had to Cambodia, and the government had to set up price controls throughout the territory. But in Laos the situation was worse than in Cambodia, because of its more isolated geographical location and because its inadequate and expensive transport system aggravated the already serious difficulties of provisioning the country. As of November 1953 it was estimated that during the preceding six months the prices of imported goods in Laotian towns had risen 100 percent and those of local

82 *Ibid.*, October 1952.
83 *Ibid.*, June 1952. For details, see Jean Maillard, "Le Laos," *Encyclopédie Coloniale*, July 1953.

produce, 50 to 70 percent.[84] Moreover, the invasion of Laos in April of the same year had increased the cost of the country's military establishment (estimated at 1,400 million piastres for 1954), drained its slim manpower resources, and resulted in the loss of some territory and food stocks to the Viet Minh.

Viet Minh and Pathetlao

The Viet Minh's successive and seemingly abortive invasions of Laos, in the spring of 1953 and of 1954, gave rise to considerable speculation. In 1953, after the tremendous effort involved in operating far from base and in mountainous jungles where the population was sparse and the food supplies almost nil, the Viet Minh troops withdrew even though no serious opposition to their advance had been encountered. The next year the same performance was repeated, with the difference that in 1954 they penetrated as far as the Mekong River and benefited by a better behind-the-lines organization. Nor was any effort made this time to capture the major towns, except for Thakhek, occupied briefly earlier in the year, and it began to look as if political objectives had come to outrank military conquest in the Viet Minh's over-all strategy.

In trying to win over the rural peoples of Laos to the Communist ideology, the Viet Minh suffered from serious handicaps. Not only were the Laotians staunch Buddhists and strongly attached to their king, but they were traditionally hostile to the Vietnamese as foreign invaders of their country. The Pathetlao movement had attracted only a handful of Laotian adherents because its leader, Prince Souvanna Vong, had been absent too long from his country to possess a numerous following, and he was too obviously subservient to Viet Minh orders. Moreover, by the end of 1953 there were signs that the Prince had become a figurehead and had lost much of his influence with the Viet Minh to younger leaders who had been trained by the Communists and, therefore, enjoyed more of their confidence. Outstanding among this group were two men—Thao Kaysorn and Thao Nou Hak. Kaysorn, who was born at Savannakhet about 1916 of a Vietnamese father and Laotian mother, had come under the influence of Giap's band of Vietnamese revolutionaries while a student at the Medical University of Hanoi during the war. Following the Japanese surrender he attended the Viet Minh Military Academy (Tran quoc Tuan). This training presumably qualified him for the posts he was later assigned—that of Pathetlao Minister of Defense and deputy commander in chief of the Laotian Liberation Army, as well as that of secretary to the Communist Lao Cu Xat Party. The other outstanding Pathetlao leader, Nou Hak, was about six years older than Kaysorn and a merchant. His business had entailed frequent trips during the war between Savannakhet and the coastal towns of Annam. It was at Vinh, the birthplace of Ho Chi Minh, that Nou Hak entered into close contact with the Viet Minh, and he was indoc-

[84] *France-Indochine*, November 1953.

trinated and trained there by them after the war ended. In October 1952 he was sent to the Peking Peace Conference as Laotian delegate, and upon his return to Indochina he was named Laotian representative on the People's Liberation Committee for Viet Nam, Cambodia and Laos, that had been formed on March 6, 1951.

Reportedly it was these men who were responsible for the Viet Minh's strategy in Laos and who organized (with the help of Vietnamese refugees and Thai political dissidents in northeast Thailand) the information and guide services, as well as the food-supply depots, which facilitated the Communists' invasion in 1954. They apparently advocated concentrating upon the rural areas in the belief that the big towns were too well defended to be worth attacking and would, in any case, fall if isolated for a long period in a region controlled by Communist forces. Because of their intimate knowledge of the country, the Pathetlao and resident Viet Minh leaders could apply methods appropriate to the different regions.[85] To keep the invasion routes open, small groups of Communist agents infiltrated the key villages and tried to cultivate friendly relations with their inhabitants. Wherever possible, they bought supplies, but when villagers proved intractable their rice was requisitioned and cached away in places known only to the Communist agents. Among the mountain tribes who inhabited the Laotian slopes of the Annamite range, the Communists were able to utilize the Khas' long-standing resentment against their Laotian masters. And in the region of Samneua, which was made the headquarters of the Pathetlao "government" in 1953, the Viet Minh actively took over. There the Communists effected a mass evacuation of recalcitrant Laotian families and replaced them with Vietnamese colonists from adjacent Tonkin. Thus, by alternately applying amiability and coercion, the Communists profited by the Laotians' credulity and timidity and were able to build up "Vietminhized zones" which, by early 1954, covered probably one-third of the whole country. In so doing they were aided by disintegration of the local administration that, independently of their efforts, had been going on in Laos since the end of the war.

The extension of Luang-Prabang's frontiers in 1946 to include the seven southern provinces was not matched by a corresponding expansion of King Sisavong Vong's authority. Successively, Laos was fought over by French and Vietnamese troops, then looted by the Chinese, and finally raided by guerrillas operating from Thailand and Tonkin. In the ensuing confusion and economic distress, the feudal families in the center and south were able to regain considerable independence of action at the expense of the central power, and they capitalized upon a regional feeling of resentment at being "annexed" to the north. The Franco-Laotian treaty of 1949 caused a further

---

85 See *Le Monde*, Feb. 26, 1954, and Yves Desjacques, "Pourquoi l'Indochine ne sera pas coupée en deux," *Indochine—Sud-Est Asiatique*, March 1954.

decline in governmental authority, for it removed the cohesive force theretofore supplied by the French Protectorate. Provincial officials became increasingly political-minded, and devoted more of their energies to promoting their
own interests than to administering their respective domains. They paid little
attention to the ethnic minorities' grievances, which grew apace after the final
transfer of services to the Laotian authorities late in 1953. Even the French
officers who still commanded rural posts, and who had often acted as arbiters
in local disputes, were now wholly absorbed by the military problems that
arose from mobile warfare. In many areas the Viet Minh, with its definite
program and close-knit organization, was able simply to step into the administrative vacuum thus created.

As had already occurred in Viet Nam, the countryside of Laos was being
taken over by the revolutionary elements, leaving only the large towns in the
hands of the French and indigenous non-Communist forces. Yet in contrast to
the manner in which this had happened in Viet Nam, the process, in Laos,
was going on against the local inhabitants' wishes. In Laos and in Cambodia,
France had made concessions to local leaders just soon enough to prevent the
formation of a solid anti-French front by its nationalist and Communist opponents. By the time the Viet Minh invaded Laos and Cambodia early in
1954, the people of those countries were no longer weakened by civil warfare
as was still the case with the Vietnamese. Hence, regardless of their military
capacity to withstand the Viet Minh's aggression, the Laotians and Cambodians then regarded the Communists as foreign invaders, not as liberators.

At the Geneva Conference in April 1954 the Laotian delegation fought
hard, though not quite so tenaciously as did the Cambodians, to convince the
world that their country's situation differed basically from that of Viet Nam
(in that there was no "independence" issue and no genuine civil war) and
should, therefore, be the object of a separate arrangement. In so doing, the
delegates had evidence of domestic support—at Vientiane a meeting of hundreds of government officials and students voiced strong approval of their
stand[86]—and they naturally enjoyed the backing of the Western powers. India
and Burma, too, were convinced that the problem of Laos (and Cambodia)
should be treated as distinct from that of Viet Nam. This conviction probably
derived from the fact that Laos and Cambodia were countries of Indianized
culture and of Hinayana Buddhism, whereas Viet Nam had a Chinese-in-
spired civilization and practiced the Mahayana form of Buddhism. Red
China, for its part, showed a willingness to compromise on the Laos-Cam-
bodian issue, despite the discomfiture of their Viet Minh allies who regarded
their western neighbors as their particular zone for expansion.[87] However, in
the final settlement Laos fared less well than Cambodia. The Pathetlao were

permitted to keep the two northern provinces, contiguous to Viet Minh territory, and the French to retain two military airfield bases and a small military
mission at Vientiane.

As had previously been the case in the Laotians' dealings with France, they
were willing to accept certain infringements of their sovereignty because they
recognized realistically the vulnerability of their country to attack. Moreover,
compromise and negotiation have long been more congenial to the Laotian
temperament than fighting, and this characteristic points the way to a possible handling of the Pathetlao situation. Early in August 1954 Premier
Souvanna Phouma announced that he had already taken steps to arrange a
meeting with his half-brother, "Premier" Souvanna Vong of the Pathetlao.
In the very unlikely eventuality that the Laotians will be left alone to work
out their own destiny, this traditional Oriental approach to the problem of
the future of Laos might have reasonable chances of success.

THE THAI OF TONKIN

Another small minority, unimportant in itself, consists of the Thai of north
Indochina, who have figured in news despatches since 1950 because of the
role they have been playing in the prolonged strife between the "Democratic
Republic" of Viet Nam and the French Union forces. Two years earlier, they
briefly attracted attention when a Thai Federation was formed under French
sponsorship in 1948.

Shortly after the Japanese surrendered, it became obvious that Ho's Viet
Nam Republic and France would compete ever more sharply for the loyalty
of the ethnic minorities of Indochina. The most important of these were
naturally the Cambodians and Laotians, for most of the remaining minorities
were primitive tribes living in inaccessible and mountainous parts of the
country. Such were the Thai of upper Tonkin, but they had two features that
distinguished them from the others—they occupied a geographically strategic
location and they were ethnically and culturally related to the Laotians and
hence to the Thai of Thailand and Yunnan and to the Shans of Burma.

Of the almost half million Thai who form the most numerous and cohesive element of the Tonkin uplands population,[88] only some 250,000 of
them live in the three provinces of Lai Chau, Son La, and Phong Tho which
constitute the Thai Federation. And even though these Thai are linked by a
common ancestry, they are divided into tribes who do not intermarry, who
live in scattered villages, and who are known by names deriving from the
color of their dress. The White Thai inhabit the northernmost mountains,
and Lai Chau is their main center; the Black Thai are in the intermediate
area of Son La; and the comparatively small and insignificant tribe of Red

[88] Pierre Gourou, "Land Utilization in Upland Areas of Indochina," Institute of Pacific Relations (mimeo.; New York, 1951).

Thai live in the south. All the peoples of the area cultivate rice and some vegetables, but only the Thai irrigate their paddy fields, which are located in the deep valleys and on the lower mountain slopes. Minority tribes, chiefly the Méos and Mans, live at higher altitudes and practice shifting cultivation. Though opium is a widespread commercial crop and there is a limited barter trade in forest products across the Yunnan frontier, the region is poor and economically isolated. Proof of its material poverty is furnished by the absence from the Thai country of Chinese immigrants as well as of French tax collectors.

Since the fourteenth century, the Thai in these inhospitable valleys have led an agrarian life that has been described as approximating the classic ideal of a communal society.[89] Theirs is a feudal type of organization, headed by an overlord who himself names his subordinate administrators and who not only owns all the best and largest ricefields but also has the right to a portion of his vassals' produce. In contrast, their eastern neighbors, the Vietnamese, are plains dwellers, living in compact and semiautonomous villages.[90] The Vietnamese both fear the mountainous regions and despise their Thai inhabitants, whom they have tried to exploit and to rule. In competing with the Viet Nam Republic after the Pacific war for the adherence of these Thai, the French started out with two trump cards—a long history of Thai resistance to the more aggressive and evolved Vietnamese and a shorter but generally cordial Franco-Thai relationship.

The French officers who conquered the Thai country in 1888–89 found that the various local chiefs owed loosely defined and sometimes simultaneous allegiances to the Laotian king of Luang-Prabang, the emperor of Annam, and the Chinese viceroy of Yunnan. Although by this time the paramount family in the region was generally acknowledged to be the White Thai Deos of Lai Chau, its head—Deo Van Tri—had had to ally himself periodically with some of the Chinese bands then pillaging in Upper Tonkin. His alliance with the Chinese Black Flags enabled him usually to assert his authority over rival Chinese groups, insubordinate Thai chiefs, and the restless Méo and Man minorities. At first hostile to the invading French, Deo Van Tri was soon won over to their side, thanks to their ridding the region of the marauding Chinese and to the diplomacy of Auguste Pavie, the "pacific conqueror" of Laos.

By an agreement he made with the French, later dignified as the "Pavie Treaty," Deo Van Tri succeeded in getting himself and his heirs recognized as heads of the Sip Song Chau Thai, or 12 Thai cantons. After his death, however, the French began cutting up the cantons into different administrative units and military territories and draining power from the hereditary chiefs.

---

[89] Sol Sanders, "The Thai Federation," *Eastern World*, January 1951.
[90] P. du Limbert, "Note sur le Pays Thai," *Chroniques d'Outre-Mer*, November 1952.

The latter became simply functionaries in the eyes of French officialdom though they continued to enjoy great prestige among their own people and considerable revenues. Some Vietnamese officials were stationed in the Thai country, and centers of colonization for Vietnamese from the overcrowded delta area were established, notably at Nghia-Lo. In 1936, when the administration of this territory had come to resemble that of the Vietnamese areas, the French made another serious error in their treatment of the Thai. To achieve even greater uniformity in the administration of Tonkin, they decided to substantiate the nominal suzerainty of the emperor of Annam over the area by making Vietnamese the compulsory linguistic medium used in Thai schools. Curiously enough, it was under the Vichy regime that this error was remedied in 1940, but that same year the French government for the first time intervened in internal Thai affairs—a step which was to have grave repercussions in the future.

Deo Van Moun, son of Deo Van Tri and successor to his brother Deo Van Khang, was removed as hereditary chief of the White Thai, and his second brother, Deo Van Long, was named provincial chief, a post which he held for five years. After the Japanese coup of March 9, 1945, three French army battalions managed to escape into southern China by way of the Thai country. Deo Van Long decided to flee with them, thus leaving the way open for Deo Van Moun to return to power. Confusion reigned for the next year while two rival Vietnamese groups—the Viet Minh and the VNQDD (Nationalist Party)—strove to win control of the area. The VNQDD was strongest at Lai Chau, whereas Viet Minh adherents were preponderant at Son La, where they named successively two provincial heads—Cam Van Duong and Sa Van Minh.[91] In the meantime Deo Van Long had returned to his own country, whither he was followed in February 1946 by the French troops with whom he had escaped almost a year before. Against little opposition these troops seized key points in the Thai country—Lai Chau, Thuan Chau, Dien Bien Phu, Phong Saly, and Samneua. Just before the French arrived at Son La, the small Viet Minh force installed there razed the town and fled, taking with them Sa Van Minh, whom they apparently intended to keep in reserve as a possible replacement for Deo Van Long should they eventually reconquer the Thai country.

The ease with which France reconquered the Thai region was due not only to the Thais' reawakened hostility toward the Vietnamese but also to a bargain that had been struck between the French and Deo Van Long, now returned to his former power. The initiator and intermediary of this new agreement was a Eurasian named Bordier, formerly an official of the Agricultural Service, who later married Deo Van Long's daughter and became organizer of the Thai partisans. Through Bordier, the French were promised by Deo

91 R. Nollet, "Une Minorité du Vietnam: Les Thais," *L'Afrique et l'Asie*, No. 21, 1953.

Van Long effective aid in ousting the Vietnamese in return for a French pledge to reactivate the Pavie Treaty of 1889. And in the years that followed, both sides loyally lived up to their bargain. France created a Thai Federation in 1948, giving it an autonomous status within the French Union, and Deo Van Long consistently aided French troops, even in defeat, and turned a deaf ear to Viet Minh blandishments.

On the heels of the establishment of the Republic, the Viet Minh launched its bid for the minorities' support. In December 1945, Ho Chi Minh called a meeting, reportedly attended by 20 delegates of the ethnic-minority groups, at which he defined the minorities' rights and duties. The Republic, he assured them, regarded the ethnic minorities as equals or, rather, as brothers and sisters of Viet Nam, and would consider any aspirations or grievances they might have.[92] But in return for this fraternal love, the minorities owed the Vietnamese support for their anticolonial front, intensified economic production, and the maintenance of friendly relations with the peoples of China. Significantly, no mention was made of any Thai among the delegates who attended this meeting.

Even before the French troops moved back into the Thai region, Viet Minh propagandists there had received a setback. Late in 1945 the Thai had driven them out of their country and torn down the Republic's red flag with a yellow star.[93] In vain did the Viet Minh later stress the Republic's constitutional guaranty (Article 8) of full and equal rights for the ethnic minorities.[94] In 1946, the Republic set up various Minority Community Offices, staffed with an inspectorate,[95] and in 1947 decided to establish a secondary school for minorities in northern Tonkin.[96] Among the writers of letters expressing loyalty that were widely publicized by the Republican radio, the Thai were again conspicuous by their absence. In fact the Thai were actively supporting the French.

Even before the Thai Federation was created, the French had successfully courted the Thai and had also trained and partly equipped several battalions of Thai tribesmen to patrol their rugged landscape and protect the area against Viet Minh infiltration. An Associated Press reporter who visited the region late in 1947 described it as an oasis of peace where, contrary to the situation prevailing in the deltas of Tonkin and Cochin China, it was possible to drive far into the countryside without escort.[97] Partly responsible for this happy state of affairs were the cultural concessions made by the French, chiefly, in-

[92] Radio of the Viet Nam Republic, Dec. 6, 1945.

[93] Sanders, *op. cit.*

[94] Article 15 pledged them the right to primary education in their own tongue; Article 24, representation in the National Assembly; and Article 66, the use of their own language in law courts.

[95] "The Republic of Vietnam: One Year of Achievement," Bangkok, October 1946.

[96] Radio of the Viet Nam Republic, Mar. 20, 1947.

[97] Stan Swinton, *Bangkok Post*, Nov. 26, 1947.

creased educational facilities designed to meet Thai wishes and needs. As of 1950, some 3,200 students attending school in the region were being taught in Thai, and were using a romanized version of their language perfected by the École Française d'Extrême Orient in 1948. Graduates of the government school at Lai Chau were made eligible for admission to the school for minorities located at Dalat, where they received a higher education of the French type.[98] But most gratifying of all to Thai aspirations was the setting up on March 1, 1948, of their own Federation and the recognition of a distinctive Thai flag.

To the public at large, which had no knowledge of the terms of the Bordier–Deo Van Long agreement, creation of the Federation stemmed from the famous speech made by High Commissioner Bollaert at Hadong in September 1947, in which France was played up as the protector of Indochina's ethnic minorities. Considerable mystery surrounded the maneuvering which led up to the first meeting of the Thai Assembly at Lai Chau in early 1948, and surprise was generally expressed when Bollaert, on March 4, announced that France had graciously acceded to the wish voiced by that Assembly for establishment of a Thai Federation. The new Federation was immediately provided with a Council and a Chamber of Representatives that were given control over its administration, courts, and budget, subject to the advice of an assortment of French officials. The Council, formed by the district chieftains and head of the judiciary, was placed under the presidency of Deo Van Long, who was responsible through his French adviser to the Commissioner for France stationed at Hanoi.[99] The constitution envisaged the creation of state assemblies and the codification of customary law, and it also defined the relations between the Federation and the minority tribes. Nevertheless, the status on which it rested was frankly provisional; the execution of certain clauses was to be postponed until cessation of the current hostilities; and the precise relationship between the Federation and other countries of the French Union was left for definition in a separate agreement between the Thai and France. These lacunae were obviously the result of juridical and practical difficulties which the drafters of the constitution had been unable to solve. Opposition in principle came from both French and Vietnamese quarters, whereas practical obstacles were encountered when it came to adjusting the relationship between the Thai and their minority tribes.

Creation of the Thai Federation was greeted by stony silence in France. Up to mid-April 1948, the only Metropolitan French newspaper which discussed its formation—and adversely—was *Climats,* which usually supported the administration in Indochina. And in Indochina itself, some French officials opposed the gratuitous granting of autonomy to the Thai on terms which

[98] Sanders, *op. cit.*
[99] *Bulletin d'Information de la France d'Outre-Mer,* Paris, April 1948.

they felt might later prove to have been overliberal. As to the Vietnamese, even the pro-French element among them was indignant. Nguyen phan Long, in his Saigon newspaper, *Echo du Vietnam,*[100] warned his compatriots to be on their guard against such a dismemberment of their country, for amputation of the major Thai provinces might herald the formation of other autonomous territories for the Man, Tho, Muong, and Moi. This, he wrote, is a colonialist maneuver designed to keep possession of our richest lands or those which offer the best possibilities for colonization. "Ethnic minorities need no special protection for they are ruled by their own chiefs under the nominal and debonair sovereignty of Vietnam," and they enjoy complete freedom and good relations with the Vietnamese. Seemingly as an afterthought, he added that in any case none of these areas could prosper without the help of Vietnamese labor.

Integration of the new Federation with the Viet Nam state appeared to be the chief stumbling block to its acceptance by France's Indochinese allies. But the problem was shortly solved by a typical Asian compromise: the Thai chiefs agreed to swear allegiance to the person of the emperor, and the latter tactfully postponed installing his representative at Lai Chau. When Bao Dai visited the region in 1952, the imperial colors were flown at Lai Chau with those of the Federation, and it was gratefully noted that he was not accompanied by the governor of Tonkin, one of whose titles was "protector of minorities."[101]

According to Nollet's analysis of the situation in December 1952, the Federation's main internal problems—the Thai-minorities' relationship and the social evolution of the population as a whole—had found no such simple formula for their solution. Like so many peoples emerging from the colonial status, the Thai have been using the same tactics as their erstwhile foreign masters in transforming or obliterating the hierarchical structure and customs of their minority tribes. In late 1952, Nollet commented that—

This is indeed a way of showing that they are foreigners to the country's administration; are they not, for example, compelled to undertake a journey sometimes of several days' duration in order to have the smallest administrative problem handled at headquarters? This evidence of their subordinate position is shown even more conclusively by the existence of "preferential" corvées and taxes. This creates dissensions and resistance, and gives rise to another important aspect of the question; for the Mans, Méos, etc., are themselves divided into groups, some of which support the Vietminh. Others among them, especially those who live well within the boundaries of the Federation—the Méos, in particular—try playing first on one side and then on the other, in an attempt to throw off the Thais' tutelage.[102]

An equally serious problem, though not one of such immediacy, was the question of training cadres and forming an indigenous middle class. Being

[100] Mar. 8, 1948.   [101] Nollet, *op. cit.*   [102] Nollet, *op. cit.,* p. 46.

essentially rural and feudal, the Thai social structure had no bourgeoisie—
there was no group or class standing "between the overlord and the man of
the river or the ricefield." With the evolution of the Thai country there would
undoubtedly be many Vietnamese and Chinese eager and willing to form
such a middle class of merchants, artisans, and administrators. But the Thai
had a well-founded fear of being submerged by those peoples in the same way
as have been their Laotian cousins. Nevertheless, as the war situation evolved
they had no element of choice in the matter, for one by one the French strong-
points in the Thai country were lost and by mid-1954 the Viet Minh had overrun the whole area.

In 1950, after a five-year interval, the Viet Minh reopened its military and
political offensive in the Thai region, where it gathered momentum with each
successive campaign. During the first year, Thai loyalty to France was demon-
strated by the aid given to French troops who had had to evacuate the Laokay-
Caobang region. In 1951 the French managed with Thai help to stave off a
strong attack on Nghia-Lo. By that time some 10,000 Thai, or almost 10 percent of the local population, were mobilized under the leadership of Deo Van
Long, Bordier, and a small force of French army officers.[103] But they were
finding the Thai territory difficult to defend on a permanent basis, for it was
exposed to Viet Minh penetration from Yenbay and Laokay provinces and to
Chinese infiltration across its northern border, and troops stationed in it had
to be provisioned and reinforced by air. At that time it was still believed that
its mountainous terrain would safeguard the Thai area from ever becoming
the scene of large-scale offensive warfare, and that its vulnerability to attack
could only be offset by building a strong guerrilla force and by maintaining
a united anti-Vietnamese feeling among its Thai inhabitants.

After the loss of Nghia-Lo in October 1952, the French began secretly to
reorganize and strengthen the Thai guerrillas, notably in the Lai Chau area.
(Reportedly it was the concentration of the Thai maquis at Lai Chau that
determined the French High Command in August 1953 to sacrifice Na San
in order to maintain its position at the White Thai capital, although the latter
town was in itself of little strategic value from the military viewpoint.) Little
was known about the existence of this new maquis until October 1953 when
it was officially given credit for much of the success of a French raid at the
time on the Viet Minh base at Laokay. The Thai maquis, it was then said, was
made up of 4,000–5,000 men specially trained for sabotage operations and for
inciting resistance to the Viet Minh among the mountain peoples. Actually it
was composed of two different organizations, one directed from Hanoi by the
French army and the other under the command of Bordier, who worked independently of, but in co-operation with, a few French liaison officers.[104] Bor-

---

[103] E. Axelraed, "Coup d'Arrêt en Pays Thai," *Indochine–Sud-est Asiatique*, December 1951.
[104] Max Olivier, "Une Histore des Partisans," *Indochine–Sud-est Asiatique*, January 1954.

dier's psychological warfare program showed that he had studied closely the methods of his adversaries. To each of his men he gave a booklet entitled *The Evangel of the Anti-Communist Group*, and every evening around the camp-fires he reportedly used it as the basis for indoctrinating his "political com-missars." The latter were to recall to the Thai people the peaceful days which they had enjoyed before the Viet Minh came to the region and to tell them that a return to their happy lives of farming and hunting would be possible only when the Viet Minh were driven out of the mountain country. Evidence of the effectiveness of such propaganda came from the Viet Minh radio which, in the latter months of 1953, conducted a violent campaign against "the traitors and colonialist spies who operate behind the lines."[105]

As the military campaign increased in intensity, both sides at high levels evinced mounting recognition of the importance of the psychological factor in their struggle. In February 1952, Jean Letourneau, the first French minister ever to visit the region, promised the Thai that the Viet Nam state would, by a formal agreement, respect its special status. The Thai chieftains responded by repeating their pledge of loyalty to the Bao Dai government and of co-operation with the French.[106] The Viet Minh countered by trying to build up anti-French sentiment among the Thai, and for this they reportedly chose Bac Cam Quy, son of a Black Thai chieftain who before World War II was said to have joined the Indochina Communist Party. No exact information is available as to what inducements the Viet Minh were holding out to Thai dissidents. And though the question seems now to be largely academic, the amount and quality of the indigenous support which the Viet Minh may be able to count on, following the military conquest of the Thai country, is worth trying to appraise.

Tilman Durdin wrote in late 1952 that the Viet Minh may have offered con-siderable autonomy to younger sons of Thai chiefs, who had nothing to gain by remaining in the French fold.[107] To convince such youthful malcontents that their inherited fears of Vietnamese exploitation were groundless, Viet Minh propaganda may well have stressed the important role they could play if they would throw in their lot with the Republic and with their Free Laotian brethren. An obvious way of gaining the adherence of the Méo and Man minority tribes in the area would be to promise them independence from Thai control. Far more difficult would be winning over the big Thai chiefs, who out of self-interest or from fear of Communist-inspired concepts of agrarian re-form, have remained loyal to the French. Yet even they might feel stirred by the creation of a great Thai state based upon the embryonic one set up in Yunnan by the Chinese Communists in 1953.[108]

The vast and prolonged military effort made by the Viet Minh in the Thai

---

105 *Le Monde*, Nov. 25, 1953.   106 *Ibid.*, Feb. 13, 1952.
107 *New York Times*, Nov. 26, 1952.   108 See p. 222.

region of Tonkin, culminating in the capture of Dien Bien Phu in May 1954, attests to the importance attached by the Communist high command to the frontier zone bordering on Yunnan. While it may be argued that in any case the Viet Minh needed a crushing victory over the French for purposes of enhancing its prestige locally and of exerting diplomatic pressure at the Geneva Conference, nevertheless it chose to accept battle on the difficult Thai terrain rather than to overrun the comparatively easier territories of Laos and Cambodia.

THE BUDDHIST BLOC AND THE THAI
"AUTONOMOUS" STATE

The spotlight thrown on Southeast Asia by military developments in Indochina during the spring of 1954 incidentally disclosed the outlines of a secondary conflict whose outcome will have a decisive influence on the region's future. Thailand and Red China are actively competing for control of an area that cuts across their political frontiers with Burma and Indochina and is inhabited by an array of minorities, of whom the most important are the Thai. The David and Goliath aspect of this struggle is disguised by the fact that it has been largely carried on in propaganda form, and has also been overshadowed by the bigger drama being played in Viet Nam.

Neither of the contestants has an immediate economic interest in the area in dispute, for it is mountainous, sparsely inhabited, and almost wholly undeveloped. Self-defense is the guiding motive for both Thailand and China, but for obvious reasons, the need of the former to create a buffer state to the east is even more imperative than the desire of Red China to establish a satellite regime along its southern borders. Moreover, Thailand's desire for an eastern zone of influence extending beyond its present border has deep roots in the past, cultural overtones, and prestige value. It is also linked to an increasingly dangerous threat to the administration looming from the northeastern provinces that have long been a major center of opposition to Pibul's rule.

Although Yunnan could not be called the cradle of the Thai race, it was nevertheless the site of the early Thai kingdom of Nangchao. In the thirteenth century, pressure from the advancing armies of Kublai Khan drove many of the Thai southward along the great river valleys of the Mekong, Menam, and Salween, but other thousands remained in Yunnan. For several hundred years thereafter, the Siamese, the Burmese, and the Vietnamese were occupied in subjecting neighboring peoples to their rule and fighting among themselves for a dominant position in the area. In the late nineteenth century, the French conquest of Indochina and the British annexation of upper Burma left Siam the only independent country in the region: the other Thai peoples—the Shans, the Laotians, and those in Yunnan—found themselves governed by three different foreign powers, Britain, France, and China.

In the late 1930's a chauvinistic spirit which swept over Siam inspired that country to expand its frontiers in order to include peoples over whom it had exercised suzerain rights a century before. In particular, Bangkok aspired to bring under its control various branches of the Thai race, as was indicated by the change of Siam's name to Thailand in 1939. And for a few years during World War II Thailand's Japanese allies gratified these ambitions by handing over to its government areas in which lived not only Thai but a goodly number of Cambodians and Malays as well. After Japan's defeat in 1945, Thailand hastily returned its ill-got British territories to Burma and Malaya.[109] But France's weakened position in Indochina and the flight of many Laotian and Khmer dissidents to Thailand permitted some Bangkok leaders to continue cherishing their dream of Thai hegemony to the east. For more than a year after the war ended Thailand vainly sought to enlist foreign support for keeping the Laotian and Cambodian territories it had acquired, and in justification of its claim to them stressed the ethnic and cultural affinities between the three countries.

Though the disputed territories were unwillingly handed back to Indochina in late 1946, the Thai government under the leadership of Pridi Banomyong continued to give protection and patronage to the Free Laotian and Khmer Issarak movements which at that time were centered in Thailand.[110] But after the coup d'etat of November 1947 caused Pridi and some of his followers to flee from the country, the Pibul administration drastically altered Thailand's policy toward its eastern and northern neighbors. Mao's victories in China during 1949 frightened Pibul into joining the Western anti-Communist bloc and into re-establishing good relations with France, which involved a formal renunciation of Thailand's irredentist claims to Cambodia and Laos. Nevertheless the dream did not die, and in late 1953 it reappeared in the form of a Bangkok-sponsored proposal to form, with Laos and Cambodia, a Buddhist bloc.

What had brought about this revival of Thailand's expansionist ambitions was a surprise move that had been made in the interval by the Mao government. Red China had taken over the concept of a Greater Thai state and by early 1951 had given it a form and orientation very different from that of its Bangkok progenitors. As it emerged from Peking's tailoring, the basic idea was inevitably altered almost beyond recognition, for not only did it have to meet international communism's requirements but also had to appeal to diverse and conflicting nationalisms. From the Chinese angle it must satisfy long-standing nationalist claims to suzerainty over adjacent portions of South-

[109] See p. 109.   [110] See pp. 173, 203 ff.

east Asia and also the Communist regime's desire to be protected to the south by satellite states. Enlisting the Viet Minh's co-operation in this project encountered a minor obstacle in that it required renunciation of the Republic's long-standing propaganda claim to be exclusively a national liberation movement. But to the Viet Minh leaders over-all Communist policy was paramount, and the prospect of reasserting Annam's former dominance over Cambodia and Laos appealed to their Vietnamese nationalism. True, execution of the master plan risked alienating the frontier peoples of Burma, Laos, and Thailand, who had both historical and current cause for fearing Chinese and Vietnamese imperialism. But the danger of arousing such a widespread hostile reaction could conceivably be minimized by utilizing the ready-made trouble spots that abounded in a region where the minorities had grievances and unsatisfied aspirations. Supporting the demands of the Kachins and Karens for their own self-governing states had the additional advantage in Peking's eyes of adding to the difficulties already plaguing the anti-Communist government of Burma. And by setting up a separate state for the Thai the Communists not only could attract elements in Thailand already hostile to the Rightist Pibul administration, but at the same time add to the troubles of the French and of the kingdoms of Laos and Cambodia. Although authentic Thai were the largest minority living on both sides of the Yunnanese frontier, the Communists began to use the term "Thai" loosely for the purpose of winning over the maximum number of dissidents possible.[111] It is not yet clear whether the various Communist-sponsored "states" set up in continental Southeast Asia are to remain nominally autonomous or are eventually to be linked together in a federation. In any case, they would certainly be tightly controlled by Peking, which, it was reported in mid-1954, was engaged in establishing important industries and a communications network in its southern provinces.

Northern Indochina was obviously the most propitious base for the radiation of Communist activity throughout the border region, but De Lattre's victories in Tonkin during the fall of 1950 apparently decided the Communist command to create another center for expansion. Northeast Burma was the logical place to choose, for the infiltration there of Chinese Nationalist troops and Yunnanese guerillas (which began late in 1949) was creating friction and shortages in an area that was already troubled by indigenous revolts and large-scale smuggling. Some time during the winter of 1950–51 one of the ablest Viet Minh political commissars, known as Nguyen van Long and by a variety of other aliases, was sent to organize in the Shan States a People's Liaison Bureau for the Liberation of Southeast Asia. Probably the "autono-

[111] For example, the Karens who set up their "Free State" in east Burma, in mid-March 1954, proclaimed that they were of the "same racial stock as the Thai and had evacuated southwards from Yunnan at the same time several centuries ago." (*Bangkok Post*, Mar. 19, 1954.)

mous Kachin State" set up in 1953 and the "Free Karen State" created in early 1954 were part of his handiwork.

In the middle zone between Burma and Viet Minh territory the Communists made faster headway, for there they could utilize groups and individuals already disposed to receive their propaganda and aid. The most important of these were the 60,000 or more Indochinese refugees who had been living in Thailand since early 1946. Not only did these refugees supply agents and funds to the Viet Minh, but their concentration in the northeast provinces of Thailand gave them regular contacts with dissident Thai leaders of the area and also easy access to adjacent Laos and Cambodia. The Free Laotian and Khmer Issarak movements, directed from headquarters in Bangkok until 1948 when they were transferred to Indochina, could be counted upon to give an authentic nationalist coloring to their objective of displacing the royal governments of Luang-Prabang and Pnom-Penh. Liaison between these movements and the Viet Minh, announced in March 1951 as a joint crusade to liberate all the Indochinese peoples from colonialist oppression, was probably furnished by—among others—the Pathetlao leader, Prince Souvanna Vong. He had lived for some years in Bangkok and the Shan States, and from Yunnan made several broadcasts endorsing the Thai "autonomous" state set up there. While the Thai region of Tonkin was slated for direct military assault, the Communists held also in reserve an indigenous chief, Sa Van Minh,[112] whom they could place in charge of a local administration to be formed after their conquest of the area.

Chinese participation in the Korean war, as well as the time required for preparatory organization, probably delayed for about a year the establishment of the first "autonomous" unit. It was not until January 17, 1953, that the New China News Agency announced the birth at Sibsongpanna in Yunnan of a Thai Nationality Autonomous People's government, the capital of which was to be at Cheli. The area of this state was said to be 20,000 sq. km., and its population, it was claimed, comprised several hundred thousand Thai living on both sides of the Yunnanese frontier. Reportedly its head was a Thai national, variously called Chao Khunsin, Chaong Khan, and So-Su-Sun. At the inaugural ceremony he was quoted as saying that his newly formed state "under the leadership of Mao Tse-tung would lead the Thai people to help other nationalities inhabiting the area to establish their own autonomous governments; strive through a common effort to smash the sabotage activities of American imperialists and Chiang Kai-shek's agents; strengthen national defense; and build a new and better life for the population of the region."[113]

At Bangkok, Premier Pibul lost little time in stressing the synthetic nature of the new "sister state" and the direct threat which its creation represented for Thailand. Although no "Cabinet" had been announced for the Sibsong-

[112] See p. 213.   [113] *Bangkok Post*, Feb. 26, 1953.

panna government, Pibul anticipated that such posts would be filled by political refugees from Thailand.[114] In the months that followed, Bangkok buzzed with speculation as to which Thai nationals might become figureheads in the new state. Since Cheli had been a big operating base for the anti-Japanese Thai resistance movement during the war, it was natural to suppose that some of the Free Thai leaders who had disappeared without trace from the Bangkok political scene might now be active there. Among these was S. Tularak, ambassador to China of the Pridi-backed government, whose whereabouts after the coup d'état of November 1947 had not been known until he turned up at the Peking peace conference late in 1952 as deputy leader of the Thai delegation. As this conference had laid great stress upon the liberation of national groups in Asia, Tularak quite conceivably might have been sent to help organize the Cheli "government." Tiang Sirikhand, another prominent Free Thai and opponent of Premier Pibul, likewise mysteriously disappeared, in December 1952, and it was thought that he too might well be among the Thai nationals who were serving the purposes of the Communists in Yunnan. But above all it was the rumor that Pridi himself was the brains behind the new "autonomous" state that gained widest credence in Thailand. The failure of various attempts by Pridi supporters to overthrow the Pibul regime may have been responsible, it was argued, for Pridi's turning to the Communists as a means of regaining power. And it was recalled that in his early years Pridi had been attracted to the Marxist creed.

Actually no one knew accurately what was happening in the border area where Chinese guerrillas, regular armed forces, refugees, and opium smugglers confusedly and sometimes destructively moved about in the no-man's-land between Yunnan, Burma, Indochina, and Thailand. The northern Thai city of Chiengmai became the major rumor center, to which gravitated Chinese "jungle generals," dealers in contraband, and Yunnanese refugees. Informants claimed that 6,000 Thai "liberation troops" were being trained in Yunnan, that three major airfields had been built in Sibsongpanna, that Cheli had a powerful radio station which disseminated propaganda it received from daily contacts with Peking, and that a new road had been built from the heart of the new Thai state to Kengtung.[115] As to the personnel of the Cheli government, a little light was shed by the former prince of Sibsongpanna, Chao Mom Lar, who had fled south when the Communists took over his area. He reported that Pridi had indeed organized the administration of the new state but that its premier, Chao Khunsin, was none other than his (Chao Mom Lar's) nephew, a man about thirty years old who had formerly served in the Chinese Nationalist government.[116] According to the same source, the Chi-

---

[114] *Ibid.*, Mar. 3, 1953.

[115] *Ibid.*, June 29, 1953; *Christian Science Monitor*, Aug. 7, 1953; *Eastern World*, January 1954.   [116] *Bangkok Post*, Sept. 15, 1953.

nese Communists, after they gained control of Yunnan, sent Chao Khunsin
to Nanking for training. There he reportedly met Mao Tse-tung and discussed
with him plans for the new state, of which he was later named premier.

Whatever the truth in all these reports, the Bangkok authorities—presumably in possession of more accurate information from their own sources—
became sufficiently alarmed to make their own bid to offset the potential lure
of the Communist Thai state. And the Bangkok government's next move
showed that it had learned a lesson from its experience in 1946–47. At that
time Thai efforts to hang on to the border provinces not only had alarmed the
French in Indochina but had alienated prominent nationalists in Pnom-Penh
and Luang-Prabang as well, for they had no wish to replace domination by
France with subordination to Thailand.[117] And those Laotians and Cambodians who then supported the Thai proposal welcomed it apparently because they saw in it a means of preventing re-establishment of the Indochinese
Federation and of diminishing the role that France was preparing to play in
their countries.

Mindful of the need to allay such fears, the Bangkok government sent up a
trial balloon in the form of a speech made by its ambassador to Cambodia at
Pnom-Penh in December 1953. In this semiofficial way, Thailand proposed,
for mutual defense against communism, the formation of a Buddhist bloc,
whose very name accentuated the most important link that bound the pious
Cambodians and Laotians to the Thai. (Creation by the French of Buddhist
Institutes and Schools of Pali at Pnom-Penh and Luang-Prabang had never
seriously diminished the influence which the Buddhist clergy of Bangkok
have perennially exercised over their Laotian and Cambodian counterparts.)
The common adherence of Thailand, Cambodia, and Laos to Hinayana Buddhism was certainly the most acceptable basis on which such a bloc could be
formed, and presumably it could later be extended to include Burma and
Ceylon, the two other Asian countries professing the same form of religion.
Furthermore, in stressing as its main objective mutual defense against communism, the proposal was guaranteed to win American approval and designed to obviate any legitimate objections being raised by France. India, both
on religious grounds and as prime advocate of Asian unity, was almost sure
to welcome Thailand's move.

Next to its cultural appeal came the economic attractions contained in Thailand's proposal to form a Buddhist bloc. Northern Laos in particular had a
great and growing need for Thailand's rice and for use of that country's rail
and river transport systems to effect commercial exchanges with the outside
world. The Cambodians were emotionally drawn to the prospect of using
Thailand's communications network though they recognized that it had cer-

[117] Namarupa (nom de plume), "Perspectives d'une Communauté de Défense dans le Sud-
est Asiatique," *France-Indochine*, March 1954.

tain economic drawbacks.[118] Out of resentment for their long-standing bondage to Saigon port and out of fear of Vietnamese expansionism, many Cambodians were willing to risk their country's becoming a satellite of Thailand
rather than let it remain a junior partner or even an associate of Viet Nam.[119]
Although Thailand had a population five times the size of Cambodia's, Viet
Nam's was eight times as great and increasing at a more rapid pace. (In the
case of Laos the demographic disproportion was even more marked.) Moreover, the Cambodians and Laotians both felt much more spiritually and culturally akin to the Indianized Thai than to the Sinicized Vietnamese.

On the other hand, the economies of Cambodia, Laos, and Thailand (as
well as of Burma) were in some respects competitive and in almost every case
so similar that there was little hope of any marked increase in their mutual
commercial exchanges even if the existing artificial barriers were removed.
And Thailand did not see eye to eye with its neighbors as regards internationalization of the Mekong River. However, Bangkok was open to compromise on this issue and it was announced in mid-March 1954 that the Thai
government was considering a plan with Cambodia and Laos for joint development of the Mekong, not only as a means of communication but for irri-
gation and hydroelectrical schemes as well.[120] Thailand's assumption of the
economic leadership of the triumvirate was implicit in a suggestion Bangkok
made at the same time that it would gladly send agricultural, fisheries, and
forestry experts to its neighbors if they so requested.

The immediate reaction of the Laotian and Cambodian premiers—who
said that they had no intention of joining any bloc of which France was not a
member—reflected prudence in the face of an inflammatory international
situation rather than their long-term attitude. There was evidence that for
some time relations between the three countries had already transcended the
bounds of simple good-neighborliness,[121] and for this the groundwork may

[118] See pp. 195 ff.

[119] Namarupa, "Perspectives d'une Communauté de Défense . . ."

[120] Agence France-Presse despatch, *Times of Indonesia*, Mar. 18, 1954.

[121] Official Thai efforts to win the Cambodians and Laotions followed this timetable in
the early months of 1954:

March—A Thai mission to co-ordinate the Thailand-Cambodia rail services arrived in Pnom-
Penh. Later that month the Thai Provincial Bank received permission to open a branch in
the Khmer capital.

April—Thai capital shared in the establishment of a Khmer Commercial Bank, also to be established at Pnom-Penh. Thailand offered to sponsor Cambodia's appeal to the United Nations regarding the Viet Minh invasion. Cambodian refugees were welcomed in Thailand
even though they were causing a food shortage in Chandburi province.

At a meeting between the Thai and Laotian governors of adjoining provinces across the
Mekong, Thailand granted permission for Laotians to use Thai boats in transporting their
merchandise. In mid-April, Thailand offered to permit Laotian and Cambodian imports and
exports to pass through Bangkok port without any transit charges. And both Laotian and
Cambodian nationals were now permitted to cross into Thailand without passports. On April

have been laid by King Norodom during his brief sojourn at Bangkok in June 1953. Since early in that year talks had been going on in regard to linking the Cambodian and Thai rail systems; in December 1953 Thailand had presented Cambodia with 2,000 rifles for arming its auxiliary forces; and the same month a good-will mission sent by Laos to Bangkok had received an exceptionally warm welcome in the Thai capital.

Recognizing the limited nature of an appeal made to its neighbors on economic grounds and of the inherently passive character of a bloc based on a common religion, Thailand soon followed through with more dynamic leadership. Although the Thai ambassador in his speech at Pnom-Penh in December 1953 had stressed the opening of commercial negotiations, he had also alluded to the eventuality of a military and political alliance.[122] While it was thought that the military aid Thailand was capable of offering Cambodia and Laos was likely to be inconsiderable, in the political field Bangkok was able to offer far more effective support to their cause. At the Geneva conference the Laotian and Cambodian delegations could and did voice their own protests against the Communists' contention that the Pathetlao regime and the Khmer Issarak were authentic national liberation movements, and in so doing they had the full support of the powerful Western bloc. Hence, it was in the United Nations—to which Laos and Cambodia had not yet gained admittance—that Thailand could speak for them, albeit indirectly. While stressing the situation in Indochina as a threat to Thailand's security and, therefore, to the maintenance of world peace, the Thai delegate on June 3, 1954, significantly and adroitly drew the attention of the Security Council to the Viet Minh's "intention of overthrowing the legal governments of Laos and Cambodia" and to the ethnic and cultural differences that separated the people of those countries from the Vietnamese.[123] He also proposed that the team of observers that he asked the UN to send into Thailand be empowered also to enter Cambodia and Laos. During the long negotiations in which a compromise was worked out on the latter issue, the French delegation showed its awareness of the "Greater Thai" overtones of Thailand's proposal, and was backed by the British in insisting that the observers' operations be restricted to Thai territory.

A curious by-product of the UN discussion of Thailand's resolution was the Thai reaction to a warning given by the Nationalist Chinese delegate to the

29, Thailand admitted 5 Laotians to study at its Police Academy and 8 other Laotians to study at its Military Academy.

May—The Thai Cabinet approved the opening of an aviation service between Bangkok and Vientiane.

June—According to Thai sources, the Laotians were ordering many books and films from Thailand which they preferred to those from other sources. "As part of a comprehensive program of aid to Laos and Cambodia," the Thai Cabinet decided to give educational facilities to theological students from those countries, and to send there a number of Thai teachers.

[122] *Le Monde*, Jan. 10-11, 1954.   [123] *New York Times*, June 4, 1954.

effect that the Thai puppet state in Yunnan was "a dark circumstance" for Thailand.[124] Although Premier Pibul himself, a little more than a year before, had described formation of the Sibsongpanna regime as a serious threat to his country, his representatives at home and abroad now played it down. Thai delegates to the UN told the press that the Yunnanese movement was made up largely of Chinese and Laotians of Thai extraction. And at Bangkok a high official (General Kharb Kunchorn) said that it "seems to have faded out. If there was such a movement, probably its leaders were not strong enough or firm enough to carry on."[125] Apparently the Bangkok government had decided by this time that admitting a serious internal weakness such as that indicated by the adherence of any dissident nationals to the Yunnanese "state" might invalidate its claim to leadership of an anti-Communist bloc consisting of neighboring Buddhist countries.

The internal situation in Thailand, at the time, hardly justified such a debonair attitude. Early in May an "unusual number" of Thai were reported to have crossed into Laos.[126] Later that month a committee headed by a police major-general was appointed to investigate rumors that a plot was being hatched in the northeast provinces by Fong Siddhitharm, a former Deputy Minister of Education, an associate of Tiang Sirikhand, and a suspect in the 1949 "separatist plot" at Ubol. On May 26 Fong was arrested on the charge of being implicated in the recruitment of Laos for fighting in Viet Nam. He was also said to be in league with the Lao Issaraks, who were working not only to overthrow the Laotian government but to create a separate state in northeast Thailand of which Fong was to be the premier.[127] On June 8, another former Thai Minister, Liang Jayakarn, who was now National Assemblyman for Ubol, warned General Phao "of the imminent danger which the northeast provinces are now facing."[128] He claimed to have evidence of a movement to recruit Laos to fight in Indochina with the Viet Minh. People in the impoverished and neglected northeast, he said, were being told that they would be better off under the Pathetlao regime. The following day, the Laotian Minister to Thailand expressed to the Bangkok press his belief that the Vietnamese refugees crossing the Mekong into the northeast provinces were part of a Viet Minh plot to set up a fifth column at strategic points in Thailand.[129] As a result of all these warnings, the Pibul administration rounded up a fresh batch of Communist suspects and declared a state of emergency in the north.

The real bombshell, however, did not explode until late July when Radio Peking broadcast an article allegedly written by Pridi Banomyong in the capital of Red China. According to this source, Pridi urged the Thai people

---

[124] *Ibid.*, June 17, 1954.
[126] *Bangkok Post*, May 10, 1954.
[128] *Bangkok Post*, June 8, 1954.

[125] *Ibid.*, June 18, 1954.
[127] Reuter despatch, Hong Kong, June 21, 1954.
[129] *Ibid.*, June 9, 1954.

to "wage a struggle against their rulers" whom he specified to be the American imperialists and their puppets, the government of Thailand.[130] This heavily publicized reappearance of Pridi, after so many years of speculation as to his whereabouts, electrified Bangkok, which saw in Pridi's appeal the first step in a well-organized Communist offensive against Thailand.

[130] Associated Press despatch, Tokyo, July 30, 1954.

Chapter Five

CHRISTIAN MINORITIES

THE SEVENTEENTH century saw the birth of Christian missionary work in Southeast Asia. It took more than a hundred years for Catholic missionaries to get a firm foothold in the area, but their pioneer work gave them a considerable advantage over Protestantism, whose missionaries—except in the Indies—did not begin to make real headway in Southeast Asia until the latter part of the nineteenth century.

From the outset, nationalism has played a role in the development of the region's mission enterprises. Many years and papal intervention were required before the bitter rivalry between Portuguese, Spanish, and French missionaries was appeased by the assignment of fairly specific areas to each group. Although the Catholic missions in Southeast Asia have kept to some degree an international character, the Société des Missions Etrangères of Paris has long been the dominant Catholic organization there. Rivalry between the national groups of Protestant missionaries in the area has never been so intense, and by informal mutual agreement respective zones and functions have been worked out between them. Within the past few years, however, the arrival of missionaries no longer able to work in China has caused some overlapping that may require a revision of the existing arrangements in Southeast Asia.

American missionaries have come to predominate among the Protestant groups working in the region, primarily because of their superior resources in money and manpower and, secondarily, because they have not been associated with colonial rule there. Among the Protestants, American Methodists are the dominant group in Malaya, Presbyterians in Thailand, Baptists in Burma, and the Christian and Missionary Alliance in Indochina. Only in Indonesia, where Dutch, German, and Swiss missionaries have long been working the field, does American Protestant missionary enterprise occupy a subordinate place. Anglicans have enjoyed official prestige and patronage in the British colonies of the area, but even in Burma and Malaya they have not been able to compete with the more recently founded American missions.

Actually the two major missionary enterprises in the whole region are those of the American Protestants and the French Catholics, and though they differ markedly as regards techniques, personnel, and resources, their experience has led them to some of the same conclusions. Both recognize that, first, educational work, and, second, medical, is the most effective means of reaching the local populations; that conversions are made almost exclusively among the minorities; and that, given the resistance offered by the major population groups to renouncing their Islamic or Buddhist religions, members of those groups in urban centers can at least be influenced in their thinking and character formation by prolonged sojourns in Christian institutions.

Differences between the Catholic and Protestant mission techniques stem from their respective church organizations, type of personnel, and basic religious philosophy. Catholic missionaries are celibates, whose vows and meager living allowances require them to live lives of austerity and asceticism, and who are stationed in posts for life with home leave granted only in cases of severe illness. This enables Catholic missions to use a sizable proportion of the funds at their disposal for keeping a large number of missionaries in the field, for material equipment, and for the expansion of their work. By operating on a shoestring they have been able to compete with the more generously endowed Protestant missions. The international character of the Catholic church not only has given organizational unity to its mission enterprises but has in large measure obviated their identification with any one national power. Finally, Catholics have concentrated on the mass conversion of families, clans, or villages in order to prevent converts from feeling cut off from their family ties and social groups, as well as to swell the number of Catholics. In some of the largest stations, newly converted Asian Catholics are brought together for a period of time so that they will not feel isolated and may undergo as a group the difficulties arising out of so radical a transition from one religion to another.

Except in Java, the Protestant approach to conversion has been the reverse. The missionary, accompanied by his family, lives in Southeast Asia according to Western standards and enjoys periodic home furloughs. This entails considerable expense to the sponsoring mission, which in consequence is limited in the number of missionaries it can send and maintain in the field. Moreover, because of the stress placed on the individual soul, Protestant missionaries have tended to concentrate on single, not group, conversions. While this method has won for them a high caliber of converts, it has not produced a numerically strong local church. It has the further disadvantage of isolating the individual Christian from his social group and thus increasing the risks of his backsliding, particularly when missionaries are no longer around. Then, too, Protestantism is everywhere hampered by its division into denominations, which makes its whole structure organizationally weak and bewilders the Asian. As a consequence of these basic differences in their mission work, Protestants in Southeast Asia have developed a larger number of strong native leaders, whereas the Catholics have developed more cohesive Christian groups and retained a bigger Occidental mission personnel and stronger European control over their native church.

The results of these two opposing processes have become clearer since the war. The Japanese occupation of Southeast Asia virtually eliminated Protestant missionary work there for five and a half years, because it was in the hands of nationals of countries at war with Japan. On the other hand Catholic missionaries, except in some areas of Thailand and Indochina, were able to remain at their posts, because they came almost exclusively from nations that were either neutral or allied with the Axis. Native Protestants, after the first shock of finding themselves cut off from foreign missionary guidance and funds, carried on the work of the missions with their own resources. Like their compatriots in political circles, they acquired during this period experience and self-confidence that were to stand them in good stead when peace returned.

Thus, in the years since the Japanese surrender, the Southeast Asian Protestants have been in a stronger position to take over the management of their churches and schools than have their Catholic counterparts. The latter are just as eager to run their own organizations, but they lack the leadership to do so. And the Catholic missionaries, now depleted numerically by warfare in the areas where they were formerly strongest, are more willing than before to effect the transfer and are trying to train more Asian Catholic leaders to take over. However, they are hampered by a late start and in so doing they risk alienating the Eurasians, who have been their staunchest indigenous mainstay and who would like the European missionaries to remain in control.

Generally speaking, the voluntary acceptance of the principle of national autonomy for Southeast Asian Christians by both the Protestant and Catholic missions has gone far to allay nationalist suspicions of Christian work. Most of the area's present politicians are Western-educated, they appreciate what the missions have done for the country, and they are eager to show the world that they are modern-minded and tolerant. The superior quality of Christian missionary education has become strikingly apparent through the emergence of native Christian leaders in numbers out of all proportion to the size of their community. Needing to utilize the abilities of every member of the numerically very limited native elite and to improve rapidly the living standards of the mass of the population, Southeast Asian nationalists have both welcomed the services of their Christian compatriots and been anxious to enlist continued mission co-operation in educational and medical work. The freedom enjoyed at present by missionaries to proselytize in connection with such work varies from country to country, but it will probably continue to be permitted at least until such time as each state feels itself able to take over the work now being done by the missions.

Foreign missionaries, for their part, are willing to go along with the national states and to turn over their work by stages to indigenous leaders, always provided that the institutions they have built up remain in nonofficial,

Asian Christian hands. To enable the latter to assume control and to give strength to them as a group, Protestant missionaries have joined together to sponsor the forming in each country of the area (except Indochina, where the Protestant community is very weak numerically) of united national organizations and of union theological seminaries for the training of local leaders in a specifically Christian institution. They have also encouraged the new national churches to link themselves to such bodies as the International Missionary Council and the World Council of Churches. A meeting of the latter organization at New Delhi in December 1952 focused its attention on the transfer of leadership of Asia's church movement. Asian delegates to this conference took an active and distinctive part in its deliberations. They showed themselves eager for larger representation in such bodies, made a strong plea that all churches in the West should take a decided stand against racial discrimination, and insisted that Christians in Asia intensely disliked the denominational walls that separated one Protestant group from another.[1]

Three years before, East Asian Christians had taken the initiative of calling a conference at Bangkok. This was the first occasion on which a regional meeting of Protestant Christians was convened with a predominantly East Asian membership, leadership, and management. Unfortunately for the sense of unity which it had been hoped could be attained there, a group of American fundamentalists who had been denied admission to the conference denounced the meeting and its sponsors (the International Missionary Council and World Federation of Churches) as pro-Communist and declared they would set up an Asian organization of their own.[2] But this development did not invalidate the significance of the meeting nor the importance of its discussions. Its 90 delegates came from 16 countries and represented churches that differed widely as to membership and evolution. They found one great bond in common, however—individually and collectively they were numerically small minorities (and in some cases ethnic minorities as well) in non-Christian countries. The Buddhist or Islamic environments in which they lived were, in varying degrees, hostile and at no point friendly to them.[3] Repeated reference was made throughout the discussions to the Christian minority's encountering a situation which was being increasingly complicated by the march of political events and widespread social revolt. And the sense of the conference was that the two main problems they faced as Christian minorities were the challenge of communism and the preservation of religious freedom.

All the national governments of Southeast Asia have given constitutional guaranties of freedom of worship, but how long and to what degree such pledges will be honored depends on whether the area's present leadership re-

[1] *New York Times*, Dec. 31, 1952.   [2] *Straits Times*, Mar. 26, 1951.
[3] "The Bangkok Conference of East Asian Leaders," *International Review of Missions*, March 1950.

mains in power and resists pressures from anti-Christian and extreme leftist groups. So long as the Communists are obviously hostile to all religious groups, no breach will probably be made in the united opposition offered extreme Marxism by all the religious bodies exposed to this common menace. But the better to meet this threat, the national governments of the area are building up the religion professed by the great majority of their people. The hopelessly outnumbered Southeast Asian Christians fear that this policy, in conjunction with the nationalisms to which it is linked, may get out of hand and become a danger to their existence as individuals and as a group.

Because of its totalitarian character, Islam is generally regarded by Christians as potentially a more dangerous enemy than Buddhism. In Southeast Asia, however, although Islam is the religion professed by about half of the area's total population—the Malays of Malaya and Indonesia—Muslim fanaticism has been very exceptional. Moreover, it is even more poorly organized than is Buddhism on both the national and international planes. In even so small a country as Malaya, unity among the Muslims has been hard to achieve because each of the nine sultans is the administrative religious head of the faithful in the area which he rules. And in Indonesia, though there has been an increasing trend during the past decade toward unity, the Muslims there are still deeply divided on fundamental issues.

The Muslims of both Malaya and Indonesia have been preoccupied with local problems and are indifferent to a world Islamic bloc as such. Pakistan as a national entity is new to the area and its efforts to make Muslim policy for Southeast Asia have had little success with the only outstanding Islamic leadership of the region—that in Indonesia. To be sure, the Indonesians have gone along with Pakistan in agitating for the independence of Islamic countries still under colonial rule, but they have done so more from a political than a religious motivation. However, a propaganda tour made by the secretary of the World Muslim Conference throughout Southeast Asia in 1953 disclosed a secular reorientation of Pakistan's policy that may prove more effective in attracting the region's Muslims than its past stress on the religious leitmotiv. The aim of the next World Muslim Conference, he said, was to transform an existing "third force," consisting of the Islamic countries stretching from Morocco to Indonesia, into a Muslim Commonwealth that would stand as a strong barrier against both aggressive communism and resurgent colonialism.[4] Though the World Muslim Conference sponsored by Pakistan has suffered from competition with the Arab-bloc organization, the number of nations attending its sessions rose from 17 in 1949 to 40 in 1953.

While Buddhism in Southeast Asia is basically divided between the Hinayana and Mahayana varieties and in Thailand and Cambodia is further subdivided into sects, it is nevertheless better organized on a national basis than is

[4] United Press despatch from London, *Bangkok Post*, Sept. 28, 1953.

Islam. And internationally, too, it has rested on longer established and more purely religious relationships. For many years the Hinayana Buddhists of Thailand, Cambodia, Laos, and Burma have exchanged cultural missions on an informal basis, and since the war there has developed a two-way exchange of sacred relics among themselves and with Ceylon and India. A World Buddhist Organization, founded as a by-product of the Asian Relations Conference at New Delhi, in the spring of 1947, evolved into the World Fellowship of Buddhists, organized in Ceylon in May 1950. It has already held meetings in Ceylon, India, and Japan, attended by a large number of laymen and monks widely representative of Asian Buddhist countries. Although these delegates have seemed mainly concerned with improvement of Buddhist literature and the supervision of holy places in India, their discussions have had significant political overtones. Preoccupation with the revival and purification of their religion has appeared to many of the pious Buddhists of Southeast Asia as complementary to, and inseparable from, their national emancipation.

In the winter of 1950–51, Dr. G. P. Malalasekera, newly elected president of the World Fellowship of Buddhists, toured Southeast Asia sounding a rallying call for Buddhist unity and advocating the training of Buddhist missionaries for work abroad. During his tour he expressed the belief that Buddhism offered a middle way between capitalism and communism that might become a power for easing world tension; that the Buddhist East could and should emancipate itself from cultural domination by the West; and that the differences between Hinayana and Mahayana Buddhism could be reconciled. He encouraged co-ordination of the work being done by individual religious scholars throughout Southeast Asia and set up a press in Ceylon (The Buddhist Publishers, Ltd.) for the purpose of producing inexpensive editions of Buddhist literature and scriptures. To underscore their cultural unity, he persuaded Asian Buddhist countries to adopt a Buddhist flag, to celebrate Visaka Buja on the same day, and to pray in unison for world peace.[5] Furthermore, plans were laid for the establishment of an international Buddhist Academy or University, the holding of a second congress of the World Fellowship of Buddhists at Tokyo in 1952, and the convening of the Sixth Buddhist Council at Rangoon in 1954.

In his presidential address at the Tokyo meeting in September–October 1952, Dr. Malalasekera again urged Buddhists to unite and to propagate through modern methods their religion at home and abroad so that Buddhism could become the active force for peace and harmony in the world that its noble principles advocated and its numerical strength permitted. But in playing a more active political and social role, he warned, Buddhists must not ape the egotistical materialism of the West but remain true to their religion, which

[5] *Bangkok Post*, May 19, 1951.

sought not to conquer the world but to live in harmony with nature.[6] Unfortunately the accomplishments of the Tokyo congress fell far short of the goals set by its leader. The two main branches of Buddhism were not united as had been hoped, and the discussion as to how Buddhism would meet the threat of the atomic age did little more than produce a few resolutions advocating the release of all war prisoners.

Though the newborn World Fellowship of Buddhists apparently lacked cohesion and sustained drive, it seemed a sufficiently important development for the Chinese Communists to make their own bid to capture the leadership of Asian Buddhists. Buddhist delegates to the peace conference held at Peking shortly after the Tokyo congress reportedly issued a joint statement which asserted that "to stop aggression and to defend peace, which is the urgent task of every man and woman, is also the task of all Buddhists."[7] And in December 1952, the chief of the newly formed China Buddhist Association announced that the objectives of this body were not only to "give Buddhism an opportunity to cleanse itself" but also to unite all Buddhists under the leadership of the People's Government . . . and to maintain contacts with Buddhists in different places."[8] As yet, however, this Chinese organization has not been able to work out a uniform policy for gaining control of the various national Buddhist movements. Although Communist directives are said to advocate ignoring religion as the most effective way of effacing Buddhism in Thailand, the Viet Minh has made a direct assault on Buddhism as well as on Catholicism in Indochina.[9]

INDONESIA

Christian groups in Indonesia are faced with several problems that have arisen out of the war and its aftermath. In chronological order they are these: the transfer of responsibilities formerly assumed by foreign missionaries to the hands of indigenous Christians; adjustment of the relations between Christians and the state; and the pressures exercised by Islamic forces, both

[6] "The world," he said, "will never live in peace until men and nations give up their selfish desires, abandon their racial arrogance, and purify themselves of their colonialist spirit which is an egotistic thirst for possessions and power. The world has had enough peace conferences, treaties, and proclamations of independence which have always been followed by massacres and the total destruction of peoples and countries . . . Only religion can achieve the necessary change of heart . . . Buddhists form a fifth of the world population, so at least one-fifth of the responsibility for the happiness and peace of the world falls on us. In Ceylon, Burma, Thailand, Laos, Cambodia, and Vietnam, we have practically Buddhist governments which together can play an effective role, at least as far as Asia is concerned. With peace established in China, a united Korea, and a revitalized Japan, Buddhists will be called upon to play an increasingly important role in world affairs. . . ." (*France-Asie*, October 1952.)

[7] Reuter despatch from London, Oct. 20. 1952.

[8] *Bangkok Post*, Dec. 23, 1953.   [9] See p. 253 ff.

inside the country and in the world at large, on the national government, which affect both directly and indirectly the position of Christians in Indonesia. The first of these problems has already been solved in large measure; the second is on its way to solution; but even the dimensions of the third are not yet clear, for the influences bearing upon it are themselves still amorphous.

The transfer of responsibility for the Christian churches in Indonesia is both an administrative and a psychological problem. The administrative aspect has been difficult for the Protestants in that it has involved setting up an organizational structure for a variety of churches, some recently founded and others long established, widely dispersed throughout the archipelago, and run by missionaries of several nationalities for communities of differing size, cultural status, and ethnic composition. For the Catholics, the existence of an over-all, supranational ecclesiastical organization has obviated the need to face such administrative difficulties. But they, like the Protestants, have had to make the psychological adjustment entailed in transferring to native Catholics more authority in regard to church management. The wartime internment of many foreign missionaries by the Japanese automatically effected this transfer in the case of those belonging to countries at war with Japan. But after the Japanese surrender, the European missionary released from internment encountered a psychological hurdle analogous to that of the liberated Dutch administrator—the need to accept as permanent the *fait accompli* of authority that was formerly theirs now being vested in Indonesians who had been under their control.

Before the arrival of the Dutch, Catholic missionaries of Portuguese and Spanish nationality were working in the Moluccas and Celebes. From the outset, they underwent persecution by the local Muslims, and the conquest of those islands later on by the predominantly Protestant Dutch dealt an almost fatal blow to the progress of Catholicism in that region. For about two centuries, the Dutch allowed no Catholic priests to go to the Indies.[10] But beginning in 1848, Catholic mission work took a new lease on life, and the number of Catholics in the Indies grew from 5,670 in that year to 63,303 in 1910. Through the establishment of churches, orphanages, hospitals, and schools, Catholicism spread to Sumatra, the Lesser Sundas, New Guinea, and Borneo. And though it gained great momentum during the twentieth century and its work was subsidized by the N.E.I. government on the same basis as were Protestant missions, its early setbacks prevented its ever catching up with the more rapid progress made by Protestantism in the Archipelago.

Protestants in contemporary Indonesia number about 1,750,000,[11] and are

[10] J. P. van Santen, "The Roman Catholic Church and Its Mission Work Among Natives," *Neerlandsch Indië*, II (1929), ch. 8.

[11] In the absence of census statistics more recent than those of 1930, there is wide divergence as to the number of Protestants and Catholics now in Indonesia. According to the National

divided into many groups. The three oldest of these, which date from the earliest days of the Dutch East India Company and which enjoyed the status of a state church until 1934, have been called simply the Protestant Church of the N.E.I. Before the war this term was used to cover the European churches (which were established chiefly in urban centers and whose membership of some 120,000 was made up of Europeans, Eurasians, and Dutch-speaking Indonesians) and the "national churches" of East Indonesia (which had likewise been founded in the days of the East India Company and whose 650,000 or so members were concentrated principally in the Moluccas, Mina-hassa, and Timor). On the fringes of the Protestant church, though not actually forming a part of it, were the 5,000-odd European and Indonesian Protestants who belonged to the Reformed (Gereformeerde) church, and who were to be found mainly in the larger cities of the Indies.

Of the indigenous Protestant churches, the most important is the Batak church of Sumatra. Founded by the German Rhenish Mission, it has been described as "the largest of all the younger churches in the world."[12] Approximately 550,000 Bataks belong to this church, both in their homeland where they include the majority of the local population, and in the branches which it has established in Java. Other indigenous Protestant groups in Java number about 70,000, and they include churches set up by the Hervirmde Mission in the eastern part of the island; the Reformed church, in the south-central area; two small churches run by the Mennonite and Salatiga missions; and the Soena church in West Java. Another category of native Protestants numbering about 400,000 comprises primitive islanders. This group includes the large churches of Sangi and Talsud, founded by the Netherlands church mission; that of the Rhenish mission of Nias; a smaller church established in Borneo by Swiss missionaries from Basle; and a variety of other churches on near-by islands. And, finally, there are the 30,000 or more members of the Chinese Protestant churches, which flourish mainly in the large cities of Java.

The aggregate size of the Protestant community in Indonesia is not only astonishing in itself—numbering nearly twice as many indigenous Protestants as those of Japan and China together—but is the more remarkable in that such dimensions have been attained in a predominantly Muslim country. Indonesia is believed to have more Christians converted from Islam than any other state in the Muslim world, and on Java alone these converts number some 65,000. True, Christian missionaries have been working in these islands for more than three centuries, but, more important, they have all, whether Protestant

Council of Churches there is a total of 2,500,000 Christians in Indonesia, of whom 1,750,000 are Protestants and 750,000 Catholics (see *Christian Science Monitor*, Feb. 20, 1954). Yet estimates given J. M. van der Kroef by the Indonesian Ministry of Religious Affairs (*Far Eastern Survey*, September 1953) indicate a total of some 5 million Christians, of whom slightly more than half are believed to be Catholics.

[12] A. J. Rasker, "Church and State in Indonesia," *International Review of Missions*, July 1948.

or Catholic, used the same techniques. Protestant missionaries in Indonesia, unlike their counterparts in Malaya, Thailand, and Burma, have followed the tactics of Catholic missionaries throughout Southeast Asia and worked toward mass conversions of families and whole villages rather than of individuals.

Not only is the Protestant church of Indonesia the product of such conversions but it is concentrated in rural rather than in urban communities.[13] A consequence of this development, which paralleled the government's policy in respect to higher education, has been the comparative neglect of the urban Indonesian intellectual. Another noteworthy difference between Protestant missionary enterprise in the Indies and that elsewhere in the area has been in the nationality of missionary personnel. Throughout the world the great majority of Protestant missionaries are American or British, but in the Indies most of them have been Dutch, German, or Swiss, in that order of numerical importance. The war brought about a change in this setup, for the internment of all Germans in the Indies in the summer of 1940 reduced the Protestant missionary forces by about one-third, and Australian, American, and South African missionaries came in to replace them.

Since the war, the ranks of the Protestant missionaries working in Indonesia have shrunk, while those of the Catholics have increased. The Catholic church has sent out many new priests and stationed more lay brothers and sisters in posts throughout the archipelago, whereas the numerical strength of Protestant missionary staffs is not even up to the prewar level. This has been due in part to the replacement of foreign missionaries by Indonesian Protestant leaders,[14] and in part to the casualties suffered by members of the European missionary personnel during the months that followed the establishment of the Republic. In this period, 30 missionaries on Java alone were killed and many Indonesian Christians were either massacred or driven from their homes.[15] Although the threat of a Muslim Holy War did not materialize, it had become obvious that the mere association of a European missionary with his flock constituted a danger to the future of that group. Thus, there was every reason to reduce the number of Protestant missionaries in the field and to confine their activities to organizing relief and welfare work.

The Catholic church, on the other hand, did not suffer from the same handicaps.[16] The international character of its organization and the inclusion in its missionary personnel of workers of many nationalities kept it from being identified in the eyes of Indonesian nationalists with the colonial government, and consequently even Catholic missionaries of Dutch origin experienced less

[13] S. C. van Randwijck, "Missions and Missionaries in N.E.I.," *Virginia Methodist Advocate*, Oct. 16, 1941.

[14] In October 1953 a Christian University was opened in Java, and a theological seminary is near completion at Makassar.

[15] Survey for 1946, *International Review of Missions*, January 1947.

[16] Survey for 1949, *International Review of Missions*, January 1950.

hostility from Indonesians than did their Protestant compatriots.[17] However, the Indonesian Catholic church did suffer from one serious weakness—its lack of indigenous clergy. As of 1951, it had only 78 students in its 3 major seminaries and 670 in training in its 19 minor seminaries, and it was only in that year that a second Indonesian bishop was consecrated.[18]

Initialing of the Linggadjati agreement with the Dutch in November 1946 greatly eased the situation in regard to Protestant mission work, but even before that, the Protestant policy-making body and personnel in the field had realized that a new relationship must be worked out with the local churches. By this time the latter had rallied from the shock of discovering that their internment throughout the war had not disrupted the work of the church which had formerly been in their charge, and they were prepared to accept a change in leadership. Early in 1946 the Netherlands Reformed Synod took the lead in making this adjustment by declaring that it recognized the need to abandon colonial relationships in the ecclesiastical field. However, it did insist that "its uncompleted spiritual mission" was one from which the Dutch church could not withdraw, and that the Republican government should officially recognize it as well as its freedom to preach the gospel. Concurrently but independently, the Catholic missionaries were working for some constitutional guaranty of freedom of religion in Indonesia.

Inasmuch as the unstable political situation made futile for the time being any such attempt to define permanently the status of missionary enterprise in Indonesia, the Protestants concentrated on the urgent task of allocating spheres of missionary and indigenous activity and of creating organizational unity out of their diverse church groups.

Early in 1947, two conferences were called in order to establish the first official postwar contacts between the missionaries and the Indonesian churches. At the first of these, held at Makassar in March, the indigenous Protestant leaders of East Indonesia decided to form a provincial Christian Council for the whole area and to found there a union theological seminary where native pastors could be trained in the Indonesian language.[19] The second conference, convened the following month at Batavia, was attended by representatives of both the Indonesian and Chinese churches in Java and by Dutch missionaries still unable to return to their posts in Republican-held territories. It was there agreed that henceforth evangelical work would be the responsibility of the local churches, and that missionaries would concentrate on such specialized tasks as theological training, the development of Christian literature in the Indonesian language, and the expansion of medical and educational services. A Council of Churches and Missions for Java, which had been originally

[17] In December 1949, President Sukarno attended the opening session of a Catholic congress at which more than 1,000 delegates from all parts of the archipelago were present.

[18] *Report on Indonesia*, May 7, 1951.   [19] *International Review of Missions*, October 1947.

formed in 1941 and which was revived in May 1946 for the area under Republican control, was assigned the task of policy-making for the Protestant churches throughout the island. For all practical purposes, the organization of these two councils eliminated the prewar distinction between the Protestant church and the churches which had grown out of the work of the missions, and in their relations with the Dutch it confirmed the autonomy of the indigenous Protestants as a whole.

At the time the two councils were formed, the hope was expressed that eventually they would be united in one body for the whole archipelago, but this did not materialize until 1950, and by early 1953 complete unity had not yet been achieved.[20] Paralleling the evolution of the political situation, the proposed ecclesiastical unity was delayed by the need to reconcile the interests of diversified groups and regional loyalties. The position of the Javanese Council was the key to the future status of the Protestant community throughout the archipelago. Though it represented only one-fourth of one percent of that island's total population, its location in the heart of the Republic and among the most culturally advanced people of Indonesia subjected it to the strongest nationalist pressures and at the same time made it suspect in the eyes of other Christians who feared Javanese domination. Specifically, the Javanese Protestants had to appear superpatriots in order to allay the suspicions of the Muslim nationalist majority around them that they were aligned with their coreligionists, the Dutch. And in identifying themselves with the Republic, they risked alienating the East Indonesian Christians, such as the Ambonese, who feared cultural domination by the Islamic Javanese.

For more than a year after the Republic was established, the Javanese Protestants opposed the return of Dutch missionaries, whom they charged with having close ties with Netherlands colonial policy and with having used denominational sects as a means of creating divisions among Indonesian Protestants. Relations slowly improved between the Dutch missionaries and Javanese Protestant leaders, but the rank and file remained cautious and aloof for a longer time. The promptness with which the mother church in Holland sanctioned national leadership of Indonesian Protestants and, later, disassociated itself from the second Dutch "police action" in December 1948 went far to eliminate lingering suspicions.

For its part, the Republic pursued a conciliatory policy in regard to religious minorities. At the first meeting of the Indonesian Parliament, in September 1945, the proposal put forward by a Muslim faction to declare Indonesia an Islamic state was rejected after fierce debate. Instead, a compromise solution was accepted to establish a Ministry of Religion, which a Christian theologian would advise on matters affecting his coreligionists. For some time, too, the

[20] Winburn T. Thomas, "The Protestant Movement in Indonesia," *International Review of Missions*, July 1953.

Republic assumed the same financial responsibilities as had its predecessor the N.E.I. government toward all the Christian clergy and even offered more support for church work and enterprises than the Protestants of Indonesia thought it advisable to accept.

The Republic has offered a subsidy to the theological school that has been reopened under the auspices of the Christian Council. It has also offered opportunities for Christian religious instruction in the government schools of the Republic. The churches, however, have not accepted this aid, preferring to be a completely neutral free church in a neutral state, and basing their decision upon observation of other lands where a similar subsidy easily resulted in a degree of political subservience to the state. Moreover, there are strong tendencies in the Republic towards the recognition of Islam as the religion of their nationalism. Islam will certainly lean that way. If that happened, a bond, such as the government subsidy, would be fatal.[21]

The position of the Provincial Council of East Indonesia differed markedly from that of its counterpart in Java. To begin with, it was much bigger, representing about a million Protestants, that is to say, a larger proportion—12 percent—of that area's total population. Furthermore, the majority of its members were primitive peoples who had no cultural development analogous to that of the Javanese and to whom Christianity came as the torchbearer of civilization. From their founding, the churches of East Indonesia were more identified than were those of Java with the Netherlands Indies government. Because of this close association and because of their superior education, Christians occupied a large proportion of high government posts in East Indonesia. This not unnaturally aroused resentment on the part of the more numerous Muslims of the area, and this, in turn, made the Christians apprehensive of their position should the Republic absorb East Indonesia. Moreover, the Protestant churches there were financially unable to forego the subsidies which they had been receiving from the Dutch.

Sumatra's Batak church, like the Protestant churches of Java, was located on an island that had an overwhelmingly Muslim population. Though the Batak Christians formed only 6 percent of the total population and though Islam was more fanatical in Sumatra than in Java, yet their position was relatively strong. In the Batak country, Christians were in the majority, they were prosperous economically, and the minority in their midst was not Muslim but primitive peoples open to Christian evangelization. Yet the Batak Christians were not wholly at ease about their future. To the northwest they were flanked by the fiercely Islamic Achinese, and like all their coreligionists throughout the archipelago, they were subject to the general suspicion that being a Christian was incompatible with being a true Indonesian nationalist.

21 Rasker, *op. cit.*

The close association between Christianity and the Dutch colonial government, which compromised Indonesian Christians in the eyes of staunchly Muslim nationalists, was based on the salaries that through long custom the N.E.I. government had paid to all members of the Christian clergy, except small groups such as the Reformed church. Aside from this, Dutch colonial policy had not been partial to Christianity, though some Muslim groups claimed that it was. Characteristic of Dutch meticulousness to respect the laws and customs of non-Christian groups was the refusal of the N.E.I. government to permit Christian missionaries to operate in Bali or Atjeh and the requirement that all missionaries must apply for an official permit before they could work in the Indies. Indeed, the Dutch in some instances even subsidized Muslim organizations and teachers where they thought that public morale needed strengthening through such religious instruction.

Government subsidies were granted to mission hospitals and schools not because they were operated by Christians but on the ground that they contributed to the public welfare. If similar grants were not made to Muslim charitable works, it was because analogous Islamic institutions either did not exist or did not measure up to official requirements. According to C. A. O. van Nieuwenhuize,[22] the only valid complaint that could be made against the policy of the prewar colonial government was that it never tried to stimulate Islamic initiative in this respect by means of initial grants. Unjustified by facts as it may have been, the Muslims nevertheless harbored a grievance first against the colonial government and later against the Republic for having given financial support to Christians. Recognizing the inadvisability of continuing to keep the Christian clergy on its payroll as government officials, the Republic in 1950 made a final grant en bloc for their support. Thus, the local Christian churches were left to fend for themselves and to seek such grants as they might receive from coreligionists outside Indonesia. That these have proved far from adequate is indicated by the difficulties which some of the Indonesian churches have been experiencing in keeping afloat. The moderator of the Christian churches of mid-Java, on a visit to the United States in the summer of 1954, claimed that the main problems facing Javanese churches today were financial.

Although this separation of the state from the Christian churches was approved by all groups concerned and has strengthened the moral position of the indigenous Christians, it has done virtually nothing to settle the basic religious question at issue between the Indonesian government and its Muslim citizens. In the eyes of orthodox Muslims from other countries, Islam in Indonesia may appear to be diluted by animism and compromised by lax observance.[23] But Indonesians themselves are very conscious of being Muslims

[22] "Religious Freedom in Indonesia," *International Review of Missions*, July 1951.
[23] See p. 66.

and many of them disapprove of the secular policy pursued by their lay leaders. Probably a great many Indonesians have regarded achievement of their country's independence as only the indispensable prerequisite to establishing a Muslim state, and have believed that the cutting off of subsidies to the Christian clergy simply heralded the allocation of bigger sums to a far wider variety of Islamic activities. As Mr. van Nieuwenhuize puts it, ". . . they feel that Islam is so much a part of independent Indonesia that the financing of every aspect of Muslim life is a part of the government's duty." For example, the heavy fiscal burden which the government assumes every year in financing the Mecca pilgrimage for thousands of Indonesians is, in their eyes, only its normal function. Indeed, they seem to have expected that the Parliament could simply legislate the Islamic state into existence.

The government has found it difficult to draw the line between what its leaders consider the legitimate obligations of the state towards the religion professed by the great majority of its citizens and what many Muslims expect. Pressure has been put upon the government to use its official machinery for collecting the religious tithe, to pay the salaries of a host of religious functionaries regardless of their qualifications, and to make Islamic instruction compulsory for students attending state schools. Indonesia's shaky economy serves as a valid excuse for resisting such encroachments, which threaten to involve the government in paying for more and more of the expenses of Islam, but Indonesia's secular-minded, humanistically trained leaders do not care to separate too sharply the functions of church and state.

Their dilemma has been sharpened by the Darul Islam movement which, for the past six years, has tried by violent means, first in West Java and more recently in south Celebes and Atjeh, to transform Indonesia into a theocratic Islamic state. On the ground that Darul Islam was in open revolt against the Republic and that it used ruthless means not condoned by the Koran to achieve its ends, the government sent troops to put down the rebellion. As President Sukarno said during a tour of East Indonesia in early 1953, the establishment of an Islamic state might lead to the secession of non-Muslim regions from the Republic. Yet the realization that Darul Islam expressed the ideal of many Indonesians, and that sympathizers with that movement had infiltrated into the army and the Masjumi Party, made an all-out attack on it inadvisable and perhaps impossible.

A corollary pressure to which the government's policy of tolerance toward all creeds was being subjected was a growing anti-Christian feeling, especially among the Muslims of East Indonesia. There the hereditary rulers, to bolster their dwindling authority, had sought the support of the majority community by championing Islam. Before the transfer of sovereignty, Muslims working together with Hindus succeeded in getting the East Indonesian Parliament to pass a regulation prohibiting Christian missionary activities which the state might consider dangerous to public order.[24] Throughout Indonesia, but particularly in the eastern islands, Christianity was forging ahead in the postwar years and Indonesian Christians were playing a role disproportionate to their numbers. The country's need for leaders who were men of training and principle thrust the Christian element to the forefront. As of 1949, the majority of ministers in the East Indonesian Cabinet were Christians. In 1950, 12 of the 200 members of the Republican Parliament were of that faith. In 1951, 4 of the 20 Cabinet Ministers of the unitary state were Christians, as were the governors of the Moluccas and Celebes. And there were several active political parties composed of Christians. In the summer of 1952, Islamic bands in south Celebes (later discovered to be a local branch of the Darul Islam movement) were reported to have been forcing Christians in certain areas to embrace Islam, and in September fighting between Muslims and Christians was said to have broken out near Makassar.[25] Since that time, south Celebes Christians have been subjected to increasing violence at the hands of Muslims, and in April 1954 the government admitted its inability to give them adequate protection.[26]

The fanatical elements which Darul Islam attracts certainly do not represent the attitude of the great majority of Indonesian Muslims, but the movement is the extreme manifestation of an ideal that many would like to see realized by other means. Centuries of communal co-operation have bred in most Indonesians a wide tolerance that is, generally speaking, averse to violence and favorable to compromise and to eclecticism in religion. Though it is hard to gauge public opinion in a country like Indonesia, most Muslims apparently are willing that their Christian compatriots should practice their religion and be cared for by their own clergy. But there is some evidence that they would like to have the government forbid foreign missionary activity on the ground that, though Christians have nothing to teach Muslims in regard to religion, Christianity might make inroads and cause trouble until such time as the standard of Islamic education in the country will have made Indonesian Muslims invulnerable to conversion.[27] Though the government has not acceded to such a demand, neither has it agreed to the reiterated request from both Protestant and Catholic missionaries to give them a constitutional guaranty of freedom to work in the country.[28] Tolerance of diverse faiths, however, is embodied in the constitution of the unitary state, of which

[24] Van Nieuwenhuize, op. cit.   [25] Times of Indonesia, July 7, Sept. 25, 1952.
[26] New York Times, Apr. 8, 1954.
[27] Van Nieuwenhuize, op. cit. A Masjumi congress at Bandung in 1952 was told by one Muslim leader that Islam needed no "foreignisms" since everything Muslims need to know can be found in the Koran.
[28] See resolutions passed by the Council of Churches at its Bandung meeting in June 1953, as reported by Antara from Djakarta, July 1953. At that time it was rumored that a citizen's right to change his faith had been deleted from the draft constitution.

a part of article 29 reads: "The state shall be based upon belief in the god of all mankind. The state shall guarantee the freedom of the people to profess and exercise their own religion." And in May 1950, Indonesia accredited its first diplomatic representative to the Vatican, and mutual guaranties of religious liberty were exchanged. Moreover, in the 1951 elections in the Djogjakarta sultanate, two Catholics were chosen by an almost solidly Muslim electorate "solely because of universal respect for their integrity and ability."[28a] During 1952–53, the need increasingly felt by both the Muslims and the Christians to band together against the recent political combine of the PNI and the Communist party induced the Masjumi and Catholic leaders to work together in Parliament.

Probably the reason why the government has been able to pursue a course that is far more liberal than are the views of the great mass of its people is that Islam in Indonesia not only has been unorganized but has been associated with the nationalist movement in a negative rather than a positive sense. Since the Dutch were careful to control only the political manifestations of Islam and not to intervene in its religious aspects, Indonesian nationalists could work to a limited extent within its framework. Prewar Islamic institutions were strongest where they offered blanket opposition to foreign domination, whether on the part of Dutch colonialism or that of Muscovite communism, and were weakest when they attempted to formulate and carry out concrete programs of action. Islam offered Indonesian nationalism a unifying force, a relatively free medium in which to operate, and support for independence from any foreign—that is, non-Muslim—influences. But Islam's failure to spearhead the nationalist movement derived in part from its organizational weakness and in part from a divergency of goals on the part of its leaders.

Lacking an over-all organization, either national or international, a formally constituted priesthood, and funds regularly and uniformly collected, Indonesian Muslims as such have found it almost impossible to formulate and carry out any nation-wide positive program. Moreover, there has been a wide gap between the few Indonesian Muslims whose education abroad has led them to interpret the Koran in a liberal and socialistic sense, and the great mass of rural Muslim teachers and religious leaders (kiais) who have felt a vague desire to see Indonesia become an Islamic state governed by Koranic law. The absence of appropriate machinery for taking united action, their lack of precision as to the form and objectives which their ideal Islamic state should have, and ignorance of developments beyond their own very limited horizon have prevented the latter group from wielding the influence which its great

[28a] Robert C. Bone, Jr., "The Future of Indonesian Political Parties," *Far Eastern Survey*, February 1954. The Catholic party holds 8 seats of the provisional Parliament's total active membership of 209.

size would warrant. Through this default, the small, educated minority has been able to direct the country's policy toward the building of a welfare state, in which secular objectives have been given priority over, and generally have been separated from, purely religious goals. A struggle that has long been going on between the conservatives and progressives in Indonesia's vast Muslim party, the Masjumi, reflects this situation.

This great body, heir to a flock of prewar Islamic parties, claims a membership of some 15 million, which though inchoate and poorly organized, is yet the strongest single political force in Indonesia today. It has been dominated, generally, by a small group known as the Religious Socialists,[29] though a few of its other leaders have broken away to form other, more conservatively orthodox Islamic parties. To hold the Masjumi together, the Religious Socialists have been forced to compromise with the rightist elements and have made some concessions, especially in regard to supporting Islamic education.

By its regulations of February 1, 1951, the government required that religious instruction be given for two hours each week in state schools, in accordance with the faith professed by at least 10 of the pupils in a class. It also assumed responsibility for appointing teachers of religious education and for the curriculum taught. In theory this was fair enough but, according to Dr. van der Kroef,[30] these regulations have been interpreted in such a way as to give free rein to Islamic orthodoxy and to neglect instruction in the faiths of the Christian and Hindu minorities. Even in minor matters, such as the Mecca pilgrimage made by Vice-President Hatta in 1952, the government was forced to compromise.[31] Though it resisted pressure to send the second-ranking executive of the state to Mecca in one of its own planes, the government felt compelled to finance sending him, along with an official entourage.

What chiefly necessitated such compromises being made by the Religious Socialists was the growth of a political alliance between the Nationalists (PNI) and the extreme left-wing parties that boded no good for the Masjumi in the forthcoming national elections. To give their program the sanction of religious authority, the Masjumi liberals convened at Medan in April 1953 a conference of *ulamas*—the most respected and learned men of the Islamic community. The "instructions" which this conference issued to the faithful, though not mandatory, were bound to have enormous influence among the villagers, from whom the Masjumi drew its main support, and they represented the first joint pronouncements of the *ulama* on matters of political (as well as of economic and social) importance. Attendance at this conference reflected the concentration of Islamic strength in the western part of the archi-

[29] See G. McT. Kahin, "Indonesian Politics and Nationalism," in *Asian Nationalism and the West* (New York, 1953), p. 75.

[30] *Op. cit.*

[31] Amry Vandenbosch, "Nationalism and Religion in Indonesia," *Far Eastern Survey*, New York, Dec. 17, 1952.

pelago as well as its weakness in East Indonesia. It also indicated the large proportion of the *ulama* that was employed in the offices of the Ministry of Religion and in consequence was aloof from the rural populations to whom the conference's instructions were addressed.[32]

These instructions required every Indonesian Muslim eligible to participate in the national elections to vote exclusively for candidates pledged to implement the teachings and laws of Islam in the state. The state, it was decided, must be based on Islamic principles, it should take the form of a republic, and its head should be a Muslim directly responsible to the people. The basic human rights of individuals should be guaranteed by the state, which must give equal and just treatment before the law to each individual in regard to education and economic and social affairs,[33] and which should lay down economic policy for the well-being of the entire population. The humanitarian and liberal tone of these instructions (as well as the absence of sanctions for failure to observe them) and their vagueness as to the division of functions between church and state pointed up weak as well as strong aspects in the Masjumi leaders' program. The passive nature of the Muslims' strength was well illustrated during the Cabinet crisis of mid-1953, when an official ban on political discussions in the mosques was effectively ignored by Muslim religious leaders.

In August 1953 the formation of a government by the Nationalists, with support from the extreme left wing and two minor Muslim parties, placed the Masjumi squarely in the opposition and accentuated fundamental divisions among the Indonesians regarding the Islamic-state question. Within a few days, mass demonstrations of mutual hostility by Muslims and Communists increased tension throughout the archipelago. On August 7, Darul Islam came out into the open in south Celebes, where it stepped up its terrorist campaign against local Christians; on August 11, Islamic leaders announced the revival of Hizbullah, a militant Muslim youth organization which had fought during the independence struggle; and on September 20, an Islamic state was proclaimed at Atjeh in Sumatra. Masjumi's Religious Socialists charged the new government with being under Communist domination, and the Communists called upon the government to arm their followers to fight Darul Islam rebels.

In July 1954 the Masjumi, beginning its pre-election campaign, launched a grass-roots movement for a United Islamic Front against continued Communist infiltration and encroachment. Caught between two fires, the government tried with some success to divert attention from its inability to attain its declared objective of restoring order throughout the archipelago. Taking a strongly nationalistic tack, it stressed measures designed to "complete the

---

[32] Information from a private source.   [33] Antara despatch, Medan, Apr. 18, 1953.

revolution" by forcibly integrating foreign-dominated business into the national economy. Moreover, it revived anti-Dutch feeling by reasserting claims to Irian (western New Guinea), pressing for dissolution of the Netherlands-Indonesian Union, and arresting hundreds of Dutch citizens, some of whom were accused of aiding Darul Islam.

Throughout the first months of 1954, religious issues in the continuing conflict between Muslims and Communists were overshadowed by party politics, nationalist sentiments, and economic unrest. Though occupying a background position in the struggle, the Christian minority could not but be adversely affected, in time, by the entry of Islam as a positive force into the political life of Indonesia.

INDOCHINA

In three respects the position of Vietnamese Catholics is analogous to that of their coreligionists in Indonesia. Because in both countries they have been identified with a colonial government that was widely and mistakenly regarded as partial to Christians, indigenous Catholics in the postwar period have had to display a patriotism that outshines that of non-Christian nationalists. Then, too, their superior education and organization as a community have given Catholics an importance far greater than their numbers would indicate. And both groups of Catholics want an autonomous church free of control by foreign missionaries. In several other ways, however, the status of Vietnamese Catholics differs from that of the Indonesian Catholics. Numerically they form a larger proportion (10 percent) of the total population, they have a larger percentage of native priests,[34] and prolonged warfare in the country has made them a notable bone of contention between the opposing forces.

It was the blood of Catholic missionary martyrs shed in the empire of Annam that was the seed of France's empire in Indochina. Their persecution—for political, not religious reasons—as the vanguard of foreign aggressors produced the very effect which the Annamite emperors had sought to avoid. The conquering French admirals not only laid the foundations for an alien rule that reduced the emperor at Hué to a figurehead, but also established the Catholic church as a temporal power in Vietnam. It was during the early years of the French regime that the Société des Missions Etrangères of Paris acquired large tracts of riceland in Cochin China and Tonkin and made its greatest headway in the conversion of a community that now numbers some 2 million Vietnamese. At the turn of the century, anticlericalism was imported

[34] As of 1948, there were 1,500 Vietnamese priests, as against 400 foreign missionaries, and some 5,000 Vietnamese nuns compared with 350 European sisters. (*La Croix*, June 1, 1948.) By 1953, 7 of Indochina's 18 bishops were Vietnamese.

from France, and the *entente cordiale* between the colonial administration and the missions in Indochina gave way to an aloofness that bordered on hostility.

The nationalist fervor that swept Viet Nam during the interwar period did not leave the indigenous Catholics untouched. During the 1930's there was a mounting demand for more autonomy for their church, and petitions to the Vatican won for it some relaxation in the controls theretofore exercised over the native clergy by French missionaries. The Republic of Viet Nam, soon after it was founded in 1945, showed its recognition of the importance of the indigenous Catholic community by making repeated efforts to win its support. Capitalizing on the long-evident desire of the Vietnamese church for autonomy, the Republic sought to identify its ecclesiastical aspirations with Republican leadership of the national struggle for independence and, conversely, to make Catholics who did not align themselves with the Republic appear to be supporters of French colonialism.

At first this policy worked well, especially at the top levels. Early in its career, the Republic declared Annamite Christian martyrs' day to be a national holiday, sent encouraging messages to the Catholic community, and accorded special privileges to its Vietnamese bishops. But in certain rural areas, Marxist militants got out of hand, attacked churches, and molested Catholics. Some of the Catholic dioceses, notably those of Phat Diem and Bui Chu, rallied quickly to organize their own defense units and peoples' committees. Their bishops protested to the Republican government and announced their intention of resisting intimidation.[35]

The Republican authorities acted quickly to make amends. A decree of September 25, 1945, imposed severe penalties on individuals ·desecrating any place of worship, and the local press was told to promote a spirit of unity and harmony with those professing Christianity. This tolerance, however, was reserved for the Vietnamese faithful and did not extend to the French missionaries, who were either interned or forced to leave thir posts.[36] Of all the foreign clergy in Tonkin, only a few Spaniards were allowed to remain in Republican-held territory.[37] The Spanish bishop of Haiphong and the four Vietnamese bishops in the area were repeatedly publicized by Republican propaganda organs as in favor of the new regime. The Viet Minh radio gave out statements attributed to them in which Catholics were urged to obey the Republic's orders, French atrocities toward the Vietnamese Christians were denounced, and Catholics throughout the world were asked to support Viet Nam's independence struggle.[38] This same audience was also frequently told

---

[35] P. Devillers, *Histoire du Vietnam* (Paris, 1952), p. 185.

[36] *La Croix,* Jan. 1, 1946.

[37] Ministère des Colonies, Bulletin No. 59, Jan. 14, 1946. In the spring of 1954, the Viet Minh released almost all of the European missionaries who were captives at that time.

[38] *Achievements of the Democratic Republic of Vietnam* (pamphlet; Paris, 1948), p. 2.

that the Republic did not have a Communist government but a democratic one, which had shown respect for all religious creeds and a special solicitude for its Catholic community, and which had as an adviser to the Cabinet a Vietnamese bishop—Mgr. Le huu Tu of Phat Diem, founder of the Vietnam Catholic League.

The outbreak of hostilities between the Republic and France in December 1946 made more acute for both sides the question of Vietnamese Catholic loyalties. Outstanding Catholics were reported by the Republican radio as holding France responsible for having launched the attack at Hanoi.[39] This was an obvious effort to absolve the Republic of the charge of having caused the death of Vietnamese priests and of having done great damage to the Hanoi vicariate during the fighting. Fearing that the violence of this period might have dissipated earlier Catholic enthusiasm for the Republic, the Viet Minh tried to mend its fences. According to a French source, the Republican Sûreté issued a communiqué to its administrative committees on April 6, 1947, in which local officials were told to show marked courtesy to and considera-tion for priests in the villages under their control, to lose no opportunity to denounce the missionaries as agents and exploiters for a foreign power, and to use every possible means to convince Catholics that the Pope supported the freedom movement for Viet Nam.[40] While the Republic was playing down the revolutionary violence of its methods and stressing its role as leader of the independence movement for both the Vietnamese state and church, the French were trying to identify the Republic with an essentially antireligious communism. And in this contest the attitude of the Vatican came to be of increasing importance to both adversaries.

It proved difficult, however, to make the Catholic church commit itself. In January 1948, High Commissioner Bollaert stopped off at Rome for forty-eight hours on his way from Paris to Saigon to see the Pope and high church officials. The Vatican showed itself reluctant to alienate the Vietnamese faith-ful by appearing to side with the French. But in view of the excesses com-mitted by some Republic Marxists and the antireligious character of the Viet Minh, it also was unwilling to declare itself in sympathy with that group. Pending clarification of the situation, the church could only urge that peace be restored in Indochina, and, after considerable delay, the Pope ex-pressed in June 1948 the hope that the "Vietnamese church would surmount its difficulties."[41] Though both sides naturally tried to interpret this statement as a papal endorsement, the first round had really ended in a draw.

In 1949, communism's successes in China, which were influencing the Re-public in an ever-more-Marxist direction, caused the Vatican to reconsider its attitude, and at the same time were instilling distrust in many Vietnamese

39 Vietnam-American Friendship Association bulletin, New York, Apr. 28, 1947.
40 *Indoclim*, Sept. 8, 1948.   41 *La Croix*, June 1, 1948.

Catholics toward the Republican leadership. A visit to Rome by Bao Dai and his Catholic empress in the fall of 1949 marked the turning point, and six months later the Vatican recognized the new Viet Nam state. Thereafter the Holy See made no secret as to where its sympathies lay. In September 1950, Bao Dai was again received in private audience by the Pope, and in May 1951, high-ranking members of his entourage attended a ceremony at St. Peter's for the beatification of Viet Nam's Christian martyrs.[42] Soon after the Vatican recognized the Viet Nam state in March 1950, two new Vietnamese bishops were named for Indochina.

In Indochina itself, events followed a similar course. In 1948, the French bishop of Saigon ordered dissolution of the Republican-sponsored Catholic League in Nambo,[43] and a few months later the attempt was made to create under French auspices a Rassemblement Catholique Vietnamien (Catholic Vietnamese Rally) which was to unite all the Catholics in the three Vietnamese cauntries. It was hoped at the time to persuade the outstanding Vietnamese Catholic layman, Ngo dinh Diem, to head this organization and line it up behind Bao Dai, but instead he refused to be drawn into politics and later left the country. It was not until mid-1954 that Ngo dinh Diem returned to his native land, as Bao Dai's prime minister.

In Cochin China, French efforts to build up militant Catholic youth brigades were for some time hampered by the uncertainty that surrounded that area's political future, by counterwooing of Catholics on the part of Viet Minh organizations, and by France's urgent need to win the support of two numerically more important non-Christian religious groups—the Caodaists and the Hoa-Haoists. Yet in Bentré province, where Catholics formed only 15 percent of the total population, a remarkable Eurasian Catholic, Jean Leroy, showed what could be done on a limited scale to organize his coreligionists to resist the Viet Minh. Catholic farmers and artisans in this area had long been a target for Viet Minh reprisals because of their strong opposition to communism. So Leroy, after three years of work, succeeded in mobilizing more than 10 percent of the available Catholic manpower into the Mobile Christian Defense Corps, which by 1950 were able to take over from the French regular army the task of pacifying and administering the area.[44] His success was not only of importance locally, but had a wider significance in that it went far to convince the French that a national Vietnamese army could be built up into an effective force for use against the Viet Minh.[45]

During this same period, Tonkin was the scene of the most dramatic and

<hr>

[42] *Vietnam* (Saigon), May 18, 1951.   [43] Radio Saigon, Feb. 17, 1948.

[44] *New York Times,* Aug. 21, 1950.

[45] In 1952, a Spanish Dominican priest organized in the Hung-Yen sector of Tonkin another Catholic "self-defense" group, in which Buddhists also participated. See an article by E. Labessière, "Les Partisans de Dieu," in *Indochine–Sud-est Asiatique,* January 1953.

crucial contest for Catholic support between the French and the Republic. The bishoprics of Phat Diem and Bui Chu were situated strategically on the periphery of the Viet Minh zone and held one of the keys to control of the rice-growing delta. Bishop Le huu Tu, forewarned by Communist violence in 1945, had utilized his position as adviser to the Republic to preserve his independence of action and to maintain the autonomy of his diocese. Strongly nationalistic as well as anti-Communist, in the early stages of the war he had compared the French occupation of Viet Nam to the Babylonian captivity of the Jewish people, and had urged that all traces of colonial rule be wiped out. But by the summer of 1949, both the bishops had decided to back the Bao Dai regime as an evil lesser than that of a Communist-dominated Republic, for the ascendancy of the Viet Minh in the Republican government was growing daily more obvious and its agents and forces were increasingly infiltrating into and encroaching on their domain. In coming to this decision, the bishops met with the opposition of some of their pro-Republican priests as well as that of the merchants of Phat Diem and Bui Chu, who found trading with the Viet Minh profitable. Nevertheless, they became so convinced that their isolation had become dangerous and that their dioceses could not be defended without outside aid that they agreed to support the Bao Dai government on specified terms.

By prior arrangement, in October 1949, Vietnamese—not French—paratroopers supplied the now urgently required reinforcements to the beleaguered dioceses, and negotiations for a more lasting agreement were begun between the bishops and the French. At first, Bishop Tu refused to receive the French commandant and would only send his deputy, Father Quynh, to discuss terms.[46] The talks dragged out, but during the following months two battalions of mobile defense units were recruited from the bishoprics. The main obstacles to the integration of the two dioceses into the Viet Nam state were both political and financial in nature. The bishops wanted the French, not their parishioners, to bear the cost of equipping and supporting the Catholic militias; they also demanded to be directly represented in the Hanoi administration; and they insisted upon preserving their independence within their territories even after the latter became provinces of North Viet Nam.

The first condition did not present insuperable difficulties. But the second eventually entailed the resignation of Governor Tri, whose Dai Viet Party was opposed to having the bishops' men taken unconditionally into the government of North Viet Nam. A visit made by the two bishops to Rome in Holy Year, where they were said to have been urged to yield on the autonomy issue, and later, the arrival of forceful General de Lattre de Tassigny as the supreme French authority in Indochina, went far to solve the final point in

---

[46] The writers are indebted for information on this period to an article by Edouard Axelraed, "Chrétientés Militantes," in *Indochine–Sud-est Asiatique*, July 1951.

dispute. Even more cogent an argument was a renewal of Viet Minh aggression in the two dioceses concerned, and by the end of 1950 the bishops gave way—convinced at long last, so the official interpretation ran, that the Bao Dai government had achieved genuine independence. Upon receiving the assurance that the French would not intervene in their domains, the bishops declared their loyalty to Bao Dai and, in May 1951, the two dioceses were merged administratively to become a province of North Viet Nam.[47] On August 31, 1953, military control of the area was transferred by the French to the Vietnamese national army.

Although the French had not yet succeeded in persuading the influential Catholic Ngo family of Central Viet Nam to forsake its neutrality in the struggle, they did win important victories in regard to Catholic support both in the north and south of the country. The Republic made a few further efforts to counter these successes by propaganda. Early in 1952, President Ho, in one of his increasingly rare public appearances, told Vietnamese Catholics that they must join the liberation movement to serve both the cause of Christ and their fatherland, and his speech was followed by a celebration of the mass over Radio Viet Minh.[48] But at the same time, some of his followers were using stronger methods to turn the people of Phat Diem against their bishop, whom they denounced as a traitor in meetings sometimes held in village churches. The bishop tried to counter this in a pastoral letter, which instructed his flock not to permit such abuse of him and told priests to prevent the use of their churches by Communists.[49] But the Viet Minh's anti-Catholic campaign was intensified, and in June 1952 fighting broke out between Viet Minh elements and Catholics in both Phat Diem and Thanh Hoa. Five months later, it was reported that the Viet Minh had arrested the Vietnamese bishop of Vinh, along with committee members of the regional Catholic League. Violent clashes were said to have followed these arrests, and Republican guards were stationed outside Catholic churches in an overt attempt to intimidate the local Christians.

The Viet Minh soon overran nine-tenths of the Bui Chu area, and it was not until the French Union forces reoccupied it in the summer of 1953 that the fate of its Catholic community became known. A report issued by the Catholic missionary agency, Fides,[50] stated that of the 189 priests in the Bui Chu area, 50 had fled to the "free zone," 12 had been imprisoned, and the remainder had been placed under "continual surveillance, often compelled to do forced labor, frequently brought to trial, and were the victims of shameful indignities." In February 1954 the French High Command reported that the Viet Minh had massacred some 1,400 inhabitants of a Catholic village near

[47] *Vietnam,* June 1, 1951. [48] *Christian Science Monitor,* Apr. 1, 1952.
[49] *Vietnam News,* Saigon, June 15, 1952.
[50] *Vietnam Information Weekly Bulletin,* Saigon, Sept. 21, 1953.

Hanoi, and at about the same time had seized 20 Catholic missionaries and nuns in central Laos.[51] Although the Viet Minh in its turn charged that the French had slaughtered Catholics in Ha Nam province during an air raid in October 1953,[52] this was not played up specifically as a French attack on religion but rather as additional evidence of the general brutality of colonialists. By this time the Viet Minh had apparently grown indifferent as to the attitude of their Catholic compatriots and had embarked on a widely antireligious policy.

Since the "cease-fire" in Viet Nam, Catholics throughout the world have expressed concern for the fate of their coreligionists now under Communist rule there. Vietnamese Catholic militiamen fought valiantly beside the French Union forces during the bloody battles for control of the Tonkinese delta that followed the fall of Dien Bien Phu, and thousands of Catholic refugees swarmed into overcrowded Hanoi in search of safety. Some of these refugees reported belated efforts made by the Viet Minh, including a radio broadcast assurance given by Ho Chi Minh on his government's policy of freedom of religion, for the purpose of persuading the Catholics of Tonkin to remain in the Communist-controlled area. They also reported being robbed by Viet Minh sympathizers, after they had decided to evacuate their homes.[53] In July 1954, the *Osservatore Romano* reflected the Vatican's "deep and unsettling fears" of large-scale persecution of indigenous Catholics and of the "heavy pressure" that would undoubtedly be exerted on the Vietnamese clergy to conform themselves to the Communist pattern.[54]

In November 1953 the Viet Minh made its first open attack on the Buddhist religion, charging that Buddhism had "drugged the people and lowered their fighting instincts."[55] The Viet Minh radio urged that monks be jailed as spies and traitors and that pagodas be burned down. Rather wistfully its spokesman admitted that it would be impossible to exterminate the religion of 90 percent of the Vietnamese people, including the wives and children of party members, but it advocated "harassing tactics," saying that by such methods the number of Buddhists within the Viet Minh zone had already been reduced to a mere 30 percent of the population there.

The Viet Minh's efforts to eliminate Buddhism, however, ran into an obstacle that could by no stretch of the imagination be attributed to Western imperialist machinations. This was a revival of Buddhism, in both its Hinayana and Mahayana forms, that had been gathering momentum throughout Southeast Asia since 1949. In the Mahayana areas, prolonged warfare appears

---

[51] United Press despatch, Hanoi, Feb. 17, 1954.

[52] Vietnam News Service, *The Burman* (Rangoon), Nov. 23, 1953.

[53] Associated Press despatch, Hanoi, July 30, 1954.

[54] *New York Herald Tribune,* July 22, 1954.

[55] United Press despatch, Saigon, Nov. 24, 1953.

to have stimulated, rather than arrested, the activities of the Buddhist associations of North and South Viet Nam, which have now expanded their program of publications and lectures and which participate in the work of the World Fellowship of Buddhists.[56] In the Hinayana regions of Laos and, to a lesser extent, those of Cambodia, Buddhism has undergone a veritable renaissance.

In Laos, where Buddhism has long been the state religion and its clergy has been organized in a hierarchy paralleling that of the administration, the initiative for reforming it was taken by an outstanding layman, Nhouy Abhay, when he was Minister of Rites and Education. In a lecture at Vientiane in May 1949, Abhay said, "We have made of Buddhism a doctrine of lethargy and of resignation that is leading to the death of our race."[57] To check this decadent trend, Abhay proposed improving the education of the Buddhist clergy and modernizing their ecclesiastical organization in such a way as to make the administration of the Laotian church more democratic and more independent of the state. At that time, the sangha (monks and novices) in Laos numbered 13,700, of whom 2,388 had administrative as well as religious duties,[58] but the whole church had no patriarch or distinctive administration of its own as did the sangha in neighboring Hinayana countries. And although Laos had two Buddhist institutes that published religious works, and 71 schools of Pali with a teaching corps of 130 monks, it had no institution of higher Buddhist learning and the educational standard of its clergy was low.

To remedy this unsatisfactory state of religious affairs, a royal ordinance in 1951 created the office of patriarch (Phra Sangharaja) and set up a Religious Council (Chao Rajagana) of five members. These high dignitaries were to be democratically elected by the whole sangha, acting as an Ecclesiastical Assembly, and though they were assigned joint responsibility for the administration of the Buddhist church in Laos, they were required to have the Assembly's consent in making decisions on certain matters. Despite the fact that no patriarch had yet been chosen, the Religious Council was inaugurated on February 26, 1953, at which time the government transferred to it financial and administrative control over the sangha. Early in 1953, also, a Higher Schol of Pali was formally opened at Vientiane with an initial student body composed of 18 monks. This institution now makes available to a far larger percentage of the Laotian clergy an advanced religious training that was formerly attainable by only a handful among them who were able to go to the higher schools of Pali learning at Pnom-Penh and Bangkok. Further evidence of the revitalization of Laotian Buddhism lies in the current movement to repair many of the country's pagodas, to create new elementary schools of Pali, and to form more regional Buddhist associations. The Ecclesiastical As-

---

[56] *France-Asie*, Saigon, April 1952.
[57] Phimmasone Phouvong, "L'Ecole Supérieure de Pali du Laos," *France-Asie*, August 1953.
[58] *France-Asie*, May 1953.

sembly, at a meeting held in Vientiane toward the end of 1952, voted to collaborate with the World Fellowship of Buddhists and to undertake a campaign for diffusing a better knowledge of Buddhism among both the Laotian elite and masses.

In Cambodia, Buddhism has developed along different lines. To begin with, it has never been so closely tied to the state as in Laos and it has been divided into two principal sects. Of these the Mohanikay, with its 2,662 wats and 77,000 monks and novices, has been more important than the Thommayutt, which possesses only 101 pagodas and a clergy numbering somewhat under 2,500. Furthermore, the postwar political turmoil in Cambodia has affected that country's clergy far more than it has touched the more docile and disciplined monks of Laos. In Cambodia, Son ngoc Thanh enlisted the support of some political-minded monks in the early days of the Japanese occupation, and he continued to make use of this influential element of Cambodian society when he was organizing his second resistance movement in 1952.[59] A "communiqué" issued in June 1953 by the monkly followers of Son ngoc Thanh from his jungle headquarters in Battambang went so far as to threaten France with a "holy war" if Cambodia were not immediately granted full independence.[60]

Apart from such secular and nationalistic activities, Cambodia's clergy shared in the cultural and religious aspects of Buddhism's postwar revival throughout Southeast Asia. In 1951–52 the state's secondary schools were opened to monks for the purpose of improving their general education, and steps were taken to transform the Higher School of Pali at Pnom-Penh into an institution of university caliber. The government offered prizes to monks who showed proficiency in religious and other examinations, and in 1953 built a hospital exclusively for members of the Buddhist clergy at Tuk Koak. Active participation in the program of the World Fellowship of Buddhists led to an increase in the number of Cambodian monks going to India for study, in the local propagation of Buddhism, and in the creation of regional religious centers "so as to show to all the world that Cambodia remains Buddhist."[61] As a tribute to the piety and learning of Cambodian Buddhists, the head of the Mohanikay sect was invited to Burma to help in the editing of Buddhist scriptures, preparatory to the convening at Rangoon in May 1954 of the Sixth Buddhist Council.

Curiously enough, the postwar revival of Buddhism throughout Indochina has been paralleled by a growth in the local Catholic and Protestant communities. The combination of persecution and increased indigenous control appears to account for the remarkable increase in the number of Vietnamese

[59] See pp. 170, 184.
[60] United Press despatch from Saigon, *Bangkok Post*, June 29, 1953.
[61] *France-Asie*, May 1953.

Catholics,[62] and the Protestant community throughout Indochina has like-wise grown during the same period. However, Protestant activity has always been very limited there, membership in that church being variously estimated as 14,000 to 25,000. French Protestant pastors, with few exceptions, have con-fined their work to caring for their compatriots in the main towns, and the only missionary enterprise in the country—aside from a small-scale effort by the Seventh Day Adventists—has been that of the American Christian and Missionary Alliance (C.M.A.), which opened its first station at Tourane in 1911. For some years the French colonial government regarded the C.M.A. with suspicion as an American attempt to gain a foothold in Indochina. But by the 1920's, the C.M.A. was able to extend its work to Cambodia and to Laos and among primitive tribes of Vietnam. In the years since World War II, it has been regarded with positive benevolence by the French authorities. This change has been due in part to the vastly altered international political outlook and in part to the addition of social-welfare activities to the C.M.A.'s theretofore wholly evangelical program.

As of 1947, the C.M.A. had 66 missionaries and 161 native workers in the country, who were ministering to 9,768 church members.[63] By that year, each of the mission's six stations had been reoccupied, but a great deal of its property had been damaged during the war and postwar hostilities, and its converts had undergone great privations and sufferings. It was the pitiable condition of their church members that induced the C.M.A. missionaries to open insti-tutions for the care of lepers and of the orphans of Christian parents who had been killed during the long-drawn-out strife in Indochina. Since the areas in which Protestantism had taken root were not—until 1953—those in which most of the fighting occurred, the C.M.A. reported a revival of religious fervor and an expansion of its work in the years 1950 to 1952.[64] In Laos alone, it was reported in February 1954, 4,000 conversions had been made during the preceding three years.[65] At the time when the Viet Minh's invasion of Laos in 1953 forced the C.M.A. to abandon its work there to native pastors, the Alliance was maintaining throughout Indochina 116 missionaries, 265 in-digenous workers, 6 Bible schools, 2 mission presses, a leprosarium, and an orphanage.[66] Despite this growth of its work, the C.M.A. was increasingly encountering financial and psychological obstacles. The war and the devalua-tion of the piastre in 1953 had so upset the local economy that its churches

[62] Survey for 1950, *International Review of Missions,* January 1951.

[63] *Report of the Foreign Department of the Christian and Missionary Alliance,* New York, May 1948.

[64] C. Bois, "Eglises et missions Protestantes d'Indochine," *Journal des Missions Evangéliques* (Paris), July-September 1952.

[65] *Christian Science Monitor,* Feb. 27, 1954.

[66] R. P. Beaver, "Christian Missions in Indochina," *Missionary Research Library Occasional Bulletin* (New York), Dec. 23, 1953.

could no longer support themselves, and some of the younger pastors felt that the United States should give them more financial aid in their time of trial. Moreover, as one commentator put it, ". . . nationalistic and communistic ideologies have confused the thinking of many Christians."[67]

This was, in a way, only a natural reaction to the rapidly deteriorating situation in Indochina, but in part it was the result of Communist propaganda which had taken some note of the Protestant community despite its small size. In 1948, Viet Minh organs reported that an appeal had been made by Vietnamese Protestants to their coreligionists throughout the world to pray for an "end to the terrible carnage being committed by the French in Vietnam, . . . in which already 5,000 [sic] Protestants have already been killed."[68] The French Protestant Church, for its part, seems to have felt a stirring of conscience in regard to the Indochina war. In January 1952, the *Bulletin de Recherche* of the Protestant parishes of France addressed a message to its readers asking them "to study urgently the serious problem of the responsibility of the Protestant churches of France regarding the war in Indochina. . . . We are responsible before God for the people where God has placed us." This appeal was signed by many pastors and teachers, but the following day it was hastily announced that this was an expression of views by a private organization and could not be considered an official Protestant statement.[69]

BURMA

Christians in prewar Burma totaled nearly 350,000, more than 80 percent of whom belonged to the indigenous peoples and about two-thirds of whom were Karens. The numerical increase noted in the Christian community during the interwar period, however, largely reflected the growth of conversions among non-Burmese peoples and the immigration of alien Asian Christians.[70] As of 1950, Christians formed roughly 3 percent of Burma's total population.[71]

Catholicism was brought to Burma almost two centuries before Protestantism; in 1721 Catholic missionaries opened their first school there. Under the guidance of the Bishop of Burma and Apostolic Vicars stationed at Rangoon and Mandalay, the mission extended its work throughout the country and among the remote hill tribes. Outstanding among Catholic medical institutions have been the Kemmendine Leper Asylum (350 inmates in 1948) and the Bishop Bigandet Home for Incurables (200 patients in 1948). Catholic missionaries have maintained free dispensaries in connection with their schools throughout Burma, and their nursing orders have supplied the staff for nonmission as well as mission hospitals. Of their many educational insti-

[67] *Ibid.*

[68] *Vietnam-American Friendship Association Bulletin*, New York, Apr. 25, 1948.

[69] *Le Monde*, Feb. 9, 1952.

[70] Christian, *op. cit.*, p. 203.   [71] Burma Press Service, Dec. 3, 1950.

tutions, the most influential has been St. Paul's School for boys in Rangoon, where many of the country's present leaders were trained. The number of Catholics in Burma rose from some 7,000 at the time of the British conquest of lower Burma in 1824 to 90,000 in 1948, when they constituted 27 percent of all the Christians in the country.

Protestantism, off to a much later start than Catholicism in Burma, quickly outdistanced its other Christian competitor, and the newest arrival among its denominations—the American Baptist Mission—was able in fairly short order to win a larger membership than any of its British colleagues. On the eve of the Pacific war, there were 260,000 Protestants in the country, of whom more than 137,000 were Baptists. That denomination, which had a marked success among the Karens, accounted for 64 percent of all the Christians then in Burma, as compared with 7 percent for its nearest Protestant rivals, the Anglicans, who numbered only some 25,000. The work of the leading Protestant groups was chiefly in the educational field, but they also operated important medical centers. Before the war, Baptist mission hospitals treated more than 62,000 patients annually.[72] Among 708 Baptist educational institutions of all types, which were attended by more than 35,000 boys and girls, the outstanding were Judson College and the Pyinmina Agricultural School. The smaller Anglican community, however, long enjoyed the prestige of being the established church, and it counted among its membership most of the British officials in the country, as well as a goodly number of Eurasians who followed their lead. On a less elaborate scale than the Baptists, the Anglicans maintained schools and hospitals, and they concentrated their work mainly among the Burmese community. There were other minor Protestant groups, such as the Scotch Presbyterians, who cared for their European members and some of the immigrant Indians; the Seventh Day Adventists, who have increased their medical work since the war; and the Methodists, both British and American, whose evangelical and educational activities have been directed chiefly toward the Chinese of Rangoon.

For both Catholic and Protestant missions, the war wrought great havoc on both their material equipment and their personnel. As elsewhere in Southeast Asia, more Catholic than Protestant missionaries were allowed by the Japanese to remain at their posts. Everywhere, however, their work was cut down, and of the staff of the Catholic mission at Mandalay, 123 were interned and several were killed during the Burma campaigns.[73] Protestant missionaries returning after the Japanese surrender managed to re-establish themselves quickly. Thanks to the money and supplies they brought with them they were able to carry out relief work that was in many ways more effective than that being done by the British Military Administration.[74]

[72] Christian, op. cit., p. 206.   [73] La Croix, Sept. 18, 1945.

[74] W. Zimmerman, "Continental Southeastern Asia" (typescript; Paris, March 1946).

In the years that have passed since the war ended, foreign missionary work in Burma has been set back by the upsurge of Burmese nationalism and hampered by the civil strife that has afflicted the country since 1948 and has particularly involved the largest indigenous Christian group, the Karens.

In theory, Burma's transition to independence has not made the position of Christians in the country dangerous or even difficult. The constitution of the Union of Burma, drafted in 1947, pledged that the state would not "impose any disabilities or make any discrimination on the ground of religious profession, belief, or status." It did, however, recognize the special position of Buddhism as the faith of about 85 percent of the population and forbade the abuse of religion for political purposes. The leaders of the dominant political party, the Anti-Fascist People's Freedom League, have consistently maintained that Burma is a secular national state, and as recently as December 1951 the premier and Parliament resisted considerable pressure to declare Buddhism the state religion. Rather, it is by indirect means that foreign missionary work in the country has been curtailed, through governmental encroachment on mission activities and through its encouragement of Buddhism.

Baptist missionaries declined in numbers from 76 before the war to 41 by 1948, and the native staff of this denomination also incurred losses. Depletion in the ranks of the indigenous Christian pastors and teachers has been due to various causes—death, the Japanese occupation, retirement for reasons of age, and transfer to more remunerative employment. But as regards foreign missionaries, ". . . government policy relating to entry and residence permits has sharply restricted the possibility of any considerable reinforcement of missionary staff."[75] Sheer necessity, arising out of the shortage of doctors in the country, made the government temporarily lenient toward medical missionaries, but the trial of Dr. Gordon Seagrave on a charge of treason in 1951 showed that this tolerance had very distinct limitations. Currently, restrictions on the entry of missionaries apply equally to medical and evangelical personnel.

It is chiefly in the educational field that foreign missions have felt the encroachments of nationalism, and this in turn has hampered the training of more indigenous leaders in specifically Christian institutions. Judson College, which before the war had more than 500 students and was the only school at collegiate level under Christian management, was absorbed shortly after the Japanese surrender into the University of Rangoon. And though many other mission schools have reopened since the war, shortage of staff and the damage done to their buildings and equipment forced a number of them to combine or to operate on a scale smaller than before the war.[76]

[75] Survey for 1949, *International Review of Missions*, January 1950.
[76] "Christian Missions in Burma," *International Review of Missions*, January 1947.

In 1946 an Educational Policy Enquiry Committee was created, and it laid down the policy that independent Burma has since set itself to follow. Its members, noting that the great majority of prewar government-aided schools in Burma had been those sponsored by foreign missions, recommended that—

without prejudice to the claim of privately owned and managed schools to recognition without aid by the government, provided that they conform to approved curricula and prescribed standards of efficiency, the system of grants-in-aid be withdrawn and that a system of schools wholly managed and financed by the state through the agency of the Education Department be adopted instead.[77]

Mission schools thus were not forbidden to operate, but the cutting off of government subsidies gave those missions with large support from their homelands a considerable advantage as regards the rehabilitation of their work in Burma. Despite the higher fees dictated by this deprivation of subsidies and by inflated living costs, mission schools are still very popular[78] because of the high standards they have maintained, especially in the teaching of English, and because the government has been encountering great practical difficulties in reviving even such state schools as existed before the war. In 1952, the government embarked on its five-year program to provide free compulsory education in all state educational institutions, including the university, but for many years the shortage of trained staff, appropriate housing, and equipment will prevent it from carrying out its obvious intention of taking over all the educational facilities in the country.

The recent history of the Methodist school in Rangoon is a case in point. During the winter of 1953–54, the mission board of governors decided to dismiss the school's headmaster—a move that was vigorously opposed by the teachers' and students' unions and by some of the pupils' parents. In consequence, the school was closed down and several thousand students demanded that the government take over the institution.[79] To avert violence, the administration did so but at the same time claimed that its tenure would be only temporary as it lacked the facilities to assume permanently such a responsibility. As of July, the controversy seemed to have died down, but it had been played up by some Rangoon newspapers as an issue between the vested interest of foreign missions as opposed to the national welfare of the Burmese.[80]

Tied in with this expansion and secularization of the school system is the problem of training indigenous Christian leaders. As a result of the policy pursued by the Japanese occupation authorities, there have been few native

[77] *Report of the Educational Policy Enquiry Committee* (mimeo.; Rangoon, 1947).

[78] As of 1953, there were 14 Christian schools in Rangoon attended by about 10,000 pupils, three-fourths of whom were non-Christian. Somewhat the same situation prevailed in the rest of Burma. (Survey for 1953, *International Review of Missions*, January 1954.)

[79] *The Burman*, May 14, 1954.   [80] *Ibid.*, May 26, 1954.

candidates for the ministry who have the proper educational qualifications. And owing to the lack of specifically Christian institutions of higher learning in the postwar period, few are now receiving a training that might fit them to take the place of foreign missionaries. Then, too, with declining missionary support and the years of strife which have impoverished Burma, there is the question of how a sizable indigenous clergy can be paid adequate salaries. The foreign missions in Burma, and elsewhere in the area, have recognized the need to replace their Western staff by local talent, but they are confronted with the dilemma which is perhaps more serious in Burma than in neighboring countries of just how and to whom the transfer will be made.

Undoubtedly many Burmese Christians share their compatriots' desire to have all their organized activities placed under national control. A Burmese pastor, the Reverend U Oh Khin, on a visit to the United States in 1948, said that foreign missionaries should turn over to Burmans such key positions as those of mission-school principalships.[81] On the other hand, some of the Christian groups in Burma seem to have been hesitant about assuming such responsibilities. A former Anglican missionary reported in 1952 that—

Rangoon diocese is learning to do without the missionary—a policy which it did not choose for itself but which is being pressed upon it by its far-seeing bishop. In Burma there has been no struggle to wrest leadership from the missionaries. Ever since Bishop Stubbs appointed John Hla Gyaw in the early 1930s to take sole charge of the Toungoo mission—leadership has been pressed on the nationals. Some have said that they were not yet ready for it.[82]

After the war, the Anglican Church moved much farther in this direction when it named a Karen (Francis Ah Mya) and a Burman (John Aung Hla) assistant bishops at Rangoon. In 1951, co-ordination of activities among all the Protestant sects in Burma was brought about through the creation of a Christian Council. By going more than halfway to meet the aspirations of Christian Burmese for ecclesiastical autonomy, the foreign missionaries have forced the growth of indigenous leadership and, at the same time, have retained the good will of their former flocks. The last-mentioned development has been of the utmost importance in preventing the Karen revolt from degenerating into a war of religion, in which the considerable Christian element among the Karens and the foreign missionaries remaining in the country might have been persecuted for a faith that the Buddhist Burmans could have interpreted as antinationalist. When the British Anglican Bishop West retired in the spring of 1954, Premier Nu paid him an extraordinary tribute. After admitting

[81] *The Burman*, July 8, 1948.
[82] G. Appleton, "Burma Revisited," *East and West Review*, October 1952.

that he had been under a serious misconception as to the Bishop's connection with the insurgents during the early days of the Karen rebellion, Nu "unhesitatingly asserted that nearly 75 percent of the spiritual progress in the country (since independence) has been due to the Bishop's efforts."[83] Despite the sincere regret widely expressed at Bishop West's departure, some journalists saw in it the "end of the Anglican epoch in Burma, though the Baptists and Roman Catholics have somehow managed to maintain the rule of Judson and Bigandet."[84]

The current revival of Buddhism in Burma may well have a far-reaching influence on the evolution of Christianity there. British colonial policy, by eliminating all indigenous opposition, undermined the Buddhist phongyis (monks)[85] in the educational field and in juridical matters, and under that policy the Anglican clergy were paid from public funds. Many Burmese nationalists deeply resented this state of things. Both as Buddhists and as nationalists they opposed proselytizing by British and American missionaries, and one of the first moves made by independent Burma was to attempt to restore the Buddhist clergy to their pre-British position. On the other hand, the new leaders of Burma were determined that the Buddhist monks should not resume the stormy political role they had played during the last years of British rule, and they stood firm against any participation in politics by the clergy.[86] With independence won, they argued, there was no further need for such activities on the part of the monks, who henceforth should devote themselves to their religious duties. The government and conservative Buddhist laymen were eager to improve their educational standards, discipline, and ecclesiastical organization so that they might become a stronger spiritual force in the country. The Buddhist hierarchy apparently concurred, and only a few individual monks and groups persisted in occasionally trying to influence political events.

It is noteworthy that very little of the impetus for the renascence of Buddhism has come from the indigenous clergy. Foreign Buddhist converts, such as Francis Story and Christmas Humphreys, have sparked the missionary movement which sent the head of the World Buddhist Missionary Society of Mandalay—himself an Italian by birth—to proselytize in the United States and sent various monks to win to Buddhism the animists of the northern hill tribes. Some private organizations have been formed to propagate Buddhism and translate appropriate religious works into Burmese, and their continued impetus has been supplied by the laity. As a whole, the Buddhist clergy has

---

[83] *The Burman*, Apr. 24, 1954.   [84] *Ibid.*, Apr. 1, 1954.
[85] There are about 120,000 monks and novices in Burma.
[86] See John Cady, "Religion and Politics in Modern Burma," *Far Eastern Quarterly*, February 1953.

remained passive and has simply gone along with efforts made by outsiders, chiefly the government, to improve their status, raise their caliber, and extend the range of their activities.

In June 1947, almost a year before Burma became independent, there was created a Department of Religious Affairs, which eventually was raised to a Ministry. At first it was given the task of devising a way of setting up ecclesiastical courts for the settlement of disputes of a purely civil nature among members of the Buddhist clergy. Its work gave rise to the Vinicchaya Thana Act of 1949, under which a beginning has been made in the establishment of such courts throughout Burma. In November 1950, a Directorate of Religious Affairs was formed, and its members were charged with taking control of the newly established ecclesiastical courts, advising the government on religious reforms they considered desirable, and supervising state religious ceremonies. The Pali Education Board founded in 1937 with both lay and clerical committeemen was transferred in June 1950 from the Ministry of Education to that of Religious Affairs. A Pali University was founded in April 1951, and at its head was placed a council of 29, of whom 22 were monks representing its constituent colleges. Six months later, a Tripitaka Translation Bureau was set up, with a five-year program which included a Burmese translation of the Pali canon, compilation of a Pali-Burmese dictionary, and the writing of a definitive biography of the Buddha. The teaching of Buddhism in state schools and Rangoon University was instituted at about the same time.

To give organizational unity to the various Buddhist groups, the Union Buddha Sasana Council was created in August 1951. It was made up of representatives of the various Buddhist associations throughout the country and of the outstanding regional Buddhist organizations. Its assigned objectives were to train workers for the propagation of Buddhism at home and abroad, to encourage the study and translation of Buddhist scriptures, to raise the moral standards of the people, and to promote relations with fellow Buddhists in foreign countries.

These long overdue and well-meaning attempts by the government to reform and revitalize Burmese Buddhism coincided with a generally conservative reorientation of national policy that occurred in the fall of 1950. And aside from the purely practical difficulties involved in carrying out its new religious program, the government encountered opposition to it both from the extreme left and from some traditionalist members of the clergy.[87] The radicals were naturally hostile on principle to any governmental commitment to back propagation of the Buddhist faith, while the conservative clergy resented the administration's refusal to make Buddhism the state religion with

[87] Cady, *op. cit.*

ifying cultural bond among the people of his country but that only
can develop a force strong enough to oppose the tide of commu-
viewpoint is predicated upon the assumption that Buddhism is
ly rooted in Burma than elsewhere in Southeast Asia and that it
veloped as the firmest possible basis for Burmese nationalism and
rnationalism. In some respects, the local Communists concur in
A secret directive reportedly issued by the Burmese Communist
March 1952 laid down a policy for Burma radically different from
followed at the same period by the Communist party in Indochina.
rective, the Communists asserted that Buddhism in Burma was the
nt" of indigenous capitalists and as such should be done away with,
warned that experience in the postwar years had shown the futility
g a frontal assault on religion. The best method for destroying re-
ey asserted, was to let it die of inanition.[90]
uent events seem to have borne out the accuracy of this analysis as
to Buddhism and Christianity in Burma. The government has
nurtured Buddhism and by indirect means has sapped the vitality
Christianity. Resurgent Buddhism in Burma is the most striking ex-
a phenomenon that has become widespread in contemporary South-
The revival of that religion throughout the area has resulted from
efforts of the government and of pious laymen, and it has owed little
ng to any spontaneous impulse toward self-reform or self-improve-
the part of the clergy themselves. Everywhere the stress has been on
ical and the pragmatic, specifically on improving the general and
education of the clergy so that they may be better able to raise the
andards of the shaken and divided people in each country and to
a cultural cement for them. It has also aimed at stimulating the clergy
rtake social service work locally and to collaborate with monkly
in other Buddhist areas. In Burma, particularly, this expansion of the
al activities of the clergy has placed them in competition with foreign
work. Thanks largely to governmental initiative and support, Bud-
n Burma has been advancing at the expense of the Christian com-
which was reported in 1953 to be declining in numbers.[91] A comple-

dhist capitalists use the argument that they are rich because they amassed merit
st existence, and they say do like us if you want to be rich in your next incarnation.
eans they suppress agitation . . . When, therefore, a people's government comes to
Burma there will be no mention of religion in the constitution. It will automatically
matter for each individual. Religion will disappear as a cloak for education. Estab-
gions must be tolerated in the beginning and even given alms, but the aim of com-
s to let religion eliminate itself in the course of time. Minorities (Christians, Hindus,
are especially sensitive on the question of religion. Their feelings must not be exac-
y arguments or discussions. They should be ignored. . . . Ignored, this issue will sink
ion." (Bangkok Post, July 1, 1953.)
ey for 1953, International Review of Missions, January 1954.

all the support for Buddhist institution:
recently formed Burma Sangha Party den
for advocating nationalization of pagod:
monks to the state's higher educational i
tive" intervention in ecclesiastical affairs.
voters to oust the government in the elec
Monks' Association endorsed these charg
new official proposal to teach Islam as a
schools and in the university.[88] Public opi
back such extremist demands, and the go
Buddhism according to the program it had

This program included a grandiose sch
Sixth Buddhist Council, an international ga
of Buddhism who would remain in sessioi
the Pali scriptures. Some opposition to t
from antireligious elements but also from
penditures involved would exert too great a
finances, and from those who feared that ;
scriptures might unduly divert the governn
matters. But by the time the Council open
classes seemed infected by a veritable relig
contributed their money or their labor to cor
tal, and other buildings required for the dele
ference these structures are to serve as the phy
Buddhist university that is to be developed f
sionary institution, Dhamma Dutta College,
cember 1952.

The new and strong stress officially placed
number of origins. In the first place, Premie
Buddhist, who has taken a deep interest in h
escorted Buddhist relics sent as gifts from Cey
place, the revival of Buddhism provided a sal
political troubles. But perhaps a far more coge
Nu shares with many other Burmese leaders—

greatest
its reviv:
nism. Tl
more de
can be c
Asian ir
this beli
Party in
that beir
In this (
"instrun
but they
of maki
ligion, t
    Subse
it appli
carefull
of local
ample (
east As
the joir
or notl
ment o
the pra
religio*
moral
provid
to un(
schola
traditi
missio
dhism
munit

[88] *The Burman,* Jan. 27, 1954.

[89] Despite his Buddhist zeal, Nu has recognized and ir
gious fanaticism. In a broadcast made when the fervor ir
Buddhist Council was at its height, Nu warned his people
interfere with the "unity and harmony among citizens o
take advantage of being a religious majority to suppress :
his extraordinary tolerance, the premier allocated public fu
gation of Catholic priests to Rome. This was described as
cially by any government in the world." (*The Burman,* Api

90 "F
in their
By this
power
become
lished
munisr
Muslim
erbated
into ob
91 S

mentary tendency, also due to official encouragement, has been an intensification of Asian solidarity that has likewise worked to the detriment of Western cultural influences.

THAILAND

Although Thailand has experienced the same sort of Buddhist revival as have other Southeast Asian countries, it has not received the same amount of official encouragement as in Burma. Because of Thailand's perennially independent status in an otherwise colonial region, Buddhism has not had to be developed there as the basis for national solidarity. And Christian missions in Thailand have never been handicapped in their evolution by being identified with an alien government. However, occasional outbursts of extreme nationalism have caused the whole Christian community trouble, and at various times the Catholics have borne the brunt of Thai resentment against France's expansion in Indochina. By and large, xenophobia has been very exceptional, and the Thai have almost always welcomed missionary work because it has been beneficial to the country. Since the war, relations between the government and the missions have been more amicable than ever before.

As in most of Southeast Asia, the Catholics pioneered Christian mission work in Thailand. Most of their personnel has been French, though in recent years the Italian Salesian Fathers have shared the field. In 1950 the Bangkok Vicariate was divided and south Thailand was assigned to a Salesian bishop with headquarters at Rajburi. Another subdivision occurred in 1944, when the growth of anti-French feeling among the Thai made it advisable to place eastern Thailand (formerly part of the Laos Vicariate) under the country's first indigenous bishop, Mgr. Cheng. On the eve of the Pacific war, there were serving in all the Catholic missions in Thailand about 35 European and 45 indigenous priests, who ministered chiefly to Chinese and Vietnamese converts.[92]

In 1885 the Catholic mission opened the first Christian secondary school in the country, Assumption College; thirteen years later St. Joseph's Convent was started; and in 1925 the Mater Dei School began classes for girls. All of these are in Bangkok and are the principal Catholic institutions in an extensive system of primary, secondary, and vocational schools throughout the country. They compete on equal terms with those of the Presbyterian mission and are generally of higher caliber than are the corresponding government schools. Less outstanding in Thailand has been Catholic work in the medical field, though the St. Louis Hospital opened in 1898 was one of the earliest of such

[92] *La Croix*, Aug. 31, 1945.

institutions, and nuns have helped to staff such non-Catholic enterprises as the Bangkok School for the Blind.

The American Presbyterian Mission is the only Protestant agency in Thailand that sponsors elementary and secondary schools with the exception of the British Disciples of Christ Mission, which operates three small schools at Nakorn Pathom. All the other Protestant groups, especially the Christian and Missionary Alliance and the Seventh Day Adventists, have confined their efforts to evangelical and medical work. The outstanding Presbyterian secondary schools are Prince Royal's College at Chiengmai, the Bangkok Christian College, and Wattana Academy which pioneered women's education in the country. Presbyterian missionaries from the United States brought the first printing press to Thailand, introduced modern medical practices there, and have done virtually the only work for lepers still being carried out in the northern and southern provinces. It is primarily in the north that Presbyterian work has been most effective as regards the number of converts, and at Chiengmai it includes not only the best secondary school but the largest hospital outside the capital.

The Presbyterians were also innovators in another very important respect—that of turning over their work to the country's nationals. (They have a mission to the Chinese in Bangkok, but their work has been done mainly with the Thai.) As regards the Presbyterian schools, the process—begun before the war—was completed in January 1947 for the Bangkok Christian College and Wattana Academy. Prince Royal's College is slated for a similar transfer, but this has been delayed by uncertainty as to that institution's future development. The mission would like to raise it to university status if assured that it would remain in Thai Christian hands. The Thai government has never before permitted a private educational institution above the collegiate level and is apparently reluctant to meet the mission's terms. Also, there has been some division of opinion among the Presbyterians themselves as to whether Bangkok, where the most wealthy and influential Thai Christians live, would not be a better site than Chiengmai. But the question at issue is not American or Thai control, and Presbyterian policy contrasts with that of the Catholic mission, which has been far slower in building up an indigenous leadership that could take over its work. Over the past fifty years the Catholics have trained only about 60 native priests, and this persistent retention of European missionary control has stood them in bad stead.

From 1938 on, Thai nationalism focused on irredentist grievances in regard to the border provinces which it had ceded to France in the early twentieth century, and showed itself increasingly hostile toward French Catholic missionaries. When armed conflict broke out between France and Thailand in July 1940, French missionaries were interned by the Thai government, and only after Bishop Peros had greatly exerted himself in their behalf were they allowed to go to Indochina. The most serious trouble of this period occurred in the Thai Lao country, where Bishop Gouin was arrested, his mission buildings were pillaged and destroyed, and even the crosses in the Catholic cemeteries were broken. The bishop and some of his priests were eventually released and they escaped into Indochina, but covert persecution of the Laotian Catholics continued even after diplomatic relations were restored between Thailand and France in July 1941.[93]

After the tide of war began to turn against the Japanese and their Thai allies in 1943, the latter became more conciliatory. When the first Thai Catholic bishop was named in 1944, and later a change in the Thai government occurred, relations between the administration and the Catholic missions became friendly once more.[94] However, the French missionaries who had escaped into Laos were less fortunate. After the Japanese coup of March 1945, those working along the Thai border were seized, Bishop Gouin was shot, and altogether some 25 members of the Laos Vicariate were killed at that time. The Catholic mission in that area has never recovered from this great loss of personnel. Though the number of Catholics in Thailand grew from some 65,000 in 1936 to about 80,000 in 1949,[95] progress has been slow compared with that of the Protestants, and its tempo is likely to be even further reduced because of the dearth of an indigenous Catholic clergy. It was not until April 1953 that a second Thai was raised to the bishopric, and he merely replaced at Chandaburi the first Thai bishop, who had died shortly before.

In the fervor of their wartime nationalism, the Thai did not leave the Protestant missions wholly untouched. As elsewhere in the region, the British and American personnel were either evacuated or interned, and the government, after declaring war on Great Britain and the United States in January 1942, took over the mission schools and hospitals. In some cases this was done to protect mission property, but in others it was a manifestation of the anti-Christian feeling promoted by nationalist reactionaries.[96] There was considerable persecution of even Thai Protestants.[97] Though there were backsliders, the Christian community in Thailand rallied. Mission schools were carried on by their native teachers under a Thai name and with funds locally raised. Although the Thai Protestants as a group remained static and did not begin to grow again numerically until after the war, they gained experience and self-confidence in operating their own institutions. This has proved invaluable to

[93] *La Croix*, July 5, 1946.
[94] It should be noted that Bangkok has never established diplomatic relations with the Vatican, and the papal delegate to Thailand (resident in Indochina) has only ecclesiastical status in the country.
[95] *Standard* (Bangkok), July 16, 1949.   [96] Zimmerman, *op. cit.*, p. 7.
[97] J. Eakin, "Mission Work in Siam," *International Review of Missions*, January 1946.

them now that they are wholly independent of missionary control and largely of mission financial support.

The Church of Christ in Siam, which was founded by the Presbyterians in 1934, is young as a national church, but since the end of the war it has gained in strength and developed its work among Thai youth in an imaginative way. Recognizing the need for training more Christian leaders in a country where Buddhism has been receiving ever stronger official encouragement, the Protestant Thai have opened hostels for Christian students in the Thai universities and have sponsored co-operative farming and youth camps in rural areas of northern Thailand. The co-operative farming venture began in 1949 as a homesteading project with 60 Christian families, all of whom had previously been agricultural tenants. The government, which gave full approval to the scheme, promised to grant title to those who worked the land for three successive years (the maximum area per family being set at 30 acres), and the Presbyterian mission supplied the machinery required. All parties concerned hoped that such co-operative farming colonies would provide "a concrete answer to the challenge of communism as it confronts rural people."[98] The Christian work camps, not started until 1951, were "to provide an opportunity for young Christians to work, play and worship together." Their success, despite objections at first from many older Thai Christians, has been so great that three more camps were started in Chiengrai province in 1952, each of which was linked with a local church.

In proportion as the Presbyterian mission has turned over its work to the Thai church and co-operated with it in new ventures, relations with the government have improved to the point of enthusiasm. Immediately after the Japanese surrender, the Free Thai government showed itself eager to make amends to the foreign missionaries for the damage done to their work during the war. With the rapidly rising demand for more educational and medical facilities, it has in every way encouraged missions to expand their schools and hospitals. Returning missionaries made themselves doubly welcome by showing no rancor and by bringing with them badly needed funds and medical supplies. The Education Department pronounced itself willing to have the missionaries propagate their religion in mission schools so long as they took from it some of the burden of teaching Thai youth and kept up academic standards.[99] The government, however, did boggle at the idea of a private Christian university and at the independence shown by some of the Catholic mission schools. Assumption College, for example, refused a government subsidy and was able to charge tuition fees at least 50 percent higher than those set for state schools because its high academic standards were attracting an

[98] "The Challenge of the Church in Thailand Today," *International Review of Missions,* July 1952.

[99] Interview by the authors with Dr. Duen Bunnag, then Minister of Education, May 2, 1947.

enrollment of over 3,000 students. But these have been only minor incidents, for the Thai government evidently does not suffer from the urge felt by newer national states to displace mission activities. More realistically, it recognizes that there is need and room for both in educational and health work, and even its present encouragement of Buddhism appears to contain no latent threat to the future progress of Christianity in Thailand.

Although the Thai government has not had to deal with internal strife as has Burma, nevertheless its leaders have been trying to tap and strengthen some unifying national emotion that would enable the country to resist the corrosive effect of communism. The obvious answer has been Buddhism, though that religion as it has developed in Thailand presents the disadvantages of being in the hands of a clergy that is apolitical, over-tolerant, split into two mutually jealous sects, and poorly educated. The Thai kings, unlike their royal colleagues in Burma, saw to it that Buddhist monks never gained political influence, and the country's sovereign status obviated the need for Thai nationalists to mobilize the clergy against a colonial administration. Indeed, any signs of political activity on the part of an occasional Buddhist monk have been followed promptly by disciplinary action, no matter what government has happened to be in power in Thailand. Actually, it has been the constitutional government that has intervened in ecclesiastical matters. Premier Pibul, during his first dictatorship from 1938 to 1944, tried to get control of church property and unite the Haha Nikay (orthodox) and Dharmayut (reformed) sects.[100] Such efforts produced an unfavorable reaction among the Buddhist clergy, made them suspicious of government interference, and retarded rather than encouraged union between them. Postwar administrations that have tried to improve the organization and education of the clergy have had to move toward those goals slowly and cautiously.

In January 1947 the Ministry of Education convened high Buddhist ecclesiastics from all the provinces in a meeting at Bangkok which was the first of its kind in Thai history. Its announced purpose was an "exchange of views beneficial to the priesthood"; actually it seems to have been called to pave the way for an administrative reorganization of the hierarchy, work out some agreement regarding church property, and initiate measures designed to improve the clergy's educational standards. Though the results of this conference were not publicized, a general compromise was apparently reached whereby the church would retain title to its property but leave administration of that property to the Ecclesiastical Department of the Ministry of Education and to laymen chosen and approved by both. It was not until 1950, two years after Pibul returned to power, that the government drafted the so-called Priests Act, which aimed at uniting the two sects in a council composed of five rep-

---

[100] Thai spelling for the same major sects as are found in Cambodia.

resentatives of each and placed under the authority of the Supreme Patriarch. Among the priesthood this bill caused considerable dissension, which came to a head in June 1951 over the choice of a president for the proposed council. The Supreme Patriarch questioned the constitutionality of the act, on the ground that the constitution's guaranty of freedom of worship conflicted with the new requirement for co-operation of the sects in missionary and other enterprises.[101] The government forthwith appointed a panel of experts who duly pronounced the bill constitutional, the Patriarch accepted this decision, and a compromise was worked out regarding the presidency of the council.

As to improved education for the clergy and their reintegration into the government school system, there was no disagreement between the ecclesiastical hierarchy and the government, particularly after the latter in 1949 allocated 10 million baht for the promotion and welfare of Buddhism. Of this sum, 2 million were to be used for the repair of temples and monasteries; 5 million for the construction at Bangkok of a hospital exclusively for monks; 2.8 million for allowances to high-ranking ecclesiastics and for subsidies to religious institutions sponsored by the Maha Makut Foundation and Chulalongkorn University. The government seemingly wanted to encourage the increased interest being shown by postwar private groups, such as the Buddhist Association and the Maha Makut Foundation, in improving the training of monks, but its long-promised sponsorship of a Buddhist University has not materialized.[102] Instead, Pibul revived a grandiose plan he had conceived during the war to make 60 square miles in Saraburi province into a world capital for Buddhism, which would be the permanent residence of the Supreme Patriarch and be organized like Vatican City.[103] Little has since been heard about this project, possibly because Burma with its plans for a Buddhist international university has stolen Pibul's thunder.

Be that as it may, the government has moved ahead in its plan to improve the religious education of the Thai people and has even made a beginning in undertaking missionary work abroad. To serve the dual purpose of remedying an acute shortage of teachers in state primary schools and of improving ethical standards among the Thai (which had deteriorated sadly during the war and postwar years), the Ministry of Education in 1949 asked monks to teach boys in elementary government schools, lecture on Buddhist precepts in secondary schools, and undertake provincial teaching-preaching tours. Thailand, which has long been the religious lodestar for Cambodian and Laotian Buddhists, is now branching out into another foreign field. In 1953, Thailand, cooperating with the World Fellowship of Buddhists program, sent four mis-

[101] *Bangkok Post,* June 27, July 11, 1951.

[102] In June 1953 the premier turned over to the Buddhist clergy a government building to serve as a school for giving theological training to monks.

[103] *Bangkok Post,* May 7, June 9, 1952.

sionaries to propagate Buddhism in Malaya and a group of scholars to Burma to help in the preparation of Buddhist scriptural texts for the projected Sixth Council to be held at Rangoon in May 1954.

MALAYA

Missionary enterprise in Malaya, both Protestant and Catholic, has followed the British flag. Starting in the Straits ports of Malacca, Penang, and Singapore, it has grown and flourished there. Only after the Malay sultans signed with the British the Treaty of Pangkor in 1874 did Christianity move into the hinterland, and there, too, it developed chiefly in the cities. Missionaries have been most successful in Malaya with the Chinese, somewhat less effective with the Indians, and not at all with the Malays. In contrast to the situation in near-by Dutch and French colonies, their relations with the administration have been good. Because the missionaries have not made determined efforts to proselytize the Malays, and because they have provided schools and hospitals of high caliber, the government has willingly helped them with facilities and grants for work in the public interest which it might otherwise have had to undertake itself.

For several reasons, missionary work was slow in getting under way in Malaya. To begin with, the country was small, sparsely populated, and inaccessible until roads and railways opened up the peninsula in the late nineteenth and early twentieth centuries. In the port towns, the population was polyglot and transient, and for many years missionaries worked there only while they were temporarily unable to get into China. It was not until the 1880's that British and American Protestant missionaries began to work among the local Chinese and Indians on a permanent basis, and neither then nor later did they make much of an effort to evangelize the Malays. Not only did the Malays present the usual Muslim invulnerability to Christian suasion, but in the Malay States of the peninsula the sultans retained, under British rule, their freedom of action in all matters pertaining to Malay customs and religion. Thus, while Christian missionary work was not expressly forbidden there and the sultans had no power to punish apostasy *per se*, they could banish outsiders considered undesirable and the missionaries could not expect their co-operation, which was indispensable for mission work. There was a strong feeling, moreover, among the British, both officials and residents, that a Christian mission to the Malays was politically undesirable and even dangerous.[104] It was only among the alien Asians and the aborigines of the peninsula that missionary work made any headway.

After a slow start, Christianity progressed rapidly, especially during the

---

[104] L. E. Browne, *Christianity and the Malays* (London, 1936), p. 68.

interwar period. By 1931, Christians in Malaya numbered slightly more than 100,000 in a population of about 5 million. By 1948 their number had grown to around 120,000 (and that of the total population to some 6 million), of whom more than half were Catholics. As the rate of growth was roughly the same among the Chinese and Indian adherents of both the Protestant and Catholic churches, it probably reflected the development of a more settled and stable population. Chinese Christians increased in numbers by 50.2 percent in the decade 1921–31, and in the latter year totaled almost 31,000, or 1.8 percent of the whole Chinese population. They were concentrated in the Straits ports, where they were nearly twice as numerous as in the Federated Malay States.[105] The number of Indian Christians, over the same period, increased from almost 24,000 in 1921 to over 36,600 in 1931—that is, in almost exactly the same proportion as did the Chinese Christians. However, the fact that Indians in Malaya were more widely dispersed geographically than were the Chinese made their conversion a more difficult task, and a larger proportion among them had adopted Christianity before leaving their own country Though the number of Christian Chinese and Indians was small in relation to the total size of both communities, the percentage loomed large beside that of the Malays. In 1936 it was estimated that there were probably at that time not more than six Christian Malays in the entire country.[106]

The fact that there are more Catholic than Protestant Christians in Malaya and that among the latter group Methodists predominate is noteworthy, for its result has been that Christianity has not been identified with the colonial administration as has been the case in adjacent colonies. Catholicism got a head start in the country with the arrival of St. Francis Xavier at Malacca in the sixteenth century, and American Methodism has been able to win more adherents in Malaya than has the Anglican church because of the larger funds at its disposal. Administratively the two Catholic parishes of Malaya are still dependent on the Portuguese Bishop of Macao, although the main missionary work for this faith is carried on by French religious orders and the Société des Missions Etrangères. As of 1951, Catholics numbered about 92,000; they included some Europeans, almost all the Eurasians, and a few aborigines, as well as sizable segments of the Chinese and Indian communities.

Among the larger of the 15 Protestant denomination groups working in Malaya, the Methodists and Anglicans number about 18,000 and 15,000 respectively; the English, Scotch, and Chinese Presbyterians together do not exceed 3,000; and next in numerical strength come the Seventh Day Adventists, whose energies and monetary resources give their work a far wider scope than the size of their membership might suggest. Before the war there was

[105] C. A. Vlieland, *A Report on the 1931 Census* (London, 1932), p. 87.
[106] Browne, *op. cit.*, p. 48.

hardly any active co-operation among the various Protestant sects, and little Asian leadership in any of them. The wartime internment or evacuation of the Protestant missionaries revealed both weaknesses. For a short time, the Japanese permitted the Anglican Bishop of Singapore to continue his work, which he widened to cover all Protestants in that city, and they even sponsored the formation of a Federation of Christian Churches in Malaya,[107] chiefly under Indian leadership. But they soon became alarmed lest this federation serve as a cover for pro-British political activities, so they dissolved it and re-interned the Bishop of Singapore. They even went so far as to issue regulations making each congregation a separate unit "in a deliberate move to prevent the Christians from becoming a united body.[108] Nevertheless, this brief experience in unity was so successful that a Christian Council for Malaya, comprising the Methodists, Anglicans, and Presbyterians, was formed in January 1948. To remedy the now obvious shortage of Asian Christian leadership, the three denominations pooled their resources to establish in 1949 a union theological seminary, called the Trinity College of Singapore, whose opening class was attended by 60 students. This college developed rapidly during the next three years. As of early 1954, its cosmopolitan student body, numbering 42 (of whom 90 percent were Chinese), included men and women from Hong Kong, Borneo, Burma, India, and Indonesia, and its sponsors believe that it has already become the spiritual training center for the future Protestant leaders of Southeast Asia.

The size of the student body at Trinity College even in its first year contrasted sharply with the 45 local priests whom the Catholics were then training in their 15 seminaries in Malaya, for until recent years there was no dearth of European missionaries willing to serve in the Far East. Because Catholic missionaries go to foreign posts for life and as single individuals, they cost their supporters far less than do Protestant missionaries, who are accompanied by their families and are granted regular home leaves. By practicing rigid economy, the Catholic missions in Malaya have managed to compete with the much more lavishly supported Protestant missions, and throughout Southeast Asia most of them were able to remain at their posts during the war. Thus, the Catholic and Protestant communities have grown at about the same pace, and now they are both facing the same problems—lack of money and of personnel to cope with the rapid increase in their membership and in particular to meet the demand from all elements of the local Asian population for more mission schools.

Malaya is widely regarded as one of the most expensive and difficult areas for foreign-mission enterprise in the Far East. Because of the many languages

---

[107] D. D. Chelliah, "Growth of Unity among the Churches of Malaya," *International Review of Missions*, October 1948.

[108] *Ibid*.

spoken, considering the small size of the total population open to Christian evangelization, a big mission staff is required. Moreover, the transiency of the Chinese and Indian populations as well as the materialistic drive that brings them to Malaya make permanent results particularly hard to achieve. First the depression, which cut deeply into all their funds, and then the war convinced all the missions that in the future they must develop far greater resources locally in money and personnel. The situation has become increasingly acute in the postwar years because of the inflated cost of living in Malaya and the declining number of recruits for mission work coming from the West. In appealing for funds in 1951, the Anglican Bishop of Singapore disclosed that only 4 of the 12 parishes in his diocese were self-supporting. And of the 2 Malayan parishes in this category, one depended upon an annual grant from the government of Singapore.[190] In 1951, also, the Catholic Bishop of Malacca bewailed the scarcity of money and Asian workers for his church. At that time there were only 70 priests in the country, of whom 9 were over sixty years of age and 45 were local men, chiefly Chinese.[110] In the interval while more Asians were being trained in Christian leadership, both Protestants and Catholics were receiving additional staff because of the ending of mission work in China. These new missionaries, however, are being absorbed by the Christian work begun recently in the resettled Chinese squatter villages and in the expansion of the missions' educational system.

Schools have been the main channel by which both Protestant and Catholic missionaries have reached the Asian population, and their success has been sensational in recent years. The number of pupils attending Catholic schools in Malaya more than doubled between 1940 (24,000) and 1949 (49,000), with the sharpest increase registered since 1945.[111] Existing schools at Penang and Malacca have been reconstructed and some new Catholic schools built, but they are not nearly enough to accommodate all the applicants. In 1940 the Methodists in Malaya had 128 schools, staffed by 894 teachers, and attended by over 22,000 pupils;[112] ten years later the enrollment was more than 35,000. As of 1951 in Singapore, there were nearly as many boys in the English schools maintained by the missions, both Protestant and Catholic, as there were in the government schools, and the girls' schools of the missions could count five times as many pupils as could Raffles Girls' School.[113] In the Catholic schools a larger percentage of the teaching is done by European missionaries and nuns than in the Protestant schools, which are handicapped by the transiency of their teaching staff—a disadvantage which is likely to grow. Lay mission teachers have become increasingly aware of the superior assets enjoyed by government teachers as regards pensions, housing allowances, and

[109] *Straits Times*, May 16, 1951.   [110] *Ibid.*, May 28, 1951.
[111] Survey for 1950, *International Review of Missions*, January 1951.
[112] *Zion's Herald* (Boston), Jan. 7, 1942.   [113] *Straits Times*, Jan. 27, 1951.

medical facilities, and further inroads are threatened by the current official plans to expand the government school system in Malaya. Moreover, the lay mission teachers have expressed growing resentment of alleged discrimination on the part of their school boards against non-Christians in the matter of salary and promotion. Although this has been vigorously denied by the heads of the missions concerned, it indicates a discontent on the part of their teachers which will probably materialize in their transfer to government schools as soon as the opportunity presents itself.

Since the end of the war, the Christian missions have begun to realize their neglect of the Malay community and to hope that the newly awakened Malay interest in English education will give them at long last a fruitful avenue of approach.[114] Islam has many of the same characteristics in Malaya as in Indonesia; it is spread thin over a tenacious animism, it experienced a revival in the early twentieth century, it became identified with nationalism, and it has never overcome the handicap of organizational weakness. But its religious revival was along more orthodox lines, and Islam has never been leavened by such liberal leadership in Malaya as in Indonesia. Nationalism in Malaya has been a very recent development, and though it has a distinctly Islamic cast, the issues around which it has developed are essentially political and economic rather than religious. The division of so small an area as the Malay peninsula into 9 sultanates (in each of whose rulers religious authority is vested and in some of which the *zakat* is collected by the government,[115] not the mosque official) has made for an even weaker ecclesiastical structure than in Indonesia. In the Malay States the British have been careful not to intervene in Muslim religious matters, but neither have they done anything to strengthen Islamic institutions there. Only in Singapore did they set up a public body to look after Muslim interests—the Mohammedan Advisory Board, on which there was not one indigenous Malay in prewar days—and in 1941 they instituted a limited amount of religious instruction in Singapore's government schools for Malays.[116]

The postwar years have brought no relaxation in Malay Muslim religious belief and practice, and in some states failure to attend the mosque for prayers or to observe the fast at Ramadan has been punished by fines. The puritanical cast of Malay Mohammedanism was shown in the resolutions passed in April 1954 by the Southeast Asia Muslim Missionary Conference held at Kuala Lumpur. Members of this conference agreed that steps should be taken to discourage gambling, drinking, lotteries, and that "indecent" literature and

---

114 R. A. Blasdell, "Renaissance in Malaya," *International Review of Missions,* January 1952.
115 In 1953, the Perak Council of Religion collected Str. $517,223 in religious taxes, of which almost half came from the *zakat.*
116 *Straits Times,* Mar. 26, 1941.

films should be banned. They also urged the Malayan government to make religious and moral education compulsory in all state and government-aided schools.[117] But new elements, both political and social, have been added to Malay Islamic life. A conservative Muslim group, Lambaga Persatuan Melayu, opposed the federal constitution of 1948 on the ground that it was "against the Islamic religion."[118] And in September 1953, the president of the All-Malaya Islamic Association resigned after his organization voted to support the UMNO-MCA alliance rather than the political group sponsored by the Mentris Besar.[119] There has been, moreover, an awakening of Malay interest in social work and religious education. In July 1947, a Muslim Welfare Committee was formed at Kuala Lumpur to render aid to the destitute and orphans, as well as to rehabilitate Muslim graves, see that Muslim religious holidays were observed, and create unity among all the Muslims of Selangor. An attempt was made in January 1948 to unite all the Muslims of Singapore so as to give representation to the whole religious community for the first time. The emotion aroused by the case of Maria Hertogh, which led to the Singapore riots of December 1950, inspired the Mufti of Johore to call a meeting of all Southeast Asia Muslims to discuss the case and to found a central missionary society. Apparently these efforts to create greater unity in the Malay Muslim community have been abortive, as was a more recent effort to get the sultans to establish a central religious organization. This met with considerable opposition from a group of religious leaders, who condemned those proposing it as "devils."[120] In February 1952 the Keeper of the Rulers' Seal delivered the coup de grâce to this idea by pronouncing it unconstitutional.[121]

The most promising of all the joint efforts yet made by Muslims in Malaya has been the active support recently given to a long-standing project to establish a Muslim College in the Federation. The existence of such an institution would remedy a serious deficiency in Malayan Islamic education by permitting future kathis and imams to receive locally a higher religious training such as has been available only to the few among them who could afford to study abroad. While some of the sultans have already contributed generously to this cause, the major donors have been not the Malays but the local Chinese. This is the more remarkable in that the great majority of the Chinese in Malaya are not Muslims and have also been financing a concurrent revival of Mahayana Buddhism in Singapore and Penang.[122]

[117] *Straits Times*, Apr. 19, 1954.   [118] *Ibid.*, Jan. 17, 1947.
[119] *Ibid.*, Sept. 28, 1953.   [120] *Ibid.*, Aug. 24, 1951.
[121] *Asia*, Saigon, March 1952.
[122] *Straits Times*, Oct. 11 and 24, 1953. See also a series of articles by Francis Story entitled "Malayan Interlude," published in *The Burman* (Rangoon), Feb. 6, 7, 8, and 10, 1953.

Though results of almost all of the foregoing efforts to bring about unity and to take a more active part in the life of modern Malaya have been disappointing, they give evidence of a new quickening of local Muslim consciousness. Probably a new political formula must be found for the country before Islam can organize a united and strong front there.

Chapter Six

CAUSES AND REMEDIES

SOUTHEAST Asia's geographical location at the crossroads between India and China, and its general development as a colonial area, are primarily responsible for the presence and the large size of its minority communities. Minorities are so complex and widespread in each country of the area that they rank among the top problems, for which the need to find a solution presses harder upon national than upon colonial administrations. So long as an alien power governs a Southeast Asian country, the situation is relatively simple—a very small minority controls other larger minorities, as well as the dominant indigenous people. But when this foreign imperialism comes to an end, or when it genuinely begins to share its power with the nationalists of the country, readjustment in relationships between the various ethnic groups becomes imperative.

In Indonesia and, to a lesser extent, in Indochina, the Japanese occupation and the subsequent establishment of national republics in both countries quickened the pace of this adjustment, for the prewar imperial powers were unable to reimpose their rule by force. The returning Dutch and French, respectively, felt that they must find some formula that would enable them to salvage what they could of their former position and at the same time to satisfy nationalist aspirations for a greater share of their power. In both cases the Netherlands and France soon came up with the same answer—federalism. At once they concentrated upon gaining the co-operation of the ethnic minorities, under the illusion that the latter held the principal key to the success or failure of the new governmental form. But in trying to establish a federal structure, the Dutch and French alienated the nationalist majorities in their former colonies and did not wholly win the allegiance of the ethnic minorities whom they were proposing to protect. The nationalists claimed that the concern now evinced by the imperialist powers for the welfare of the ethnic minorities did not ring true nor was it necessary, and that federalism was but a postwar version of the old policy of divide-and-rule. Later events were to prove the half-truths in these conflicting contentions, as well as the fact that a federal government offered no practical solution to the problem of the ethnic minorities—at least in the current stage of their evolution.

Throughout the area, the ethnic minorities had at some time in the past suffered—or felt that they had suffered—from exploitation and aggression at the hands of the dominant people. And to the ethnic minorities the colonial power, whose conquest of the whole country had arrested the process, appeared either as a savior or as the lesser of two evils. Nearly all of these minorities were quite small numerically and lived in inaccessible regions that possessed no known resources of great value. Consequently, the European power intervened little in their affairs, and the few contacts that it had with such minorities were superficial and agreeable.

In instances where the ethnic minority concerned was relatively strong and less isolated from the majority communities, as were the Karens in Burma, it had been used by the colonial power as an ally and as an auxiliary military force in order to serve as a counterpoise to the national majority. As for many of the Karens, as well as the Ambonese in Indonesia, this link between themselves and the foreign administrators was strengthened by their common adherence to the Christian religion. Not unnaturally the close ties thus developed between the British and the Karens and between the Ambonese and the Dutch aroused the resentment of the Burman and Indonesian nationalists, who held the Europeans responsible for alienating their "brothers" from them. Furthermore, they blamed the ethnic minorities for adding local strength to the imperial powers and helping to perpetuate their rule. Thus, the breach between the indigenous majority and minority communities, which antedated European rule, was widened by the fear and suspicion engendered as a by-product of the policy pursued by the colonial regimes.

When the erstwhile imperial powers proposed federalism as a logical solution to the ethnic-minorities problem in the postwar period, the national majorities immediately expressed strong opposition. They maintained that the barriers separating them from the other indigenous communities were essentially artificial and that this would be clearly evident once "the third party to the dispute" had withdrawn from the field. Simply through its association with foreign imperialism, federalism was anathema to them. Furthermore, they wanted the largest possible area and population to be included under their own rule. They regarded the domain formerly governed by the imperial power as their own legitimate national territory even when it comprised, as in the case of western New Guinea, peoples far removed from the national majority, both ethnically and geographically. This insistence was due to the belief that their national prestige was involved and that the inclusion of even disparate ethnic groups living in isolated and undeveloped areas would be a source of strength to their new rule.

Burma, as the first colonial country in Southeast Asia to attain independence in the postwar world, was determined to convince its many ethnic minorities that the British had been responsible for the country's segmentation. Burmese nationalists first turned their attention to the frontier areas which before the war had been under direct British rule and administered separately from the rest of Burma. In 1947 the Burmese drafted a constitution that provided self-

government for the Shans, Kachins, and Chins within their respective territories, under loose ties with the central Union government. The formula was
ingeniously devised and it proved for some years generally acceptable and
satisfactory to the frontier peoples.

Unfortunately, the Burmese majority did not move with comparable speed
and tact in their dealings with the ethnic minorities that had formed an integral part of Burma before the war. Though an opportunity for autonomy
was offered the Karens, this widely scattered community did not form a compact minority, and the resultant administrative difficulties were so great that
the government, beset by many other problems, made the grave mistake of
procrastinating. Similarly, because the Arakanese lived in a distant and inaccessible area, the Burman nationalists failed to appreciate their intense regionalism, until the situation in Arakan became so confused as almost to defy
solution. Moreover, the violently asserted claims of the Karens and the Arakanese to self-government incited other minorities, such as the Mons, to follow
their example. Thus, through a combination of inexperience, preoccupation
with other problems judged to be more urgent, and a dilatory and unequal
application of theoretically generous terms to the indigenous minorities, the
Burman majority has had to face armed revolt on the part of Karens, Arakanese, and Mons. Centrifugal forces have undermined the governmental structure of the so-called Union of Burma, and they have largely discredited among
the Burmese the principle of federalism.

Everywhere in Southeast Asia, the new national governments have tended
to ignore the problems of the ethnic minorities once the foreign imperial
power has been eliminated. Their concern for such minorities is aroused only
when they fear that outside elements may be using minority grievances as an
excuse to re-establish foreign rule. When two British adventurers began
supplying the Karens with arms and advice, and when a Dutch journalist was
planning to aid the Ambonese rebels, the Burmese and Indonesians became
incensed and sounded the old alarm of "imperialist intervention." The fact
that neither the British nor the Dutch government was involved in these
ventures—indeed it was the British ambassador at Rangoon who revealed the
"plot" to the Burmese Cabinet—was not generally appreciated by the local
nationalists, and in consequence of this rebirth of suspicion Anglo-Burmese
and Indonesian-Dutch relations deteriorated.

Moreover, such suspicions have intensified the nationalists' distrust of the
minority involved and their determination to tighten the controls exercised
by the central government. Probably the trend toward authoritarian government would have reasserted itself in any event, given the tradition of absolute monarchies throughout the area and its perpetuation by colonial administrations, not to speak of the need to stamp out widespread crime and to
unify the diverse peoples living in each of the new national states. Even where

the nationalist leaders have sincerely aimed at introducing democratic institutions in their respective countries, the practical difficulties involved have
been too much for them. It took Indonesia only eight months after achieving
sovereignty to replace the federal structure, set up under the terms of its agreement with Holland, by that of a unitary state. And signs are not wanting that
the Viet Nam state, should it have free rein in its own territories, would eliminate the legal measures devised by the French to safeguard the status of the
Cambodian minority in Cochin China.

From the viewpoint of the national governments, the claims of their minority groups require attention and satisfaction, not on the grounds of abstract
justice but in proportion to the kind and degree of outside help that an individual minority can muster. An extreme case is represented by the Eurasians,
who can count on virtually nothing but their own resources, which are limited
both economically and spiritually. Such support as they have received from
Europeans has derived from the generally slight degree of moral responsibility
felt toward them by individuals or imperial governments involved, and even
this is rapidly coming to an end. Pure-blooded Southeast Asians have shown
a readiness to utilize the services of those Eurasians who are willing to merge
with the country's nationals, for they are generally better educated and more
skilled professionally than the bulk of the population. With the exception of
some aboriginal tribes, Eurasians are numerically the smallest minority in
each country of the area, only a handful among them can leave the country and
reside elsewhere, and the great majority must remain and fend for themselves. In brief, the Eurasians have no recourse but to live on the terms offered
to them by their nationalist half-brothers. At present these terms are generous,
but they will probably be progressively less so the longer the Eurasians delay
in accepting them.

The next easiest type of minority for the national governments to handle is
that in which the outside aid, solicited or given, comes from another Asian
country. This is the case of the Mujahids in northern Arakan and to a lesser
degree that of the Malays in southern Thailand. In regard to the former, the
Asian powers involved—Burma and Pakistan—are both still strongly conscious of the recency of their colonial past and are determined that the Mujahid question will not become a bone of contention between them. However,
the sharing of a common frontier that dates only from the colonial period
means that some nationalist claims and counterclaims arise out of the more
distant past. More serious, the two minorities in dispute correspond to religious differences between the Buddhist Burmese and the Muslim Pakistani.
Fortunately the area and the number of persons involved are small and relatively unimportant, and the whole Arakan problem is peripheral to the major
concerns of the governments of both Burma and Pakistan.

The Malays of southern Thailand, like the Mujahids in northern Arakan,

have received support from nonofficial sources among their ethnic and religious relatives across the frontier which they share with Malaya. Here, too,
the situation is influenced by claims arising out of the historical past, when
both groups of Malays enjoyed far greater independence before they were
annexed by the Thai and British respectively. So far the appeals of the Thai
Malays for aid, whether from the United Nations or the British, have proved
unavailing. The United Nations does not want to develop into a court of
petty claims, and London has consistently felt that its interest lay more in
preserving the friendship of Thailand than in adding more Malay states to
its peninsular possessions. The only outside support which the Thai Malays
have received in their efforts to improve their semicolonial status vis-à-vis
Bangkok has come from Kelantan and from scattered groups in Malaya and
Singapore. This help not only has been ineffectual but has alarmed moderate
Malay nationalists in Malaya into disavowing any responsibility for it. In
consequence, the Thai have been concerned, by fits and starts, to meet the
aspirations of their Muslim minority only when it appeared that Malay
restiveness in the border area might serve as an excuse for secession or for the
annexation of the region by British Malaya.

The full cycle of revolt, suppression, and concessions has not been experienced by all the ethnic minorities in Southeast Asia, but dissidence is generally endemic among them. Not all of them are strong enough either by
themselves or through outside support to rebel, but the transition from a
colonial to a national government has everywhere made them restive. In almost every case they are less concerned for their political rights than for the
preservation of their cultural integrity. What chiefly complicates the ethnic-
minority problem is that racial divergencies between them and the majority
community are often accompanied by religious differences. The Muslim
minorities in Buddhist countries have little to fear from the proselytizing zeal
of the tolerant Buddhist clergy, but they are fearful of the impact of Buddhist-
inspired law upon their family institutions, particularly in the matters of inheritance and marriage. In some but not all cases, they want to preserve linguistic and sartorial distinctions, but primarily it is their insistence on religious
autonomy that determines their other desiderata. Throughout Southeast Asia
the Muslim minorities are weak organizationally, and no international Islamic
leadership has yet appeared that satisfies their aspirations.

Indigenous Christians, too, fear for their cultural survival among societies
that are predominantly Muslim or Buddhist. In strongly Islamic countries,
there is the additional threat of persecution at the hands of Muslim fanatics,
as in Indonesia where such extremists not only resent the prominent role that
Christians are playing in the country's public life but in some regions have
terrorized Christian communities and forcibly converted them to Islam.
Where Buddhists are the majority people, there is no such threat of physical

violence, but inroads are being made obliquely on the Christian community, and its capacity to expand is being undermined by the state's absorption of institutions that had previously been under Christian management. Though foreign missionaries are withdrawing from positions of leadership, the Buddhist governments are covertly disputing control of the educational field with native Christians. This promises to be a long-term struggle, for none of the states involved is yet able to take over the institutions which were started and to some extent are still supported by foreign missions. Already evident, however, is the governments' intention of strengthening the organization and educational standards of the Buddhist clergy, as is the identification of Buddhism with the local nationalism as a unifying force capable of resisting aggression from inside and outside the country. The ethnic minorities, should they be sealed off from foreign support and required to share the cultural, religious, and legal institutions of the majority community, would eventually have no choice but to become merged with the latter. The pattern has been clearly established, and the only remaining question is as to the rate at which this assimilation will take place, for it depends on both internal and international events. As to internal influences, the tempo would be determined by the understanding and tact displayed by the national government and majority people and also by the extent of willingness to compromise shown by the ethnic minority concerned. From the international angle, the pressures—or absence of them—exerted by outside forces with which the minority could actually or conceivably ally itself would either retard or speed up the process.

If the working out of the future of ethnic minorities requires time and a profound psychological adjustment, that of the alien minorities is even more complex. Besides involving far-reaching political and social considerations, it has psychological overtones and also demands a more rapid solution. By and large, the Indian minority no longer constitutes a problem, for it has so shrunk in numbers and economic importance as to have ceased to arouse hostility, even in such countries as Burma (and, to a far lesser degree, Malaya), where formerly it was a major issue. India's attainment of sovereignty has made Southeast Asian Indians even less interested in local politics than they previously were, except at Singapore and in some of the recently formed trade-unions in Malaya. Even the Indians permanently settled in the area, whose proportion to the total Indian population has grown in recent years, are playing a passive rather than an active role in current public affairs. They remain generally aloof from other Asian communities in the country, and cling to their Indian culture and ties with the homeland. Though they are essentially foreigners in Southeast Asia, their unassimilability is not aggressive, and their prosperity is not so marked as to arouse the jealousy of the other Asian communities. Moreover, Nehru has urged his overseas compatriots to identify themselves clearly either with India or the country of their residence, and in any case his great personal popularity among the region's nationalists largely offsets the distaste or indifference they feel toward the Indian minorities in their midst.

The Chinese minority, on the other hand, is far from being such a self-liquidating problem. Their numbers in the area have grown, even without fresh immigration; their economic importance has increased despite official efforts to control it; their cultural unassimilability remains adamant; and their political future is ominously unpredictable. Though they continue to be divided among themselves by language, provincial origin, and political affiliations, they are nevertheless very strong as a community. In themselves they inspire admiration and envy on the part of Southeast Asians, and in view of the rise of Communist China they are feared by local nationalists as a potential fifth column for the conquest or absorption of the area by its northern neighbor. Most of the local governments have done little beyond making ineffectual attempts to curtail the economic and political activities of their Chinese minorities. The only country which has arrived at a more constructive approach to the problem is Malaya, where the unique composition of the population has made it imperative to work out a compromise between its two numerically equal components—the Chinese and the Malays. Under British guidance and arbitration, some of the farseeing members of both communities struck a bargain in which, roughly speaking, the Chinese bartered some economic power for a greater share in the political privileges held by the Malays. Unfortunately, this arrangement has not worked out as well as it might have, for it was not widely accepted by the Malays or the local Chinese. But it pointed to what at present seems to be the only solution possible in a region where, to a large extent, the economy is in the hands of Chinese aliens and political power is monopolized by the indigenous peoples.

The minorities, both ethnic and alien, are in the region to stay, whether the national majorities like it or not. Unless the individual governments offer them enough of a stake in the country to induce them to merge with the majority people in a common nationality, the national majorities may revert to the status of being once more subject peoples in their own lands.

BIBLIOGRAPHY

Achievements of the Democratic Republic of Vietnam. Paris, 1946.

Andrus, J. Russell. *Burmese Economic Life.* Stanford University Press, 1947.

Asian Relations. New Delhi, 1948.

Awbery, S. S., and Dalley, F. W. *Report on Labor and Trades Union Organizations.* Kuala Lumpur, 1948.

Baxter, James. *Report on Indian Immigration.* Rangoon, 1941.

Beaver, R. P. *Christian Missions in Indochina.* Missionary Research Library, New York, December 23, 1953.

Browne, L. E. *Christianity and the Malays.* London, 1936.

Cady, John; Barnett, Patricia; and Jenkins, Shirley. *The Development of Self-Rule and Independence in Burma, Malaya, and the Philippines.* New York, 1948.

Christian, John. *Modern Burma.* University of California Press, 1942.

Dev, D. Y. *Our Countrymen Abroad.* New Delhi, 1940.

Devillers, Philippe. *Histoire du Vietnam.* Paris, 1952.

Dobby, E. H. G. *Southeast Asia.* London, 1950.

Economic Survey of Asia and the Far East—1950, —1951, —1952. United Nations.

Elsbree, Willard H. *Japan's Role in the Southeast Asian Nationalist Movements, 1940–45.* Harvard University Press, 1953.

Ethnic Groups of Northern Southeast Asia. Yale University, 1950.

Gourou, Pierre. *Land Utilization in Upland Areas of Indochina.* New York, 1951.

Hammer, Ellen. *The Struggle for Indochina.* Stanford University Press, 1954.

Kahin, George McT. *Nationalism and Revolution in Indonesia.* Cornell University Press, 1952.

Kondapi, C. *Indians Overseas.* New Delhi, 1951.

Landon, K. P. *The Chinese in Thailand.* Oxford University Press, 1941.

Leach, E. R. *Political Systems of Highland Burma.* Harvard University Press, 1954.

Levi, Werner. *Free India in Asia.* University of Minnesota Press, 1952.

Lévy, Roger. *L'Indochine et ses Traités.* Paris, 1946.

Lewis, Norman. *A Dragon Apparent.* New York, 1951.

———. *Golden Earth,* New York, 1952.

Nanjundan, S. *Indians in Malayan Economy.* New Delhi, 1951.

Purcell, Victor. *The Chinese in Southeast Asia.* Oxford University Press, 1951.

Report of the Educational Policy Enquiry Committee. Rangoon, 1947.

Silcock, T. N., and Abdul Aziz, Ungku. *Nationalism in Malaya.* New York, 1950.

Singapore Department of Social Welfare. *A Social Survey of Singapore.* Singapore, 1948.

Skinner, G. William. *Report on the Chinese in Southeast Asia.* Cornell University, 1950.

Smith, T. E. *Population Growth in Malaya.* London, 1952.

Souvanna Phouma, Prince. *Projet de Développement Economique du Laos.* 1947 (typescript).

Tufo, M. V. Del. *Malaya—A Report on the 1947 Census of Population.* London, 1949.

Zimmerman, Walter. *Continental Southeastern Asia.* Paris, March 1947 (typescript).

PERIODICALS AND BULLETINS

Asia (Saigon)

Burmese Review (Rangoon)

Eastern World (London)

Economic Development and Cultural Change (Chicago)

Encyclopédie Coloniale (Paris)

Far Eastern Survey (New York)

France-Asie (Saigon)

Great Britain and the East (London)

Guardian (Rangoon)

Indochine Française (Paris)

Indochine–Sud-est Asiatique (Saigon)

Indoclim (Paris)

International Review of Missions (Edinburgh)

Ministère de la France d'Outre Mer. *Bulletin* (Paris)

———. *Chroniques d'Outre-Mer* (Paris)

Pacific Affairs (New York)

Report on Indonesia (New York)

Southeast Asia Review (Bangkok)
Standard (Bangkok)
Vietnam-American Friendship Association bulletin (New York)
Vietnam News (Saigon)

CURRENCIES (OFFICIAL RATES)

U.S. (approx.)

Burma: 1 kyat (from mid-1952) or 1 rupee (pre-1952) $0.21

Thailand: 1 baht 08

Malaya: 1 Straits dollar 33

Indonesia: 1 rupiah 09

Indochina: 1 piastre (devalued in May 1953 from U.S.
$0.059) 035

INDEX

All-Burma Indian Congress, 79
All-Burma Muslim League, 75, 79. *See also* Burma Muslim Congress
Ambonese: Christianity among, 165, 237, 239, 240, 241, 281; Dutch policy toward, 165, 166, 167, 168, 281; revolt against central government, 165, 166–68, 169, 282
American missionaries, 229–30, 238, 257–58, 259, 260, 263, 267, 268, 269, 270
Anglo-Burmans, 146–48
Anglo-Indians, 143, 146
Annamites. *See* Vietnamese
Arakanese: Communist activity among, 153, 154, 155; economic status, 151, 152, 157, 158; Indian community's relations with, 67, 151–52, 153, 154, 155, 156; separatist movements, 30, 67, 153–57, 282
Associated States. *See* Cambodia; Geneva Conference; Indochina; Laos; Pau conference; *and* Viet Nam
Azad Hind movement, 64, 77–79, 99–100, 108, 109 n., 119, 126, 129, 130

Bao Dai, 4, 131, 132, 133, 181, 182, 205, 216, 218, 251, 252, 253
Baxter Report on Burman Indians, 73–74, 152
Bose, Subhas Chandra, 78, 79, 99, 152
Buddhism, 71, 170, 173, 194, 197, 210, 220, 224, 225, 226, 227, 233–35, 254–56, 260, 262, 263–66, 267, 271–73, 278, 283, 284–85
Buddhist bloc, 194, 220, 224, 225, 226, 227
Burma: Buddhist revival, 260, 263–67, 273; Christian community, 165, 229, 258–67; education, 55–56, 89, 158; elections, 82, 90, 156, 157; Eurasians (Anglo-Burmans), 146–48, 259; immigration restrictions, 54, 55, 59, 62, 72–73, 75–77, 81, 90, 93, 96–97, 152; Kuomintang troops in, 15, 19, 24–28, 54, 55, 92, 221; missionaries in, 229, 258–63; relations with China, 8, 10–11, 12, 15–16, 19, 20–21, 24–28, 29–30, 61–62, 91, 92, 221; relations with Great Britain, 91, 162, 281, 282; Relations with India, 61, 62, 63, 67, 68, 69–70, 71–75, 76–77, 79–80, 84, 85, 86, 87, 89–93, 127; relations with Pakistan, 67, 68, 153, 154–55, 155–56, 283; revolts, 19, 25, 26, 27, 28, 67, 85, 86, 91, 92, 148, 153–57,

Burma (*cont.*)
165, 168, 221–22. *See also* Arakanese; Chinese, overseas; Indians, overseas; Kachins; Karens; Shans
Burma Indian Congress, 79
Burma Muslim Congress, 81, 82
Burma Muslim League, 82

Cambodia: Buddhist revival, 255, 256, 272; Chinese community, 57, 58, 172, 180, 182; constitution of 1947, 178–79, 179–80; economic situation, 170–71, 172, 180, 181–82, 183, 193–96, 224–25; elections, 172, 177, 178, 179, 183, 184, 192, 196, 197; political parties, 178, 179, 183, 184, 185, 186, 188, 192, 193, 195; relations with France, 57, 58, 149, 170, 171, 172–73, 174, 175, 176, 177, 178, 179–80, 181, 182, 185, 186–87, 188, 189–90, 190–92, 193, 194, 211; relations with Thailand, 170, 172, 173–74, 180, 182, 184, 189, 193, 194, 195, 197, 220, 224–26; relations with Viet Nam, 134, 170, 171, 172, 179, 180–82, 183, 184, 185, 187, 189, 191, 192, 193–94, 195, 197, 211, 221, 225; revolutionary movements, 173–74, 175–77, 180, 182, 183, 184–85, 186, 187–88, 189, 190, 191, 193, 196, 256; Viet Minh invasion, 134, 177, 191, 192, 196, 210, 225 n., 226; Vietnamese community, 170, 171, 174–75, 195. *See also* Buddhism; Buddhist bloc; Geneva conference; Indochina; Kmer Issarak; Pau conference
Central Indian Association of Malaya, 98, 112, 115
Cheng-Lock Tan, Sir, 36, 37, 40
Chettyars. *See* Moneylenders, Indian
Chiang Kai-shek, 31, 222. *See also* China, Nationalist
China, Communist (People's Democratic Republic of China), 3, 6, 7, 8, 9, 10–25, 26, 44, 46, 49, 51, 52, 56, 62, 63, 91, 210, 219, 220–21, 223–24, 227, 235, 286
China, Nationalist, 2, 4, 8, 10, 11–12, 13, 15, 16, 19, 20, 21, 24–28, 44, 46, 47, 54, 55, 56, 57, 60, 92, 201, 223, 226. *See also* Kuomintang troops

Chinese, overseas: attitude toward Chinese regimes, 3, 9–11, 12–14, 18, 31–32, 46, 49–
50, 53, 56; in Burma, 3, 5, 6, 8, 9, 10–11, 15,
19, 54–56, 259; business activities, 3, 4–5,
6–7, 9, 10, 22, 23–24, 31, 33, 39, 40 n., 49,
110, 131, 172; in Cambodia, 57, 58, 172,
180, 182; communalism, 3, 6, 9, 32, 37, 43–
44, 50 n., 286; economic status, 3, 4–8, 24,
31, 40, 286; in Indochina, 3, 5, 6, 8, 9, 10–
11, 12, 24, 56–58, 131, 172, 180, 182, 197;
in Indonesia, 4, 5, 6–7, 9, 10–11, 12, 31, 48–
54, 237, 239; in Laos, 197; in Malaya, 4, 5,
6–7, 8, 9, 10–11, 12, 18, 32–44, 94, 95, 96,
97, 98, 99, 100, 101, 102, 103, 104, 105, 106,
107, 108, 110, 111, 112, 113, 114, 165, 273,
274, 275, 276, 278, 286; political activities,
3, 8–11, 32, 36, 37–41, 50, 97, 100, 101,
102, 103, 104, 105; in Thailand, 3, 5, 6, 7,
8, 9, 10–11, 12, 20, 22, 30–31, 44–48, 223,
267, 268. See also Education, Chinese; Labor: Chinese
Chins, 28, 281–82
Chittagonians. See Indians, overseas, in Burma
Chou En-lai, 11, 15, 17, 30, 31, 32, 61, 196
Christian minority: Eurasians, position of, 137,
144, 237; status in Burma, 165, 229, 258–
67; status in Indochina, 232, 235, 248–58;
status in Indonesia, 165–69, 235–45, 246,
247, 248; 284; status in Malaya, 137, 229,
273–77; status in Thailand, 267–71. See also
Missionaries
Citizenship issue, 8, 10–11, 34, 35–36, 37, 38,
39, 40, 44, 47, 50–52, 55, 57–58, 62, 78, 80–
81, 88, 100, 101, 102–3, 105, 107–8, 120,
140, 141, 142, 147, 148, 149, 150–51
Colombo conferences, 15, 21, 61, 65, 68, 93,
124, 128, 133
Communalism. See Chinese, overseas; and Indians, overseas
Communist Party: Burma, 30, 67, 92, 153, 154,
155, 156, 266; Chinese, in Malaya, 33, 100,
101, 103, 104; Indian, in Singapore, 101;
Indochina, 218, 266 (see also Viet Minh);
Indonesia, 16, 19, 22, 54, 247, 248; Malayan,
98, 100–101, 105, 113, 114; Thailand, 16,
22, 29. See also China, Communist; Chinese,
overseas: political activities; Communist
propaganda; Malaya: Communist revolt; Soviet Union
Communist propaganda: in labor organizations,
9, 10, 16–17, 100–101, 104, 113, 114
Communist propaganda: in schools, 8, 9, 10,
11, 12, 16, 42, 48, 50, 53, 56, 58
Co-operatives, 6, 7–8, 85–86, 169
Council of Joint Action (Malaya), 36, 102, 103,
104, 108

Darul Islam, 243, 244, 247, 248
Delhi conferences, 60–61, 91, 124, 128, 131

Education: Chinese, 3, 8, 9, 11, 12, 16, 34, 39,
40, 41–44, 45, 47–48, 50, 52–54, 55–56, 58,
115, 116, 117, 118, 119, 142; Eurasian, 135,
137, 138, 141–42, 143, 144, 145, 148, 149,
150; Indian, 75, 82, 89, 98, 102, 114–19,
127–28. See also Missionaries
Eurasians: in Burma, 146–48, 259; economic
status, 135, 136–37, 138, 139, 140, 141, 142,
143, 144, 145, 146–47, 148, 149, 283; education, 135, 137, 138, 141–42, 143, 144, 145,
148, 149, 150; homeland projects, 137, 139,
140, 146, 148; in Indochina, 149–50, 251;
in Indonesia, 51, 138–43, 237; in Malaya,
136, 143–46, 274; occupations, 135, 136,
137, 138–39, 140, 142, 144, 145, 146–47,
148, 149; political status, 139, 140, 141, 144–
45, 145–46, 147–48, 149–50; social status,
1, 135–36, 137, 138, 141, 142, 143–44, 145,
146, 149; in Thailand, 135, 150–51

Federation of Indian Organizations (Malaya),
105–6
France: relations with China, 17–18, 24, 56–57,
58
"Free Cambodian" movement. See Khmer Is-
sarak
"Free Laotian" movement. See Lao Issarak
"Free Thai" regime. See "Thai Autonomous
State"

Geneva conference, 17, 32, 61, 62, 128, 133–
34, 196, 210, 219, 226
Great Britain: relations with Burma, 91, 162,
281, 282; relations with Thailand, 158, 159–
60, 162, 269, 284. See also Malaya

Hatta, 20, 65, 66, 166, 246
Ho Chi Minh, 4, 130, 131, 132, 133, 199, 201,
205, 208, 211, 214, 253, 254

Immigration: Chinese, 3, 4, 5, 19, 33–34, 40,
45–46, 49, 54–55, 56–57, 72, 96, 113, 207,
286; Indian, 59, 62, 68, 72–73, 75–77, 81,
90, 91, 93, 94–95, 96–97, 107, 111, 113,
121, 122–23, 125, 129, 151–52, 153, 154
Independence of Malaya Party, 37, 38, 106,
108, 146
India: Colombo conferences, participation in,
15, 21, 61, 65, 68, 93, 124, 128, 133; Delhi
conferences, 60–61, 91, 124, 128, 131; policy
toward overseas Indians, 59–63, 69, 72, 73,
74–75, 76, 77, 80, 84, 85, 86, 91, 94–95,
101, 102, 112, 119–21, 127, 285; relations

India (*cont.*)
with China, 101; relations with Indochina, 61, 62, 63, 69, 129, 131–34, 210; relations with Indonesia, 62, 63, 65, 69, 123–25; relations with Malaya, 62, 63, 93–95, 119–21; relations with Thailand, 63, 125, 126, 127, 128, 224; relations with Viet Minh, 131, 132, 133. *See also* Burma

Indian Democratic League, 101

Indian Independence Leagues, 78, 98, 99, 101, 125, 126, 129, 159

Indians, overseas: in Burma, 3, 55, 60, 64, 67, 69–93, 151–52, 283, 285; business activities, 59, 64, 70, 72, 74, 75, 77, 80, 83, 84, 85, 87, 93, 97, 98, 109–11, 122, 123, 127, 130, 131; communalism, 62, 64, 70–71, 81, 82, 83, 100, 102, 103–4, 106–7, 126, 155, 285; economic status, 40 n., 59, 64, 69, 70, 71, 74, 75, 79, 81, 83–89, 95, 96–97, 102, 108–14, 123; in Indochina, 69, 129–34; in Indonesia, 69, 122–25; in Malaya, 38, 39, 40 n., 60, 64, 69, 93–121, 126, 273, 274, 275, 276, 285; political activities, 38, 39, 64, 71–72, 74, 79–83, 98–108, 120, 125–26, 129, 130, 285; in Thailand, 125–28, 159. *See also* Education, Indian; Labor, Indian; Moneylenders, Indian; India: policy toward overseas Indians; Remittances, Indian

Indochina: Buddhism, status of, 254–57; Chinese community, 3, 5, 6, 8, 9, 10–11, 12, 24, 56–58, 131; Christian community, 232, 235, 248–58; education, 58, 150, 206, 213, 215; Eurasian community, 149–50, 251; immigration restrictions, 54, 56–57, 129, 207; Indian community, 69, 129–34; Kuomintang troops in, 3, 19, 24, 57, 199, 200, 201, 202; missionaries in, 229, 231, 232, 248–58; relations with China, 4, 10–11, 12, 17–18, 24, 62; relations with India, 63, 69, 129, 130–34. *See also* Cambodia; Geneva conference; Laos; Pau conference; "Thai Autonomous State"; Thai of Tonkin; Thailand: relations with Indochina; Viet Minh; Viet Nam State

Indo-European League (Indonesia), 139

Indo-Europeans, 51, 138–43, 237

Indonesia: Chinese community, 4, 5, 6–7, 9, 10–11, 12, 31, 48–54, 237, 239; Christian community, 165–69, 235–45, 246, 247, 248, 284; Communist revolt (1948), 19; Darul Islam revolt, 243, 244, 247, 248; education, 50, 52–54, 138, 141, 143, 246, 247; elections, 50 n., 165, 166; Eurasian community, 51, 138–43, 237; immigration restrictions, 49, 54, 122–23; Indian community, 69, 122–25; Islam, position of, 66–67, 235–36, 237, 238, 240, 241, 242–43, 244, 245–48, 284;

Indonesia (*cont.*)
missionaries in, 229, 230, 235–48; Moluccas revolt, 165, 166–68, 169, 282; relations with China, 4, 6, 8, 10–11, 12, 15, 16, 19–20, 21–22, 23, 50, 51, 52; relations with India, 62, 63, 65, 69, 123–25; relations with Netherlands, 165, 166, 167–68, 69, 280, 281, 282, 283; relations with Pakistan, 65–66, 67, 122, 123, 233; trade with Communist China, 6, 22–23. *See also* Ambonese

Islam, 70–71, 82, 100, 103–4, 122, 153, 154, 155, 166, 169, 233, 235–36, 237, 238, 240, 241, 242–43, 244, 245–48. *See also* Indonesia: Islam, position of; Malays of Malaya; Malays of south Thailand; *and* Pakistan's position in southeast Asia

Japanese occupation, effects of, 4, 9, 33, 75, 77–79, 83, 85, 88, 95, 98–100, 108, 109, 112, 116, 125–26, 129–30, 136, 139, 149, 151, 152, 159, 170, 171, 175, 197, 199, 201, 220, 231, 236, 259, 260, 269, 275, 280

Kachins, 15, 19, 25, 28–29, 29–30, 221–22, 281–282

Karens: Christian community among, 165, 258, 259, 260, 262, 281; revolt, 26, 27, 30, 91, 155, 165, 168, 221–22, 260, 262, 263, 282

Khmer Issarak (Free Cambodians), 30, 173–74, 175–76, 176–77, 179, 180, 182, 183, 184, 187, 189, 190, 191, 193, 203, 204, 205, 220, 222, 226

Kuomintang. *See* China, Nationalist

Kuomintang troops: in Burma, 15, 19, 24–28, 54, 55, 92, 221; in Indochina, 3, 19, 24, 57, 199, 200, 201, 202

Labor: Chinese, 5, 9, 10, 12, 14, 16–17, 34, 64, 100, 101, 104, 111, 112; Eurasian, 139, 147, 148; Indian, 34, 59, 64, 69, 70, 73, 74, 75, 76–77, 79, 87–88, 94–95, 96–97, 98, 99, 100–101, 102, 108, 111–14, 117, 119, 120, 121, 122, 123, 152

Landownership: in Burma, 6, 62, 71, 83–85, 86–87, 93, 157; in Indochina, 6, 62, 130, 212; in Indonesia, 6, 49, 51, 62, 141; in Malaya, 6, 34–35, 40 n., 62, 95, 108; in Thailand, 6, 62

Lao Issarak (Free Laotians), 30, 184, 198, 199, 200, 201, 202, 203–5, 218, 220, 222, 227. *See also* Pathetlao

Laos: Buddhism, reform of, 255–56, 272; Chinese community, 197; Christian community, 254, 257, 269; economic situation, 197–98, 203, 205, 206, 207–8, 224; elections, 202, 203, 206; Issarak movement, 184, 198, 199,

Laos (cont.)

200, 201, 202, 203–5; Kuomintang troops in, 199, 200, 201, 202, 209; relations with France, 57, 149, 190, 191, 197, 198–99, 200, 201–2, 203, 204, 205, 206, 209–10, 211; relations with Thailand, 173, 198, 202, 203–5, 224, 225–26; relations with Viet Nam State, 57, 197, 206, 207, 210; Viet Minh invasions of, 134, 188, 189, 190, 191, 196, 200–201, 205, 206, 208, 209, 210, 221, 226, 257; Vietnamese community in, 197, 199, 201, 203, 207, 209. See also Buddhism; Buddhist bloc; Geneva conference; Indochina; Pau conference

Luang-Prabang, Kingdom of. See Laos

Malaya: Central Indian Association of, 98, 112, 115; Christian community, 137, 229, 274–77; Communist revolt, 4, 18, 23, 33–34, 35, 36, 38, 97, 101, 105, 113–14, 120, 121, 161, 162; Council of Joint Action, 36, 102, 103, 104, 108; education, 8, 35, 41–44, 115–19, 121, 144, 145, 273, 275, 276–77, 278; elections, 37–38, 39, 40–41, 104, 106, 107, 120, 145; Eurasian community, 136, 143–46, 274; Federation of Indian Organizations, 105; immigration restrictions, 33–34, 40, 59, 94–95, 96, 107, 111, 113, 121; independence of Malaya Party, 37, 38, 106, 108, 146; Islam, position of, 273, 277–79; missionaries in, 229, 273–77; Nanyang University, 43–44; Pan-Malayan Muslim Indian League, 103, 104; relations with China, 10–11, 12, 18, 22–23 (see also Chinese community); relations with India, 62, 63, 93–95, 119–121; relations with Thailand, 158, 159, 160, 161–62, 163–64, 284; Thai community in Kedah, 160–61; United Malays National Organization, 102, 106. See also Chinese, overseas, in Malaya; Indians, overseas, in Malaya; Malays of Malaya; Malays of south Thailand

Malayan Chinese Association, 34, 36, 37, 38, 39, 40, 42, 43, 105, 106, 278

Malayan Democratic Union, 104, 105, 146

Malayan Indian Association, 105

Malayan Indian Congress, 39, 101, 102, 103, 104, 105, 106, 107, 117, 120

Malays of Malaya, 5, 18, 32, 33, 35, 36–37, 38, 39, 40 n., 42, 43, 64, 95, 103, 112–13, 115, 117, 118, 158, 159, 160–61, 162, 163, 233, 273, 274, 277–79, 284, 286

Malays of south Thailand: autonomy movement, 30, 158, 161, 162–63, 164, 283–84; British policy regarding, 158, 159, 160, 161, 162, 284; economic status, 159, 164; irredentism of Malaya Malays toward, 159,

Malays of South Thailand (cont.)

160, 161, 162, 284; Thai attitude toward, 158–59, 159–60, 161, 162–63, 164, 284

Mao Tse-tung, 17, 19, 20, 24, 220, 222, 224

Masjumi party (Indonesia), 22, 66, 243, 245, 246, 247–48

Méos, 1, 212, 216, 218

Missionaries: Buddhist, 234, 263, 264, 265, 272–73; Catholic, 136, 150, 229–32, 236, 237–38, 238–39, 244, 248–49, 253, 254, 258–60, 263, 267–68, 268–69, 270–71, 273, 274, 275, 276; education, role in, 229–30, 231, 236, 239, 241, 242, 257, 258–59, 260–62, 267, 268, 269, 270, 271, 273, 275, 276–77, 285; Indian, 89, 91; medical work, 89, 91, 229–30, 231, 236, 239, 242, 257, 258, 259, 260, 267, 268, 269, 270, 271, 273; Protestant, 229–32, 236, 237–38, 239–40, 241, 244, 259–60, 261, 262, 267, 269–70, 273, 274–75, 276. See also Christian minority

Moluccan revolt. See Ambonese

Moneylenders: Chinese, 6, 7, 9; Indian, 8, 59, 62, 64, 71, 75, 76, 79, 83–87, 90, 91, 93, 98, 108–9, 120, 129, 130, 131

Mons, 26, 27, 30, 282

Mujahids. See Indians, overseas, in Burma

Nanyang University (Singapore), 43–44

Nehru, Jawaharlal, 11, 15, 59, 60, 61, 62, 63, 65, 66, 74, 80, 90, 91, 93, 101, 102, 104, 105, 120, 121, 123, 124, 127, 128, 130, 131, 132, 133, 134, 285

Norodom Sihanouk, King, 170, 171, 176, 181, 183, 184, 185, 186, 187, 188, 189, 190, 191, 192, 193, 196, 202, 226

Nu, 11, 15, 16, 20, 21, 25, 26, 28, 29, 62, 65, 68, 91, 92, 93, 155, 157–58, 262, 263, 265

Onn bin Jafaar, Dato, 36, 37, 38, 96, 121

Pakistan's position in southeast Asia, 59, 64–68, 81, 156, 233

Pakistanis. See Indians, overseas

Pan-Malayan Muslim Indian League, 103, 104

Pathetlao (neo-Lao Issarak), 205, 208–9, 210–11, 222, 226, 227. See also Lao Issarak

Pau conference, 57, 181, 188, 194, 206

"Peace" propaganda, Chinese, 14, 235

Peking conferences, 14, 15, 18, 26, 31, 209, 235

Phetsarath, Prince, 199, 200, 204, 205

Pibul Songgram, 16, 20, 22, 46, 47, 159, 161, 174, 204, 219, 220, 221, 222, 223, 227, 271

Pridi Banomyong, 173, 174, 203, 220, 223, 227–28

Remittances: Chinese, 10, 11, 13–14, 15, 46, 69; Indian, 64, 68–69, 71, 84, 93, 95

Shans, 24, 25, 26, 27, 28, 29, 220, 281–82
Singapore. *See* Malaya
Sisavong Vong, King, 198, 199, 200, 202–3, 209
Son ngoc Minh, 176, 177, 184, 193, 196
Son ngoc Thanh, 170, 171, 173, 175, 176, 184, 185, 186, 187, 191, 193, 256
Soumokil, role in Moluccas revolt, 166, 167, 168
South Moluccas Republic. *See* Ambonese
Southeast Asia Treaty Organization (SEATO), 22, 62, 133
Souvanna Phouma, Prince, 204, 205, 206, 207, 211
Souvanna Vong, Prince, 204, 205, 208, 211, 222,
Soviet Union, role of, 10, 16–17, 18, 25, 134, 202
Squatters, Chinese, in Malaya, 6, 34–35, 276
Sukarno, 7, 20, 65, 124, 169, 239 n., 243

Taipeh meeting of overseas Chinese, 31
"Thai Autonomous State," 19, 30, 218, 220–21, 222, 223, 224, 227
Thai Federation, 211, 214, 215–16
Thai of Tonkin: Chinese policy toward, 1, 19, 214, 217, 219; economic status, 212; educational facilities, 213, 214–15; French policy toward, 211, 212–18; relations with Vietnamese, 212, 213, 214, 216, 217; social structure, tribal, 211–12, 216–17; Thai Federation, 211, 214, 215–16; Thailand's policy toward, 1, 219, 220; Viet Minh activities among, 213, 214, 216, 217, 218–19
Thailand: Buddhism, status of, 267, 271–73; Chinese community, 3, 5, 6, 7, 8, 9, 10–11, 12, 20, 22, 30–31, 44–48, 223, 267, 268; Christian community, 267–71; education, 8, 45, 47–48, 127, 128, 160, 163; elections, 164; Eurasian community, 135, 150–51; immigration restrictions, 45–46, 125; Indian community, 125–28; Khmer Issarak, activities of, 173–74, 184, 185, 187, 188, 220, 222; Lao Issarak, activities of, 198, 202, 203–4, 204–5, 220, 222; missionaries in, 229, 231, 267–71; relations with China, 4, 10–11, 12, 16–17, 19, 20, 22, 24, 27, 30–31, 46, 47, 219 (*see also* Chinese community); relations with France, 220, 224, 226, 267, 268–69; re-

Thailand (*cont.*)
lations with Great Britain, 158, 159–60, 162, 269, 284; relations with India, 63, 125, 126, 127, 128, 224; relations with Indochina, 31, 128, 170, 172, 173–74, 180, 181–82, 184, 187, 189, 193, 194, 195, 197, 198, 202, 203–4, 204–5, 207, 209, 220, 224–26, 267; relations with Malaya, 158, 159, 160, 161–62, 163–64, 284; Thai-Bharat Cultural Lodge, 125, 126, 128; Vietnamese community, 202, 204, 209, 227, 267. *See also* Malays of south Thailand; "Thai Autonomous State"; Thai of Tonkin
Trade with Communist China, 6, 20, 22–24, 31

United Malays National Organization, 37, 39, 40, 42, 102, 106, 278
United Nations and UN specialized agencies, 4, 6, 20, 21, 22–23, 25, 26–27, 30, 31, 62, 66, 85, 86, 91, 124, 128, 131, 134, 167, 168, 173, 183 n., 186, 189, 200, 207, 225 n., 226, 284
United States, 16, 17, 20, 22, 25, 26, 27, 62, 65, 92, 128, 133, 168, 182, 186, 189, 195, 196, 202, 206, 224, 257, 263, 269

Viet Minh (People's Democratic Republic of Viet Nam): relations with China, 17–18, 24, 30; relations with India, 131, 132, 133; relations with Khmer Issarak, 171, 175–77, 184–85, 187, 191, 193, 222; relations with Lao Issarak and Pathetlao, 197, 199–200, 201, 202, 204, 205, 208–9, 211, 222, 227; Thailand, use as base, 29; Viet Nam, military and political activities in, 7, 17, 24, 57, 130, 150, 211, 212, 213, 214, 216, 217, 218, 219, 235, 249–50, 251–52, 253–54, 258. *See also* Cambodia; Ho Chi Minh; Laos
Viet Nam: Cambodian minority, 174, 180–81, 283; relations with Cambodia, 134–70, 171, 172, 180–82; relations with France, 24, 57, 182; relations with Laos, 57, 197, 206, 207, 210; Vietnamese attitude toward China, 3, 57; Vietnamese community in Cambodia, 170, 171, 174–75, 195; Vietnamese community in Laos, 197, 199, 201, 203, 207, 209; Vietnamese community in Thailand, 202, 204, 209, 227, 267. *See also* Bao Dai; Geneva conference; Indochina; "Thai Autonomous State"; Thai of Tonkin; Viet Minh

World Federation of Trade Unions, 14, 15